the world's population
problems of growth

the world's

population

problems
of
growth

Edited by Quentin H. Stanford

Toronto/New York   Oxford University Press   1972

ISBN-0-19-540193-X

© Oxford University Press (Canadian Branch) 1972

Printed in Canada by

John Deyell Company

2 3 4 5 6—7 6 5 4 3

Contents

8 9

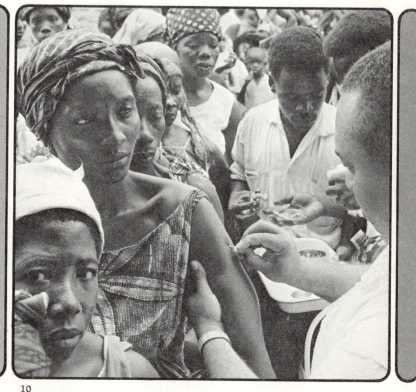

11   12

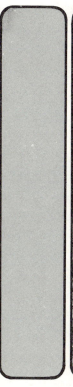

THE PHOTOGRAPHS ILLUSTRATE:

Cover: The home of an East-Pakistan refugee — A water pipe in Calcutta. MILLER SERVICES.

1. Family-planning instruction in India. AUTHENTICATED NEWS INTERNATIONAL.
2. A family-plannning clinic in Delhi, India. AUTHENTICATED NEWS INTERNATIONAL.
3. Refugee squatter community in Hong Kong. UNITED NATIONS.
4. Social worker distributing milk to school children in Colombia. UNITED NATIONS.
5. A malnourished Philippine child. AUTHENTICATED NEWS INTERNATIONAL.
6 & 7. World Food Program supplies being distributed in Chile. UNITED NATIONS.
8. A soil chemist, at the College of Agriculture of the University of the Philippines, experimenting with plants of low-land rice. AUTHENTICATED NEWS INTERNATIONAL.
9. Construction work on the Nagarjunasagar Dam in India. AUTHENTICATED NEWS INTERNATIONAL.
10. Smallpox vaccination at Coquilhatville, Congo Republic. UNITED NATIONS.
11. An alley in Karachi, West Pakistan. UNITED NATIONS.
12. The Tuberculosis Chemotherapy Centre in Madras, India. UNITED NATIONS.
13. Shanty town, Hong Kong. AUTHENTICATED NEWS INTERNATIONAL.
14. A refugee group at a dispensary, South Kasai, Congo Republic. UNITED NATIONS.
15. Refugee camp clearance at Elizabethville, Congo, 1962. UNITED NATIONS.

Preface

The current rate of world population growth is one of today's major problems and constitutes a threat to the future of all mankind. Over three and a half billion people live on our small, in places overcrowded, planet, and if the present rate of growth continues this figure will double within the next thirty to forty years. This development has been described as 'the population explosion'. Why does it constitute a threat? Growth in itself is not necessarily bad; it has been the basis for much human progress in the past. What concerns us is that a very large proportion of this growth is concentrated in certain areas of the world and can be linked to the appalling conditions of deprivation endured by millions of men, women, and children in these areas. Though the impact of the population explosion is presently restricted to only certain segments of mankind, there is every indication that its future consequences may affect all of us.

Deprivation acquires vivid meaning for us when it is reported in terms of individual suffering. Emotion is easily aroused by cases that are reported from various countries in Asia, Africa, and Latin America: photographs or films of starving children are heartrending, as are reports of women who practise infanticide because they simply cannot support an extra child; and it is shocking to learn of tens of thousands of homeless and jobless people, particularly in certain large cities, who are forced to live as best they can literally on the street. It is extremely difficult, however, for those of us who live in affluence (or are at least surrounded by affluence) to comprehend such conditions as these, which are associated with the population explosion. Despite the best of intentions most of us find that we cannot sustain our emotional response to them—perhaps because we feel that as individuals we cannot do very much, or because the number and frequency of such reports deaden our responses in time, and blunt whatever promptings of conscience we feel.

What can we do about all this? Certainly we as individuals cannot shoulder the burdens of all our fellow men; but we should feel sufficiently concerned to want to seek an understanding of the nature of these burdens and to support actively those programs, both public and private, that are attempting to ease them. It must be remembered, however, that at the present time the paths to understanding are obscured by ignorance, controversy, and apathy.

While humanitarianism alone should cause us to feel concern and make us want to understand the population crisis, there are other reasons why we should not ignore it. Many authorities feel that the lack of economic progress in the impoverished or underdeveloped countries, which is in great measure attributable to their rapid rate of population growth and has divided the world into rich and poor nations, is a major factor contributing to political and military strife between and within nations. In other words, population control is something that must be achieved if we are to make any progress towards permanent peace in the world. Thus, in pragmatic terms, it is in our own interests to be concerned, for without peace and international stability no one anywhere in the world can afford to feel secure. This relationship between economic growth and peace and our responsibilities as citizens of a rich nation has been succinctly summarized by Lester Pearson, the former Prime Minister of Canada:

> Peace is progress, peace is growth and development. Peace is welfare and dignity for all people. The nations—developed and developing—must work together; each side has its responsibility to this end. They must do so not merely by transferring resources from those who have to those who have not, in conditions which make progress possible. There must be international, economic, and financial policies which recognize the interdependence of all nations and will help the poorer ones to grow. If after the political, economic, and financial experiences of recent years we still think that states, however proud and independent they may feel, can go it alone in these matters, ignoring each other's interests and above all the interests of the impoverished and backward states, then we are beyond redemption. Before long, in our affluent, industrial, computerized jet society, we shall feel the wrath of the wretched people of the world. There will be no peace.[1]

Thus, whether we view the population problem in humanitarian or pragmatic terms, there can be little doubt that the present staggering rate at which the world's population is increasing has implications not only for those who live in the underdeveloped countries and are directly involved but for all of mankind. Yet people are still reluctant to accept the warnings, which are now issuing from many different sources, that mankind is in trouble. When there is so much at stake it hardly seems

[1] Lester B. Pearson, *Peace in the Family of Man.* The Reith Lectures 1968, Oxford University Press, 1969, and The British Broadcasting Corporation.

reasonable to stand idly by and hope for the best. We have failed to solve today's problems from lack of foresight. We can solve those of tomorrow only if we agree to be responsible for them today.

The principal purpose of *The World's Population* is to offer an organized approach to a complex and often very controversial subject by means of a variety of articles from periodicals and excerpts from books. The volume of material written on the subject of population in the past few years has been immense; from this literature every effort has been made to choose not only the best and most readable selections, but also those that are fairly recent and most representative of writings on the subject. (It should be explained that commentaries and introductions relating to these selections have been provided. They appear in sanserif type.) While some of the more controversial works or those that are unquestionably biased have, with perhaps one or two exceptions, been omitted, all controversy has not been played down. In general the overall intention has been to present issues as clearly, carefully, and, on occasion, as starkly as possible.

The subject of this book is not easily organized. The various aspects that have contributed to, or are a part of, the population crisis are interrelated in an often complex and sometimes confusing fashion—there is no logical beginning and end. For this reason it is important to indicate here the principal contents of *The World's Population*.

The book is divided into three parts. Part 1 contains various topics that offer some of the more important information one must acquire in order to examine in detail the problems of population growth. These include demographic terms and techniques, readings on the history of growth, predictions of future growth, the distribution of the present world population, and the theories of demographic regulation and transition.

Part 2 begins by examining the roots of the population dilemma. Why is it that in many parts of the world where death rates have been substantially reduced, birth rates remain very high? Why has it been relatively easy to achieve measures of death control and yet so difficult to effect any kind of control over births? Then the implications of present trends in the growth of the world's population are examined. After all, how do we know that there is a population problem? What are the implications of continued population growth, particularly at the rates that presently exist?

Part 3 is entitled 'Towards a Solution' and considers, first, the difficult and controversial question of controlling births. The concepts of birth control, family planning, and population control are briefly examined, not only in terms of their practicality but also in ethical terms. While the population dilemma can be tackled by trying to reduce births, another and very important part of the solution lies in economic development, a subject that takes up the major portion of Part 3. Various aspects of the problems of economic development are covered in a series of articles that describe some of the measures that have already been advocated—or taken—to improve the situation and that emphasize the inadequacy of present levels of international assistance.

part one

the population problem

---

background

Introduction

The English economist and sociologist Robert Thomas Malthus (1766-1834) is generally considered to be the first writer to examine the growth of human population. Although others before him had commented on the importance of population size, Malthus was the first to set down a consistent theory in his *Essay on the Principles of Population*, first published in 1798. His theory was based on two propositions: 'Population, when unchecked, increases in a geometrical ratio. Subsistence only increases in an arithmetical ratio.' Thus the means of subsistence set the limits to the population any area can support, and as these means are extended the population will always press against them unless prevented by some very powerful checks. For Malthus the only possible checks were moral restraint, 'vice' (i.e. measures of birth control, of which Malthus did not approve), and misery (war, famine, and disease). Malthus' view was clearly a very pessimistic one that aroused much criticism in his time and has been a source of controversy ever since. Since he did not believe moral restraint would work and could not accept birth control, his thesis ran contrary to the generally optimistic view of his time that science and reason could produce a better world for all—thoughts expressed in the writing of such eighteenth-century philosophers as Rousseau and Condorcet.[1]

When Malthus wrote his *Essay* the population of the world was about 900 million and that of England about 8.5 million. Despite these relatively small numbers (the present world population is 3.6 billion and that of England and Wales is approximately 48 million) poverty and famine had been endemic in Europe for centuries. While Malthus' *Essay* seemed appropriate for the conditions of his day, he could not foresee the vast and varied technological developments that began in the nineteenth

---

[1] There are many articles and books written about Malthus, and also recent editions of his *Essay*. For example, see Louise B. Young (ed.), *Population in Perspective*, Oxford University Press, New York, 1968, pp. 3-29, and Garrett Hardin (ed.), *Population, Evolution, Birth Control*, W. H. Freeman & Co., San Francisco and London, 1969, pp. 3-16.

century and constituted what is generally referred to as the Industrial Revolution. The principal consequences of these developments, in the Western world at least, were an enormous increase in population combined with an equally impressive improvement in standards of living.

As a result of these events, the conflict that Malthus postulated between the increase in population and that of the means of subsistence was averted for a time. But only for a time, for it now appears that a new day of reckoning is at hand. In a sense we have come full circle since Malthus wrote his essay. The population of the world has increased fourfold in 170 years and this increase shows no signs of abating. In some parts of the world this growth is unquestionably outstripping the availability of the basic necessities of life and in such areas poverty and famine are widespread.

The ideas that Malthus expressed were based on conditions he saw in England in the late eighteenth century. There were few population statistics and little information about population. Indeed for many areas of the world there was *no* information available on population. Today, however, we do not have this limitation. In our attempt to understand the population problem we have access to almost unlimited information. In fact the vast amount of material now available on the subject constitutes a problem in itself.[1]

The object of Part 1 is to provide background information on various subjects that are related to the central issue. These include such topics as the history of population growth, population projections into the future, the distribution and density of the world's population, the relationship between economic productivity and population growth, and important theories in demography. Such topics can be regarded as constituting a minimum basis essential to an understanding of the principal aspects of the population problem that are discussed in Parts 2 and 3.

---

[1] For any topic dealt with in this book there are many additional references that may be consulted if more information is required. Some of the more important of these are listed in the Bibliography at the end of the book.

1 | Terms and Techniques in Demography

Before examining some of the basic information—facts, figures, and theories—essential to any study of the problems of population growth, this opening section considers, briefly, a number of terms and techniques that are commonly used in studies of population growth.

The subject that is referred to as *demography* or *population studies* is one whose scope can be interpreted in two basic ways. In its most formal sense demography is a very technical and highly mathematical study of the vital statistics of human population (especially births, deaths, and migration), as well as of the characteristics of population structure (including age, sex, and marital status) as they contribute to an understanding of population change. In recent times, however, a broader meaning has been applied to the field, so that it refers to any population study. In this sense, one authority describes the field of demography as focusing its attention on

> three rather common-place and readily observable human phenomena: (a) change in population size (growth or decline), (b) the composition of the population, and (c) the distribution of population and space. It is interested not only in size, composition, and distribution of the population at the present time, but also in changes in these aspects over time. Moreover, it is concerned with seeking explanations of why a particular combination of population conditions exists at a given time and why the conditions are changing. . . . Therefore, the field of demography may be defined as the description of current status and of changes over time in the size, composition, and distribution of populations, and a development of scientific explanations of these events.[1]

Thus, in addition to those who regard themselves as being solely demographers, other disciplines—including economics, sociology, human ecology, geography, anthropology, statistics, biology, medicine, and

[1] From D. J. Bogue, *Principles of Demography*. Copyright © 1969 John Wiley & Sons, Inc., New York. Reprinted by permission.

human genetics—have within their ranks those who are concerned with the study of different aspects of population and, therefore, may also be properly called demographers.

POPULATION CHANGE

The most fundamental fact about a population is its rate of growth, which is more accurately referred to as population change. Change, of course, may involve either an increase or a decrease. Since there are few instances where the population of countries is not increasing, in the absence of a + or — symbol with a statistic, positive change may be assumed.

The simplest way of measuring population change is by calculating absolute change; that is, the growth or decline in population for a country over a period of time. For example, in India there was the following absolute change:

1960	432,750,000
1950	359,250,000
	73,500,000

The United Kingdom, on the other hand, had an absolute change of:

1960	52,508,000
1950	50,616,000
	1,892,000

This information becomes more meaningful if the change is shown relative to the size of the population. Thus for India and the United Kingdom the relative change in population would be:

India $\quad \dfrac{73,500,000}{359,250,000} \times 100 = 20.5\%$

United Kingdom $\quad \dfrac{1,892,000}{50,616,000} \times 100 = 3.7\%$

Such growth figures are commonly found in the literature on population and are referred to as the *intercensal growth rate* or intercensal rate of increase if census years are used, or simply the *decennial growth rate* if ten-year periods are involved, as they commonly are in United Nations' statistics. Growth rates, of course, can also be expressed in terms of percentage change for any period of time.

To get some idea of the significance of what might appear to be small annual growth rates, Table 1 shows the population of the world projected to the year 2200 on the basis of the present growth rate of approximately 2% per year. (The actual growth rate of the world's population has remained constant at 1.9% for the years 1967, 1968, and 1969.)

Table 1
PROJECTED POPULATION OF THE WORLD BASED ON ANNUAL INCREASE OF 2% PER YEAR

Year	Estimated Population (billions)
1960	3.0
1970	3.7
1980	4.5
2000	6.7
2050	17.8
2100	47.9
2200	430.6

This table clearly shows why the present rate of growth is described as explosive. We should not be misled by statements suggesting that if the present rate of population growth for the world were reduced—for example, to 1%—the problems of growth would be solved. A rate of growth of 1% would mean that the world's population would double in 70 years: the problem would thus be postponed, not solved. Realization of this fact has led many people to advocate zero population growth as an essential objective: they contend that we should devote our energies to stabilizing the world's population, with zero growth as the ultimate objective.

THE COMPONENTS OF POPULATION CHANGE

Population change for any individual country is computed by assessing four factors: fertility, mortality, emigration, and immigration.[1] The difference between fertility and mortality (births and deaths) is known as the *reproductive change* or *natural increase*. The balance of emigration and immigration is called *net migration.* Thus there are only two ways in which a population can change: through reproductive change and through net migration. As an example, Table 2 shows how the population of the United States changed during the periods 1950-60 and 1960-70.

The method of tabulating population change illustrated in Table 2 is sometimes referred to as 'demographic bookkeeping' and indicates the way in which a nation can keep track of its population growth between census years. In the United States such a population estimate was produced for each year following both the 1950 and 1960 censuses, using reported figures on birth, death, and migration. By adding and subtracting year by year as required, an estimate was produced for the increase in population between 1950 and 1960 (27,719,000) and 1960 and 1970 (24,352,000), as indicated in line 9 of Table 2. Since there are some

[1] The terms 'fecundity' and 'fertility' are constantly found in the literature of population and are very often confused. Fecundity refers to reproductive *capacity,* while fertility indicates the amount of reproduction that has actually occurred. The terms 'emigration' and 'immigration' are also often confused. The former describes the action of a person going away *from* his own country or native region to settle elsewhere; the latter refers to that of a settler coming *into* a country or region.

Table 2

ESTIMATES OF POPULATION CHANGE IN THE UNITED STATES FOR THE PERIODS 1950-60 AND 1960-70 (IN THOUSANDS)

	1950 to 1960	1960 to 1970
1. Births	40,963	39,033[1]
2. Deaths	15,608	18,192[2]
3. Natural Increase	+25,355	+20,841
4. Immigrants	2,500	3,899[3]
5. Emigrants	261	N.A.[4]
6. Net movement of armed forces abroad	-330	-540
7. Excess of arrivals over departures from Puerto Rico and other outlying U.S. territories	+455	N.A.[4]
8. Net migration	+2,364	+3,511[5]
9. Expected net increase in population (3+8)	+27,719	+24,352
10. Population 1 April 1960 and 1970 (as determined by the Census)	179,323	203,166
11. Population 1 April 1950 and 1960 (as determined by the Census)	151,326	179,323
12. Net increase	+27,997	+23,843
13. Error of closure	+278	-509

[1] Births preliminary after December 31, 1968.
[2] Deaths preliminary after December 31, 1967.
[3] Immigration preliminary after July 1, 1968.
[4] Data not available.
[5] Since data is missing for 5 and 7, this figure cannot be derived from the data included in this table.

inaccuracies in the reporting of such vital statistics, an error was building up in this bookkeeping process during the years between censuses. The extent of this error (known as the error of closure) is indicated by comparing the expected population for the census years with the actual population as determined by the census. The extent of the error of closure in both cases is remarkably small. In other countries where the reporting of vital statistics is reasonably complete, the error of closure is normally somewhat greater, although in most instances it is less than 1 per cent.

In both Canada and the United States a form of demographic bookkeeping is used to program a population clock. In Canada this clock stands in the foyer of the Dominion Bureau of Statistics Building, Ottawa. On 15 October 1970, when the clock showed a population of 21,500,000, it was operating on the following base figures: one birth every 1 minute 23 seconds; one immigrant every 3 minutes 16 seconds; one death every 3 minutes 21 seconds; and one emigrant every 9 minutes 23 seconds.

A world population clock (if one existed) would show for 1969 a gain of 2.2 persons per second or 190,000 per day, based on an average of 3.9 births per second and 1.7 deaths. Thus the estimated population of the world on 1 July 1969—3,551 million—increased by 72 million to 3,623 million by 1 July 1970.

In order to express the components of change in the form of rates, *birth rates*, *death rates*, and *migration rates* are used. The first two are the simplest and the most commonly used statistics. They are sometimes referred to as the crude birth and death rates, and are simply the result of dividing the number of births or deaths that occur in one year by the population count in the middle of that year. This number is then multiplied by a thousand to show the figure per 1,000 people (the figure commonly used for this purpose). For example, the crude birth rate in Canada for the period 1 July 1969 to 1 July 1970 was 17.4 per thousand, while the crude death rate was 7.3 per thousand.[1] The difference between the two, the crude rate of reproductive change, was therefore 10.1 per thousand population in Canada in the year 1970. (This rate then can be expressed as 1.01%.) Similarly the immigration rate and the emigration rate can be found, and the difference between the two would give the crude rate of net migration.

Note the use here of the cautionary word 'crude'. When the birth and death rates for different countries are compared by using such figures, these statistics *are* crude because they take no account of the age structure of a population. In countries such as France and England, for example, the proportion of the population in the child-bearing years is smaller than it is in, say, India or China. In order to take this difference into account, a statistic known as the *fertility rate* is used, which measures the births per year per thousand women in their reproductive ages (15 to 45). An even more detailed breakdown of this kind of information is provided by the *specific fertility* rate, which gives the fertility rate of women in different age groups in their reproductive years.

AGE STRUCTURE

Crude birth and death rates, then, can be misleading. In order to assess more accurately the growth potential of a particular country, it is necessary to examine the population structure; that is, the numbers of people in different age groups as well as the specific fertility rates for these different age categories.

The structure of a population is commonly illustrated by means of pyramids (Figure 1). While these pyramids (two bar graphs placed back to back with a vertical centre line representing zero) can be constructed to show absolute numbers in different age groups, they are more often constructed to indicate the proportion of the total population in each of the age groups. In the latter case, when the population structure of two countries is compared, the area of the pyramids will be identical, but the shapes will differ. It is this difference in shape that makes it possible to contrast either the population structure of different countries or the change in structure of one country's population occurring over a period of time. Both of these situations can be seen in the pyramids in Figure 1.

[1] Dominion Bureau of Statistics, *Vital Statistics*, July 1970, Vol. 18, No. 7.

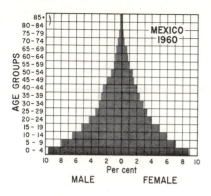

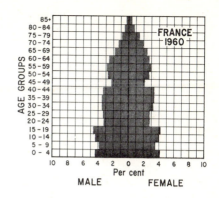

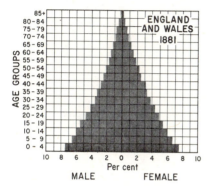

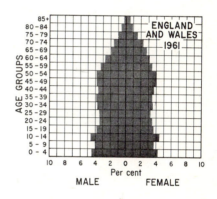

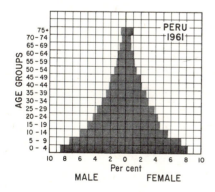

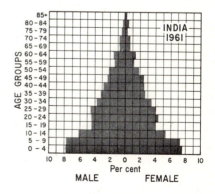

Continued over

FIGURE 1 Population pyramids.

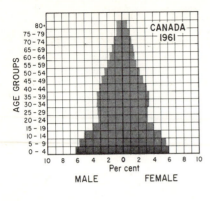

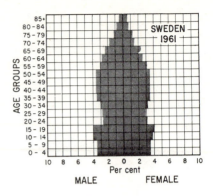

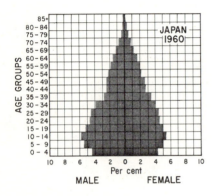

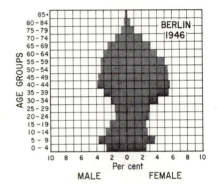

FIGURE 1 *Continued.*

It is possible by comparing the shapes of pyramids for different countries to recognize certain classes of population structure. Each of the numbered sections below describes a class,[1] and each of these is shown diagrammatically in Figure 2.

(1) The regular triangular-shaped pyramid is typical of those countries that have high birth and death rates. While such a pyramid was common for most countries before the seventeenth and eighteenth centuries, there are very few in this category now. The population pyramids for England and Wales in 1881 and India in 1961 on p. 9 show some resemblance to this shape.

(2) The second pyramid, with its bowed sides, is typical of those countries where death rates have begun to fall, particularly in the age group 0 to 5, while birth rates remain high. Such a situation is typical of the underdeveloped countries, as the pyramids for Mexico and Peru (Figure 1) indicate.

[1] This classification is based on that used by W. S. Thompson and D. T. Lewis in their book *Population Problems*, McGraw-Hill Book Company, 1965.

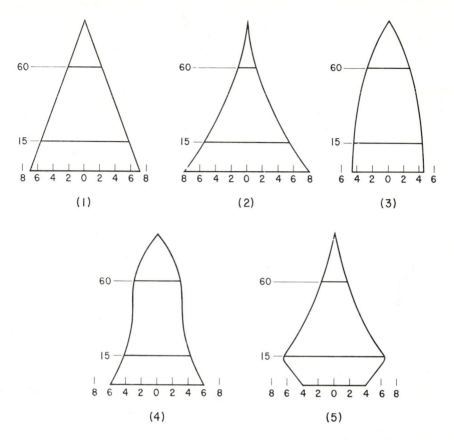

FIGURE 2   Five types of national population structure.

(3) This beehive-shaped pyramid is associated with those countries that have low birth rates (a narrow base) and low death rates (a very slight indentation for each age group from the youngest to the oldest). Sweden and England and Wales are the best examples of this type (Figure 1).

(4) A bell-shaped pyramid represents a population that, after experiencing a considerable period of time with low birth and death rates, has increased its birth rate. This shape is often associated with the more developed countries, such as Canada and the United States, that are undergoing rapid economic growth.

(5) The last pyramid represents a situation where a marked and rapid decline in fertility has occurred. Japan is the only major country in the world at the present time with a pyramid such as this, although a number of western European countries had similar pyramids in the 1930s.

Note that none of these shapes represents permanent situations, although some are clearly more transitional than others. For example, as modern medical techniques have been made available to underdeveloped

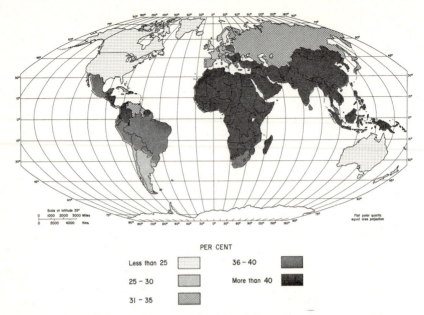

PER CENT

Less than 25 | 36 – 40

25 – 30 | More than 40

31 – 35

FIGURE 3   Percentage of population under fifteen years of age.

countries the characteristic shape of their pyramids has quite quickly changed from (1) to (2). Similar relationships can be found between (2) and (5) and (3) and (4). Pyramid (3) represents the most stable situation.

Compare the diagrammatic pyramids with the actual ones shown in Figure 1. Further examples of each type can be roughly determined from the population information included in the Appendix on pp. 322-8.

It should also be noted that similar variations in population structure, as well as many additional types, exist for areas within countries. For example, the structure of an urban population is normally quite different from that of a rural one; and within cities the population structure of a suburban community will likely differ considerably from that of an older residential community nearer the centre of the city. In some cases the population structure is not a result of normal variations in births, deaths, and migration. An example is the pyramid for Berlin in 1946 (Figure 1). Clearly some very unusual influences have caused this particular structure.

An understanding of a most important aspect of the population problem can be gained by comparing the graph of an underdeveloped country such as Mexico or Peru with that of a developed nation—for example, Sweden or England and Wales. In the former countries the proportion of the population under fifteen years is between 40% and 50%, while in the latter the figure is much lower, usually between 20% and 30%. Thus in the underdeveloped countries, as this younger group gets older the childbearing fraction of the population increases and, even if the number of births per female were reduced (which is occurring in most instances), the rate of absolute population increase would almost certainly rise. In developed countries such as Sweden, however, the proportion of the population in each age group under fifteen years is little different from the proportion in the age groups between fifteen and forty-five; clearly a reduction in the fertility rates would have an immediate effect on the rate of population growth. Thus in most developed countries a reduction of the birth rate will result in a decrease in the rate of population growth, whereas in most underdeveloped countries even a substantial reduction in the number of births per female will not immediately reduce the rate of population growth because of the disproportionate segment of the population under fifteen years. In these countries it could well take several decades before a reduction in birth rates would actually bring about a slowing down of the rate of population growth.

2 | The Growth of the World's Population

The time of man's emergence on the earth is uncertain. Reliable sources merely indicate that what we call *Homo sapiens* ('Thinking Man') first appeared about 50,000 years ago and for most of the time since sustained himself by hunting and foraging. Such a means of existence was certainly one factor that effectively restricted population growth; at any time in the first forty millennia of man's existence, therefore, the total human population of the world was very small (see Table 3).

The first step towards a more secure and permanent existence occurred between 10,000 and 6,000 years ago when the first crude attempts at agriculture were made in a few areas of Asia and Africa. The impact of this and subsequent developments in the history of man and the growth of human population are briefly analysed in the following extract.

A BRIEF HISTORY*

John D. Durand

[1958]

The development of agriculture, even in a simple form, enormously increased the population-carrying capacity of the earth and at the same time made possible a great improvement in the conditions of life. L. R. Nougier's article on the prehistoric population of France, which appeared in the French journal *Population*, gives some idea of the population increase which took place in some regions during the neolithic era. Basing his calculations on a detailed survey of the archaeological findings in different parts of the country, he concluded that the population of the area which is now France prior to the 'neolithic revolution' probably never amounted to more than about 20,000. During the fourth millennium B.C., when the first agricultural settlements appeared, he esti-

*Reprinted with permission of The Macmillan Company from *Population and World Politics*, edited by P. M. Hauser. © 1958 by The Free Press, a Corporation.

Table 3*
ESTIMATES OF WORLD POPULATION: 1,000,000 YEARS AGO TO A.D. 2000.

Years Ago	Cultural Stage	Area Populated	Assumed Density Per Square Kilometre	Total Population (Millions)
1,000,000	Lower Paleolithic (hunting-gathering)	Africa	0.00425	0.125
300,000	Middle Paleolithic (hunting-gathering)	Africa and Eurasia	0.012	1
25,000	Upper Paleolithic (hunting-gathering)	Africa and Eurasia	0.04	3.34
10,000	Mesolithic (hunting-gathering)	All continents	0.04	5.32
6,000	Village farming and early urban	Old World	1.0	86.5
		New World	0.04	
2,000	Village farming and urban	All continents	1.0	133
310 (1650)	Farming and industrial	All continents	3.7	545
210 (1750)	Farming and industrial	All continents	4.9	728
160 (1800)	Farming and industrial	All continents	6.2	906
60 (1900)	Farming and industrial	All continents	11.0	1,610
10 (1950)	Farming and industrial	All continents	16.4	2,400
A.D. 2000	Farming and industrial	All continents	46.0	6,270

* From Edward S. Deevey, Jr, 'The Human Population', *Scientific American*, September 1960. Copyright © 1960 by Scientific American, Inc. All rights reserved.

mated that the population grew to about half a million, and in the next thousand years—4000 to 3000 B.C.—it jumped to five million.

A still greater impetus to population growth in some regions may have been given by the next great step in social and economic evolution, namely, the creation of the market economy and of city-centred societies of exchange. Trade over wide market areas permitted the division of labour to a degree that would not have been possible under the neolithic regime, with its small, self-sufficient villages. At this stage, the advance of civilization not only opened the way for population growth, but was itself encouraged by the increase of numbers. In fact the society of exchange requires a certain minimum population size and density within the trading area to permit extensive specialization of functions. Furthermore, the growth of population under this regime made it possible to mobilize large forces of labour for works such as drainage, irrigation, and terracing, which greatly extended the useable land in some regions. In ancient Egypt, for example, the areas of farmland along the Nile were originally very small; in spite of their remarkable fertility they could not support much population until the swamps had been drained and irrigation works constructed on a large scale.

By the time of Christ, agriculture was being practised in most of Europe and Asia, in large parts of Africa, and in much of Central America and northern South America. Societies of exchange with dense agricultural population and sizeable cities had been organized over a great area in the eastern hemisphere, extending from Spain to China and from India to the Baltic Sea. The trend reached culmination in the military and trading empires of ancient Rome, Persia, India, and China. Similar developments were beginning in Middle America and the Andes. These accomplishments were reflected by a large increase of world population. At this time the total is believed to have been between 200 and 300 million. If so, the average increase during the preceding six thousand years was at least 6 per cent and perhaps as much as 10 per cent per century.

The growth during the next sixteen centuries was slower. Willcox's estimate for 1650 A.D. is 470 million. Professor Carr-Saunders has estimated 545 million. If we accept a range from 450 to 550 million, it appears that the rate of increase between the time of Christ and 1650 was from 2.5 to 5 per cent per century. This was a period when the pace of social and economic development was comparatively slow. There were no innovations that could be compared in importance with the invention of agriculture or the development of the exchange economy, nor with the subsequent development of the industrial economy. Progress took the form chiefly of extending earlier advances to regions which had been retarded in their development. The growth of population likewise was confined mainly to the outlying regions. Within the historic centres of high culture, available estimates show little net increase during the first centuries of the Christian era or the Middle Ages.

MODERN GROWTH

Since 1650, the rate of increase has risen far above what was estimated for any previous period. It has averaged at least 65 per cent per century during the last 300 years. This enormous spurt, like the smaller one in pre-Christian times, has been linked with important new developments in the social and economic spheres. Industrialization, with a whole host of connected improvements in techniques of production and social organization, has again added to the carrying capacity of the earth. Again, the course of economic development has demanded a growing population to supply markets and a labour force for production on a larger scale with ever finer specialization of employments.

How has the link between population increase and economic and social development been made? Is it a rising birth rate or a falling death rate which has permitted population to expand when expansion was feasible and useful? How has expansion been checked when development slowed down?

For the pre-modern period, the answer is unknown. According to one hypothesis, the mores of almost all peoples have been oriented since very ancient times to the maintenance of a high birth rate, in order to

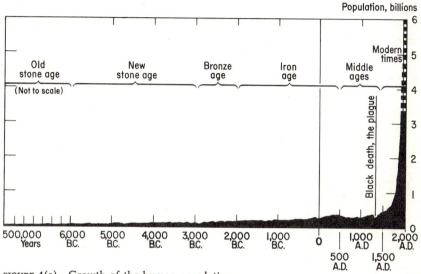

FIGURE 4(a)   Growth of the human population.

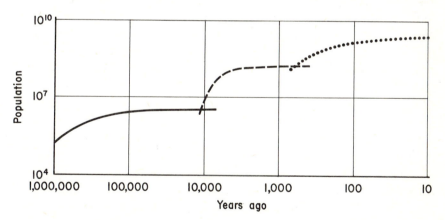

FIGURE 4(b)   This graph showing the growth of the human population has been drawn using logarithmic scales. In addition to showing a longer time span than Figure 4(a), it reveals a step-like growth in human population that is not evident in the arithmetic graph. The steps mark three population surges, which reflect the toolmaking or cultural revolution (solid line), the agricultural revolution (broken line), and the scientific-industrial revolution (dotted line). (Adapted from Edward S. Deevey, Jr, 'The Human Population', *Scientific American*, September 1960. Copyright © 1960 by Scientific American, Inc. All rights reserved.)

guarantee survival in the face of high mortality risks. These mores are slow to change, according to the hypothesis, and therefore adjustments in the population trend have been effected chiefly by changes in the death rates. But it is now well known that various means of regulating the birth rate, including abortion, infanticide, coitus interruptus, limitation of marriage, and taboos affecting sex relations, have long been known and practised by many peoples, both primitive and 'civilized', in different parts of the world. It seems possible, therefore, that changing birth rates have had as much to do with population trends as changing death rates.

The same uncertainty applies to the acceleration of population growth in the early part of the modern period, that is, before records of vital statistics were established. However, so far as the recent past is concerned, the statistics have already demonstrated that it is rapidly falling death rates, and not rising birth rates, which have been primarily responsible for a faster increase of numbers.

Not everyone realizes how much death rates have been reduced in recent times. Two hundred years ago a new-born child could look forward on the average to only thirty-five or forty years of life, even in the countries where conditions of health were most favourable. Estimates for former times, including calculations of the life expectancy in medieval Europe, ancient Greece, and Egypt, and in prehistoric times, show a still more dismal picture of early death. At present the expectation of life in many countries exceeds sixty-five years and all over the world it is being lengthened, thanks mainly to a great reduction in the number of children who die in infancy. This progress of death control is one of the most important achievements of the modern age. It is without any precedent in the past, and it has a powerful effect on the population trend.

Major reductions of death rates were first recorded in the vital statistics of various countries in northwestern Europe early in the nineteenth century. There were probably substantial reductions during the eighteenth century also, before the national systems of birth and death registration were established in most of the countries concerned. The trend was quickly communicated to the more prosperous areas of European settlement overseas, and, subsequently, to the countries of southern and eastern Europe. With minor interruptions, it has continued ever since; the average death rate today for European countries—around ten deaths annually per 1,000 population—is less than one-third of what it was in the early nineteenth century.

The initial effect on the population of Europe was a veritable mush-rooming. The birth rates at first remained almost unchanged while the death rates fell. It has been estimated that between 1750 and 1900 the population of Europe and its emigrant offshoots overseas multiplied nearly four-fold.

The phase of rapid growth in the European population was finally brought to an end by falling birth rates. By 1900 the small-family idea was well established in the leading industrial countries of western, northern, and central Europe, and also in the United States, Canada, Australia, and New Zealand. Thirty years later the number of births in many of these countries was no longer sufficient to replace the population permanently, and their governments were beginning to consider the need for vigorous measures to avoid the threat of de-population. That threat has now disappeared, at least for the time being, thanks to

Table 4
ESTIMATES OF WORLD POPULATION BY REGIONS: 1650 TO 1969

Source of estimate and year	World total	INDUSTRIALIZED REGIONS				DEVELOPING REGIONS			
		Total	Europe and USSR	Northern America	Oceania	Total	Asia	Latin America	Africa
A. ESTIMATED POPULATION (MILLIONS) United Nations estimates									
1969	3552	943	700	224	18.9	2669	1988	276	315
1960	3008	857	640	200	16.5	2151	1685	211	255
1950	2509	756	576	267	13.0	1753	1384	162	207
1940	2249	730	573	146	11.3	1519	1212	131	176
1930	2015	671	532	135	10.4	1338	1072	109	157
1920	1811	613	487	117	8.8	1198	966	91	141
Carr-Saunders/Wilcox estimates									
1900	1590	510	423	81	6	1079	886	63	130
1850	1131	302	274	26	2	829	698	33	98
1800	912	200	192	6	2	712	596	21	95
1750	711	147	144	1	2	564	456	10	98
1650	507	106	103	1	2	402	292	10	100
B. IMPLIED AVERAGE ANNUAL RATES OF GROWTH									
1950-1960	1.83	1.26	1.06	1.82	2.41	2.07	1.99	2.68	2.11
1940-1950	1.10	0.35	0.05	1.35	1.41	1.44	1.31	2.15	1.64
1930-1940	1.11	0.85	0.75	0.79	0.83	1.28	1.21	1.86	1.15
1920-1930	1.07	0.91	0.89	1.44	1.68	1.11	1.05	1.82	1.08
1900-1920	0.65	0.92	0.71	1.86	1.93	0.52	0.43	1.86	0.41
1850-1900	0.68	1.05	0.87	2.30	2.22	0.53	0.48	1.30	0.57
1800-1850	0.43	0.83	0.71	2.98	0.00	0.31	0.32	0.91	0.06
1750-1800	0.50	0.62	0.58	3.65	0.00	0.47	0.54	1.50	-0.06
1650-1750	0.34	0.33	0.34	0.00	0.00	0.34	0.45	0.00	-0.02

SOURCE: Data for 1920-1969 from United Nations, *Demographic Yearbook*. Data for 1650-1900 are based on average of estimates by Carr-Saunders/Wilcox, as modified by United Nations and reported in *The Determinants and Consequences of Population Trends*.

a revival of birth rates. But Europe still appears on the world map as a region of low human fertility, and its rate of population growth is now only about one-half the world rate. The United States, Canada, Australia, New Zealand, and the Soviet Union have somewhat higher birth rates; their rate of increase is about the same as the world average, or slightly higher.

Any slackening of world population growth which might have been caused by lower birth rates in Europe was more than offset by falling death rates in other parts of the world, where birth rates were still high. The progress of death control in Latin America, Asia, and Africa has been most remarkable during the last few decades. Latin America as a whole now has a death rate not much higher than the average for Europe. The effect of this combined with the higher birth rate of the Latin American peoples is to make Latin America the fastest growing region of the world today. Most countries in that region have recently been adding to their population rates between 2 and 3 per cent per annum: that is, about twice the world average. The same is true of many countries in Asia and Africa: Egypt, Turkey, Ceylon, and the Philippines, for example.

In other Asian and African countries, the population is growing more slowly at present, not because they have lower birth rates than the countries above, but because they have higher death rates. Consider India as an example. The death rate in that country at present is two or three times as high as in the United States. Even with a birth rate far above the world average, the population of India grows at a comparatively modest rate: somewhere between 1 per cent and 1.5 per cent per year.

For a long time the consensus of expert opinion has been that China's population was growing rather slowly. The death rate was presumed to be high even in good years, and it was thought to rise from time to time when there were large floods, famine, or other catastrophes. In this way the effect of a high birth rate was presumed to be counterbalanced. But the presumption could not be verified for lack of any reliable statistics. In 1953 a census was taken on the mainland, and data on births and deaths as well as population were obtained. It was reported in the newspapers that the birth rate was found to be thirty-seven per 1,000 and the death rate seventeen per 1,000. If these are the correct figures, they mean that the Chinese population is now growing at 2 per cent per annum. But the figures should be taken with some reserve; experience has shown that birth and death statistics collected in censuses are subject to substantial errors.

China's population is about one-fourth the world total; with the rest of Asia it accounts for more than half of all mankind. If this huge population begins to multiply at the rate demonstrated in Latin America, the result will be a large boost to the rate of world population increase. If the Chinese census figures are correct, this has nearly come to pass already in China; and if not, all that is needed to bring it about there, and in all Asia, is a repetition of what has happened in countries like Ceylon. With modern techniques and materials for public health work, it is entirely possible, and within a few years. Increasing at 2 per cent a year, Asia's people would add a billion to the world population in less than thirty years.

In Latin America, too, there is room for progress in cutting down death rates. In many cases they are still noticeably higher than the rates for the most advanced countries in Europe, for example. The fact is that death rates can be reduced in practically every part of the world; and it is virtually certain that this will happen in the years to come— always barring the possibility of calamities such as another World War.

What can be said about the possibility that birth rates, too, will be reduced so that the rate of population growth will be kept at the present level or diminished? An effort in this direction will be made in some countries where too rapid an increase is found to be hindering progress toward a satisfactory level of living. India has announced a policy of taking steps to moderate the growth of population in accordance with the needs and capacity of the economy. Egypt is considering a similar policy; Japan already has a national system of birth-control clinics, and other countries may follow suit. But it is not easy to make such a policy effective in an underdeveloped country with a low level of income and popular education, and poor facilities for the distribution of either ideas or materials. In view of the difficulties, it seems unlikely in the near future that any reduction of birth rates in underdeveloped countries will be great enough to counterbalance their falling death rates.

In the parts of the world where birth rates are lower—generally speaking, Europe, North America, and Australia—fertility may rise or fall; it is difficult to predict. But fewer births in those regions, representing only about one-third of world population, would hardly be sufficient to balance the acceleration of growth which seems almost inevitable in Asia, Africa, and Latin America.

PROJECTIONS NOT PREDICTIONS*

Louise B. Young

The above title summarizes in three words the caution one must employ when utilizing population projections, a point made quite clearly in Louise B. Young's excellent introduction to the subject of population growth. It is followed by a discussion of the United Nations' projections of the world's population to the year 2000.

[1968]

The projection of a future population from a present growth rate is a hazardous undertaking at best. These rates contain many variables and are sensitive to small changes in these variables. Furthermore, since population growth is cumulative, very slight changes in present rates can make enormous differences when projected 100, 200, or more years into the future.

In reading some of the more extreme predictions about the crowded state of our planet many centuries from now, we are reminded of Mark Twain's amusing comment about using present rates of change to calculate what happened in the past or will happen in the future:

In the space of one hundred and seventy-six years the Lower Mississippi has shortened itself two hundred and forty-two miles. That is an average of a trifle over one mile and a third per year. Therefore, any calm person, who is not blind or idiotic, can see that in the old Oolitic Silurian Period, just a million years ago next November, the Lower Mississippi River was upward of one million three hundred thousand miles long, and stuck out over the Gulf of Mexico like a fishing-rod. And by the same token any person can see that seven hundred and forty-two years from now the Lower Mississippi will be only a mile and three-quarters long, and Cairo and New Orleans will have joined their streets together, and be plodding comfortably along under a single mayor and a mutual board of aldermen. There is something fascinating about science. One gets such wholesale returns of conjecture out of such trifling investment of fact.[1]

Actually, in projecting present rates of growth into the future most demographers are not making predictions in the sense of something which they believe will happen. Rather they are putting into vivid terms

---

*From Louise B. Young (ed.), *Population in Perspective.* Copyright © 1968 by Oxford University Press, Inc., New York. Reprinted by permission.
[1] From Mark Twain, *Life on the Mississippi*, 1883.

the dangers of a present course of action, realizing that a knowledge of this danger will help to alter the outcome. As Philip Hauser expresses it:

> Projections of future populations are admittedly fictions. No one can actually predict future population and anyone who claims he can is either a fool or a charlatan. Yet the projections of the demographers are more than exercises in arithmetic: they make it possible for us to see the implications of observed rates of growth. The fact that man is able to consider these implications is one reason why the projected numbers will never be reached, for recognition of the problems posed by his birth rate will move man to modify it. Such a modification, however, will not be automatic. It requires policy decisions and implementation of policy . . .[1]

No effective policy can be created without a careful appraisal of the goals that we want that policy to achieve. Do we want to stabilize the population as rapidly as possible and attempt to hold it at that level? Many people fear that the concept of stability in population connotes stagnation and old age. A declining population is often considered to be a symptom of decadence. On the other hand, stability as it is used in physics to describe a condition of equilibrium would allow for future population growth as new discoveries made available more natural resources. A population balanced with the means of subsistence would be in a constantly changing state of equilibrium.

Furthermore, there are other and more significant kinds of growth than the purely physical growth involved in population expansion. Cultural and spiritual growth could continue, indeed might even be favoured, in a society with a relatively stable population, just as the individual human being achieves full physical growth quite early in life and thereafter goes on growing in other ways for many more years before old age and decadence set in. The prime of creativity comes long after physical growth has ceased. A wise population policy would involve planning not only for a comfortable physical balance between population and the means of subsistence but also for the fostering of those special qualities which give human existence its creative and dynamic character.

Achievement of this goal can be accelerated by a more widespread understanding of the dangers and difficulties involved and an appreciation of the many complex factors that influence the fertility of a

---

[1] From Philip Hauser, *Population Perspectives*, Rutgers University Press, New Brunswick, N.J., 1961.

people. It is our belief that perspective on the problem will contribute toward the formulation of an intelligent and consistent long-term policy. Therefore, the readings in this book have been planned to encourage the individual to think through the various issues himself, to question stereotypes, and to be aware of the future which is being created today by the actions and decisions of individuals everywhere on earth. 'The world's greatest need,' says C. P. Snow, 'is an appetite for the future . . . All healthy societies are ready to sacrifice the existential moment for their children's future and for children after these. The sense of the future is behind all good policies. Unless we have it, we can give nothing either wise or decent to the world.'[1]

WORLD POPULATION PROJECTIONS 1965-2000*

Robert C. Cook

[1965]

The United Nations demographers have gazed into their modern statistical crystal balls and come up with some startling projections. [See Tables 5, 6, and 7 at the end of this article.] If the present trend of population growth continues, world population will reach 7.4 billion by the year 2000. If certain other trends develop, the world total could fall short of this by 2 billion. As matters now stand, the higher figure appears to be the more likely, barring famine, nuclear war, disintegration, or some new and 'miraculous' form of fertility control.

The gain of 4.1 billion in only thirty-five years would exceed the present total world population of 3.3 billion by nearly a billion! The current trend, long continued, is viewed as 'calamitous'.

The United Nations estimates revealed that over 85 per cent of the increase will be in the high-birth-rate, 'developing' countries of Asia, Africa, and Latin America. This continues a trend which has been building up since 1900. Then, with world population totalling only 1.6 billion people, just over two-thirds lived in Asia, Africa, and Latin America; less than one-third lived in Europe and northern America. By 1965 these proportions had shifted to three-fourths and one-fourth respectively.

Projections to the year 2000, based on current trends, indicate that

[1] From C. P. Snow, 'What Is the World's Greatest Need?', New York Times Magazine, 2 April 1961.
*From Population Bulletin, Vol. XXI, No. 4, October 1965. Copyright © 1965, Population Reference Bureau, Inc. Reprinted by permission.

four-fifths of the world's people will then be living in Asia, Africa, and Latin America. Northern America and Europe (including the U.S.S.R.) will have shrunk to less than one-fifth of the total. World projections are somewhat moot because of the big question regarding Mainland China, discussed below.

The ranking of the ten largest nations will also show some interesting changes by the year 2000. In 1965, the list included five 'developed' countries. (See Figure 5.) By 2000, this number may be reduced to three, with West Germany and the United Kingdom being replaced by Nigeria and Mexico. The total population for the 'top ten' nations will grow to 4.7 billion if present trends continue.

The United Nations Report, from which these projections are taken, represents the fourth time the UN has scanned the demographic radar. The previous reviews were published in 1951, 1954, and 1957.

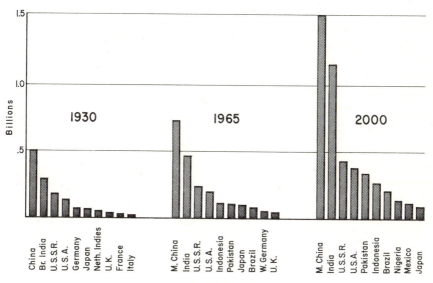

FIGURE 5   'Top Ten' nations in population: 1930, 1965, and 2000.

HOW PROJECTIONS ARE MADE

The construction of population projections, using the most advanced demographic techniques, is not an exercise in crystal gazing. It is a sophisticated and ingenious procedure which can be outlined here only very sketchily.

The starting point is population data—the more detailed and accurate, the better—for a nation, for a region, or for the world. The essential information includes the total population, and such components as breakdowns of the population by age and sex; death rates for the total population and for its age-components; birth rates and other special measures of fertility.

Most of the developed countries have the essential census and vital statistics data in considerable detail. While many countries of the world have taken censuses since 1960, there are still important gaps. Vital statistics are still far from adequate in many countries. Where such data are lacking, much skill and ingenuity is employed in developing from other data estimates adequate to fill these gaps.

The basic demographic data for a nation or a region being at hand, the projection process computes the movement of this population into the future, usually in five-year intervals: so many babies are born; so many people die in each age-cohort. The surviving 0-4-year-olds in 1965 become the 5-9-year-olds in 1970, etc.

If birth rates and death rates never changed, it would be a simple matter to forecast future populations with great accuracy. That vital rates may—and do—change greatly complicates matters. Future population depends on how these variables shift and the rate and magnitude of the shifts.

To meet this difficulty a series of projections is prepared which, hopefully, will bracket the range of possibilities. These are based on

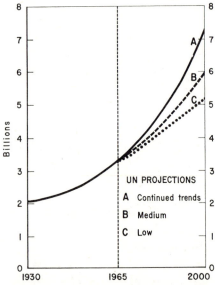

FIGURE 6 World population growth, 1930 to 1965 and projected to 2000.

different sets of assumptions regarding changes in birth and death rates both for the world and for regions, especially for the two main demographic groupings. The thinking on which some of these assumptions are based is set forth in the UN Report:

Plausible prospects of future population growth differ substantially for populations of the two types. Barring events that cannot now be foreseen, the scope of plausible future variations, both in fertility and in mortality, is much wider in the 'developing' than in the 'developed' regions. In the former, failure of mortality to decline where it is still high would certainly be regarded as a calamity and is not contemplated in this report. An even greater calamity would eventually ensue, at least in the remote future, if fertility decline were to be postponed indefinitely while mortality decline continued. Declines of both fertility and mortality must therefore be assumed in the 'developing' countries, though the assumption has to be varied from area to area as regards plausible timing and speed of declines. In the 'developed' regions, currently prevailing trends may continue well into the future, though reasonable allowance has to be made for possible changes in trends, particularly as there remains some scope for moderate variations of fertility in response to changes in economic and social circumstances.

The big question—what will happen to fertility *and* mortality?—cannot be disposed of by verbal fiat. The assumption that mortality will continue to decline is made in the face of ominous developments in certain stress areas, discussed below. In the UN projections, a continuing mortality decline is assumed for developing countries.

The 'high', 'medium', and 'low' projections are based on different assumptions regarding the timing of fertility declines in Asia, Africa, and Latin America. Birth rates there have maintained their previous high level in the 40-50 range, with a few relatively minor exceptions— Chile, Taiwan, Ceylon, Singapore, and Hong Kong. During the past fifty years, death rates have declined by 50 per cent or more, and now stand at 25 to 30 in Asia and Africa, and even lower in Latin America. The 'continued recent trends' projection assumes that this pattern will persist. If it does, world population could considerably exceed 7 billion by the year 2000.

Depending mainly on how rapidly fertility declines in developing areas, the 'low' and 'medium' projections show a world population ranging from 5.3 to 5.9 billion in the year 2000; the 'high' projection totals 6.8. Even were the 'low' projection to be realized, the sobering fact remains that this shows a two-thirds increase over present world population.

In evaluating these 'radarscopings' of future population growth, it cannot be too strongly emphasized that the realization of the projections depends on many additional factors too complex and unpredictable to measure. The major assumption which is not explicitly stated is that there will be nothing more than brushfire wars, no economic crises, no major pandemics, etc., etc. The statement quoted above that 'calamity ... is not contemplated in this report' and that 'declines of both fertility and mortality must therefore be assumed' borders on verbal magic. These and other calamities may not be contemplated, but they could happen.

Also necessarily ignored in these assumptions is the alarming fact that food production around the world is not keeping up with population growth. If the projections of population growth in the developing countries are to be realized, a massive revolution in agriculture on a scale apparently not now contemplated must be achieved. The looming threat of famine cannot be exorcised merely by ignoring it.

The value of projections of future population growth is that they do give a picture of what might happen if everything went according to 'plan'—if the assumptions were realized; if none of the calamities happened.

In the past, UN projections have tended to be low. The addition of a new 'continued trends' projection may indicate that the projectors are not too sure that calamity-averting declines in fertility will take place.

With death rates still declining and persisting birth rates, a population of 7.4 billion people thirty-five years hence is definitely a possibility. If this prospect is indeed 'calamitous', then humane and effective steps to avert it are indicated. This review of the areas and a few of the major nations is geared to the 'continued trends' projection. . . . The 'high' and the 'continued trends' do not differ greatly.

THE 'CONTINUED TRENDS' PROJECTION

World population is estimated to be growing at a rate of 2.1 per cent a year. Each year about 125 million babies are born, 55 million people die, leaving some 70 million human beings added to the world's total population. If this trend continues, *world population will gain over 100*

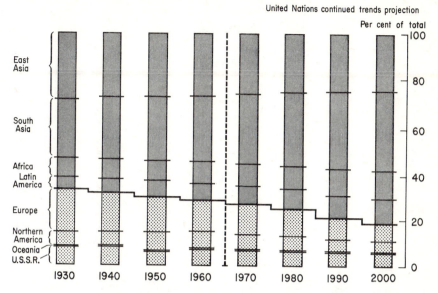

FIGURE 7 Percentage distribution of world population, 1930-2000. In 1930 the developed regions (separated from the undeveloped regions by the step-like line across the graph) had 32.7 per cent of the world's population. This had shrunk to 27.5 per cent by 1965 and is projected to shrink to 18.8 by 2000.

million each year by 1980 and over 200 million by 2000: a number that would exceed today's total U.S. population.

In the first half of the nineteenth century, the rate of world population growth was less than 1 per cent per year. It took fifty years—from 1900 (1.6 billion) to 1950 (2.5 billion)—to add one billion more people. If current trends proceed unchecked, the next billion will be added in only thirteen years—by 1978.

World population is projected to increase by 125 per cent between 1965 and 2000. During the previous thirty-five years (1930-1965), the comparable increase was 60 per cent. Latin America had the highest increase (130 per cent) and Europe, the lowest (25 per cent). In the next thirty-five years, Latin America's population is expected to triple, while Europe's would increase by slightly more than one-fourth.

'Continued trends' show every continent having a larger increase between 1965 and 2000 than between 1930 and 1965. Africa is expected to increase by 177 per cent, compared to 90 per cent in the previous three decades. Asia would jump from a 64 per cent to a 139 per cent increase. Among the developed areas, the U.S.S.R. is expected to have the highest gain from a previous 31 per cent to an anticipated 72 per

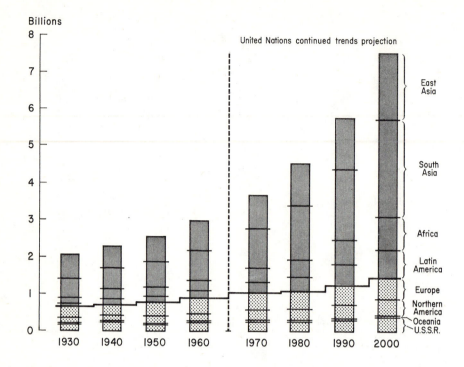

Billions

United Nations continued trends projection

East Asia

South Asia

Africa

Latin America

Europe

Northern America

Oceania

U.S.S.R.

1930 1940 1950 1960 1970 1980 1990 2000

FIGURE 8   Numerical growth of world population, 1930-2000.

cent. Northern America's growth would increase from 60 to 80 per cent; Europe's gain would be least, from 25 to 29 per cent.

Latin America's high rate of population growth gives it the dubious distinction of being the fastest-growing major area in the world. Its average annual rate of growth between 1930 and 1965 was close to 2.5 per cent. At this rate of growth, a population doubles in less than 29 years. A continuation of present trends would give Latin America a rate in excess of 3.5 per cent. This would mean a doubling of the population in 20 years, or a tripling in only 31 years.

In comparison, Europe's rate of growth over the past 35 years has been about 0.7 per cent. The same rate is projected to the year 2000. At this low rate of growth, Europe's population will take some 100 years to double.

In terms of massive numerical gains, Asia, with her huge population base, far exceeds Latin America. One half of the world's 2 billion people lived in Asia in 1930; a growth rate of 1.4 per cent annually produced 1.8 billion by 1965. The overall projected growth rate of 2.5 per cent to the year 2000 would result in about 4.4 billion people in

Asia alone. This would be a billion more people than the entire world population today.

Latin America, whose present population is 248 million, and Africa, with 311 million, would each accumulate over a half billion more people by 2000. The U.S.S.R. (234 million) and northern America (215 million) would both add about 170 million; Europe (443 million) about 128 million; and Oceania (17 million) only 16 million.

Table 5
POPULATION PROJECTIONS: WORLD AND MAJOR AREAS 1965-2000

World and Major Areas	Mid-1965 Estimated population	1970 Continued trends	1970 Medium	1970 Low	1980 Continued trends	1980 Medium	1980 Low	1990 Continued trends	1990 Medium	1990 Low	2000 Continued trends	2000 Medium	2000 Low
WORLD	3,308	3,626	3,574	3,515	4,487	4,269	4,071	5,704	5,068	4,659	7,410	5,965	5,296
Asia	1,842	2,033	2,000	1,959	2,557	2,404	2,279	3,317	2,840	2,606	4,401	3,307	2,969
East Asia	867	941	910	882	1,139	1,038	963	1,419	1,163	1,036	1,803	1,281	1,114
South Asia	975	1,092	1,090	1,077	1,418	1,366	1,316	1,898	1,677	1,570	2,598	2,023	1,855
Africa	311	348	346	344	458	449	434	620	587	546	860	768	684
Latin America	218	284	282	278	387	374	352	537	488	429	756	624	514
Europe	443	460	454	450	496	479	467	533	504	482	571	527	491
Northern America	215	230	227	222	272	262	248	325	306	274	388	354	294
Oceania	17	18	19	19	22	23	22	27	27	25	33	32	27
U.S.S.R.	234	253	246	243	295	278	269	345	316	297	402	353	316

Table 6
PROJECTED ANNUAL RATE OF INCREASE 1960-2000

Per Cent

World and Major Areas	1960-1970 Continued trends	1960-1970 Medium	1960-1970 Low	1970-1980 Continued trends	1970-1980 Medium	1970-1980 Low	1980-1990 Continued trends	1980-1990 Medium	1980-1990 Low	1990-2000 Continued trends	1990-2000 Medium	1990-2000 Low
WORLD	2.1	2.0	1.8	2.4	1.9	1.6	2.7	1.9	1.4	3.0	1.8	1.4
East Asia	1.9	1.5	1.1	2.1	1.4	0.9	2.5	1.2	0.7	2.7	1.0	0.8
South Asia	2.7	2.7	2.5	3.0	2.5	2.2	3.4	2.3	1.9	3.7	2.1	1.8
Africa	2.7	2.7	2.6	3.2	3.0	2.6	3.5	3.1	2.6	3.9	3.1	2.5
Latin America	3.4	3.3	3.1	3.6	3.2	2.6	3.9	3.1	2.2	4.1	2.8	2.0
Europe	0.8	0.7	0.6	0.8	0.6	0.4	0.7	0.5	0.3	0.7	0.5	0.2
Northern America	1.6	1.4	1.2	1.8	1.5	1.2	1.9	1.7	1.0	1.9	1.6	0.7
Oceania	1.7	1.9	1.8	1.9	2.1	1.7	2.1	2.0	1.4	2.2	1.8	1.2
U.S.S.R.	1.8	1.5	1.4	1.7	1.3	1.0	1.7	1.4	1.0	1.7	1.2	0.7

Table 7

POPULATION PROJECTIONS BY 24 REGIONS AND 5 SELECTED COUNTRIES 1965-2000

Region and Selected Country	Mid-1965 Estimated population	1970 Continued trends	1970 Medium	1960-1970 Annual rate of increase continued trends	1980 Continued trends	1980 Medium	1970-1980 Annual rate of increase continued trends	1990 Continued trends	1990 Medium	1980-1990 Annual rate of increase continued trends	2000 Continued trends	2000 Medium	1990-2000 Annual rate of increase continued trends
	millions			%	millions		%	millions		%	millions		%
EAST ASIA													
Mainland Region	715	776	748	1.9	942	850	2.1	1,180	949	2.5	1,509	1,045	2.8
China (Mainland)	710	770	742	1.8	935	843	2.2	1,171	940	2.5	1,498	1,034	2.8
Japan	98	103	101	1.1	114	111	1.0	122	118	0.7	127	122	0.4
Other East Asia	54	61	60	3.2	83	77	3.6	117	96	4.1	166	116	4.2
China (Taiwan)	12	14	14	3.5	20	17	3.9	28	21	4.1	39	25	4.0
S. Korea	29	33	33	3.5	46	43	3.8	65	55	4.3	94	67	4.4
SOUTH ASIA													
Middle S. Asia	656	732	730	2.6	945	900	2.9	1,255	1,072	3.3	1,709	1,252	3.6
India	484	542	541	2.3	694	662	2.5	914	783	2.8	1,234	908	3.0
Pakistan[1]	106	121	121	2.7	162	154	2.9	223	189	3.2	314	227	3.5
Southeast Asia	251	283	283	2.9	370	364	3.1	140	133	3.6	193	168	3.8
Southwest Asia	68	77	77	3.0	103	102	3.4	503	472	3.6	697	603	3.9
AFRICA													
Western Africa	100	114	113	3.3	156	150	3.7	220	202	4.1	318	277	4.5
Eastern Africa	83	91	190	2.1	114	113	2.6	147	143	2.9	193	183	3.1
Middle Africa	31	33	33	1.8	40	41	2.1	50	51	2.5	64	65	2.8
Northern Africa	76	87	87	3.2	117	116	3.5	161	153	3.8	228	192	4.1
Southern Africa	20	23	23	3.0	30	30	3.3	41	39	3.6	58	51	3.9
LATIN AMERICA													
Tropical S. America	133	154	153	3.7	214	205	3.9	302	271	4.1	431	350	4.3
Middle America	56	65	65	3.8	92	90	4.2	133	125	4.5	195	166	4.6
Temperate S. America	36	39	39	2.0	47	46	2.0	57	53	2.0	68	61	2.0
Caribbean	23	26	25	2.8	34	32	3.1	45	39	3.4	62	48	3.6
NORTHERN AMERICA	215	230	227	1.6	272	262	1.8	325	306	1.9	388	354	2.0
United States[2]	194	211	208	1.6	252	241	1.8	301	288	1.8	362	338	1.9
EUROPE													
Western Europe[3]	139	144	144	0.7	152	152	0.6	161	160	0.6	172	168	0.6
Southern Europe[4]	123	129	127	1.0	141	135	0.9	154	142	0.8	165	149	0.8
Eastern Europe	102	106	105	1.0	116	114	1.0	126	122	0.9	136	128	0.8
Northern Europe[5]	80	81	79	0.7	87	81	0.7	92	82	0.6	98	84	0.7
SOVIET UNION	234	253	246	1.8	295	278	1.7	345	316	1.7	402	353	1.7
OCEANIA													
Australia & N. Zealand	14	15	15	1.6	17	18	1.7	20	21	1.8	24	24	1.8
Melanesia[6]	2	3	3	—	3	3	—	4	2	—	5	5	—
Polynesia & Micronesia[6]	1	1	1	—	2	2	—	3	2	—	4	3	—

[1] According to U.S. Bureau of Census report on Pakistani population, the continued trends projection is 114 million (1965), 136 million (1970), and 230 million (1985).

[2] For the U.S., continued trends is based on the post-Word War II high fertility pattern. Recently U.S. fertility has been declining slightly and a continuation of this trend approximates the medium projection.

[3] Medium assumes net immigration of 100,000 per year.

[4] Medium assumes net emigration of 150,000 per year.

[5] Medium assumes net emigration of 130,000 per year.

[6] Rough conjectures based on arbitrarily assumed rates.

3 | Spatial Characteristics of the World's Population

Up to this point we have been concerned primarily with numbers. Before going any further it is important to consider how these numbers are distributed on the earth's surface: in other words, to introduce a spatial dimension to the study of population.

DISTRIBUTION AND DENSITY*

Glenn T. Trewartha

[1969]

The concepts of distribution and density as applied to population are not identical, yet they are so closely interrelated that there is good reason to discuss them simultaneously. Population distribution is most often represented by two kinds of maps: one employing dots or points for numerical values, and the other making use of different density categories derived from ratios of number of people to area.

Both dot and density maps are relatively simple and unsophisticated, for they involve only numbers of people and disregard their character- istics. Thus they assume men of various cultures and backgrounds are equal in their acquired characteristics, and no account is taken of their great variety of skills, technological levels, physical well being, and edu- cational accomplishments, or of their capacities as producers and con- sumers. Such maps also disregard the fact that areas of comparable size may vary strikingly in their resource potentials for supporting human life. Most population maps therefore have serious limitations, for they assume a standardization of both people and areas that does not exist.

The dot (or point) map is especially effective in representing details of spatial distribution pattern that ordinarily cannot be picked up on

*From G. T. Trewartha, *A Geography of Population: World Patterns.* Copyright © 1969 John Wiley & Sons, Inc., New York. Reprinted by permission.

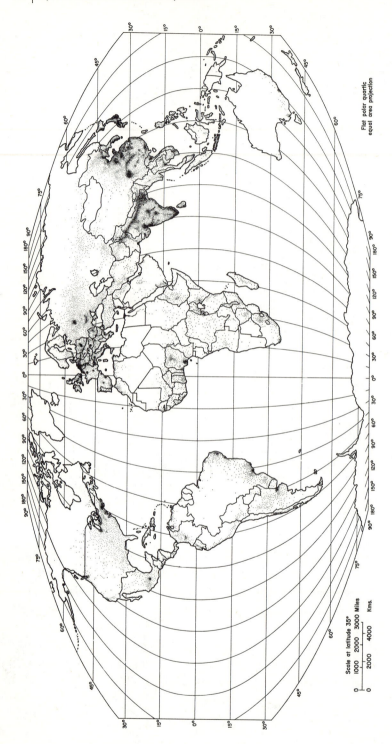

FIGURE 9 Distribution of population. Each dot represents 100,000 people.

most density maps (Figure 9). Offsetting this advantage, however, is the disadvantage that the dot map is not quantitative—it shows only *relative* degrees of crowding not expressed quantitatively. This the density map does; on the other hand, it is a blunter instrument for showing details of pattern distribution.

By far the most common population density map is the one whose ratio compares total population to total area. This is spoken of as *arithmetic* [or simple] *density*. Its weaknesses have already been noted. Its merits for showing spatial distribution patterns increase as the size of the statistical areas decrease. A density map of the United States by states has little merit; by minor civil divisions it is far more useful. The almost universal use of arithmetic density reflects the fact that the data required by this ratio are by far the most readily available (Figure 10).

A somewhat more refined form of density is expressed by the ratio *total population/arable area*. This is sometimes called *nutritional density*, or *physiological density*. Here there is eliminated from the denominator all land not fit for tillage. Of course it errs in eliminating all productive nonarable land, including not just waste or barren land but also forest, wild pasture, mining land, and scenic areas. It likewise does not recognize the great variations in the output of various arable lands having different climates, soils, and drainage characteristics. Still, it provides a better indicator than does arithmetic density of the degree of crowding in a region compared with its physical potential for producing food and agricultural raw materials. Japan's arithmetic density in 1960, for example, was 655 per square mile; its nutritional density was an unbelievable 4,680, a fact which suggests the necessity for significant imports of food and vegetable raw materials.

Occasionally density maps are compiled by employing the ratio agricultural population/arable land. Here the nonfarmers in the population are eliminated. This ratio is especially useful for indicating a more realistic population density in regions where farm families constitute a large share of the total population.

Certain noteworthy features concerning arithmetic density distributions, on a world scale, may be observed from Figure 10 and Table 8. The most conspicuous feature of current population spread is its extreme unevenness. About half the earth's people are crowded onto some 5 per cent of the earth's land area. By contrast, some 50-60 per cent of the land area probably contains only 5 per cent of the earth's inhabitants. Although the ratio of men to area shows a wide range of variability,

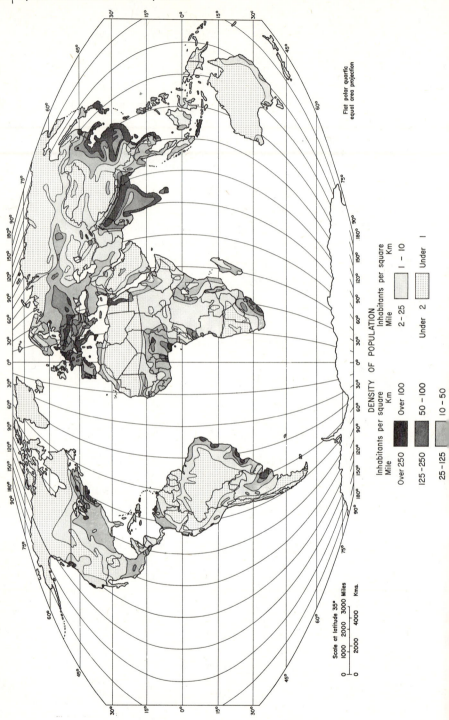

this is irreducible to any simple formula. An easily recognizable and repeated world pattern, more particularly of the high population densities, does not seem to prevail. Crowded and sparse characteristics are common to traditional societies and to those that are technologically advanced, to white and coloured races, to the Old World and the New, and to tropics as well as middle latitudes. Java is an overcrowded island with traditional culture in the wet tropics; Belgium and the Netherlands are high-density states with Western culture, located in middle latitudes; population-saturated Egypt is an agrarian riverine state that developed in an arid environment. Significantly dense populations are lacking in high latitudes. The map shows that the largest areas of high density (>250 per square mile or 100 per square kilometre) are to be

Table 8

AREA, POPULATION, AND POPULATION DENSITY BY REGIONS OF THE WORLD IN 1960 AND 1980 (MEDIUM VARIANT ESTIMATES)

Regions	Area (Sq. Km.)	Population (Million)		Density Per Sq. Km.	
		1960	1980	1960	1980
MORE DEVELOPED COUNTRIES					
Australia and New Zealand	7,973	13	18	1.6	2.2
Temperate South America	4,124	33	46	8	11
Northern America	21,515	199	262	9	12
U.S.S.R.	22,402	214	278	10	12
Northern Europe	1,636	76	81	46	50
Southern Europe	1,314	117	133	89	101
Eastern Europe	989	97	114	98	115
Western Europe	992	135	152	136	153
Japan	370	93	111	252	300
LESS DEVELOPED COUNTRIES					
Melanesia	539	2.2	3.1	4	6
Middle Africa	6,607	28	41	4	6
Southern Africa	2,670	18	30	7	11
Northern Africa	8,484	66	116	8	14
Tropical South America	13,666	112	210	8	15
Eastern Africa	6,301	75	113	12	18
Western Africa	6,165	86	150	14	24
Southwest Asia	3,968	59	102	15	26
Middle America	2,512	47	90	19	36
Polynesia and Micronesia	45	0.9	1.7	20	38
Southeast Asia	4,492	219	364	49	81
East Asia (Mainland region)	11,097	654	850	59	77
Middle South Asia	6,774	587	954	86	133
Caribbean	235	20	32	85	136
Other East Asia	259	47	80	178	297
More Developed Countries	61,315	977	1,195	16	19
Less Developed Countries	73,814	2,021	3,075	27	42
World Total	135,129	2,998	4,332	22	32

SOURCE: United Nations, *World Population Prospects*, Chap. 6.

found in eastern and southern Asia, western Europe, and northeastern United States. In some parts of these high-density regions the ratio rises to 500, 1,000 per square mile, and even higher. In Europe and Anglo-America, both regions of advanced technological culture, high densities are characteristically linked with a strong degree of urbanization. But this is not the case in Asia, where (Japan excepted), on fertile alluvial plains, high densities usually represent predominantly rural farm people.

Very low densities of under 2 per square mile are typical of much more extensive areas than are very high densities. The near-empty lands are largely confined to drought regions, cold high-latitude and high-altitude lands, and some, but by no means all, wet-tropical environments, particularly those in South America. The sparsely populated Anglo-American dry lands are representative of regions with a high Western standard of living; the emptier Amazon Basin symbolizes a primitive agrarian culture.

The present highly irregular spatial distribution and arrangement of the earth's people as revealed in Figure 10 and Table 8 can only be a consequence of the adjustment of population to resources, and to the impact of cultural and demographic influences, over the millenniums of human history. But the present distribution certainly is only a temporary condition, for it is hard to believe that spatial distribution will not change in the future as it has in the past. Just how much and in what ways cannot be predicted. It is probably true that the blocking out of the world in terms of its productive capacity, and hence in a measure its population density, has at present been achieved to a degree not known previously. The discovery of new resources and the development of new technologies for their utilization have today progressed so far that the people of the world are more nearly where they seem to belong than ever before, taking into consideration their cultural level and organization. But that is not to say that a static condition in spatial distribution has been reached. There is no limit, apparently, to terrestrial and extra-terrestrial discoveries, and man's inventiveness seemingly has no bounds. Hence the resource base will change as men's ideas change, and, of course, the spatial features of population will too. Over the past few decades amazing new discoveries of mineral resources have occurred, and unbelievable new storehouses of energy have been envisioned in atomic and hydrogen sources. Whether such energy will be used to obliterate population or to multiply it and change its concentrations is problematic.

The factors that affect the spatial aspects of population are as complex and varied as are the patterns of distribution. Three main classes of factors may be recognized:

1. Physical or natural factors, including climate, terrain, water, soils, minerals, as well as space relationships.

2. Cultural factors, embracing social attitudes and institutions, stage of economic development, and political organization.

3. Demographic factors, involving differential birth and death rates and the currents of migration.

Characteristically the factors affecting population distribution do not operate singly, but always in combinations. Consequently, it is nearly impossible to segregate and assess the effects of one single factor. Moreover, it is recognized that the interplay of the various influences is highly complex, and that their effects are brought to bear upon population usually indirectly and through a slow process of adaptation. Probably it is correct to say that *the role of physical factors in spatial distribution of population declines in direct importance as civilization advances in complexity.* As a rule, in simple agrarian societies, primitive and otherwise, where differential population numbers and densities depend very largely on the direct food-producing potentials of the land, physical factors exercise a relatively greater influence. For example, agrarian societies are more subject to the vicissitudes of nature than are technologically advanced urban cultures. Also, the importance of physical factors is somewhat less in modern times than it was earlier, when science and technology were less advanced. In large measure the significance to a population of the natural earth is determined by its culture. Consequently changes in the technological efficiency, aspirations, and objectives of a people require a constant reassessment of the role of the physical resource base.

DISTRIBUTION BY ECUMENE AND NONECUMENE*

Glenn T. Trewartha

To understand better the basic nature of the distribution of the world's population, it is necessary to examine the concepts of *ecumene* and *nonecumene.* The former refers to the permanently inhabited areas of the world, while the latter includes those areas that are uninhabited, sparsely inhabited, or intermittently inhabited. In the following article Trewartha discusses these concepts and some of the complex factors that account for the characteristics and location of these areas. Obviously in a study of population it is important not only to appreciate the distribution and density of the world's population, but also to ponder the implications of increasing population densities and expanding the boundaries of the

*From G. T. Trewartha, *A Geography of Population: World Patterns.* Copyright © 1969 John Wiley & Sons, Inc., New York. Reprinted by permission.

ecumene. Both of these changes are occurring and will continue to occur as the world's population grows. Which will be the most important in absorbing future population growth? To what extent is Trewartha correct when he states that the role of physical factors affecting the spatial distribution of population declines as civilization increases in complexity? Can we look forward to large populations in the polar and equatorial regions? Even if large-scale settlement in such physically hostile regions is possible, should we consider this desirable?

[1969]

On first thought it may seem a simple matter to differentiate ecumene and nonecumene and represent them on a world map (Figure 11). Actually it is very difficult, for neither the occupied nor the unoccupied land is a compact, continuous surface. In addition, the boundary separating the two is not easy to demarcate. The great ice caps of Antarctica and Greenland represent the more complete and continuous nonecumene. But much of the nonecumene is in the form of isolated unoccupied or intermittently occupied regions of variable size—desert wastes, cold barrens, high mountains, swamps, primeval forest in both tropics and subarctic—which punctuate the ecumene. Hence the boundaries separating ecumene from nonecumene are vague and complex; precise data for many parts are lacking. Even any quantitative assessment of the relative proportions of the earth's land surface that should be classed as occupied is subject to serious error. Of the earth's land area of about 149 million square kilometres, Hassinger estimates that some 27 million (31 to 32 per cent) are barren waste, either cold or dry, and without appreciable human settlement.[1] Large areas within the primeval forest are also population empty, and these and other islands of nonecumene may reduce the ecumene to 80-90 million square kilometres or only 55 to 60 per cent of the total land area.

Even allowing for the dubious accuracy of the preceding figures, it becomes clear that a goodly proportion of the earth's solid surface is largely without permanent human settlement. About four-fifths of the earth's population occupies less than one-fifth of the surface of the continents. Still, the nonecumene is smaller today than ever before, for an established feature of human history has been an ever-expanding ecumene. This has been accelerated during the last few centuries, a period which has seen a spread of European settlement on a scale never

[1] *Handbuch der geographische Wissenschaft, Allgemeine Geographie*, Zweiter Teil, *Das Leben auf der Erde*, Akademische Verlagsgesellschaft Athenaion M.B.H., Potsdam, 1933.

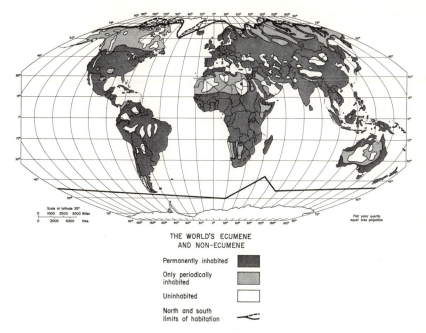

THE WORLD'S ECUMENE
AND NON-ECUMENE

Permanently inhabited

Only periodically
inhabited

Uninhabited

North and south
limits of habitation

FIGURE 11   Generalized distribution of ecumene and nonecumene. (After map by Hassinger, in *Allgemeine Geographie*, Vol. 9.)

before equalled. The expansion of Western peoples many times was not into completely empty areas, but rather a filling in with permanent settlements by a technologically higher culture of regions previously occupied either thinly, or only intermittently, by weaker and less resistant ones. A rapidly shrinking nonecumene is less typical of the present; actually the current settlement frontier is a fluctuating one, advancing in some places and stationary, or even retreating, in others.

In view of the burgeoning world population and the diligent probing for new settlement areas during the past few centuries, it would appear that those lands that still remain empty, or only periodically or very sparsely occupied, must be those that are definitely marginal in resource character and present serious physical obstacles to human settlement. (The only other explanation of the present extensive nonecumene is that people, and especially those of European culture, have been myopic in judging the resource potential of certain environments.) With few exceptions, these obstacles are basically climatic in origin, although drainage, soil, rough terrain, and wild vegetation are often auxiliary factors. In some high cordillera the prevalence of steep slopes admittedly is a deterrent to settlement. But still, it is the highest, and therefore coldest, windiest, and bleakest highlands that are most empty, suggesting that climate is the main obstacle.

As a generalization further differentiating ecumene and nonecumene, it can be pointed out that the extensive coterminous empty regions are overwhelmingly a consequence of defects in the resource base. Their environments are hostile to man. By contrast, within the ecumene the wide variations in density of settlement are both cultural and physical in origin. Socio-economic causation is there much more to the forefront. For example, one can scarcely make a good case for the resource base being responsible, even indirectly, for over half of humanity being crowded into the rimlands of eastern and southern Asia, or for another one-fifth's being lodged in Europe.

LANDS HOSTILE TO MAN—THE NONECUMENE

Three types of climate—the cold, the dry, and the hot-wet—embrace most of the earth's empty lands (Figure 12). Of these three types, it is those which are deficient in heat that provide the most negative conditions for human settlement. Next in order are the rainfall-deficient dry lands. But where underground or surface water is available in these climatically dry lands, settlement usually is dense. No comparable local temperature exceptions exist in the cold lands. Least hostile to man seem to be the hot-wet lands.

THE COLD LANDS

It is high latitudes that provide the largest share of the cold nonecumene. Smaller and more discontinuous areas of low temperature exist at high altitudes in all latitudes. Completely without permanent settlement are the extensive ice caps of Antarctica and Greenland and some of the northernmost island tundra lands of both North America and Eurasia. In the still more extensive tundra and forested boreal lands on the mainlands of those two continents farther south, some areas are completely without settlement; more are classified as only periodically occupied. Permanent settlement in boreal Eurasia is mainly confined to the river valleys. The Arctic and subarctic cold desert north of about the 65° parallel certainly contains fewer than a million inhabitants.

Chief climatic handicaps in the cold ecumene are a completely absent, or at best very short, annual freeze-free interval, a cool summer, and a long annual period without sun. On the ice caps the average tempera-

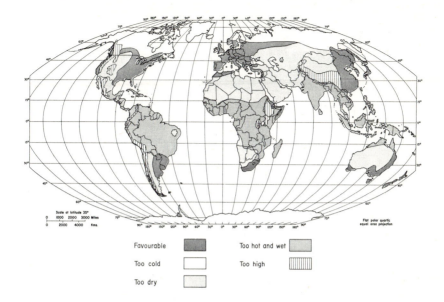

FIGURE 12 Lands attractive and hostile to man. Most of the lands unoccupied or sparsely occupied by human beings have environments that are hostile to man—too cold, too dry, too hot and wet, or too high and rugged. Some hot and wet regions, especially in the Old World tropics, are densely peopled. (Modified from map in *Focus*, September 1959, published by the American Geographical Society. From *Elements of Geography* by Trewartha, Robinson and Hammond. McGraw-Hill.)

tures of all months are below freezing, so there is no growing season for plant life. In the tundra, where by arbitrary definition the average temperature for at least one month rises above 32° (but not over 50°), a lowly plant cover consisting of mosses, lichens, sedges, and some bushes provides meagre forage for a sparse nomadic-herding population of polar peoples, based mainly on reindeer in Eurasia. In the North American sector the polar peoples are chiefly hunters and fishers. In the boreal climates south of the tundra, where average temperatures for one to three summer months creep above 50°, an extensive forest, predominantly of needle trees, prevails. Only along the southernmost margins of the subarctic forest, and following some of the river valleys in Eurasia, is the summer warm enough and long enough to permit a modest amount of tillage. Fur-trading posts, more recently mining and lumbering camps, and infrequent military and scientific establishments occasionally break the monotony of the forest or tundra, but the total aggregate population is small. Auxiliary handicaps associated with the niggardly polar and boreal climates are the extensive development of a permanently frozen subsoil (permafrost), large areas of swamp and bog, a thoroughly leached and poor-texture topsoil, and large regions of ice scour. Inaccessibility adds a further element of discouragement.

Prospects for future important and widespread permanent new settlement in the subarctic and tundra, and a concomitant shrinking of the cold nonecumene, are bleak indeed. It now appears that only isolated islands and strips of durable settlement can be expected, and the cold environment as a whole is likely to remain an ecumene frontier.

THE DRY LANDS

On this frontier of the ecumene the great obstacle to durable settlement is an annual deficiency of water in the form of precipitation. Supplementing this is the unreliability of the rainfall, and the sparseness and low utility of the wild-vegetation cover. Desert soils, where they exist, may be high in mineral plant foods, although they are usually coarse, stony, and deficient in organic matter. Within the deserts are extensive isolated regions devoid of population, imbedded within a larger matrix of territory which is only very thinly or periodically occupied by nomadic peoples. This generally empty landscape stands in stark contrast to the dense settlement present in a few oases where a durable supply of surface or underground fresh water is available.

During the past half century or more, application of modern engineering techniques to irrigation projects has resulted in appreciable expansion of settlement within the dry lands. Some of these projects have been expensive multipurpose operations involving not only irrigation but also development of hydro-electric power as well as recreation and navigation facilities. Many times these have been costly projects involving large capital outlays that only a national government could finance. This type of expensive reclaimed land tends to attract mainly high-value crops, for instance, fruits and vegetables. Doubtless the irrigated desert can be somewhat further expanded, but only at high cost, and mainly through the impounding of surface drainage behind huge dams.

Other dry-land reclamation possibilities involve the providing of fresh irrigation water by the desalinization of sea water, and the augmentation of normal rainfall using cloud-seeding techniques. Fresh water produced by desalinization methods, although expensive, is not prohibitively so for municipal use. At present, desalinized water can be produced at a cost of about $65 to $100 per acre-foot *at the plant*, but this is well in excess of what can be afforded for irrigation water for crops.

Still, 'there seems to be little question that the market for nuclear desalting will extend into agricultural territory.'[1] This will be some time in the future, and in the beginning will be used in limited quantities only, and for high-value crops only. It is not yet known whether costs can be reduced sufficiently to make desalinized water useful in growing basic food crops.

The costs involved in producing precipitation water by cloud-seeding methods are relatively cheap compared with desalinization. In cloud seeding the question is not so much one of cost, but rather the physical ability to cause appreciable rainfall in dry climates by this method. There are serious limitations, for rainfall can be increased only from clouds that are already raining or about to rain, and such clouds are scarce indeed in dry climates. There are still no known ways to stimulate useful precipitation from cloudless skies, a condition so common in deserts, or even from clouds too thin to contain much water. The likelihood of utilizing either desalinization or cloud-seeding methods for importantly augmenting the water supplies of desert agriculture in the foreseeable future do not seem bright, but neither are they hopeless.[2]

There are those who believe that despite these obstacles dry lands will eventually be conquered. For example, a Russian scientist[3] points out that spatial distribution of solar radiation at the earth's surface is one of the two greatest determinants of earth resources for human use, since the energy of solar radiation is utilized by the biosphere. Annual solar energy receipts are greatest in the tropical and subtropical dry lands and the savannas. But there a serious shortage of water exists, just where solar radiation is at a maximum. Still Pokshishevskii writes: 'But humanity is acquiring more and more skill and technical facilities for the redistribution of water, and the control of run-off; thus in the final analysis and in the far future, the zones with most abundant solar radiation may be expected to become the richest in the bio-energetic sense, which is specially important for food production. A time may be foreseen when the present-day deserts and the zones of tropical (but not equatorial) forests will become the main granaries of the earth. . . .'

[1] R. Philip Hammond, 'Nuclear Desalting for Agricultural Water', *Nucleonics*, Vol. 23, September 1965, pp. 51-5.
[2] W. R. Derrick Sewell (ed.), *Human Dimensions of Weather Modification*, University of Chicago, Dept. of Geography Research Paper No. 105, Chicago, Ill., 1966, pp. 31, 65.
[3] V. V. Pokshishevskii, 'The Population and Resources of the World'. Paper submitted to a Symposium on the Geography of Population Pressure on the Physical and Social Resources, Pennsylvania State University, September 17-23, 1967.

Most agronomists would probably consider this forecast dangerously optimistic.

The semi-arid lands surrounding the deserts serve as transition belts between desert and humid climates. They are also transitional between ecumene and nonecumene. Those of middle latitudes have been partially settled by people of Western culture during the last century, so that by far the greater share of the steppe is now under permanent, although relatively thin settlement. In fact in some areas the dry frontier of tillage moved too far toward the desert, and has been forced to withdraw.

THE HOT-WET LANDS

Unlike the other two types of extensive nonecumene, the wet tropics, instead of being plagued with seemingly insuperable climatic deficiencies, are afflicted with a superabundance of climatic energy in the forms of solar radiation, heat, and precipitation. It is the excess of climatic energy and the associated features of a lush, wild vegetation and low-grade soils which appear to have retarded settlement over extensive parts of the wet tropics. Annual receipts of solar energy reach a maximum in the tropical and subtropical latitudes,[1] and in the wet tropics rainfall and heat are both abundant, and the heat is continuous throughout the year. There is no dormant season for vegetation because of cold, and in equatorial latitudes none because of drought, so that the cover of wild vegetation is luxuriant. A dense broadleaf evergreen forest dominates in those wetter parts lacking a significant dry season; deciduous trees and tall grasses prevail where the rainfall is more seasonal. Nowhere else do plants grow as quickly and luxuriantly as in the wet tropics, and since it is from plants, directly, or indirectly through herbivorous animals, that man derives his food supply, the dense and prolific vegetation is an indicator of a large potential food-producing capacity, capable of supporting large populations.

There are offsetting features, however. Abundant rainfall in the presence of constant heat acts to remove the soil's soluble plant foods so that mature soils are highly deficient in those elements. Under tillage they deteriorate rapidly and need a long fallow period for recuperation. Beneficial soil organisms are scarce. Growth of weedy plants in tilled fields is rapid, tending to suffocate crops not carefully tended. Heat and

[1] This does not occur close to the equator, where the abundant cloudiness somewhat reduces the solar energy received at the earth's surface.

humidity make for great physical discomfort, hasten spoilage and decomposition, and create an environment stimulating to parasites and bacteria injurious to plants, animals, and men.[1]

Unlike the dry and the cold nonecumene where population is either lacking, exceedingly thin, or only periodic, the humid tropics exhibit all gradations of settlement density, from emptiness to severe crowding. The New World tropics, on the average, are less well peopled than those of the Old World, particularly those of Asia. Just why is not clear. But in both the Eastern and Western Hemisphere tropics there are plenty of examples of both high and low population densities. The vast Amazon Basin is illustrative of the relatively empty tropics, and Java, lowland India, and Puerto Rico of the crowded sections. But the very fact that such variations in density actually do exist clearly indicates that the humid tropics do have potentialities for future settlement probably far in excess of those possessed by either the cold or the dry lands. Kellogg has estimated that 20 per cent of the unused tropical lands within the Americas, Madagascar, Borneo, and New Guinea, amounting to nearly 400 million hectares, could be brought into cultivation if suitable land-use systems can be developed.[2] It is in the humid tropics, most likely, that the nonecumene will suffer its greatest shrinkage in the decades to come. The speed of reclamation is another matter.

A frightening aspect of modern population is its soaring rate of growth. A concomitant feature is that this burgeoning is not accompanied by a significant settlement on new lands. Quite the opposite, for the added population is mainly piling up in previously settled areas to create higher densities and greater crowding. This seems to suggest that in terms of man's present productive skills, the contemporary world pattern of ecumene-nonecumene may better reflect the quality of the resource base than it did in earlier periods. Still, one should guard against myopic judgements. In the man-resource relationship both factors are constantly changing. Not only is population dynamic in both numbers and potentialities, but the resource base is as well. The resource base changes with succeeding scientific inventions and discoveries, and with each new plant-breeding success. The population optimum in a complex scientific civilization depends not alone on area of crop land, manpower, and loaves of bread, but even more upon the relationship between

---

[1] Jen-Hu Chang, 'The Agricultural Potential of the Humid Tropics', *Geographical Review*, Vol. 57, July 1968, pp. 333-61.
[2] C. E. Kellogg, *Food, Soil and People*, The Manhattan Publishing Co. (with UNESCO), New York, 1950, p. 21.

human intelligence, horsepower, and computers, whose limits certainly have not been reached. So, most likely, the potentialities of the earth for supporting population will change in the future as they have in the past. The new tools constantly being fashioned by science cannot help but modify our present concepts of the man-land relationship.

THE ECUMENE

As pointed out earlier, great variations in the degree of population concentration exist within the inhabited sections of the earth. Moreover, areal variations in density of settlement within the ecumene, while by no means unrelated to the qualities of the physical environment, are more frequently and more strongly influenced by socioeconomic factors. Thus, whereas the nonecumene appears to be largely physically conditioned, the variety in population density within the ecumene has stronger attachment to cultural causes. Four of the ecumene's main population clusters are particularly noteworthy.

Some 70 to 75 per cent of the earth's population is contained within four primary clusters: two in Asia, one in Europe, and one—the smallest—in Anglo-America. Together the two Asiatic concentrations, one in East Asia and the other in tropical South Asia, account for about 46 per cent of the world's inhabitants (this rises to 52 to 53 per cent if intervening Southeast Asia is included). Largest of the four, the cluster in eastern Asia has about 26 per cent. Its main political units are China with over 700 million inhabitants, Japan with about 100 million, North and South Korea, and Taiwan. Together India (some 525 million), Pakistan (about 125 million), and Ceylon comprise a great share of the South Asia cluster, whose approximately 675 million people make up about 20 per cent of the world's total. The European concentration (roughly 650 million, including European U.S.S.R.) is almost of the same magnitude as that in South Asia. Smallest of all (less than 6 per cent) is the cluster in central and eastern Anglo-America, which includes most of the United States' entire 200 million and Canada's 21 million.

Of the ecumene's four main population concentrations, the one in Europe is centred at about 50°N, the one in Anglo-America about 10° closer to the equator, and that in East Asia at about 35°N. Only the cluster in South Asia is distinctly tropical in location. Two of the population concentrations border upon the Atlantic Ocean, one on the Pacific, and one on the Indian.

The four population concentrations pair off in other important respects as well. The Anglo-American concentration, developed as a result of a budding off from Europe, expectedly bears the stamp of European culture, including its distinguishing features of economic development. These two population clusters are far advanced in a scientific, machine-age civilization, individual wealth is relatively great, living standards are high, regional specialization is well developed, and urbanization—the offspring of industry and commerce—is far advanced, with the consequence that urban dwellers make up a large proportion of all the people. The two Atlantic clusters include a great majority of the more developed countries, in which 20 per cent of the world's population controls 80 per cent of the world's wealth.

By contrast, the pre-modern world still exists to a large degree in the two Asiatic clusters. Here the people are predominantly poor peasant farmers engaged in intensive subsistence agriculture. Population presses closely upon the food supply; poverty and malnutrition are omnipresent; birth rates are still depressingly high, while death rates, although still high by Western standards, are falling. Consequently the rate of natural increase in population is large and, of course, in absolute numbers it is tremendous. Urban population comprises a small fraction of the total. Japan is the single political unit within the two Asiatic clusters which has experienced the demographic transition accompanying the Scientific-Industrial Revolution, with the result that it resembles Europe and Anglo-America both in its birth and death rates and in its emphasis on manufacturing and trade.

What is remarkable about the Asiatic population is that it has become so vast and so dense while at the same time remaining overwhelmingly rural. It has not been greatly affected by the processes of industrialization and urbanization to which the large and dense populations in the West can be attributed. This unique situation in Asia has its origin partly in the fact that its intensive agriculture is almost completely oriented toward the vegetable kingdom, and does not significantly involve animal feeding. Such an agriculture in which crops are consumed directly by human beings can support several times more people than a mixed crop-animal type in which much of the crop output is fed to animals, whose products subsequently are consumed by humans. Thus it is the vegetarian diet that has allowed the rural Asians to become so numerous and so dense. Supplementary factors are the great antiquity of Asiatic civilization, its intensive subsistence agriculture, a prevalence of almost universal marriage, and the early age at which marriage takes place.

4 | Population Growth and Economic Development

Although economic development has already been referred to several times, it is very important to note that one of the most fundamental aspects of the population problem is the relationship between such development and population growth. The article that follows clearly underlines this and, in so doing, succinctly summarizes the great demographic dilemma.

A distinction between the developed or industrial countries and the underdeveloped or non-industrial ones is mentioned in many places in this book. It should be pointed out, however, that many levels or stages of development exist. The term 'underdeveloped' is a relative one; that is, certain countries are underdeveloped in relation to more industrialized and economically more complex countries, notably those in North America and western Europe—commonly referred to as the *'developed countries'* *(DCs)*. However, the general and much-used expression *'underdeveloped countries' (UDCs)* refers to those that are characterized, among other things, by a low level of industrialization, a low gross national product, and a high rate of illiteracy. These differences are discussed further in the article that follows and also in those on pp. 54 and 170.

THE GREAT DEMOGRAPHIC PROBLEM*

Donald J. Bogue

[1969]

The United Nations has prepared estimates of world population and growth for each continent and for world regions (subdivisions of the continents). Data for each continent and region are reported in Table 9. . . . From this table . . . it is readily seen that more than one-half of the earth's inhabitants (56 per cent) live in Asia (excluding U.S.S.R.). Europe comprises a little less than one-seventh of the world population,

*From D. J. Bogue, *Principles of Demography*. Copyright © 1969 John Wiley & Sons, Inc., New York. Reprinted by permission.

Table 9

WORLD POPULATION, VITAL RATES, DISTRIBUTION, AND DENSITY BY CONTINENTS, DIVISIONS, AND REGIONS: 1966

Major divisions and regions of the world	ESTIMATED POPULATION 1966		VITAL STATISTICS 1960-66		PER CENT DISTRIBUTION		Density per square kilometre 1966
	Mid-year population (millions)	Annual rate of growth	Crude birth rate	Crude death rate	World's population	World's land area	
WORLD TOTAL	**3,356**	**1.9**	**34**	**16**	**100.0**	**100.0**	**25**
AFRICA	318	2.3	46	23	9.5	22.3	11
Western Africa	100	2.3	50	27	3.0	4.5	16
Eastern Africa	88	2.4	45	21	2.6	4.6	14
Northern Africa	76	2.4	43	19	2.3	6.2	9
Middle Africa	33	1.9	42	23	1.0	4.9	5
Southern Africa	21	2.5	42	17	0.6	2.0	8
AMERICA	470	2.2	32	11	14.0	30.9	11
NORTHERN AMERICA	217	1.5	22	9	6.5	15.8	10
LATIN AMERICA	253	2.8	41	13	7.5	15.1	12
Tropical South America	135	2.9	43	14	3.9	10.1	10
Middle America	59	3.5	45	10	1.8	1.8	24
Temperate South America	36	1.8	28	10	1.1	3.0	9
Caribbean	23	2.4	38	14	0.7	0.2	99
ASIA	1,868	2.0	38	18	55.7	20.3	68
EAST ASIA	864	1.4	33	19	25.7	8.6	73
Mainland Region	710	1.4	35	21	21.1	8.2	64
Japan	99	1.0	17	7	3.0	0.3	267
Other East Asia	55	2.8	40	12	1.6	0.2	214
SOUTH ASIA	1,004	2.5	43	18	30.0	11.7	64
Middle South Asia	681	2.5	43	18	20.4	5.0	101
South East Asia	255	2.6	43	17	7.6	3.3	57
South West Asia	68	2.4	42	18	2.0	3.4	15
EUROPE	449	0.9	18	10	13.4	3.6	91
Western Europe	145	1.2	18	11	4.3	0.7	147
Southern Europe	124	0.8	21	9	3.7	1.0	94
Eastern Europe	101	0.6	17	9	3.0	0.7	102
Northern Europe	79	0.7	16	11	2.4	1.2	48
OCEANIA	17.9	2.1	26	11	0.5	6.3	2
Australia and New Zealand	14.3	2.0	22	9	0.4	5.9	2
Melanesia	2.5	2.4	44	20	0.1	0.4	5
Polynesia and Micronesia	1.1	3.0	40	10	—	—	36
U.S.S.R.	233	1.4	22	7	6.9	16.5	10

SOURCE: United Nations, *Demographic Yearbook, 1966,* Table 1.

as do the Americas combined. Africa, U.S.S.R., and Oceania together comprise the remaining one-sixth. Columns 5 and 6 of Table 9 give the percentage of the population and the land area of each continental region.

A glance at column 3 of Table 9 reveals a very surprising fact. With respect to fertility behaviour the world is divided into two distinct groups: the European region, which has moderately low birth rates— 16 to 21 per thousand population—and the Afro-Asian-Latin American group, which has high birth rates—35 to 50 per thousand population. In this grouping, North America, the U.S.S.R., and Oceania tend to fall between the two clusters at 22 to 26 per thousand. This is closer to the European than to the Asian-African-Latin American group. It is a very surprising fact that at the present time there are no regions where the birth rates fall in the high 20s or low 30s. In other words, birth rates tend to be either very high or moderately low, with no regions falling in between.

To summarize, if we group the world regions according to their level of birth rates, we have the following division:

LOW BIRTH-RATE REGIONS

Europe (all regions)
Northern America
U.S.S.R.
Oceania

HIGH BIRTH-RATE REGIONS

Asia
Africa
Middle America
South America

We see immediately that this list also rather neatly divides the world along economic lines into the 'economically underdeveloped' and the 'economically developed' or industrialized nations.[1] (Inasmuch as nearly all of the nations in the former group are in a highly dynamic condition of rapid economic development, we shall call them 'developing' rather than 'underdeveloped' nations.)[2] The following social and economic characteristics are commonly associated with these two types of economies:

INDUSTRIALIZED ECONOMIES

High level of literacy and educational attainment
Material comfort: high per-capita income
Predominantly urban
Dominant occupations: white collar, skilled, and government
Much communication and transportation

[1] There are, however, some outstanding exceptions. Argentina, Japan, Israel, Cyprus, and the Ryukyu Islands are now quite industrialized and resemble the European group more than they do the region in which they are located.
[2] While accepting Bogue's point, the terms 'underdeveloped' and 'developed' are used throughout this book. (ed.)

Much spatial mobility
Much use of electricity and fuel
Intensive medical care: high ratio of doctors and hospitals to population

DEVELOPING ECONOMIES

Low level of literacy
Poverty: low per-capita income
Predominantly rural
Dominant occupations: farming, labour, and service
Low development of communication and transportation
Low spatial mobility
Low consumption of electricity and fuel
Insufficient medical care: low ratio of doctors and hospitals to population

We arrive, therefore, at the following generalization: at the present stage in the world's history there is a very strong inverse relationship between the level of economic development and the birth rate; *in the less developed nations the birth rates are high, whereas in the industrialized nations they are low.*

Let us weight the vital rates as of 1960-1966 for these regions by population size and compute a set of weighted average rates for the industrialized and the developing regions:

Rate	Developing regions (high birth rate) (A)	Industrialized regions (lower birth rate) (B)	Difference (A MINUS B)
Crude birth rate	39.3	20.1	19.2
Crude death rate	18.1	9.0	9.1
Rate of reproductive change	21.2 per thousand	11.1 per thousand	10.1 per thousand

Like the birth rate, the death rates in the developing countries are much higher (more than twice as high as in the industrialized areas), and the rate of growth is also higher.

The reason why the developing nations are growing faster than the industrialized nations is that their death rates have fallen quickly, while their birth rates have remained higher or have declined only slightly. As will be shown in more detail later, high death rates may be reduced very quickly and at very moderate cost, whereas much more effort, time, and cost are required to lower birth rates. Inasmuch as the death rates in the developing nations are still quite high and inasmuch as all these nations have ambitious programs for improving sanitation, public health, and medical care, there is every reason to believe that in the years immediately ahead the death rates will continue to decline in this group. Unless the birth rates of the developing nations also begin to decline, and soon, the rate of world population growth will rise even higher!

The great demographic problem in the modern world may now be stated: *A disproportionate share of the current population growth in the world is concentrated in the poorer regions and is inundating them just as they are making a major effort to improve their economic condition. Thus not only is the world growing at an explosive pace, but its growth is concentrated in exactly those spots where it can be afforded least (from the point of view of reducing world poverty and raising levels of living).*

FERTILITY AND MORTALITY IN THE DEVELOPED AND UNDERDEVELOPED COUNTRIES*

Kingsley Davis

The article above notes the differences in birth rates between the DCs and the UDCs, concluding that one of the most important aspects of the great population dilemma is the inhibiting effect of rapid population growth on economic growth in the poorer countries. In the following article, Kingsley Davis, a noted demographer, examines trends in births and deaths in the developed and underdeveloped countries. In particular, he is concerned with a population paradox: the most impoverished and most crowded nations are also the most rapidly growing countries of the world.

The principal purpose of this article is to examine population growth in various countries both in terms of its evolution in time and its present variation from country to country.

[1963]

The first step in the demographic evolution of modern nations—a decline in the death rate—began in northwestern Europe long before it started elsewhere. As a result, although population growth is now slower in this area than in the rest of the world, it was here that the unprecedented

*From Kingsley Davis, 'Population', *Scientific American*, September 1963. Reprinted with permission. Copyright © 1963 by Scientific American, Inc. All rights reserved.

upsurge in human numbers began. Being most advanced in demographic development, northwestern Europe is a good place to start in our analysis of modern population dynamics.

In the late medieval period the average life expectancy in England, according to life tables compiled by the historian J. C. Russell, was about 27 years. At the end of the seventeenth century and during most of the eighteenth it was about 31 in England, France, and Sweden, and in the first half of the nineteenth century it advanced to 41.

The old but reliable vital statistics from Denmark, Norway, and Sweden show that the death rate declined erratically up to 1790, then steadily and more rapidly. Meanwhile the birth rate remained remarkably stable (until the latter part of the nineteenth century). The result was a marked increase in the excess of births over deaths, or what demographers call 'natural increase.' In the century from about 1815 until World War I the average annual increase in the three Scandinavian countries was 11.8 per 1,000—nearly five times what it had been in the middle of the eighteenth century, and sufficient to triple the population in 100 years.

For a long time the population of northwestern Europe showed little reaction to this rapid natural increase. But when it came, the reaction was emphatic; a wide variety of responses occurred, all of which tended to reduce the growth of the population. For example, in the latter part of the nineteenth century people began to emigrate from Europe by the millions, mainly to America, Australia, and South Africa. Between 1846 and 1932 an estimated 27 million people emigrated overseas from Europe's ten most advanced countries. . . .

In addition to this unprecedented exodus there were other responses, all of which tended to reduce the birth rate. In spite of opposition from church and state, agitation for birth control began and induced abortions became common. The age of marriage rose. Childlessness became frequent. The result was a decline in the birth rate that eventually overtook the continuing decline in the death rate. By the 1930s most of the industrial European countries had age-specific fertility rates so low that, if the rates had continued at that level, the population would eventually have ceased to replace itself.

In explaining this vigorous reaction one gets little help from two popular clichés. One of these—that population growth is good for business—would hardly explain why Europeans were so bent on stopping population growth. The other—that numerical limitation comes from the threat of poverty because 'population always presses on the means of subsistence'—is factually untrue. In every one of the industrializing countries of Europe economic growth outpaced population growth. In the United Kingdom, for example, the real per-capita income increased 2.3 times between the periods 1855-1859 and 1910-1914. In Denmark from 1770 to 1914 the rise of the net domestic product in constant prices was two and a half times the natural increase rate; in Norway and Sweden from the 1860s to 1914 it was respectively 1.4 and 2.7 times the natural increase rate. Clearly the strenuous efforts to lessen population growth were due to some stimulus other than poverty.

The stimulus, in my view, arose from the clash between new opportunities on the one hand and larger families on the other. The modernizing society of northwestern Europe necessarily offered new opportunities to people of all classes: new ways of gaining wealth, new means of rising socially, new symbols of status. In order to take advantage of those opportunities, however, the individual and his children required education, special skills, capital, and mobility—none of which was facilitated by an improvident marriage or a large family. Yet because mortality was being reduced (and reduced more successfully in the childhood than in the adult ages) the size of families had become potentially larger than before. In Sweden, for instance, the mortality of the period 1755-1775 allowed only 6.1 out of every 10 children born to reach the age of 10, whereas the mortality of 1901-1910 allowed 8.5 to survive to that age. In order to avoid the threat of a large family to his own and his children's socio-economic position, the individual tended to postpone or avoid marriage and to limit reproduction within marriage by every means available. Urban residents had to contend particularly with the cost and inconvenience of young children in the city. Rural families had to adjust to the lack of enough land to provide for new marriages when the children reached marriageable age. Land had become less available not only because of the plethora of families with numerous youths but also because, with modernization, more capital was needed per farm and because the old folks, living longer, held on to the property. As a result farm youths postponed marriage, flocked to the cities, or went overseas.

In such terms we can account for the paradox that, as the progressive European nations became richer, their population growth slowed down. The process of economic development itself provided the motives for curtailment of reproduction, as the British sociologist J. A. Banks has made clear in his book *Prosperity and Parenthood*. We can see now that in all modern nations the long-run trend is one of low mortality, a relatively modest rate of reproduction and slow population growth. This is an efficient demographic system that allows such countries, in spite of their 'maturity', to continue to advance economically at an impressive speed.

Naturally the countries of northwestern Europe did not all follow an identical pattern. Their stages differed somewhat in timing and in the pattern of preference among the various means of population control. France, for example, never attained as high a natural increase as Britain or Scandinavia did. This was not due solely to an earlier decline in the birth rate, as is often assumed, but also to a slower decline in the death rate. If we historically substitute the Swedish death rate for the French, we revise the natural increase upward by almost the same amount as we do by substituting the Swedish birth rate. In accounting for the early and easy drop in French fertility one recalls that France, already crowded in the eighteenth century and in the van of intellectual radicalism and sophistication, was likely to have a low threshold for the adoption of abortion and contraception. The death rate, however, remained comparatively high because France did not keep economic pace with her more rapidly industrializing neighbours. As a result the relatively small gap between births and deaths gave France a slower growth in population and a lesser rate of emigration.

... The emphasis in Ireland's escape from human inflation was on emigration, late marriage, and permanent celibacy. ...

The Irish preferences among the means of population limitation seem to come from the island's position as a rural region participating only indirectly in the Industrial Revolution. For most of the Irish, land remained the basis for respectable matrimony. As land became inaccessible to young people they postponed marriage. ... Marriage was also discouraged by the ban on divorce and by the lowest participation of married women in the labour force to be found in Europe. The country's failure to industrialize meant that the normal exodus from farms to cities was at the same time an exodus from Ireland itself.

Ireland and France illustrate contrasting variations on a common theme. Throughout northwestern Europe the population upsurge resulting from the fall in death rates brought about a multiphasic reaction that eventually reduced the population growth to a modest pace. The main force behind this response was not poverty or hunger but the desire of the people involved to preserve or improve their social standing by grasping the opportunities offered by the newly emerging industrial society.

Is this an interpretation applicable to the history of any industrialized country, regardless of traditional culture? According to the evidence the answer is yes. We might expect it to be true, as it currently is, of the countries of southern and eastern Europe that are finally industrializing. The crucial test is offered by the only nation outside the European tradition to become industrialized: Japan. How closely does Japan's demographic evolution parallel that of northwestern Europe?

If we superpose Japan's vital-rate curves on those of Scandinavia half a century earlier (Figure 13), we see a basically similar, although more rapid, development. The reported statistics, questionable up to 1920 but good after that, show a rapidly declining death rate as industrialization took hold after World War I. The rate of natural increase during the period from 1900 to 1940 was almost exactly the same as Scandinavia's between 1850 and 1920, averaging 12.1 per 1,000 population per year compared with Scandinavia's 12.3. And Japan's birth rate, like Europe's, began to dip until it was falling faster than the death rate, as it did in Europe. After the usual baby boom following World War II the decline in births was precipitous, amounting to 50 per cent from 1948 to 1960— perhaps the swiftest drop in reproduction that has ever occurred in an entire nation. The rates of childbearing for women in various ages are so low that, if they continued indefinitely, they would not enable the Japanese population to replace itself.

In thus slowing their population growth have the Japanese used the same means as the peoples of northwestern Europe did? Again, yes. Taboo-ridden Westerners have given disproportionate attention to two features of the change—the active role played by the Japanese government and the widespread resort to abortion—but neither of these disproves the similarity. It is true that since the war the Japanese government has pursued a birth-control policy more energetically than any government ever has before. It is also clear, however, that the Japanese people would have reduced their childbearing of their own accord. A marked decline in the reproduction rate had already set in by 1920, long before there was a government policy favouring this trend.

As for abortion, the Japanese are unusual only in admitting its extent. Less superstitious than Europeans about this subject, they keep reasonably good records of abortions, whereas most of the other countries have no accurate data. According to the Japanese records, registered abortions rose from 11.8 per 1,000 women of childbearing age in 1949 to a peak of 50.2 per 1,000 in 1955. We have no reliable historical in-

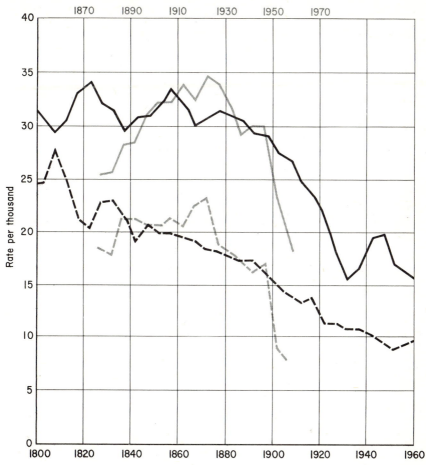

FIGURE 13 Birth and death rates for Denmark, Norway, and Sweden combined (black lines and dates) are compared with Japanese rates (grey lines and dates) of 50 years later. Japan has been passing through a population change similar to that which occurred earlier in Scandinavia. Area between respective birth-rate curves (solid lines) and death-rate curves (broken lines) shows natural increase, or population growth that would have occurred without migration. In past few years both Japanese rates have dropped extremely rapidly.

formation from Western countries, but we do know from many indirect indications that induced abortion played a tremendous role in the reduction of the birth rate in western Europe from 1900 to 1940, and that it still plays a considerable role. Furthermore, Christopher Tietze of the National Committee for Maternal Health has assembled records that show that in five eastern European countries where abortion has been legal for some time the rate has shot up recently in a manner strikingly similar to Japan's experience. In 1960-1961 there were 139 abortions for every 100 births in Hungary, 58 per 100 births in Bulgaria, 54 in Czechoslovakia, and 34 in Poland. The countries of eastern Europe are in a developmental stage comparable to that of northwestern Europe earlier in the century.

Abortion is by no means the sole factor in the decline of Japan's birth rate. Surveys made since 1950 show the use of contraception before that date, and increasing use thereafter. There is also a rising frequency of sterilization. Furthermore, as in Europe earlier, the Japanese are postponing marriage. The proportion of girls under 20 who have ever married fell from 17.7 per cent in 1920 to 1.8 per cent in 1955. In 1959 only about 5 per cent of the Japanese girls marrying for the first time were under 20, whereas in the U.S. almost half the new brides (48.5 per cent in the registration area) were that young.

Finally, Japan went through the same experience as western Europe in another respect—massive emigration. Up to World War II Japan sent millions of emigrants to various regions of Asia, Oceania, and the Americas.

In short, in response to a high rate of natural increase brought by declining mortality, Japan reacted in the same ways as the countries of northwestern Europe did at a similar stage. Like the Europeans, the Japanese limited their population growth in their own private interest and that of their children in a developing society, rather than from any fear of absolute privation or any concern with overpopulation in their homeland. The nation's average 5.4 per cent annual growth in industrial output from 1913 to 1958 exceeded the performance of European countries at a similar stage.

As our final class of industrialized countries we must now consider the frontier group—the U.S., Canada, Australia, New Zealand, South Africa, and Russia. These countries are distinguished from those of northwestern Europe and Japan by their vast wealth of natural resources in relation to their populations; they are the genuinely affluent nations. They might be expected to show a demographic history somewhat different from that of Europe. In certain particulars they do, yet the general pattern is still much the same.

One of the differences is that the riches offered by their untapped resources invited immigration. All the frontier industrial countries except Russia received massive waves of emigrants from Europe. They therefore had a more rapid population growth than their industrializing predecessors had experienced. As frontier countries with great room for expansion, however, they were also characterized by considerable internal migration and continuing new opportunities. As a result their birth rates remained comparatively high. In the decade from 1950 to 1960, with continued immigration, these countries grew in population at an average rate of 2.13 per cent a year, compared with 1.76 per cent for the rest of the world. It was the four countries with the sparsest settlement (Canada, Australia, New Zealand, and South Africa), however, that accounted for this high rate; in the U.S. and the U.S.S.R. the growth rate was lower—1.67 per cent per year.

Apparently, then, in pioneer industrial countries with an abundance of resources, population growth holds up at a higher level than in Japan or northwestern Europe because the average individual feels it is easier for himself and his children to achieve a respectable place in the social scale. The immigrants attracted by the various opportunities normally begin at a low level and thus make the status of natives relatively better. People marry earlier and have slightly larger families. But this departure from the general pattern for industrial countries appears to be only temporary.

In the advanced frontier nations, as in northwestern Europe, the birth rate began to fall sharply after 1880, and during the depression of the 1930s it was only about 10 per cent higher than in Europe. Although the postwar baby boom has lasted longer than in other advanced countries, it is evidently starting to subside now, and the rate of immigration has diminished. There are factors at work in these affluent nations that will likely limit their population growth. They are among the most urbanized countries in the world, in spite of their low average population density. Their birth rates are extremely sensitive to business fluctuations and social changes. Furthermore, having in general the world's highest living standards, their demand for resources, already staggering, will become fantastic if both population and per-capita consumption continue to rise rapidly, and their privileged position in the world may become less tolerated.

Let us shift now to the other side of the population picture: the nonindustrial, or underdeveloped, countries.

As a class the nonindustrial nations since 1930 have been growing in population about twice as fast as the industrial ones. This fact is so familiar and so taken for granted that its irony tends to escape us. When we think of it, it is astonishing that the world's most impoverished nations, many of them already overcrowded by any standard, should be generating additions to the population at the highest rate.

The underdeveloped countries have about 69 per cent of the earth's adults—and some 80 per cent of the world's children. Hence the demographic situation itself tends to make the world constantly more under-developed, or impoverished, a fact that makes economic growth doubly difficult.

How can we account for the paradox that the world's poorest regions are producing the most people? One is tempted to believe that the under-developed countries are simply repeating history: that they are in the same phase of rapid growth the West experienced when it began to industrialize and its death rates fell. If that is so, then sooner or later the developing areas will limit their population growth as the West did.

It is possible that this may prove to be true in the long run. But before we accept the comforting thought we should take a close look at the facts as they are.

In actuality the demography of the nonindustrial countries today differs in essential respects from the early history of the present indus-trial nations. Most striking is the fact that their rate of human multipli-cation is far higher than the West's ever was. The peak of the industrial nations' natural increase rarely rose above 15 per 1,000 population per year; the highest rate in Scandinavia was 13, in England and Wales 14, and even in Japan it was slightly less than 15. True, the U.S. may have hit a figure of 30 per 1,000 in the early nineteenth century, but if so it was with the help of heavy immigration of young people (who swelled the births but not the deaths) and with the encouragement of an empty continent waiting for exploitation.

In contrast, in the present underdeveloped but often crowded coun-tries the natural increase per 1,000 population is everywhere extreme. In the decade from 1950 to 1960 it averaged 31.4 per year in Taiwan, 26.8 in Ceylon, 32.1 in Malaya, 26.7 in Mauritius, 27.7 in Albania, 31.8 in Mexico, 33.9 in El Salvador, and 37.3 in Costa Rica. These are not birth rates; they are the *excess* of births over deaths! At an annual natural increase of 30 per 1,000, a population will double itself in 23 years.

The population upsurge in the backward nations is apparently taking place at an earlier stage of development—or perhaps we should say *un*development—than it did in the now industrialized nations. In Britain, for instance, the peak of human multiplication came when the country was already highly industrialized and urbanized, with only a fifth of its working males in agriculture. Comparing four industrial countries at the peak of their natural increase in the nineteenth century (14.1 per 1,000 per year) with five nonindustrial countries during their rapid growth in the 1950s (32.2 per 1,000 per year), I find that the industrial countries were 38.5 per cent urbanized and had 27.9 per cent of their labour force in manufacturing, whereas now the nonindustrial countries are 29.4 per cent urbanized and have only 15.1 per cent of their people in manufacturing. In short, today's nonindustrial populations are growing faster and at an earlier stage than was the case in the demographic cycle that accompanied industrialization in the nineteenth century.

As in the industrial nations, the main generator of the population upsurge in the underdeveloped countries has been a fall in the death rate. But their resulting excess of births over deaths has proceeded faster and farther, as a comparison of Ceylon in recent decades with Sweden in the 1800s shows (Figure 14).

In most of the underdeveloped nations the death rate has dropped with record speed. For example, the sugar-growing island of Mauritius in the Indian Ocean within an eight-year period after the war raised its average life expectancy from 33 to 51—a gain that took Sweden 130 years to achieve. Taiwan within two decades has increased its life expectancy from 43 to 63; it took the U.S. some 80 years to make this improvement for its white population. According to the records in 18 underdeveloped countries, the crude death rate has dropped substantially in each decade since 1930; it fell some 6 per cent in the 1930s and nearly 20 per cent in the 1950s, and according to the most recent available figures the decline in deaths is still accelerating.

The reasons for this sharp drop in mortality are in much dispute. There are two opposing theories. Many give the credit to modern medicine and public health measures. On the other hand, the public health spokesmen, rejecting the accusation of complicity in the world's population crisis, belittle their own role and maintain that the chief factor in the improvement of the death rate has been economic progress.

Those in the latter camp point out that the decline in the death rate in northwestern Europe followed a steadily rising standard of living. Improvements in diet, clothing, housing, and working conditions raised the population's resistance to disease. As a result many dangerous ailments disappeared or subsided without specific medical attack. The same process, say the public health people, is now at work in the developing countries.

On the other side, most demographers and economists believe that economic conditions are no longer as important as they once were in strengthening a community's health. The development of medical science has provided lifesaving techniques and medicines that can be transported overnight to the most backward areas. A Stone Age people can be endowed with a low twentieth-century death rate within a few years,

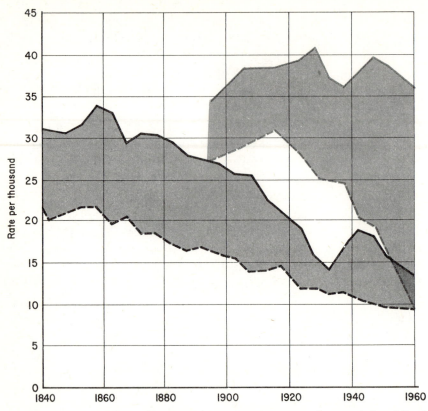

FIGURE 14   New demographic pattern is appearing in the non-industrialized nations. The birth rate (solid line) has not been falling significantly, whereas the death rate (broken line) has dropped precipitously, as illustrated by Ceylon (grey line). The spread between the two rates has widened. In nations such as Sweden (black), however, birth rate dropped during development long before death rate was as low as in most underdeveloped countries today.[1]

without waiting for the slow process of economic development or social change. International agencies and the governments of the affluent nations have been delighted to act as good Samaritans and send out public health missionaries to push disease-fighting programs for the less developed countries.

The debate between the two views is hard to settle. Such evidence as we have indicates that there is truth on both sides. Certainly the newly evolving countries have made economic progress. Their economic advance, however, is not nearly rapid enough to account for the very

[1] i.e. Birth rates fell as economic development proceeded and the spread between birth and death rates was never as great as it is in most underdeveloped countries today. (ed.)

swift decline in their death rates, nor do they show any clear correlation between economic growth and improvement in life expectancy. For example, in Mauritius during the five-year period from 1953 to 1958 the per-capita income fell by 13 per cent; yet notwithstanding this there was a 36-per-cent drop in the death rate. On the other hand, in the period between 1945 and 1960 Costa Rica had a 64-per-cent increase in the per-capita gross national product and a 55-per-cent decline in the death rate. There seems to be no consistency—no significant correlation between the two trends when we look at the figures country by country. In 15 underdeveloped countries for which such figures are available we find that the decline in death rate in the 1950s was strikingly uniform (about 4 per cent per year), although the nations varied greatly in economic progress—from no improvement to a 6-per-cent annual growth in per-capita income.

Our tentative conclusion must be, therefore, that the public health people are more efficient than they admit. The billions of dollars spent in public health work for underdeveloped areas has brought down death rates, irrespective of local economic conditions in these areas. The programs instituted by outsiders to control cholera, malaria, plague and other diseases in these countries have succeeded. This does not mean that death control in underdeveloped countries has become wholly or permanently independent of economic development, but that it has become temporarily so to an amazing degree.

5 | The Theories of Demographic Regulation and Transition

From Davis's article it can be observed that societies are capable of regulating their own growth and that this process of regulation, which occurs as a result of various factors, follows a fairly recognizable pattern or series of stages. As certain conditions are met, a society will move from one stage to another along a fairly predictable course.

On the following pages two theories are set out that seek to explain these aspects of population growth. The theory of *demographic regulation* maintains that all societies are capable of regulating their population and that such regulation is a result of certain social norms and economic conditions. It is a positive assertion that a society facing the probability of overpopulation inevitably finds a *natural* means of regulating its own increase. (If this assertion does not have universal application, we must assume that the regulation of the world's population can only be achieved by other means; that is, by the forceful actions of national or international agencies.) The theory of *demographic transition* is an attempt to describe the conditions that, over long periods of time, bring about changes from high birth and death rates to low ones, and the ways in which these changes occur. The two theories are very closely related: in fact the theory of transition is only valid if we assume the operation of a process of regulation.

THE THEORY OF DEMOGRAPHIC REGULATION*

Donald J. Bogue

[1969]

This theory may be stated as follows: *Every society tends to keep its vital processes in a state of balance such that population will replenish losses from death and grow to an extent deemed desirable by collective*

*From D. J. Bogue, *Principles of Demography*. Copyright © 1969 John Wiley & Sons, Inc., New York. Reprinted by permission.

norms. These norms are flexible and readjust rather promptly to changes in the ability of the economy to support population. Almost everywhere this adjustment takes the form of first minimizing death rates to the greatest extent possible under the given state of technology and then regulating birth rates in such a way that the desired balance or rate of growth is accomplished. In societies where death rates are high there is comparatively little need for regulation of fertility . . . because high fertility is required to offset high mortality. In technologically advanced societies, where death rates have been brought to a very low level, high birth rates . . . cause the size of the family to be larger than that deemed desirable by the prevailing norms. As a consequence, in such societies the regulation of fertility comes to be identified with group (as well as individual) welfare and becomes a positive good and a part of the culture. The steps by which this process of adjustment through fertility regulation takes place as death rates decline are such that fertility regulation inevitably lags behind mortality regulation. As a direct result, during the period of adjustment there is a phase of rapid population growth. This growth may not be anticipated or desired by the group.

In a sense, this theory is merely an extension to man of the principle of the 'balance of nature' as enunciated by Charles Darwin, but it is a sociological version of that principle. It has two facets that are missing in the balance-of-nature principle as it exerts its force on other forms of life: (a) the theory of demographic regulation asserts that the species itself has a norm that implies, at any given time, what constitutes 'good' or 'desirable' population trends and that this norm can and does change with changes in demographic conditions; (b) whereas the balance of nature is *imposed* by the rigours of the environment on other forms of life by the action of death rates, human societies tend to avoid this drastic type of control through starvation and the action of 'fang and claw' by *imposing upon themselves* the desired balance by regulation of the birth rate. The avoidance of death is everywhere a social value; with only minor exceptions all societies readily accept practices that reduce mortality. Almost no society imposes death on members as a means of controlling growth, except by occasional use of infanticide and except for the indirect effects of war. Adaptive action has consisted primarily of attempting to change fertility behaviour. The extent of this type of regulative action has increased steadily as populations have increased in size and density; and the intensity of the desire for strict regulation rises rapidly as a state of social maladjustment that threatens the standard of life, or life itself, is reached.

The phase of rapid population growth that emerges during the period of readjustment and regulation following mortality reduction is of extraordinary concern to demographers. Their studies have taught them that this phase is inevitable whenever death rates fall. In every such case the decline in the birth rate lags behind the decline in the death rate. This happens for two major reasons. First, the mortality reduction occurs first in time; it is the stimulus to which fertility regulation is a response. . . . Second, the adjustment of fertility to reduced mortality is not a simple automatic reflex, but is an entire *process* of social change, which consists of several different steps or phases. If death rates fall, the population must sense the fact by realizing that average family size is increasing. Merely attaining this awareness would require a period of several years . . . . Next, the implications of this change for individual and group welfare must be appreciated, and defined as undesirable. Finally, some socially acceptable solution (mode of fertility control) must be devised, diffused throughout the population, and adopted as socially acceptable behaviour. Even under the most favourable circumstances substantial time would be required for a population to go through these steps. If there are strong forces resisting the regulation of fertility, the process is slowed even more. Resistance may exist either in the form of active opposition or in the form of cultural or bureaucratic inertia.

The amount by which the population grows during this phase is determined by the extent of the disparity between the birth rate and the death rate and by the number of years the disparity persists.

The theory of demographic regulation is premised on the assertion that every society has a set of norms that guide population growth. *These norms are not explicit opinions about desired population size or the optimum rate of growth. Instead, they are opinions concerning what constitutes the ideal size of completed family, or the number of surviving children a couple ought to have when it reaches the end of the reproductive period.* . . . Any society whose average members believe that it is good or desirable to have four or more surviving children either will grow rapidly or must face very high mortality. A society whose members agree to bear no more than two children is one that expects to suspend further growth, and expects very low mortality. Recent studies have demonstrated that these attitudes of ideal family size definitely exist and can be clearly verbalized by all but a small minority of the adult population. . . .

The effort required to achieve a particular average size of desired completed family varies with the mortality condition that exists. If death rates are high, many of the children will die before they reach adult-hood, and a couple must 'overbear' in order to attain the ideal family size. If death rates are very low, the couples need bear only the number of children they desire in their family of ideal size.

Readjustment to a condition of lower mortality therefore requires a double change in social attitudes:

1. A lowering of the ideal size of completed family to match the growth rate indicated by the present conditions.

2. A lowering of the estimated amount of 'overbearing' of children necessary to overcome mortality and attain the desired family size.

Such a double adjustment cannot be arrived at instantaneously. It involves the solution by trial and error of what is actually a rather complex set of demographic calculations, and a modification of the customs, attitudes, and outlook to conform to the new pattern. More-over, the social organization itself must change to facilitate the carrying out of the changed ideals. For example, fertility control must be admitted as a normal part of health and medical services, and medical and health organizations must become prepared, technologically and psychologi-cally, to offer such services. On the other hand, there is nothing in the situation that would prevent a rather rapid adjustment in the course of a very few years, or even months. The speed with which the change can take place depends on many factors, not the least of which are the intensity and the degree of uniformity of the old fertility attitudes and the extent of communication, discussion, and social consensus.

It may be presupposed that such a change can be accomplished today in much shorter time than in any previous period, because of the existence of several new factors that were not previously acting:

1. Modern demographic science can and does keep the national leadership fully informed of its present and prospective future popu-lation. As a result, there is a widespread social consciousness of the demographic balance and the need for regulation.

2. Modern methods of communication make it possible to circulate new ideas rapidly through the population. Awareness of the need for regulation can be rapidly diffused throughout the society. Information about how this regulation may be achieved can be diffused just as rapidly.

3. Social change has permeated society to such an extent that entire nations are now growing accustomed to making changes almost con-tinuously. Resistance to change is being lowered everywhere.

4. The techniques for limiting fertility (contraception) are now num-

erous, varied, and cheap, so that every couple has available at least one method that will be both effective and acceptable to it. Further technological progress along these lines may be expected in the very near future.

5. Major and powerful institutional groups are placing the weight of their prestige and influence in favour of fertility regulation. They include medical groups, economic planners, religious groups, and political leaders and educators. The resistance to fertility regulation is rapidly becoming identified with an outmoded way of thinking and behaving.

Because of the combined action of these forces, it may be supposed that the efficiency and degree of success with which a population can realize its ideals in practice are much greater today than ever before and will increase even more as further advances are made in contraceptive technology and experience in its use. Within our lifetime we may see fertility control become an integral part of the morals and culture, with highly developed social organizations for maintaining it, in all societies of the world. In other words, the theory of demographic regulation is a positive assertion that nations, when faced with serious overpopulation, will undergo adaptive social change to lower fertility rates and in so doing will invent and adopt a technology of contraception. Moreover, this theory asserts that *modern man is able to foresee demographic catastrophe long before it arrives and takes adaptive action long before it is forced on him by the brute forces of nature.*

THE PROCESS OF DEMOGRAPHIC TRANSITION

From a historical examination of population statistics it appears that every country has experienced or is experiencing regulation of its population. This occurrence is known as the process of demographic transition; that is, a transition occurs over a period of years during which time a condition of high death and birth rates changes to one of low death and birth rates.

There is probably no large area in the world today where this process of transition is not under way. Before it began in any particular country, both birth and death rates were very high and—as seen in the examples included as Figures 15 and 16—fluctuated considerably from year to year. Averaged over several decades, however, the numbers of births and deaths are approximately the same; the population growth in these times was therefore very close to zero.

The early stage of the transition process is marked by a falling death

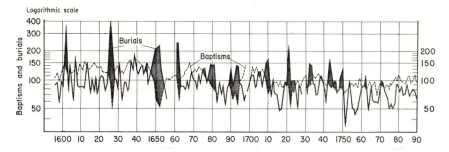

FIGURE 15 Number of baptisms and burials for the French parish of St Lambert des Levées during the seventeenth and eighteenth centuries. (Adapted from Marcel R. Reinhard and André Armengaud, *Histoire général de la population mondiale*, Paris: Editions Montchrestien, 1961, p. 126.)

rate—caused in large measure by improved medical and public health services—with little or no change in birth rates. The result is a rapid increase in the rate of population growth. After a period of time the birth rate begins to drop (owing in part to literacy, urbanization, and industrialization) and eventually is brought more into line with the death rate. This is not to suggest that a condition of zero growth is achieved, but certainly the rate of population increase becomes quite low.

Such a demographic transition can be clearly seen in Figure 16, where the birth and death rates for Sweden, available back to 1720, have been plotted from that date to the present. In general the transition process is nearing its end in most of the DCs, while the UDCs are generally in Stages 2 and 3 as described below.

STAGES IN THE DEMOGRAPHIC TRANSITION[1]

Stage 1. Pre-transitional. Before the process of transition begins, populations have high birth rates and high and fluctuating death rates. The overall rate of population growth varies from year to year but averages close to zero. The few areas that are still at this stage of development are among the most backward in the world.

Stage 2. Early Transitional. Death rates begin to drop but birth rates remain high or may even increase as a result of the improved health of women in the reproductive ages. Many of the Asian and African countries are at this level.

Stage 3. Mid-transitional. Death rates continue to drop, and while birth rates may be reduced somewhat, the rate of population growth is high.

---

[1] Using the birth- and death-rate estimates contained in the Appendix, it should be possible to classify most of the countries of the world according to these stages in the demographic transition.

Some of the Asian countries are passing into this stage, as are many of the nations of Latin America and North Africa.

Stage 4. Late Transitional. Death rates are low and changing little, and birth rates are steadily declining, with a resulting decrease in population growth. A relatively small number of countries fall into this category, but some examples would include Ceylon, Malaysia, Chile, and possibly the People's Republic of China.

Stage 5. Post-transitional. Birth and death rates are low and fairly steady. (In the long run birth rates will fluctuate much more than death rates.) Population growth is relatively low—in a few cases near zero. North America, much of Europe, the U.S.S.R., Australasia, and Japan are in this stage.

The demographic transition confronts mankind with perhaps its most crucial problem. Having entered only the early stages of the transition process, will the UDCs be able to reduce their rate of population growth to Western levels without disrupting or permanently ruining their econo-mies? In the opinion of many demographers, the amount of time avail-

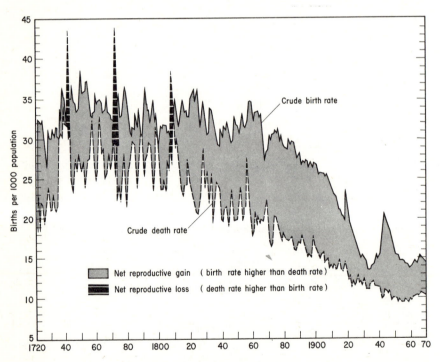

FIGURE 16 Crude birth rates and crude death rates for Sweden: 1720 to 1962. (*Historisk Statistik för Sverige, Befolkning: 1720-1950.* Stockholm: Statistika Centralbyrän, 1955. United Nations, *Demographic Yearbook, 1962.*)

able to the UDCs to reach stage 5 in the process of transition is substantially less than the time that has been taken by those DCs, such as
the nations of western Europe, that have more or less completed the
process. This problem is discussed more fully in the following article.

DEMOGRAPHIC TRANSITION: THREAT TO DEVELOPING NATIONS*

G. A. Schnell

[1970]

The demographic transition, so-called, serves to illustrate the notion
that population growth is self-corrective, given the means to increase
agricultural and industrial production, the accompanying process of
urbanization, and an improved level of living. For northwestern Europe,
as well as the other advanced nations of today, such modified fertility
and mortality patterns helped to bring about the change from a pre-industrial balance to a modern balance in demographic trends (Figure 17).
High birth and death rates, resulting in low rates of natural increase,
characterized the former status; whereas the latter or modern balance
achieved approximately the same low rates of reproductive change but
through significantly reduced rates of birth and death.

The ultimate results of such modified demographic behaviour not-

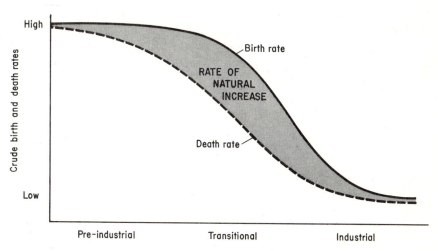

FIGURE 17 Model of demographic transition, illustrating a generalized version of
trends in vital rates in northwestern Europe during industrialization.

*Copyright © March 1970 *Journal of Geography*. Reprinted by permission.

withstanding, it is of the utmost importance to recognize that, in gaining modern demographic status, the populations of northwestern Europe passed through periods of transition during which growth rates were higher than in either the pre-industrial or industrial stages. As Figure 17 depicts, this explosive period of growth was the result of a relatively early and steep decline in rates of mortality, as the rates of fertility remained at or near their pre-industrial levels.[1] Table 10 lists for a specific example, England and Wales, trends in vital rates and resultant natural increases for selected periods. Assuming the rates shown are generally accurate, it is clear that fertility remained high long after mortality had declined.

Perhaps the logistic- or s-curve describes with a fair amount of accuracy the cumulative trends in Europe's growth of population during

Table 10
CRUDE BIRTH AND DEATH RATES AND NATURAL INCREASE, ENGLAND AND WALES, SELECTED PERIODS

Year	Births/1,000	Deaths/1,000	Natural Increase/1,000
1751-55	35.0	30.0	5.0
1801-05	34.0	23.0	11.0
1851-55	33.9	22.7	11.2
1905-09	26.7	15.1	11.6
1950	15.9	11.6	4.3

Taken from data in Carlo Cipolla, *The Economic History of World Population* Penguin Books, Baltimore, 1962, pp. 78-9.

successive stages of demographic transition.[2] In pre-industrial and industrial phases of demographic transition the curve was quite flat, representing moderate growth levels at most. By contrast, during the transitional stage, the curve climbed steadily, becoming more nearly horizontal in aspect only as it approached the end of the stage. In spite of the similarity cited (rates of population growth during the initial and terminal stages being the product of nearly equivalent vital rates), a most significant difference is evident—the number of inhabitants at the outset was small, gaining rapidly through transition and although the curve becomes quite flat in the industrial stage, the size of population became very large. Thus, the absolute number of inhabitants

[1] Although some diversity of opinion exists, it is generally agreed that disease control and its impact upon mortality was extremely important in the growth surge of Europe. See P. Deane and W. A. Cole, *British Economic Growth 1688-1959*, Cambridge University Press, 1967, pp. 5-12 and 106-34.
[2] This does not imply that the general growth of the human population adheres to the s-curve; rather that this device is appropriate to describe growth during transition. The more general statement is attributed to Pearl who, after experimenting with fruit-fly reproduction, transposed his findings to the human population. See R. Pearl, *The Biology of Population Growth*, Knopf, New York, 1925.

increased tremendously during demographic transition, despite the eventual reduction in rates of reproductive change.

The disparity in time between the decline of the death rate and the birth rate in response to economic development might be aptly described as an example of cultural lag—the absence of action taken to modify social values and attitudes as the economy evolved from agrarian to urban-industrial. Thus, new and more effective methods of disease control and a rising level of living, which effected decreases in mortality, had little or no immediate influence on the high levels of fertility. (It has been estimated by some that, in the case of England and Wales, average birth rates actually increased during the eighteenth century.)[1]

The substantial emigration from Europe during the last century and the early portion of this reduced somewhat the impact of population growth during demographic transition.[2] England, for example, experienced a total gain in numbers of inhabitants from approximately 10 million in 1800 to over 50 million in 1950. It has been estimated that over 100 million persons of English descent lived abroad in 1950,[3] an obvious boon to English economic development at home.

As the English example indicates, the population of Europe was not great at the beginning of the Industrial Revolution, and the effects of an improved agriculture were lasting. In addition to its central role in raising living levels, agricultural advancement created the labour supply so vital to urban-industrial development by reducing the intensity of farm labour requirements and, ultimately, the rural population. These and other factors contributed mightily to the positive results finally achieved by northwestern Europe as it passed through demographic transition.

DEMOGRAPHIC TRANSITION:
CURRENT TRENDS AND IMPLICATIONS

Demographic transition seems to have succeeded, on the heels of urban industrial growth, in bringing about quite positive results in much of Europe. Turning from the historical to the present, however, one might ask how such a sequence of trends in demographic behaviour might affect the nations of Africa, Asia, and Latin America. To answer this

[1] Deane and Cole, op. cit., p. 127.
[2] The effect of emigration notwithstanding, estimates of relative change for Europe indicate that the rate of growth increased through much of the period (1750-1900). See A. M. Carr-Saunders, *World Population*, Oxford University Press, New York, 1936, p. 42.
[3] K. Sax, *Standing Room Only, the World's Exploding Population*, Beacon Press, Boston, 1955, pp. 53 and 54.

question is difficult, to say the least: however, by restricting our view to what is known about past trends in vital rates and their relationships to economic development, certain inferences can be drawn. It is convenient, therefore, to begin with a discussion of the current demographic situation in the world, directing special attention to patterns of fertility, mortality, and natural increase.

Table 11 lists, for the major areas of the world, annual rates of reproductive change from 1960 to 1966, the excess of births over deaths expressed as a rate. The rates range from very high annual growth (say, 3.0 per cent or more) to very low (0.9 per cent or less). The very slowly growing populations include those resident in northern, western, and eastern Europe only, the rates of natural increase for these areas ranging from 0.5 per cent per year to 0.8 per cent in northern and eastern Europe, respectively. The category of from 1.0 to 1.4 per cent, representing 'low' growth applies to the following regions—southern Europe, North America, East Asia, and Australia and New Zealand. The remaining middle latitude and/or developed regions, the Soviet Union and temperate South America, are shown as being in the 'moderate' class, along with Middle Africa (1.5 to 1.9 per cent). The categories of high growth apply, in varying degrees, to the remainder of the regional populations shown on Table 11. These range from 'very high' in Middle America, Polynesia, and Micronesia (3.0 per cent or more) to 'moderately high' (2.0 to 2.4 per cent), which characterizes the inhabitants of much of Africa and South West Asia. All of South Asia, tropical South America, and Southern Africa are shown to be in the 'high' category, with populations increasing at a rate of from 2.5 to 2.9 per cent annually.

The application of current-trend projections to existing populations reveals the disparities among these regional groups in terms of future growth. For example, it would require only about 20 years for the population of Middle America to double (assuming its current rate of 3.5 per cent annually prevails).[1] By contrast, northern Europe's rate of 0.5 per cent would require 140 years in order to increase that population to twice its present number.

Finally, with reference to Table 11, one might generalize, for the various major areas shown, the stages of demographic transition they now occupy. Utilizing three stages, those regions with high birth and

---

[1] The following equivalents may be applied to other populations to determine the time it will take them to double at current rates: 1.0 per cent per year–70 years to double; 2.0 per cent per year–35 years; and so forth.

Table 11
SELECTED DEMOGRAPHIC INDICATORS, THE WORLD AND MAJOR AREAS[1]

Area	Estimated Population (000,000's) 1960	Estimated Population (000,000's) 1966	Births/1,000 Per Year 1960-66	Deaths/1,000 Per Year 1960-66	Annual Rate of Nat'l Increase[2] 1960-66 (per cent)
WORLD TOTAL	3,005	3,356	34	16	1.8
AFRICA	278	318	46	23	2.3
Western	88	100	50	27	2.3
Eastern	76	88	45	21	2.4
Northern	66	76	43	19	2.4
Middle	30	33	42	23	1.9
Southern	18	21	42	17	2.5
NORTH AMERICA	199	217	22	9	1.3
LATIN AMERICA	214	253	41	13	2.8
Tropical S. America	113	135	43	14	2.9
Middle America	48	59	45	10	3.5
Temperate S. America	33	36	28	10	1.8
Caribbean	20	23	38	14	2.4
ASIA	1,659	1,868	38	18	2.0
East	794	864	33	19	1.4
Middle South	587	681	43	18	2.5
Southeast	219	255	43	17	2.6
Southwest	59	68	42	18	2.4
EUROPE	425	449	18	10	0.8
Western	135	145	18	11	0.7
Southern	117	124	21	9	1.2
Eastern	97	101	17	9	0.8
Northern	76	79	16	11	0.5
OCEANIA	15.7	17.9	26	11	1.5
Australia & N.Z.	12.6	14.3	22	9	1.3
U.S.S.R.	214	233	22	7	1.5

[1] SOURCE: United Nations, *Demographic Yearbook, 1966.* Major areas are based upon the component regions listed on p. 19 of the source.
[2] Natural increase rates are based upon the excess of births over deaths and do not include effects of migration.

death rates, such as West Africa, could be catalogued pre-industrial. High birth rates and low death rates, as exemplified by Middle America, qualify those populations as transitional in stage of development. The last stage, industrial, is obviously illustrated by the populations of northern, eastern, and western Europe, where mortality and fertility rates are both extremely low.

Note that none of these areas has a population which exhibits all three characteristics that, on purely demographic grounds, allows direct comparison to pre-industrial Europe — high birth rates, high death rates, and low rates of reproductive change. Thus, for the sake of comparison to Europe prior to and during the early phase of industrialization, the underdeveloped lands of today have populations in an early period of transition at least, evidenced by their mortality rates, which have fallen somewhat from strictly pre-industrial levels, and birth rates which remain quite high. Such disparate vital rates combine to produce rather high rates of natural increase, unlike the faltering growth rates of

Europe in the period prior to development. By placing generalized demographic trends of an underdeveloped population in the twentieth century next to population trends of western Europe as it evolved through the stages of demographic transition, the disparities cited above become readily apparent (Figure 18). Notice the precipitous decline in mortality for the underdeveloped population, as compared to the more gradual reduction in Europe. Notice also the difference in vertical space between births and deaths, indicating much greater reproductive change in the early stages of transition in the underdeveloped population.

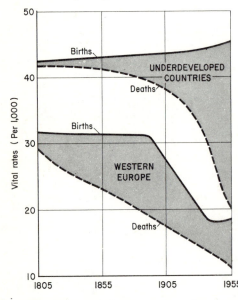

FIGURE 18 Comparison of western Europe during demographic transition and trends in vital rates in underdeveloped countries in the twentieth century. (After Sauvy, *Fertility and Survival*, Collier Books, New York, 1963, p. 68.)

The thesis of this paper can be argued more emphatically, it seems, if examples drawn from today's scene are utilized and the merits of demographic transition as it might affect them are discussed. Illustrated on Figure 19 are the vital rates of 15 nations, selected because they represent various stages of development. When arranged according to crude death rate, in descending order, the stages associated with demographic transition provide an appropriate classification scheme reflecting the economic, as well as the demographic, status of each nation included. Furthermore, this rank-order produces a pattern of natural increase rates which is somewhat similar to the model of demographic transition based upon the European experience. (Compare Figures 17 and 18.) Significantly, the major difference between the early transitional (pre-industrial) and transitional groups is found more in their rates of mortality than in their fertility.

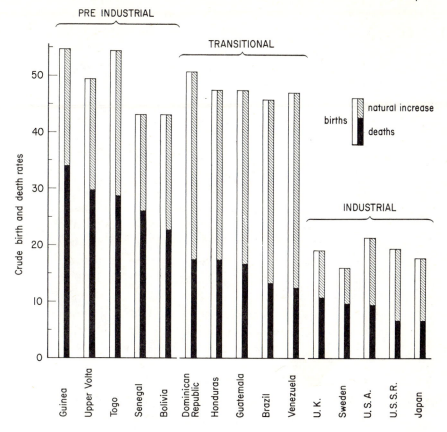

FIGURE 19 Vital rates for fifteen selected countries c. 1964 illustrates, in addition to birth and death rates and rates of natural increase, the status of these examples in terms of demographic transition.

The current demographic status of pre-industrial nations is such, that the application of trends in vital rates similar to Europe's during demographic transition would result in much larger future populations than current-trend projections suggest. Table 12 includes a summary measure illustrative of just such trends—the number of years required for the population of each nation and each group of nations to double at existing rates of natural increase. The differences in average doubling time among the groups suggest serious implications for these pre-industrial nations, should they arrive at the transitional stage of increased growth when their death rates will have decreased to even lower levels while births remain high. Viewed in this way, demographic transition becomes a dismal theory for populations such as those of West Africa included in the examples, requiring, it seems, that their population problems grow worse before they improve!

Although the association between declining mortality and improved economic status (the latter represented crudely by GNP per capita) is supported somewhat by the inverse relationship apparent on Table 12, a comparison of today's pre-industrial nations and pre-industrial Europe suggests that sufficient discordance exists to discourage the idea that demographic transition will do for currently developing countries what it did for Europe in the past. The initial difference of note is that the European pre-industrial balance between mortality and fertility does not exist today among the underdeveloped nations. (See Figure 18.) Although, for example, Senegal's vital rates are the least disparate among the group selected of pre-industrial examples in Figure 19, the rate of natural increase of 17.5 per 1,000 inhabitants is hardly derived from traditionally balanced fertility and mortality. Estimates for England and Wales indicate, by contrast, that the average rate of natural increase rose from less than 2.0 per 1,000 in the period 1701 to 1750 to 14 per 1,000 inhabitants in the period from 1801 to 1830.[1]

The second difference of note concerns the role played by population trends in Europe's economic development as compared to such forecasts for existing underdeveloped lands. Despite rather general agreement that population growth in Europe was caused by and, in its turn, contributed to economic expansion, such reciprocity is improbable today. Indeed, given the poor levels of life and the lack of demographic balance so common among the inhabitants of underdeveloped countries, as these already rapidly expanding populations continue to grow (and at an increasing rate, if trends following demographic transition are applied), an annual increment of economic growth equivalent to the increment in population becomes necessary just to maintain current standards.

Listed in Table 12 are the infant mortality rates for the selected nations. This table serves well in accentuating an extremely important consequence of infant mortality control. Innovations in preventive medicine and other measures which reduce mortality can be readily applied in underdeveloped countries (and have been in many cases); and, unlike Europe in the past, the effects of such programs are more nearly immediate. Moreover, as mortality decreases, it is common for the attendant improvements in medicine and health to cause the greatest gains in survivorship among the youthful populations rather than the aged.[2]

---

[1] These estimates of natural increase are from data found in Deane and Cole, op. cit., p. 127.
[2] A. J. Coale, 'How a Population Ages or Grows Younger', in Ronald Freedman (ed.), Population: The Vital Revolution, Doubleday, New York, 1964, p. 50.

Table 12[1]
DEMOGRAPHIC AND ECONOMIC DATA FOR SELECTED NATIONS, c. 1964
(Ranked in descending order by crude death rate)

Nation	Deaths Per 1,000	Births Per 1,000	Natural Increase Per 1,000[2]	Number of Years for Population to Double[3]	Infant Mort. Per 1,000 Live Births	GNP Per Capita (U.S. $)
PREINDUSTRIAL NATIONS (EARLY TRANSITIONAL)						
Guinea	34.0	55.0	21.0	24	220	60
Upper Volta	29.5	49.0	19.5	33	175	45
Togo	29.0	54.5	25.5	29	—	75
Senegal	26.0	43.5	17.5	31	—	200
Bolivia	22.5	43.0	20.5	50	145	154
Weighted Mean[4]	28.1	48.3	20.2	34	179	106
TRANSITIONAL NATIONS						
Dominican Rep.	17.5	51.0	33.5	20	90	269
Honduras	17.5	47.5	30.0	22	54	216
Guatemala	17.2	47.7	30.5	22	93	284
Brazil	13.5	45.0	31.5	23	—	196
Venezuela	12.5	47.5	35.0	21	68	728
Weighted Mean	13.8	45.6	31.8	22	76	249
INDUSTRIAL NATIONS						
United Kingdom	11.3	18.8	7.5	100	21	1,564
Sweden	10.0	16.0	6.0	140	14	2,046
United States	9.4	21.2	11.8	44	24	3,083
U.S.S.R.	6.9	19.6	12.7	41	29	1,202
Japan	6.9	17.7	10.8	78	20	626
Weighted Mean	8.2	19.7	11.5	55	25	1,773

[1] SOURCE: The Population Reference Bureau, *World Population Data Sheet*, December 1965.
[2] Natural increase rates were computed from the crude birth and death rates shown in this tabulation and, therefore, do not reflect migration.
[3] The estimate of doubling time is based upon the assumption of continued growth at the average annual rate of increase of each nation from 1958 to 1963.
[4] Means for each of the three groups are weighted according to the population of each component nation.

The survival to puberty and beyond, therefore, of greater numbers of female infants will serve to swell the ranks of the next young adult generation and raise fecundity and possibly fertility to new and higher levels. Such trends in infant mortality would thus cause the population to grow increasingly younger and, as a result, produce a generation of females whose absolute numbers might be sufficient to negate the effects of decreasing rates of fertility.[1]

In addition to the differences cited above, legislation often denies the inhabitants of today's developing nations the freedom to migrate. Related to this, as well, is the lack of suitable land in most under-

[1] It is interesting and quite revealing to compare the infant mortality rates of the nations listed on Table 12 with those of England at an earlier time in its development. Figures on infant mortality per 1,000 baptisms for selected English parishes show an almost steady decline—from a high of 242 per 1,000 in 1691-1700 to 184 per 1,000 in 1731-40. See D. E. C. Eversley, P. Laslett, and E. A. Wrigley, *An Introduction to English Historical Demography*, Basic Books, New York, 1966, p. 59.

developed or developing countries for pioneer settlement, as was the case in North America, Australia, and Argentina, among others.[1] It seems reasonable, therefore, that these nations, lacking such methods of relieving population pressures, must themselves do all that is possible rapidly to attain properly adjusted vital rates and, simultaneously, develop means to insure continuous and vigorous economic expansion.

SUMMARY

When demographic trends based upon European experience during industrialization are applied to projections for pre-industrial nations of today, it seems quite clear that such an exercise will not produce a similar forecast. Perhaps the underlying cause is the marked dissimilarities between eighteenth-century Europe and currently underdeveloped countries. With rates of reproductive change already far in excess of pre-industrial Europe's, *advancement* to later stages of the demographic transition by existing pre-industrial populations would place the tremendous burden of more rapidly expanding numbers upon economies hard pressed to maintain extant levels. Therefore, it is imperative that the vital rates of these countries be controlled to prevent further surges in growth rates. Hopefully, as (or before) mortality continues to decline in the near future, as it probably will, every effort will be made to reduce fertility commensurately. Perhaps then, relieved of the task of keeping up with ever-increasing numbers of inhabitants, economic planners might enjoy greater success.

[1] W. Zelinsky, 'The Geographer and His Crowding World: Cautionary Notes Toward the Study of Population Pressure in the Developing Lands', *Revista Geografica*, No. 65 (December 1966), p. 19.

part two

the population problem

---

causes
and
implications

Introduction

The present annual increase in the population of the world (72 million in 1969) is incredibly large; and, according to many authorities, existing rates of growth cannot be allowed to continue. The greatest growth is occurring in the poorer regions of the world and this growth is making it extraordinarily difficult to achieve any significant improvement in the general economic situation and, consequently, in the well-being of the people living in these regions. This is the demographic dilemma in its simplest terms, and it can only be comprehended if we examine the following two aspects. First, although the basic cause of the population problem has been identified as changes in birth and death rates, it is important to discover what has caused mortality rates to decline almost everywhere, while birth rates have not altered to the same extent. Or, to put it another way, why has the break-through in death control not been matched by similar achievements in birth control? Second, although most people will freely accept that a condition of overpopulation exists, particularly in underdeveloped countries, an understanding of the problem can be gained only if we consider the specific reasons. Why do the present numbers and rates of growth constitute a problem? It is also important to consider whether overpopulation is a concept related to stages of economic development and achievements in technology or whether there are, in fact, absolute standards of overpopulation that are determined by such factors as resources, food-production capabilities, or even the stress that affects people living in crowded conditions.

1 | Factors Affecting Mortality

The discussion of the demographic transition in Part 1 described the relationship between man's increasing control over mortality and the present population crisis. The lowering of death rates began in the Western countries in the nineteenth century and in recent years has levelled off at approximately 7 to 12 deaths per thousand population per annum. In a recent study[1] it was estimated that the causes of this decline could be attributed to the almost equal effects of each of the following — (i) improved levels of living and the emergence of stable governments, (ii) environmental sanitation and improved personal hygiene, and (iii) the developments of modern medicine and public health programs. In the UDCs, a similar decline began more recently—for the most part since the Second World War—and mortality rates dropped very rapidly. Today the rate of mortality decline in many of the UDCs has also slackened, although there is still considerable variation from country to country, with annual death rates ranging from approximately 10 to 20 per thousand. While the same three causes noted above have been chiefly responsible for this decline, the developments in modern medicine and public health programs have certainly been most important in the UDCs.

The article below examines various aspects of man's control over mortality in both the developed and underdeveloped countries of the world, while the extract that follows it—'Increase in Life Expectancy Due to Modern Medicine'—deals more specifically with the medical aspects of this achievement. In examining these articles, two important questions should be kept in mind. First, in what way were the conditions leading to the rapid lowering of death rates in the UDCs different from those that were responsible for the same kind of change that occurred earlier in the DCs? Second, how may these and other differences affect the future progress of the UDCs in completing the demographic transition?

---

[1] Philip M. Hauser (ed.), *The Population Dilemma*, Prentice-Hall, Englewood Cliffs, N.J., 2nd ed., 1970.

THE CONTROL OF MORTALITY*

T. E. Smith

[1967]

The circumstances of death, as the inevitable termination of human life, have changed out of all recognition in the past one and a half centuries. Until the early nineteenth century, the death of one out of every four or five infants in the first year of life was common experience, and expectation of life at birth[1] was seldom more than thirty to forty years. At present, ninety-eight out of every hundred infants survive the first year of life in many of the countries of Europe, North America, and Oceania, while in much of Asia and Latin America and in some parts of Africa there have been big declines in infant mortality. Partly as the result of this much lower infant mortality and partly as the result of lower mortality rates for older age-groups, expectation of life now exceeds seventy years in the healthiest countries and is well in excess of fifty years in many countries with relatively low standards of living. The annual death roll in areas of low birth and low death rates now consists of the elderly for the most part; in the technically most advanced countries of Europe, 65 to 70 per cent of all deaths now occur in persons over sixty-five years of age, in contrast to the earlier position of communities with high birth and high death rates in which a considerable proportion of the deaths were those of infants and young children. Where the birth rate remains very high and the population consequently remains young, and where the death rates are at a level such that expectation of life at birth is in the region of forty to forty-five years, deaths appear to be divided in roughly equal proportions between children and adults. For example, in Egypt for the period 1936 to 1940, when expectation of life at birth was less than forty years, 55 per cent of all deaths occurred in persons under five years of age.

The main causes of death have changed and continue to change with the rising expectation of life and new discoveries in the fight to control diseases. In most of the countries with low death rates the cancers and heart diseases have become the principal causes of death, whereas a few decades ago tuberculosis ranked first as a cause of death. For instance in Czechoslovakia at the beginning of the twentieth century, 15 per cent

*From *Annals of the American Academy of Political and Social Science*, Vol. 369, January 1967. Reprinted by permission.
[1] Expectation of life at birth measures the average number of years of life for the individuals in a population, assuming static death rates for every age-group of each sex.

of all deaths, and 60 per cent of deaths of persons between twenty and thirty years of age, were caused by tuberculosis. Cholera, plague, diphtheria, smallpox, typhoid fever, scarlet fever, and other dangerous infectious and parasitic diseases are in most parts of the world no longer the mortal scourges they once were.

MORTALITY REDUCTIONS IN DEVELOPED COUNTRIES

The damage to human life which has at times been caused by war, famine, and disease can be simply illustrated by a few examples. The Taiping rebellion in China in the 1850s is thought to have led to the deaths of 30 million people. In Ireland, the Great Famine of 1846-7 caused close to one million deaths out of a population of eight million as the result of starvation and accompanying diseases. The influenza epidemic of 1918 caused 15 million deaths in a population of just over 300 millions in the Indian subcontinent alone.[1] In all countries, the cities tended to be such insanitary and unhealthy places, until well into the nineteenth century, that urban death rates were usually far higher than rural death rates. In general, while medicine remained an undeveloped science and the mass of the population had a low level of living, death rates were always very high by current standards, and the occasional disasters, whether caused by disease, war, or famine, resulted in periods of actual population decline.

It was only in the second half of the nineteenth century that the average expectation of life at birth in the countries of western Europe, North America, and Oceania began to rise much above forty years. Average expectation of life in Denmark, England and Wales, France, the Netherlands, Norway, Sweden, and the State of Massachusetts in the United States was 41 years in 1840 and had advanced only as far as 43.5 years by 1870.[2] Outside these areas, high mortality rates and a correspondingly low expectation of life continued to be the general experience throughout the nineteenth century. For instance, expectation of life at birth in 1896-7 in European Russia was only about thirty-two years.

The early mortality decline in the more advanced countries was associated with rising standards of living, including better diets, improved environmental sanitation, and the provision of safe water supplies, particularly in the cities; the introduction of smallpox vaccination and other advances in medicine; and the virtual elimination of famine, even

[1] Kingsley Davis, *The Population of India and Pakistan*, Princeton University Press, Princeton, N.J., 1951, p. 33.
[2] *Population Bulletin of the United Nations*, No. 6, Table IV. 1, p. 49.

on a local basis, as the result of high agricultural productivity and improved communications. A recent analysis[1] of the reduction in death rates in England and Wales in the nineteenth century has revealed that almost the whole of the decline could be attributed to fewer deaths caused by tuberculosis, typhus, typhoid, scarlet fever, cholera, and smallpox, those particularly affected by the improvement being persons over the age of one and under forty-five. The reduction in deaths from tuberculosis accounted for nearly half of the total mortality reduction, and this led the authors to the conclusion that the rising standard of living was the most influential factor in the decline. On the other hand, a prominent American expert holds the view that

the great mortality movements of the West appear to have been initiated by medical advances, particularly as applied by governments. Improving economic conditions were important, but much more as permissive elements than as precipitating factors.[2]

Continuing research on nineteenth-century demography may lead to an improved evaluation of the relative importance of the social, economic, and medical factors involved in the mortality decline; such research is, however, necessarily difficult, because of the geographical and historical limitation of usable mortality statistics, and particularly cause-of-death statistics.

The pace of the mortality decline accelerated in the first half of the twentieth century, and a growing number of countries were involved. In general, the slower starters among the more developed countries experienced a more rapid decrease in death rates and hence a more rapid rise in life expectancy than had those countries which led the field. For instance, expectation of life at birth in Czechoslovakia had only reached about forty years at the turn of the century, compared with fifty or more in Scandinavia; in the mid 1950s, the Scandinavian peoples were still among those with the lowest death rates in the world, but their expectation of life (about seventy-two years) exceeded that of the population of Czechoslovakia by only three years.

MORTALITY REDUCTIONS IN DEVELOPING COUNTRIES

In developing countries, as in the industrially more advanced countries,

[1] Thomas McKeown and R. G. Record, 'Reasons for the Decline of Mortality in England and Wales during the Nineteenth Century', in *Population Studies*, Vol. XVI, No. 2 (November 1962), pp. 94-122.
[2] George J. Stolnitz, 'Comparison between Some Recent Mortality Trends in Underdeveloped Areas and Historical Trends in the West', in *Trends and Differentials in Mortality*, Milbank Memorial Fund, New York, 1956, pp. 26-34.

there has been considerable variation in the rapidity of the decline in mortality and in the factors associated with it. It has sometimes been assumed that very high death rates persisted in all developing countries until the use of antibiotics and insecticides became widespread after World War II. This is not, in fact, the case; countries as widely separated as Malaya and Jamaica have long enjoyed an effective public health organization and good urban sanitation, and mortality had been gradually declining in those countries for some decades before the war. In many tropical and sub-tropical countries, however, malaria eradication programs and other public health measures since the war have made a major contribution to the reduction of the death rate. Ceylon and Mauritius are good examples of the spectacular effect of such programs in compact, fairly densely populated countries; in both of these countries, crude death rates[1] are only about one-third of their pre-war level. The reduction in Ceylon in recorded crude death rates has been from 24.5 for 1935-9 to a current level of about 8.5, and in Mauritius, from 27.3 for 1935-9 to about 8.6. More recently, malaria eradication has been a factor in the continued gradual reduction of the death rate in India. Many writers have pointed out that the declines in mortality in developing countries have not, for the most part, been accompanied by improvements in living standards, and can therefore be attributed entirely to advances in medical and health work. It should be noted, however, that there have, at the same time, been very considerable advances in education and in road communications in these countries, and it seems doubtful whether mortality reduction would have been so rapid in the absence of educational development and improved infrastructure.

MORTALITY BY AGE AND SEX

How has the mortality decline affected different age-groups of each sex? In the first place, mortality rates for females at all ages are, in general, lower than the corresponding rates for males in countries of low mortality, and the decline has had the effect of increasing male excess mortality. In the United States, for instance, it has been calculated by the use of age-adjusted death rates that the ratio of male to female mortality rose from 1.08 in 1920 to 1.60 in 1958, the largest increases in the ratio by age-groups affecting those between fifteen and twenty-four and between forty-five and sixty years of age. An examina-

---

[1] The crude death rate measures the number of deaths in a given year per one thousand population living in the middle of the year.

tion of death rates in the United States by cause of death revealed that trends in motor vehicle accidents, maternal mortality, and tuberculosis mortality could largely account for the changed ratio for the younger of these groups, while trends in deaths due to cancer and heart diseases were important causes for the increase for the older age-group. In some of the countries of high mortality in South Asia, there is still female excess mortality at some ages, but cause-of-death statistics are too poor to establish with confidence the reasons for this state of affairs.

When the decline of mortality in modern times is studied with regard to different age-groups, it is found that the greatest reductions in death rates have been those affecting children and the younger adults, and that the death rates of the elderly have been cut down in smaller pro-

Table 13

AGE SPECIFIC DEATH RATES FOR EACH SEX. (RATES PER 1,000 POPULATION OF SPECIFIED SEX AND AGE)

Age	Mauritius 1960	United States 1959	Japan 1959	France 1960	Malaya 1957
MALES					
Under 1	86.3	33.3	37.0	31.5	109.9
1-4	9.8	1.2	3.0	1.3	11.4
5-9	1.7	0.6	1.1	0.5	3.1
10-14	1.1	0.6	0.7	0.4	1.8
15-19	1.5	1.3	1.2	0.9	2.3
20-24	1.7	1.8	2.2	1.2	3.1
25-29	1.9	1.7	2.3	1.6	3.7
30-34	3.3	2.1	2.5	2.1	4.8
35-39	4.4	2.9	3.0	2.7	6.4
40-44	8.2	4.6	4.2	3.9	9.0
45-49	13.5	7.5	6.4	6.6	13.7
50-54	26.2	12.2	10.2	11.0	18.0
55-59	33.5	18.8	16.8	16.9	30.9
60-64	54.3	27.7	25.9	25.6	39.0
65-69	67.3	43.6	41.8	37.4	66.6
70-74	79.6	62.8	67.5	57.9	⎫
75-79	147.4	86.0	107.6	92.6	⎬ 100.1
80-84	263.3	132.1	162.5	149.4	⎭
85 plus	150.0	203.1	241.0	258.6	
FEMALES					
Under 1	70.4	25.6	30.6	23.9	84.6
1-4	11.6	1.0	2.6	1.1	11.2
5-9	2.3	0.4	0.9	0.3	3.3
10-14	0.8	0.3	0.5	0.3	1.8
15-19	2.0	0.5	0.8	0.4	3.0
20-24	4.4	0.7	1.4	0.7	4.2
25-29	4.9	0.9	1.7	0.8	5.6
30-34	4.4	1.3	2.0	1.1	6.4
35-39	6.3	1.8	2.4	1.6	7.9
40-44	6.2	2.7	3.2	2.3	8.7
45-49	5.4	4.1	4.5	3.6	12.1
50-54	11.3	6.2	6.8	5.3	12.7
55-59	17.3	9.4	10.3	7.7	25.1
60-64	32.9	14.4	15.7	12.0	26.0
65-69	54.5	24.3	26.6	19.9	48.8
70-74	57.8	39.1	45.9	34.0	⎫
75-79	111.4	59.1	77.7	60.9	⎬ 81.0
80-84	216.3	105.6	123.6	108.9	⎭
85 plus	310.6	203.3	200.9	206.3	

SOURCE: *United Nations Demographic Yearbook, 1961.*

portions. When expectation of life at birth increases from thirty to seventy years, mortality of persons up to about the age of forty is reduced by 90 per cent or more, the percentage reduction slowly declining with age, while at age seventy-five the reduction would be likely to be of the order of one half only. In the words of a United Nations publication: 'More has been accomplished in eliminating premature death than in lengthening the life-span of persons who survive beyond middle age.[1] Age-specific death rates for each sex are compared for a few countries in Table 13. It will be seen that the risk of death is usually lowest for the ten to fourteen age group.

VARIATIONS IN MORTALITY BY ECONOMIC AND SOCIAL STATUS

Mortality differentials still persist in many countries between socio-economic groups, between different ethnic groups in the same country, and between urban and rural populations. Such differentials are, however, usually on a much reduced scale when compared with the pre-war position. For children, the general rule is still that those whose parents are well-off socially and economically have a better chance of survival than those whose parents are poor. A recent analysis of infant mortality levels by social class in England and Wales has shown that the inverse relationship between infant mortality and class still persists, though the gap has narrowed in recent years. The author of this analysis[2] attributed the variation to such matters as housing, parents' educational level, and parents' own health and physique rather than to wealth as such. One result of the arrival of the 'affluent society' seems, however, to be a tendency for the middle-aged of high socio-economic status to suffer a death rate above that of those at a lower socio-economic level. For instance, a study of occupational and social class differences in the United States found that, above the age of fifty-five, death rates for professional workers were greater than those for technical and administrative workers, and those for skilled workers greater than those for semiskilled.

Differentials in mortality between ethnic groups exist in almost all countries in which two or more races live side by side without much intermarriage. In the United States, for example, the death rates of

[1] *Population Bulletin of the United Nations*, No. 6, United Nations, New York, 1963, p. 53.
[2] J. N. Morris, 'Some Current Trends in Public Health', in *Proceedings of the Royal Society*, Vol. 159B (London, December 1963), pp. 65-86.

nonwhites are higher than those of whites for all age-groups up to middle age and for all occupational classes. A similar situation is to be found in Malaysia where death rates for Malays are considerably higher than those for Chinese, and in New Zealand where age-specific death rates for Maoris are higher than those for the whites, though crude death rates for Maoris and whites are approximately equal owing to the younger age structure of the Maoris. In all three instances cited, the poorer community has the higher mortality rate, but cultural differences almost certainly are important, as well as the differences in wealth.

Differences in mortality experience between urban and rural areas and between different regions in the same country form a fascinating field of study. In the nineteenth century, as has been noted, death rates were higher in urban than in rural areas in those countries for which statistics are available. The situation has now changed to some extent, but not completely. In Sweden, for instance, women now enjoy a higher expectation of life in the cities than in the rest of the country, but the reverse is the case for the men. In some of the developing countries, the cities do better than the rural areas, but in others the opposite is true. Poor communications and inadequate health services in parts of the rural areas are sufficient to account for some of the regional differences in mortality within developing countries, but they do not explain regional differences in cancer mortality in countries such as Japan and the Netherlands; here, soil conditions are believed to be partly responsible. The general tendency in the more developed countries seems, however, to be in the direction of national uniformity in mortality.

These differences within nations are the complement of differences between nations. The longest-lived peoples in the world are still, on the whole, those who, nationally speaking, are in the upper income bracket, though there is not an exact correspondence between the league table of expectation of life at birth and that of national income per head. The United States is behind quite a few European countries, as well as New Zealand, in the former table. It is, however, correct to say quite unequivocally that the average life expectancy in the less developed countries of the world is still much lower than in the economically more advanced countries, despite the fact that the gap has been narrowed in recent years.

THE PRESENT SITUATION

The position now is that, in the more developed regions of the world, crude death rates range between seven and twelve deaths per one thousand population per annum, and expectation of life at birth exceeds sixty-five years in virtually all the countries of these regions, and exceeds seventy years in a number of them. In the developing areas of Asia, Africa, and Latin America, the country-by-country range is much wider, but regional average crude death rates vary from a low of about ten for temperate South America to the mid-twenties for central and western Africa. Some of the developing countries can claim lower crude death rates than those of many European countries, but the age-specific mortality rates of the European countries are, nevertheless, lower. The higher average age of European population as compared with that of developing countries explains this paradox and emphasizes the danger of relying on crude death rates as a measure of mortality when comparing one population with another.

The expectation of life at birth of countries in Asia (other than Japan and Israel) and South America varies between the lower and upper limits of forty and sixty-five years. In Africa, life expectancy at birth is in some countries below forty years, and there are probably very few African countries in which it exceeds fifty years. In the developing countries, however, estimates of present levels of mortality must necessarily be subject to a very wide margin of error, owing to fragmentary coverage or the complete absence of registration of deaths. Examples of current measures of mortality in selected countries with reasonably good vital statistics are given in Table 14; this selection necessarily excludes countries with the highest death rates, because these countries do not possess adequate statistics for the calculation of ex-

Table 14
MEASURES OF MORTALITY FOR SELECTED COUNTRIES

Country	Year	Crude Death Rate	Infant Mortality Rate	Expectancy of Life at Birth		
				Date	Males	Females
1. Sweden	1964	10.0	13.6	1962	71.32	75.39
2. Netherlands	1964	7.7	15.8	1956-60	71.4	74.8
3. New Zealand	1964	8.8	19.1	1955-57	68.2	73.0
4. United States	1964	9.4	25.2	1963	66.6	73.4
5. U.S.S.R.	1963	7.2	30.9	1960-61	65.0	73.0
6. Japan	1964	6.9	20.4	1963	67.21	72.34
7. Italy	1964	9.6	35.5	1954-57	65.75	70.02
8. Portugal	1964	10.2	73.1	1959-62	60.73	66.35
9. Taiwan	1964	5.7	26.4	1959-60	61.33	65.60
10. Trinidad	1963	6.7	38.5	1957	59.88	63.35
11. Malaya (former Federation of)	1963	8.9	56.7	1956-58	55.78	58.19
12. India	1951-61	22.8	139.0	1951-60	41.89	40.55

SOURCE: *United Nations Demographic Yearbook, 1964*, Table 3. (See notes to that Table for bases of data of individual countries.)

pectation of life at birth, infant mortality, and other rates. Thus, no African countries appear in Table 14, though estimates of mortality rates for some of them have been made on the basis of sample survey data of questionable accuracy.

CHIEF CAUSES OF DEATH

In order to examine the prospects for further improvement in life expectancy in each of these two groups of countries, a closer look at the chief causes of death and at current trends in age-specific mortality is required. Considering first the countries with the lowest death rates, one finds that infant mortality is now at the very low level of fifteen to twenty infant deaths per one thousand live births, and looks as though it will stay at about this level until further progress is made in reducing deaths due to birth injuries and congenital malformations. In these very low mortality countries, deaths in infancy and early childhood attributable to environmental factors and lack of infant care have all but disappeared. In later childhood and the earlier decades of adult life, deaths caused by violence, most of which are accidental, predominate; indeed, for the fifteen to twenty-four age group, in particular, the much bigger risk of males than of females dying from violence leads to age-specific death rates for males which may be up to three or four times as high as those for females. In low mortality countries, the reduction of mortality for the older children and younger adults thus depends largely on progress in reducing accidental deaths, particularly deaths on the roads. The possibilities of reducing deaths from motor vehicle accidents in the United States can be illustrated by comparing the record with that of countries such as Sweden, the United Kingdom, and New Zealand. In 1964, 24.5 persons in every 100,000 died as a result of motor accidents in the United States, compared with 15.3 in the United Kingdom, 16.5 in New Zealand, and 17.5 in Sweden.

Deaths due to violence increase with age after childhood, but not so rapidly as mortality rates from all causes, so that at the older ages violent deaths form quite a small proportion of total mortality. When life expectancy at birth exceeds seventy years, deaths caused by heart disease and cancer form about half of total deaths at all ages, and the proportion is well in excess of one half for the older age groups. In the countries of low mortality, the prospects for further reduction in mortality rates for the elderly must, therefore, be measured largely in terms of decreases in mortality from cancer and heart diseases. On the basis of trends in the last few years, the prospects, particularly for the older men, do not look particularly bright. Above age sixty-five years for men and seventy-five years for women, mortality from diseases of the heart has increased in recent years, and between the ages of forty-five and sixty-five has remained about static, though there is, of course, considerable variation between different countries with low death rates. Men above the age of forty-five years have also suffered increased death rates from cancer recently in some of the low mortality countries, though the rates for middle-aged and elderly women have declined in line with the general decline in mortality from all causes. So prominent among the causes of death are the heart diseases and the cancers that one calculation made at the 1965 World Population Conference in Belgrade was to the effect that the total elimination of all other causes of death in the countries of low mortality would not increase expectation of life at birth by more than ten to twenty years. Clearly, no further major reductions in adult mortality in these countries can be expected in the absence of major break-throughs in the treatment of the cancers and the heart diseases. At present, treatment of the heart diseases, which cause more deaths than the cancers, has the effect of postponing death, and not of curing the disease.

FUTURE PROSPECTS

In some of the developing countries the pace of mortality decline appears to have slackened in the last two or three years, and the question which demographers are naturally asking is whether important improvements in living standards are a necessary condition for any further large reductions in the death rate. Is there, in other words, some kind of a barrier in the process of mortality decline beyond which populations with an average per-capita income of less than a very few hundred dollars per annum cannot be expected to go? Or can the use of the most modern medical and public health techniques reduce mortality rates in the developing countries to the lower European levels in the absence of any improvement in economic conditions? No definite answers can be produced, but it seems likely, on present trends, that mortality decline in the developing countries, as in the countries of currently low morality, will proceed at a slower pace in the next few decades than in the twenty years since the end of the Second World War.

INCREASE IN LIFE EXPECTANCY DUE TO MODERN MEDICINE*

Harrison Brown

[1954]

Two thousand years ago the average baby born in the heavily populated city of Rome had a life expectancy of little more than 20 years. His contemporaries who were born in the provinces of Hispania and Lusitania, away from the unhealthy congestion of the capital of the empire, could expect to live for a considerably longer time—girls had a life expectancy of about 35 years, and boys, of about 40 years. In Roman Africa the chances of survival were even greater. Girls could expect to live about 45 years, and boys had nearly a 50-year life expectancy.

Life expectancy did not rise appreciably above those levels until very recent times. In 1850 the life expectancy at birth of a girl born in Massachusetts was little more than 40 years—only a little greater than that in ancient Hispania and Lusitania. In England, at the same time, the life expectancy at birth was very nearly the same as in the United States. Between 1850 and 1900 some decrease in mortality was achieved, and female life expectancy at birth rose to 47 years in England and to 50 years in the United States. Nevertheless, the life-expectancy figures at the turn of the century were not far removed from those which had existed in Roman Africa.

During the first half of the twentieth century enormous reductions were made in mortality rates in the United States[1], particularly in the younger age groups. Female infant mortality decreased from approximately 110 deaths per thousand births in 1900 to 26 per thousand in 1946. In 1900 only 80 per cent of the girls who were born could be expected to reach the age of fifteen. In 1953 over 96 per cent of all white girls born were expected to reach the onset of the breeding period. In 1900 only 65 per cent of newborn girls could be expected to survive until the end of the breeding period. In 1953 over 90 per cent of all white girls born in the United States could expect to reach their forty-fifth birthday.|The most important single factor associated with the enormous decrease in mortality during the past 50 years has been the increase in knowledge, which permits us to control many epidemic and endemic infections which are themselves associated with the existence

*From *The Challenge of Man's Future* by Harrison Brown. Copyright © 1954 by Harrison Brown. Reprinted by permission of The Viking Press, Inc. and McIntosh and Otis, Inc., New York.
[1] Most of the specific references to the United States apply equally as well to Canada and the countries of western Europe. (ed.)

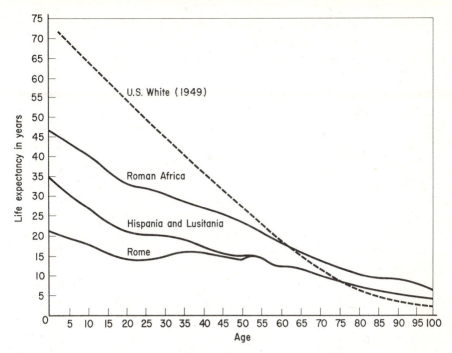

FIGURE 20   Female expectation of life in the ancient Roman Empire.

of civilization—diseases which were practically unknown in primitive societies. As we have seen, civilization has resulted in the crowding of many people into small areas. This, in turn, has created conditions for rapid incubation and spread of disease.

Since the time of Pasteur[1] we have accumulated a vast amount of knowledge concerning the nature of various infections and the ways in which they are spread. Our knowledge permits us to control infections by blocking the routes by which germs enter the body, by inducing immunity to diseases through inoculation, and by reducing the mortality of diseases, once contracted, through the use of drugs and proper hospital care.

A classic example of the application of the principles of immunology has been inoculation against smallpox, which was practiced irregularly long before the time of Pasteur. Prior to the introduction of vaccination, few people in Europe escaped having smallpox—and usually 1 out of 12 infected persons died. Today, by contrast, smallpox is a medical curiosity in the Western world. Following Pasteur's work, the principles of immunology have been extended to the point where we have today,

[1] Louis Pasteur, the eminent French chemist and bacteriologist (1822-85). (ed.)

in addition to smallpox vaccination, highly effective and preventive serums for a diversity of diseases, including typhoid fever, tetanus, rabies, scarlet fever, and diphtheria.

The most dramatic changes in mortality patterns during the past half-century have been connected with the control of infections in children. The pasteurization of milk alone has been largely responsible for the drop in frequency of diarrheal diseases in children under five years of age—a drop which has resulted in a decrease from 40 deaths per thousand children from this cause alone to a negligible number. During the early part of this century diarrhea and enteritis ranked as the chief causes of death of children under one year of age. Today these diseases rank fifth in importance as causes of death.

Death rates due to other diseases of childhood have likewise declined steadily through the years—some rapidly, others more gradually. The introduction of diphtheria antitoxin treatment in 1895 has led to a reduction of deaths resulting from that disease to a negligible proportion. Deaths resulting from scarlet fever, measles, and whooping cough have likewise decreased to levels which are low compared to those which existed at the turn of the century. We have now reached the point at which death rates among infants are determined, in the main, by causes other than infection—premature births, congenital malformations, and injury at birth. But the main causes of death during the second year of life are still diseases over which we have some, but not complete, control—bronchitis, pneumonia, measles, whooping cough, diarrhea, and enteritis.

In the Western world there is a clear relationship between mortality rates for the diseases of childhood, and economic class or 'standard of living'. For example, the infant death rate in England resulting from bronchitis and pneumonia in families of the poorest economic group was found recently to be seven times greater than that in families belonging to the professional class. Similarly, the ratio of deaths resulting from measles and whooping cough in the two groups were in the ratio of 15 to 1 and 7 to 1 respectively.

It seems likely that with further increased general medical care and further elevations of standards of living, death rates among children will be reduced to even lower levels than those which prevail today. Whereas at the present time we can expect approximately 96 per cent of the girls who are born to survive to the age of fifteen, it is not unlikely that two or three decades from now 98 per cent of the girls who are born will reach maturity. With further advances in the techniques of caring for

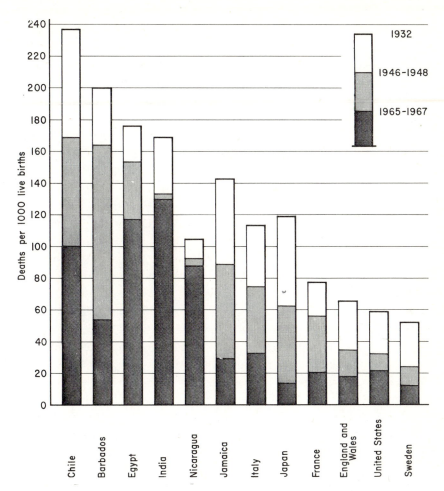

FIGURE 21   Deaths of infants under one year of age.

prematurely born infants, a 99-per-cent survival to the age of fifteen might be possible. Further reductions of infant and child mortality will be difficult, however, because of the limits imposed by congenital mal-formations and by congenital debility.

The principal reductions in mortality during the years from age fifteen to age forty have likewise been brought about by the control of in-fectious diseases. Perhaps the most outstanding achievement in this connection has been the virtual elimination of typhoid fever as a cause of death in the United States. Mortality from typhoid fever was highest in adolescence and early adult life, and its elimination has therefore substantially increased the proportion of persons who live through the breeding period.

During the latter part of the last century deaths from typhoid fever in Chicago were approximately 50 to 100 per year per 100,000 inhabitants. During occasional major outbreaks, mortality rose to even higher levels. Following the installation of filters in the water system in 1906, the inauguration of water chlorination in 1913, and the introduction of pasteurized milk, the number of typhoid deaths dropped precipitously to extremely low levels. In the United States as a whole, the further protection given by typhoid inoculations has reduced the annual mortality from the disease to less than 1 death per 200,000 persons.

Tuberculosis still remains one of the greatest of all threats to the lives of young adults, yet the decrease in mortality during the last fifty years has been dramatic. In the United States in 1900 nearly 200 out of every 100,000 persons were killed each year by the disease. With the spread of increased facilities for treating the disease and improved methods of early diagnosis, mortality has been lowered to one-sixth the former number.

It is likely that mortality from tuberculosis will be decreased still further in the future, for we know that the death rate depends greatly upon the environment. Recently, for example, the tuberculosis mortality rate in the poorest class in England was found to be greater than twice the mortality rate in the wealthiest class.

It seems likely that with continued improvement of living conditions, coupled with continued increase in the general availability of adequate nutrition and medical care, death rates resulting from diseases such as tuberculosis, bronchial and lobar pneumonia, and rheumatic fever will be decreased to levels much lower than those which exist today, even if no really specific cures for the diseases are found. When this point is reached, the main barriers to further decreases in mortality will be deaths from such phenomena as childbirth, accidents, virus diseases such as influenza, . . . cancer, and 'degenerative' diseases such as hypertensive vascular disease. It is quite possible that further research on the nature of virus diseases will disclose more effective controls than those which exist today. Further, it seems likely that death rates resulting from childbirth will be reduced to a level considerably lower than that now prevailing. In addition, growing awareness of the considerable incidence of accidental death has resulted in the establishment of accident-prevention programs of increasing scope and effectiveness.

When we take all of these factors into consideration, it is probable that the adult mortality curve of a century from now will be determined in the main by such diseases as cancer, nephritis, heart disease, cerebral hemorrhage, and diseases of the arteries. When that time arrives, we can expect approximately 96 per cent of all girls born to reach their forty-fifth birthday.

Beyond the age of forty-five a high percentage of death results from degenerative diseases. The human body, like other highly organized living structures, will apparently serve for only a limited period of time before certain processes start which we are helpless to combat—at least at the present time. A part of our helplessness results from our lack of understanding of the nature and the causes of the processes associated with aging. Nevertheless, a good case can be made for the view that although medical science is making it possible for ever-increasing numbers of people to live out their natural life span, the ultimate 'limit' of the human life span is not being increased appreciably.

It seems likely that every human being is genetically endowed at conception with a certain 'life potential'—a natural life span which could be fulfilled in the absence of physical or biological accidents and which seems to vary greatly from individual to individual. At one end of the scale are those babies who are born with biological weaknesses that terminate their lives within a few minutes or hours. At the other end of the scale are those relatively few individuals who live to pass the century mark. The bodies of most individuals are of intermediate stability and appear to be sufficiently well constructed to permit them to function for at least seventy-five years (barring physical or biological accidents) before degenerative processes bring about death.

The record of decreasing mortality during the last half-century attests to the difficulty of increasing the life expectancy of the aged. Since 1900 we have lowered the mortality rates of infants, children, and young adults to one-fifth the previous number, but our success in reducing mortality rates in older age groups has been less spectacular. The probability of an eighty-year-old woman dying during the course of a year is only 20 per cent less today than it was 50 years ago. In spite of our greatly increased medical knowledge and our improved facilities for the care of the aged, the decrease in mortality rate for ninety-year-old persons is so slight as to be only barely observable.

It seems clear that the primary reductions in the mortality rates of older persons have resulted from the same developments which lowered the death rates of young people. But with older persons the probability of death due to degeneration and resultant stoppage of any one of the innumerable functioning components of the body is large compared

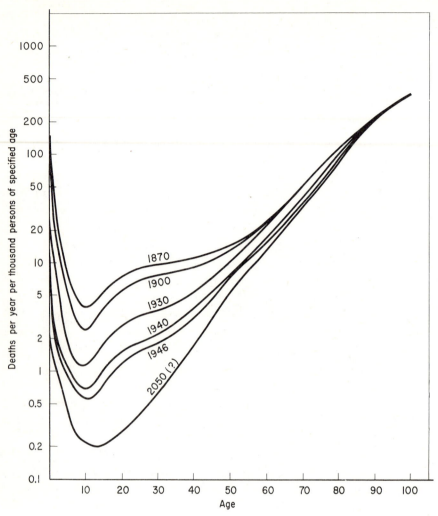

FIGURE 22   Mortality rates, United States white females.

with the probability of death due to infectious diseases. Consequently, although the deaths due to disease have been reduced considerably, the decreases have had but small effect upon the overall death rates of older groups.

It is unlikely that the general situation with respect to the degenerative causes of death will change very rapidly in the future. Some progress has been made in the treatment of certain types of cancer and heart disease, but the overall demographic effect has been small. When the body grows old, there are many possibilities of failure. An older man might be saved one day from death from cancer, but he might die soon afterward of nephritis or heart failure.

Our knowledge of the processes of aging and degeneration must be considerably greater than it is today if the human life span is to be increased much beyond that which exists at present. And even when we understand the processes of aging, it may well turn out that there is little that can be done about it. However, in the unlikely event that new biochemical discoveries result in our attaining greatly increased life spans, the demographic consequences will be small when compared with the consequences of the biological discoveries that have already been made. Even if we are able at some future time to increase the average life expectancy to 150 years, the long-range consequences will be merely a doubling of Western population. When we compare this with the population increases which are made possible by our existing techniques, it appears that an increased natural life span would make a relatively unimportant contribution to future population changes.

The increased life expectancy that has been made possible by the technological developments of the past century has strongly affected two aspects of population growth. First, an increasingly large fraction of new-born girls survives to reach the breeding age. Second, and quite independent of birth pattern, the long life span has resulted in increased population solely because more people are living longer. The latter effect has produced, in addition to its contribution to population increase, a marked change in the composition of the population.

One hundred years ago over 50 per cent of all persons living in the United States were under the age of twenty, a mere 2.6 per cent were over the age of sixty-five, and the median age of the population was only 18.8 years. By 1900 the median age had risen to 22.9. During the last 50 years the proportion of persons in the United States under twenty years of age has dropped to 34 per cent, the proportion of persons over sixty-five has increased to approximately 7 per cent, and the median age of the population has risen to 30.1. These changes are still under way, and during the course of the next few decades we can expect the proportion of persons over sixty-five years of age to increase further and approach 15 per cent.

One hundred years ago the population age distribution in the United States and in the rest of the Western world was very much the same as it is in the Far East and in many other areas of the world today. Even in the United States and in England we can expect further population increases, solely on the basis of increasing the average life span, even if the net reproduction rates should drop again to the neighbour-hood of unity and remain there. However, these expected increases are small when compared with the increases that would result from this effect alone in India and China if the mortality rates in those areas were lowered to the rates which we now know are medically possible. Given adequate food and medical care, the populations of those countries would double even if birth rates were drastically lowered to the levels prevailing in the West.

2 | Factors Affecting Fertility

The various factors that have contributed to the world-wide decline in mortality are not too difficult to explain—the desire to reduce deaths and thereby extend life is a practically universal one. It is much more difficult to understand what affects the number of births, because birth rates are determined by individual decisions, and obviously such decisions will be influenced by a variety of interrelated social, economic, and religious factors. Even in those countries where there are population policies designed to either increase or decrease the number of births, such policies function by appealing to the individual through education or the provision of different kinds of incentives. Therefore, in order to understand why fertility rates have changed, it is necessary to examine those factors, including official policies, that have influenced people's attitudes to family size.

ECONOMIC AND SOCIAL FACTORS AFFECTING FERTILITY*

United Nations

The following material is from an early but excellent United Nations' population study. The first section deals with the factors affecting a declining fertility in those regions (principally Europe, North America, and Oceania) that have passed through the demographic transition and thus have relatively low but often fluctuating fertility rates. The second examines the situation in regions that are in the early or intermediate stages of the transition (principally Latin America, Africa, and Asia) and have high and steady fertility rates.

The following four generalizations[1] attempt to explain why fertility rates differ in developed and underdeveloped regions of the world. These points—which, it should be stressed, require considerable

*From *Determinants and Consequences of Population Trends*. United Nations, New York, 1953.
[1] Based on A. J. Coale, 'The Voluntary Control of Human Fertility', *Proceedings of the American Philosophical Society*, Vol. III, No. 3, 1967.

amplification—should serve as an organizing framework for the articles that follow.

(1) In an urban industrial society children are less of an economic advantage than they are in rural societies.

(2) Industrialization and modernization in general cause infant death rates to decline. The proportion of surviving children in a DC is therefore increased and the number of births needed to achieve a given family size is lower than in a UDC.

(3) The educational level of women and their opportunities for employment outside the home are much greater in an industrial society. Such factors certainly work against uncontrolled fertility.

(4) In underdeveloped countries, where illiteracy is high, education is usually a family process and behaviour is likely to be determined by tradition—large families are generally considered desirable. In developed countries the influence of rationality is stronger; one result of this is that couples are much more likely to realize the advantages of a small family.

[1953]

AGE STRUCTURE AND MARRIAGE PATTERNS

Considerable attention has been given to the question of whether changes in the age composition and marital status of the population have contributed to the decline in the birth rate. Existing studies indicate that the decline in the crude birth rate has not resulted from a decline in the proportion of persons within the reproductive age group. In fact, the proportion of women of child-bearing age increased somewhat in many countries during the period when the birth rate declined. Not only has the ratio of births to women of child-bearing age declined, but frequently its decline has been even greater than that of the crude birth rate.

It is evident also that the decline in the crude birth rate does not reflect to any considerable extent a change in the tendency to marry, or the age at which marriage takes place. Except in Ireland, the proportion of all women aged 15 years or over who are married and the proportion of women within the child-bearing age have not declined. In other analyses of marital status it has been found that in general there has been little change in the proportion of women who remain unmarried until the end of the child-bearing period, and no increase in age at first marriage during periods of fertility decline. Ireland is the exception in this connection since in that country the reduction in the proportion of women marrying probably caused most of the early decline of the birth rate.

Other factors, such as the rates of dissolution of marriages by divorce or by death of husband or wife, and the rates of re-marriage, have been viewed as less important in long-term changes in fertility. Owing to the decline in death rates, marriages have been dissolved less quickly by death in recent decades than formerly. This change has operated to increase the average number of births which may be expected within the duration of marriage. The increase in divorce has exercised an influence in the opposite direction, but usually to a lesser degree.

SOCIAL AND ECONOMIC FACTORS

THE CHANGING ATTITUDE TOWARDS FAMILY LIMITATION Some writers have been concerned primarily with explaining how the idea of limiting the number of children and spacing births has come to be generally accepted in industrialized countries, replacing the traditional idea of having the number of children which 'nature' provided. Other writers, however, view the problem as essentially that of explaining why people now desire fewer children than formerly. These different approaches to the problem underlie, in part, the differences among authors as to the role played by various factors in bringing about the decline in family size.

It has been pointed out, for example, that differences in approach influence the importance to be attributed to the decline in infant mortality. If people plan to bring up a definite number of children, a reduction in infant mortality will clearly cause a reduction in the number of births. Whether a reduction in infant mortality might cause the idea of family planning to be widely accepted is much more doubtful.

A related problem is the distinction between the causes of the decline in the birth rate and the motives present in the minds of married couples today when they decide how many children they should have. Reasons frequently given by couples for not having children—such as fear of unemployment, lack of money, inability to obtain satisfactory housing accommodation—are often discussed at length in works which try to answer the question: by what policies can the birth rate be raised? These reasons are sometimes described as causes of the low birth rate or even causes of family limitation. They should be distinguished, however, from the causes which brought about the reduction of the birth rate and the spread of family limitation.

Usually the decline in family size is treated as a single process. Occasionally, however, different phases have been distinguished which require separate analysis. If the problem is seen as a fundamental change in attitude—the acceptance of family limitation—one may distinguish between the origin of the attitude and its subsequent spread throughout society. From this point of view it is significant that family limitation was accepted first in the higher social classes of society, and by techniques of fashion and social example probably spread to other segments of society. The differences in fertility between different groups may reflect the extent of the contact of other classes with the classes who lead the way in the decline of family size. For example, the more rapid decline in cities may be due to the closer contact of the lower classes in cities with the classes who first practised family limitation. If the decline in the birth rate is treated as a fundamental change in the attitude toward family limitation, other processes which may have operated to reduce family size besides the great increase in the proportion of persons practising family limitation are occasionally distinguished. Such processes include changes in the numbers of children regarded as desirable; changes in the number planned by those practising family limitation; and changes in the effectiveness of birth control among those practising it. Few detailed discussions of these topics, however, appear in the literature.

It is a striking feature of the literature on the decline in fertility that many explanations of the decline which appear different at first sight turn out upon closer inspection to be fairly similar. Most recent authors believe that the decline in fertility is due to a complex of interrelated causes, acting upon one another and jointly bringing about the decline. They generally agree that the decline in fertility is closely connected with the changes which have fundamentally transformed European society in the last two centuries, but attempts to associate the decline exclusively with a particular aspect of these changes, such as, for example, urbanization, have not proved satisfactory. Those writers who attribute the decline in fertility to 'civilization' as a whole have perhaps most clearly shown this to be true.

The connection between the fall in the birth rate and such developments as urbanization or the change in the status of women reflects in a general way the period in which the birth rate declined. The decline has in addition been associated with particular historical events. For example, the French Revolution and the far-reaching changes which it brought are believed to have greatly stimulated the attitude favourable to family limitation. In Great Britain, the serious depression in the years after 1875 and the influence on public opinion of the trials of Bradlaugh-Besant[1] in 1877-8 for spreading propaganda for birth control are thought to have been connected with the beginning of the decline in the birth rate about 1880. Also, in Sweden and Australia the public scandals connected with birth control propaganda may have contributed to the spread of family limitation at that time.

URBANIZATION The decline in fertility has been preceded and accompanied in all countries by a great shift of the population from the country to the city. It has often been suggested that the rapid increase in the proportion of the population living in cities is closely connected with the decline in fertility. The evidence that families are larger among rural than among urban populations in many countries, has been cited in support of this contention.

The relation between the process of urbanization and low fertility is complex. Families tend to be larger in certain highly urbanized countries than in some other less urbanized countries. Also, the practice of family limitation has spread within rural communities, the French peasantry representing a much discussed example. Formerly, it is likely that the populations of cities did not practice family limitation to any large extent. Within European and American cities, different segments of the population began practising extensive family limitation at different times, and even today large differences in the size of their families are known to exist.

Without necessarily emphasizing urbanization, most writers concerned with the causes of the decline in family size believe that modern large cities have provided a particularly favourable environment for the development of the attitudes motivating family limitation. Several have regarded the urban environment as an essential condition for this development and have believed the decline of family size elsewhere to be a consequence of the diffusion from cities of certain aspects of urban living and the urban mentality.

Many factors believed to promote family limitation in cities to a greater extent than in the country have been suggested. First, it has

---

[1] Annie Besant (1847-1933), an ardent British feminist, and Charles Bradlaugh (1833-91), a British politician and social reformer, stood trial in 1877 for their part in the reprint of a pamphlet entitled the *Fruits of Philosophy*, which contained references to sex and birth control. They challenged the police to arrest them in order to gain publicity for the birth-control movement. While the verdict of the subsequent trial went against the defendants, it did achieve the results they desired—publicity for their cause. The verdict was later set aside on a legal technicality. (ed.)

been pointed out that family life in the city is less cohesive, because family members participate in other institutions and have a broader range of contacts outside the family. Second, children are not regarded as an economic asset in the city as they are in the country. A smaller proportion of children, especially young children, generally contribute to the family income in the city, and those who contribute do so on a smaller scale. Third, status aspirations, the achievement of which may be handicapped where support of a large family is mandatory, are probably more prominent in the cities, as are the opportunities to gratify such ambitions. Further, the importance of the spirit of 'rationality' and 'independence of tradition' prevailing in cities has also been emphasized. These points, frequently treated as 'causes' of the spread of family limitation, are discussed in greater detail below.

SOCIAL MOBILITY The desire to improve one's position in the social scale has been stressed as an important motive for family limitation. The argument is particularly associated with the name of Dumont, who in the latter half of the nineteenth century devoted an extensive series of studies to this phenomenon, which he termed 'social capillarity' (capillarité sociale). Just as a column of liquid must be thin in order to rise under the force of capillarity, so also must a family be small to rise in the social scale. He and many others have argued that during the period when family size declined, the mobility between social classes increased greatly, and new attitudes toward social mobility developed. Whereas formerly most men took their social position for granted, concern with improving one's own position or that of one's children became an ever-pressing preoccupation in those countries where family limitation spread. The effect of social mobility on fertility appears to be attributed in general to the fact that rearing children absorbs money, time, and effort which could otherwise be used to rise in the social scale. Social mobility is thus more feasible with one or two children than with a larger number.

OTHER FACTORS

Changes in the status and role of women have been advanced as a reason for the decline in family size. Many changes are believed to have worked against women's acceptance of their traditional role as home-maker and the bearer of children. Factors frequently mentioned as contributing to the changing attitude among women are the increased education and equality for women in many spheres of public life, the emphasis upon the woman's role as a companion with equality in marriage, and the opportunity for personal development and independence.

Families are smallest in those countries where levels of living are highest. Within the period of declining fertility, the average real income has been rising, and the rich have generally had fewer children than the poor. It has therefore been suggested that increasing wealth decreases fertility. Others have pointed out that there is no simple relationship between income levels and fertility levels. It has been noted that following the decline in fertility among the rich, the decline has also spread to the poorer groups. Particularly has this been true in large cities as witnessed by the large decrease in fertility among the relatively poor.

Various reasons have been suggested as to why an increase in wealth alone should produce a decline of fertility. One theory is that the balance between competing sources of pleasure changes as wealth increases. Greater income makes possible a wider selection of leisure-time activities. Child care may be considered an interference with the satisfaction of other desires, and hence the incurring of such responsibility may be limited.

It is also often assumed that a decline of religious interest has been conducive to the limitation of family size. Inferred is the notion that religious interest has declined as traditional values have given way to rationalist modes of thinking. Thus, the control of family size is believed to be less within the jurisdiction of religious institutions and increasingly within the domain of the family itself.

The decline in mortality among infants and young children has been advanced as a factor responsible for the decline in family size. The proportion of children born who survive has increased, which would indicate a greater burden for their support were the practice of family limitation not resorted to. Since it has been noted in certain statistical studies that there is a tendency for couples to have another child to 'replace' a child who did not survive, it is possible that a greater rate of survival among children has caused couples to limit the number of children born. Generally, the lowering of infant mortality has been regarded as only one element in the total social situation favourable to the development of family limitation.

The decline in mortality among adults has also been suggested as a factor promoting family limitation. Thus, the slower elimination of the aged from the labour force is said to have made the economic situation more difficult for those in the reproductive ages. Further, the dependency burden may have increased because of the greater survival of the aged and thereby have encouraged smaller families.

Other causes suggested for explaining the decline in the birth rate are housing shortages, poverty, economic insecurity, unemployment, and fear of war. Objections to such causes have been advanced on the grounds that there has been no intensification of such factors in most countries where the birth rate has declined. Standards of housing on the whole have improved, average income has increased, and there is no evidence that wars have become more frequent. If such factors have caused a decline in the birth rate, this must have been due to changes in people's mentality which altered their reactions to these conditions. While individuals often give these as reasons to explain why they are not having more children, the genuineness of such motives as fear of war has been doubted by some authors.

FACTORS AFFECTING HIGH FERTILITY

Where data are available they generally show that, in countries of high fertility, marriage of women occurs at an early age and is nearly universal. For example, the proportion of women ever married in the age group 45-49 years was 99 per cent in India in 1931 and 97 per cent in Ceylon in 1946. In Egypt a figure of 99 per cent was recorded for the age group 40-49 years in 1946. That the age at marriage is low may be illustrated by the fact that among women aged 20-24 years, 71 per cent were or had been married in Ceylon and 95 per cent in India. For Egypt within the age group 20-29 years the figure was 88 per cent.

Latin-American countries appear to be exceptions to the rule that where fertility is high almost all women marry at an early age. However, the great number of consensual marriages in these countries may render invalid any comparisons of their official data on marital status with those of other countries. Available census data on the number of children borne by each woman show that women begin childbearing early. For example, census data for 1943 in Jamaica show that 48 per cent of women aged 20-24 years had borne one or more children. In Trinidad and Tobago in 1946, 62 per cent of women aged 20-24 years were recorded as having borne children. In Brazil and Peru in 1940 the corresponding figures were 46 per cent and 52 per cent.

Much of the literature concerned with the high fertility in the regions under consideration has been primarily concerned with similar factors to those considered in discussion of the decline of the birth rate in the

West. For example, just as this has generally been attributed to family limitation, it has been the general opinion that Orientals have many children because they marry early and do not practise family limitation. Some have believed that reproduction in these countries is near the limit of that which is biologically possible. Others have argued that all societies have institutions and customs which reduce fertility substantially below the physiological maximum. The delay of marriage beyond puberty or the avoidance of marriage altogether, and the ban on the re-marriage of widows in India, lower fertility in some degree. There are, furthermore, practices which reduce the fertility of married persons, such as abstention from intercourse at certain times for ritual and other reasons, and the prolongation of lactation. The practices of infanticide, abortion, and birth control are also found in some cases.

Much attention has been devoted to economic, social, and cultural pressures making for high fertility. The discussions reflect, to some extent, the variety of the explanations which have been given for the decline of the birth rate in the countries of low fertility. For example, Dumont has discussed the obstacles to social mobility—such as the caste system and property rights—in India, China, and Russia in order to show why social capillarity . . . did not operate in those countries.

More recently writers have been concerned with the questions as to whether the high-level fertility is likely to decline as it has in the West and whether measures could be taken to bring about or hasten such a decline. Among the factors mentioned as favourable to high fertility are general conditions which are believed to foster attitudes making for large families—such as illiteracy, heavy dependence on agriculture, isolation, a low standard of life, a fatalist attitude. Other conditions mentioned concern more directly the motives to have many children, such as religious injunctions, the form of family organization, a widespread desire for heirs, a high mortality resulting in small numbers of surviving children even where many are borne and the absence of economic incentives to limit the number of children where children can contribute to the family income and where the cost of satisfying the children's needs is small. It has been emphasized that various elements of social organization form an interlocking system, and the combined result is a very strong pressure to reproduce. For example, Stycos[1] has suggested that while Puerto Ricans have small-family preferences, institutional and cultural patterns work counter to low fertility levels. Within the

[1] Dr J. M. Stycos is Director of the International Population Program, Cornell University. (ed.)

society, differential sex statutes and rules are such that high fertility may result because the woman's effective role is minimal. On the other hand institutional mechanisms outside the immediate family serve as palliatives to relieve the pressure of numbers on resources and the psychological disequilibrium between the marriage pair.

At the time when the French birth rate was conspicuously lower than that of any other country, certain writers argued that as civilization spread to other European countries, their birth rates would fall to the French level. A similar argument has been widely applied in recent decades to peoples of non-European civilization. European civilization has begun to affect many if not all countries and it is widely believed that the economic, social, and cultural conditions of many lands will in the future become similar to those of western Europe today. It is generally expected that such a development will eventually result in a reduction of fertility. The same attitudes, values, and ideas and the same economic incentives which have caused the spread of family limitation in Europe will then become effective in the countries of high fertility.

It is expected that industrialization may soon take place on a fairly large scale in several economically retarded countries where birth rates are high. If their experience is like that of other countries which have undergone industrialization, their birth rates will decline as industrialization proceeds. However, there may be a considerable time lag between industrialization and the fall of the birth rate, and the length of this time lag may vary with the cultures in question. The reduction of fertility, through changes in marriage customs and family limitation, requires fundamental changes in the individual's outlook and values. These values are deeply embedded and rigidly enforced by social sanctions. Even under the impact of a rapidly changing environment, such values may change only gradually.

CHILDREN BECOME AN ECONOMIC LIABILITY*

Katherine and A.F.K. Organski

[1961]

The wonders of industry have not, as one might expect, produced a higher birth rate. Had the old peasant values favouring large families remained, this might well have happened, for surely, being richer,

*From *Population and World Power* by Katherine and A.F.K. Organski. Copyright © 1961 by Katherine and A.F.K. Organski. Reprinted by permission of Alfred A. Knopf, Inc.

mankind can afford more children. But peasant values went the way of the peasants, and falling birth rates followed on the heels of industrialization (Figure 23).

The decrease in fertility requires more explanation than does that in the death rate. Death, after all, is man's oldest enemy, and the desire to combat hunger and disease as is old as human history. It is to be expected that improved technology would be used to lengthen life, but it is more difficult to explain its use to cut family size. It is by no means easy to find clear 'causes' for anything as complex as a change in human values, which is what we are dealing with here. Looking backward, it is relatively easy to provide plausible explanations for what has happened in the past; but we do not know which factors were the key ones or what minor changes might have produced a different result.[1] Some of the reasons for the declining rate of human reproduction can be suggested, however.

Consider the cost of raising children in the modern way compared to what it costs a landed peasant family. Except in times of famine or where the shortage of land is acute, peasant children put little economic strain upon their parents; indeed, they might almost be considered an economic asset. Six-year-old boys can tend goats and fetch wood and water; eight-year-old girls can serve as full-time nursemaids; twelve-year-olds can sweep and mend. Their usefulness increases with years. In many pre-industrial societies grown sons stay home and work the land of their fathers, bringing home their wives to live and do the most unpleasant chores.

Compared to their peasant ancestors, modern children are an expensive if highly attractive luxury. They do not work: they play and go to school. Their full support—and full it is—must be provided until they reach maturity. At that point, sheltered, groomed, ready to give as well as to receive, they leave home and make their contribution elsewhere. Families with eight or ten children were not uncommon in the past, but who can afford such families today?

The social cost of a large family has also changed. In a peasant society a man's position is determined by his birth. Childlessness may bring him pity and derision, a large family, universal congratulation; but his social standing remains about the same. Not so for modern man: in an industrial society the family's standing depends heavily upon the

[1] Recent studies suggest that the relationship of lower fertility to industrialization and urbanization may not be as automatic as was previously assumed. See Frank Lorimer, *Culture and Human Fertility*, UNESCO, Zurich, 1954, Chap. vi.

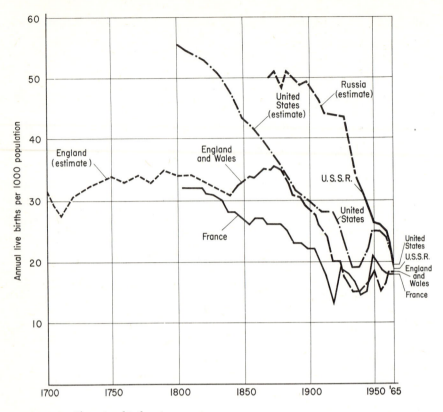

FIGURE 23 Changing birth rates.

occupation of the head of the household and upon the standard of living of the whole family as evidenced by the material goods it can display. A family with eight children cannot live in as good a neighbourhood as a family with two; it cannot dress as well, drive as new a car, have as many conveniences and luxuries, or travel as much. The children will not receive as expensive an education, and this is particularly important in determining their social status when they become adults. False values? Perhaps modern men should feel, as do Indian peasants, that the family with eight children is richer than that with two—richer by six children. But that is not the way men count their wealth today or measure out esteem.

Industrial society, moreover, has invented new roles for women, holding out the lure of money and importance for work that takes them far from home. The training and education of women today directs them towards new goals. The current American pattern, for example, tends to minimize the differences between boys and girls in the early years and to provide a glamour pattern for young women. As a result, the role of aging mother-wife and housekeeper—'only a housewife', the phrase goes—is not as attractive as it used to be. Oddly enough, the Soviet pattern works in the same direction, although glamour is not the goal. The Russians put tremendous emphasis on careers for women because of the national shortage of labour. Be she capitalist or communist, modern woman finds herself faced with a choice of jobs that did not exist for her grandmother; and children, particularly if they are numerous, would bar her way to a career.

For all these reasons, and for many subtler ones as well, modern man for all his wealth has cut his birth rate. Planning his life, his work, his world, he has also begun to plan his family.

In their transition from the peasant world to the world of industry, Western nations have experienced falling birth rates, falling death rates, and a gap between them that has produced the largest population growth in history. Russia has followed such a pattern at a somewhat later date, and so has Japan, the only Asiatic land thus far to industrialize.

Experts have reasoned that if these population changes always accompany industrialization, similar changes may be in store for the rest of the world in the not-too-distant future.

POPULATION POLICIES*

Hope T. Eldridge

The theory of demographic regulation maintains that societies are capable of regulating the growth of their population by natural means; the process of demographic transition describes how this has occurred. However, the existence of world population problems suggests that demographic regulation is not occurring quickly enough in many countries, which remain in the early stages of the transition process. In those countries that have not passed through the transition, governments have established legislative measures and administrative programs, and taken other forms of action to reduce population growth. While it is the reduction of growth rates that concerns us in this book, there have also been instances in certain countries (described in the article below) where policies have been formulated to counteract declining populations. In addition to these quantitative aims, it should be noted that population policies can also be

*'Population: Population Policies' by Hope T. Eldridge. Reprinted with permission of the Publisher from The International Encyclopedia of the Social Sciences, David L. Sills, ed. Vol. XII, pp. 382-8. Copyright © 1968 by Crowell Collier and Macmillan, Inc.

concerned with eugenics (biological quality), distribution, and other qualitative aspects of population.

The following article considers some of the different population policies that have been devised by various countries and assesses, in general terms, the effect such policies have had on population growth. (Part 3, in the section entitled 'The Means of Controlling Births', considers in more detail those measures that have been tried or proposed to control population growth.)

[1968]

Government concern over matters of population is not a new phenomenon. State intervention, in the form of laws or decrees encouraging marriage, taxing the unmarried, subsidizing families with children, regulating immigration and emigration, fixing a legal minimum age for marriage, and the like, have existed since ancient times. In general these measures represented a populationist philosophy that equated power and prosperity with large numbers.

The expansionist motivation in population policy reached a climax in Germany, Italy, and Japan during the period between the two world wars. Intensive pronatalist propaganda, cash payments to families with children, the rewarding and honouring of motherhood, the repression of birth control, the regulation of emigration, and the enactment of 'eugenic' laws, all reflected the drive for larger native and racially 'pure' populations, and they were directly associated with the political and territorial ambitions of the Axis powers.

During the same period, policies with a somewhat similar content but a different rationale were taking shape in other countries where very low rates of growth were evoking fears of an impending decline in numbers. Fertility rates were below replacement levels in many of these countries, and although only France and Austria actually recorded an excess of deaths over births, it was considered but a matter of time until most of western Europe would be experiencing a natural decrease of population. At the same time, sustained economic depression was precipitating a new concept of social justice, and governments were taking steps to protect workers against the risks of unemployment and to guarantee a minimum family wage that would take account of the number of dependents supported by each worker.

Although it was not clear to what extent the low birth rates then current were a continuation of the secular trend and to what extent they were a temporary phenomenon, it was thought that low marriage rates and low fertility within marriage had an essentially economic explanation. Consequently, the attempt to sustain or increase the birth rate became linked to the development of social-security programs, particularly those aspects of social security that contribute to the economic security of the family. Because of this linkage, it is sometimes difficult to say whether measures favouring the family, maternity, and infancy have a demographic as well as a welfare intent, unless the government concerned specifically so states. Insofar as these programs do have a demographic intent, they are distinguishable from the populationist policies described above, in that they are not expansionist in the imperialist sense but, rather, are animated by a desire to avoid population decline or, at most, to achieve a gently increasing population.

Similar programs have developed in the Soviet Union and eastern Europe, as an integral part of the plan to build the socialist state. The populationist overtones of these programs stem in part from the old controversy between Malthus and Marx, in which Marx took the position that 'overpopulation' was a misnomer for imperfect social organization, and in part from a felt need, in the Soviet Union at least, for a larger population. But in these countries, as elsewhere, the nature of population policy—and even the question of whether a policy exists —is to some extent a matter of the interpretation a government chooses to make of its actions and programs. Thus, a nation's stated policy is not necessarily an exact statement of its purposes of the moment. Indeed, the prevailing pattern of social and political organization is such that much of national policy in any area takes form through a series of compromises between contending pressures and hence has elements of ambiguity, not to say of ambivalence.

After World War II, with the emergence of new nations and a growing awareness of the economic problems of underdeveloped countries, population policies that represented a different point of view began to develop. In many of the underdeveloped countries mortality was falling rapidly, as a result of large-scale preventive measures, but fertility remained high and rates of increase as great as 2.5 to 3.0 per cent per annum were either recorded or in prospect. Such rates were without precedent in Western experience. They implied a possible doubling of population within a generation and aroused fears that the effort to raise levels of living would be impeded by the necessity to provide subsistence for the increasing numbers. Policies that favour reducing or stabilizing the rate of population growth have therefore begun to evolve in some of the densely populated underdeveloped countries of the Far East and the Caribbean.

ELEMENTS OF POLICY

Ideally, population policy involves the examination of past and current demographic trends and their causes; an appraisal of the future demographic changes implied by these trends; an evaluation of the social and economic consequences of expected patterns of change, in the perspective of what is regarded as the national interest; and finally, the adoption of measures designed to bring about desired changes or prevent undesired ones. Demographic trends are a function of changing relations between the forces of fertility, mortality, and migration, whether in the population as a whole or differentially in its various segments. Policy makers are therefore logically concerned with understanding the factors of change in these three processes and with ways and means of influencing the direction and amount of change in each of them. However, practical considerations are such that most of population policy, as it exists today, is directed at influencing fertility, although the trends and effects of migration and mortality may also be carefully studied, for changes in them can be the precipitating factors that render population a 'problem'.

MIGRATION Control of international migration as a means of adjustment between high-density countries and low-density countries holds only limited possibilities, principally because of the national feelings, political differences, ethnic preferences, problems of assimilation, and fears of the economic consequences of inundation from abroad. The immigration laws of the so-called countries of immigration (Australia, New Zealand, and most of the countries of western Europe and the Americas) are generally restrictive, setting limitations upon the number and source of immigrants and barring those who, for political, social, or medical reasons, are considered undesirable. Although some migration from high-density to low-density countries is encouraged, it is carefully controlled, often through bilateral agreements between the governments concerned. In these programs quantitative aims are present, but nonquantitative considerations usually take precedence.

From the point of view of the densely populated underdeveloped countries, there are, thus, no available outlets that could possibly siphon off the current and prospective increases in numbers. In effect, the solution of what are regarded as demographic problems is almost strictly a national affair. Adjustments of population to resources or to a program of economic development must be effected principally within national borders. . . .

MORTALITY Broadly defined, population policy includes measures intended to affect the death rate. But the purpose of such measures is to improve the health of the population, not to control the rate or direction of numerical change. To include the totality of such measures would be equivalent to identifying health policy with population policy. Manipulation of the death rate in order to control the rate of growth is not feasible, because there is only one policy in relation to mortality that is socially acceptable—namely, to reduce it. . . .

CONTROL OF FERTILITY

Under present political, cultural, and technological circumstances, the principal focus of efforts to influence population trends necessarily centres on the control of fertility. It so happens that, in general, countries wishing to stimulate growth are low-fertility countries and countries wishing to restrain growth are high-fertility countries.

Only three countries can be said to have coherent, carefully constructed, and frankly stated population policies: France, representing a strong pronatalist view; Sweden, representing a more tempered pronatalist view; and India, representing an antinatalist view. A much larger number of countries have taken cognizance of population problems in one way or another: by appointing commissions to study the question and make proposals; by issuing statements of official attitudes; or by enacting legislation which probably has inherent demographic aims, although other objectives may be the only ones acknowledged. A brief description of the policies of France, Sweden, and India, along with some indication of similar or relevant specific measures taken in other countries, should give perspective on how developments in this area are moving in the world in general.

FRANCE The essentials of French population policy are set out in the Code de la Famille, which came into force in 1940 ('Décret relatif à la famille . . .', 1939). Its purpose is both to encourage family formation and childbearing in numbers sufficient to maintain a moderate increase in population and to counteract the general aging of the population. Specific provisions to this end include, on the one hand, positive measures for financial aid to marriage and child rearing and, on the other hand, repressive measures restricting the use of induced abortion and contraception. Subsequent legislation has introduced some changes in the program, the general effect of which has been to improve its administration and increase its benefits.

The principal economic measure is the system of family allowances. Monthly cash allowances are payable to all families having two or more children under 15 years of age; in special circumstances the age limit is as high as 20 years. Reflecting pronatalist intent, allowances are higher for the third and subsequent children than for the second child. . . .

Further benefits to married couples include government loans for various purposes, tax reductions, and rebates on the costs of public services. Social services in aid of the family have taken the form of subsidies to school canteens, boarding schools, vacation camps, day nurseries, and kindergartens, the provision of household help; and family counselling. Certain benefits, available to persons covered by the social-security scheme and contingent upon attachment to the labour force, are regarded as part of France's program to compensate family expenses and have been regularly included in the computation of the costs of France's population policy. Principal among these benefits are reimbursement for most of the cost of the medical care of the spouse and children of the insured, including maternity care of insured women and spouses of insured men, paid maternity leave for insured women, and leave with pay for the father at the time of the birth of a child.

On the repressive side, the Code de la Famille re-embodied earlier legislation which made birth-control propaganda, sale or advertisement of contraceptives, and incitement to abortion illegal. . . .

Supplementing the pronatalist policy is the encouragement of immigration of a type that is considered compatible with both manpower and demographic needs. A final aspect of French policy is the existence of the Institut National d'Etudes Demographiques, created in 1945 to conduct research in problems relevant to population, follow studies and developments in other countries, and explore all possible means of increasing the number and improving the quality of the population.

SWEDEN Demographically, Sweden is similar to France and most of the other countries of western Europe. Like France, Sweden has a closely reasoned, highly developed population policy that is oriented towards sustaining the birth rate. But in Swedish policy, consideration of individual welfare and personal freedom have taken precedence over pronatalist aims wherever the two were in conflict. Also, much more emphasis is placed on payments in kind and on the provision of institutional or social services in behalf of the family.

Government action in matters of population began in 1935, with the appointment of a population commission. On the basis of the deliberations and recommendations of that commission and of a second commission, which functioned from 1941 to 1946, Sweden has developed a well-coordinated program, the themes of which are voluntary parenthood and child welfare. Family allowances are payable in behalf of each child under the age of 16. Reflecting a welfare, rather than a pronatalist, emphasis, this is a flat-rate allowance beginning with the first child, and the rate per child does not increase with the number of eligible children. The amount relative to the cost of child care is somewhat lower than that paid in France, but the system of supplementary services and allowances in kind is much more exhaustive. The supplementary aids include marriage loans for the purchase of household equipment, a comprehensive system of maternal and child welfare centres, housing and fuel grants for families of moderate means with two or more children, free school meals, home-help services, holiday travel for mothers and children of families in difficult circumstances, and tax relief. The sickness and maternity insurance scheme covers all resident citizens and registered aliens. Maternity leave is compulsory, and the costs of confinement are borne by the state. Women employees may not be dismissed because of pregnancy or childbirth.

In keeping with the aim of voluntary parenthood, contraceptive advice is given at hospitals and health centres, contraceptives may be purchased at all pharmacies, the laws against induced abortion have been relaxed, and sex education has been made a regular part of the school curriculum. The object of this part of the program is to improve the quality of the population, as well as influence population growth in the direction desired. Abortion has been legalized to the degree that medical boards may authorize the interruption of pregnancy on rather broadly defined therapeutic or eugenic grounds, taking into account the general social, medical, and psychological circumstances of the woman involved. Sterilization may be authorized for similar reasons. It was hoped that the more lenient attitude toward induced abortion would in the end reduce the number of such abortions; however, it is not yet possible to ascertain whether this program has had the desired effect.

INDIA   In India, population policy is oriented toward restraining the rate of increase, on behalf of economic development and of raising the level of living of the people. This policy was initiated in 1952, with the first five-year plan, and subsequent action has put increasing emphasis upon the need to reduce the widening gap between a lowering death rate and a persistently high birth rate. The third five-year plan, promulgated in 1961, stated, 'The objective of stabilizing the growth of population over a reasonable period must be at the very centre of planned development'. The plan calls for a large-scale program of education and motivation for family planning, provision of birth-control advice and contraceptive supplies, and government-sponsored research in demographic trends, contraceptive methods, and family-planning motivation. Family-planning clinics have been established in a large number of rural areas, and family-planning services are available at urban medical and health centres. These activities are steadily expanding, with the government subsidizing the manufacture and distribution of contraceptives. The question of how to make the program more effective is under constant study. At the request of the government, the United Nations sent a team of experts to India in 1965, 'to assess the problems involved in accelerating the adoption of family planning by the people and to advise the Government on action that might be taken for this purpose'.

The law against induced abortion has not been relaxed, and pregnancy may be artificially terminated only to save the life of the mother. Voluntary sterilization, however, is regarded as an acceptable means of preventing births, and the practice seems to be spreading. Another facet of the Indian policy has to do with the effort to raise the average age at marriage. In this connection, the third five-year plan places special emphasis on the education of women and on the provision of new employment opportunities for women.

PROGRAMS IN OTHER COUNTRIES In Europe all the rest of the countries have adopted programs that resemble those of France or Sweden in various ways and to varying degrees, but in none of them has population policy been as fully developed or as clearly stated. These countries have family allowance schemes and social insurance or national health service systems that cover all or part of the costs of maternity and the medical care of workers and their dependents.

Measures in the Roman Catholic countries of western and central Europe and in the Netherlands are similar to those in France but less intensive. They may be characterized as favouring natality and as repressing the practices of birth control and abortion. Family allowances are generally of the progressive type; laws regarding birth-control propaganda and the sale of contraceptives tend to be restrictive; induced abortion is prohibited. Although pronatalist influences contributed to the enactment of these measures, they do not necessarily have an announced or a sustained pronatalist intent. Two countries—Italy and the Netherlands—have been encouraging emigration.

Programs in the Scandinavian countries, the United Kingdom, and Finland are similar to those of Sweden. The general attitude is pronatalist, but demographic considerations take second place to considerations of immediate welfare. . . .

Policies in the Soviet Union and in eastern Europe since World War II have been pronatalist in tone. Family allowances of the progressive type predominate, and special awards for mothers of large families are a persistent feature. Since 1955, legislation against abortion has been greatly liberalized in most of these countries; in some the operation is obtainable at the woman's request. The change was made on humanitarian and health grounds and was declared a measure intended to combat the dangers and frequency of induced abortion. The use of contraception, rather than abortion, is strongly advocated. The new policy does not necessarily indicate abandonment of the anti-Malthusian point of view, but there have been some expressions of the opinion that rapid population increase may interfere with economic development. . . .

Policies resembling that of India are emerging in a number of other densely populated underdeveloped countries. Intensive government-sponsored programs to promote family planning have been launched in Pakistan and the Republic of Korea. In Taiwan the government gives informal support to a program that is conducted by private organizations. The first five-year plan of Turkey reversed prior policy and provides for family-planning education. Iran's third plan mentions the need to popularize family planning. In Tunisia a policy favouring birth control is under study and a family-planning campaign has been started. In the United Arab Republic the charter promulgated by the president in 1962 stated that family planning was one way of alleviating the problem of low per-capita production. Official interest has also been demonstrated, by government approval or support of planned parenthood programs, in Hong Kong, Malaysia, Thailand, Barbados, Ceylon, and the Philippines. China has liberalized its laws on abortion and sterilization and, despite strong commitment to anti-Malthusianism, has begun to encourage birth control and advocate late marriage.

EFFECTS OF POPULATION POLICY

Not much can be said about the effects of population policy. As far as the three countries with well-defined policies—France, Sweden, and

India—are concerned, evidence that the desired effects are being produced is inconclusive. In France fertility is above pre-war levels, and
French analysts believe that French policy accounts for that fact. In
Sweden, however, the crude birth rate of 1960 was the lowest in
Europe and probably the lowest in the world. Growth rates remain high
in India. Elsewhere current levels and recent trends in national birth
rates appear to bear no consistent relation to the presence, purpose, or
content of national policy.

It seems clear that once the majority of a population has recognized
at the personal level the desirability of controlling family size, it will
act without much regard for the position of the law or official policy.
Thus, the secular fall in Western fertility took place over a period when
birth control was officially opposed and policy, if any, favoured increase.
The experience in Japan since World War II is another case in point.
Japanese law on abortion and sterilization was liberalized between
1948 and 1954, and at the same time the use of contraception, rather
than abortion, was urged upon the population. Recorded abortions
increased rapidly and soon were approaching the number of live births.
By 1960 the birth rate had fallen to a level comparable with that in
Western industrial countries. But the resort to abortion and the fall in
the birth rate began before 1948; the practice had undoubtedly existed
on a wide scale for some time. Legalization may have caused some of
the increase in the number of abortions, but the important fact, from
the sociological point of view, is that a great many people wanted to
limit the size of their families. In other words, when such a conviction
has arrived, ways and means of attainment will be found. An antinatalist policy has the problem of instilling that conviction; a pronatalist policy, of dispelling it. The question of whether governments
can or will provide incentives strong enough to change behaviour in
this area is still open.

The period of the 1960s was one of rapid development in the area of
population policy, especially among underdeveloped countries. Many
influences—social, political, economic, religious—were at work, both
in and outside of government and at both national and international
levels. For instance, the U.S. Congress, in passing the 1966 Food for
Freedom bill, specifically authorized the president to use the local
currencies acquired in sales of food under the Food for Freedom program
to set up birth-control clinics in any nation covered by the program,
if its government so requested. In January 1967 President Johnson,
in his State of the Union message, formally endorsed the 'export' of

birth control as a continuing policy. The elements of a domestic population policy also began to emerge, with the deepening involvement of the U.S. Department of Health, Education, and Welfare in birth-control activities, and the support of these activities by certain members of the Congress. But the Roman Catholic church, in spite of mounting internal criticism and considerable evidence that many Catholics either were using or wished to use some form of 'artificial' contraception, still had not modified its traditional stand by mid-1967. In the meantime, most governments of Latin America—the region with the world's highest rate of population growth—had yet to evolve population policies, although privately sponsored conferences in 1965 and 1967 allowed, for the first time, some public expression of concern. During the same period, other governments, such as that of the United Arab Republic, whose natural resources seemed inadequate to support their rates of population growth, were undertaking extensive birth-control programs for the first time.

But it was impossible to foresee the net impact of these forces upon the content and effectiveness of official policy in matters of population. A contemporary survey of government opinion[1], covering 53 countries in various stages of economic development, found that while many governments were aware of problems associated with population changes, there were differences between them in the interpretations they gave to such changes and in the policies they considered acceptable for dealing with the problems that are created. It must be concluded that knowledge about the interaction between population trends and economic growth is still imperfect and that there is plenty of room for honest disagreement about which population policies will be most effective in securing the general welfare.

---

[1] United Nations, Economic and Social Council 1961, *Inquiry Among Governments on Problems Resulting From the Interaction of Economic Development and Population Changes*. Report of the Secretary General E/3895/Rev. 1. United Nations, New York.

3 | The Implications of Present Population Trends

To this point it has been assumed that the present rates of population growth constitute a problem. While few would contest this assumption, it is essential now to consider more specifically how this problem manifests itself; in other words, to examine the implications of present population trends. We must answer the questions: What is the basis for thinking that there is a population problem? What criteria are used to establish the problem? What consequences are predicted if present growth rates continue?

Several factors have to be considered. First and foremost is the matter of sheer numbers: the population of the world is growing at an increasing overall rate that stands in 1971 at approximately 2%. Ignoring for the moment the problem of providing food and resources for the additional number of human beings that are born each year, or their impact on the quality of the total world environment—or, for that matter, the mental well-being of each individual—we must recognize that the present universal rate of growth will lead by the year 2000 to a world population in excess of 6 billion. By A.D. 2050, within the lifetime of people recently born, the figure will exceed 15 billion (over four times the present population of the world). Clearly there must be a limit, for in time growth will exhaust the earth's space. While most demographers agree that we do not know what this limit is, or more importantly what an ideal or optimum population may be, there can be little doubt that it is essential to proceed under conditions of controlled growth. The important question, then, is whether growth can be controlled by reducing the number of births on a world-wide basis. The inhumane and therefore unacceptable alternative would be to rely on an inevitable increase in death rates. Outside of migration to other planets, there are no other alternatives.

Other criteria can be used to establish the existence of a population problem. There are certain absolute limits in the capability of the physical and biological environment to support mankind. Although these are difficult to assess accurately, we appear to be approaching some of the limits now, particularly in the availability of basic resources and the quality of the environment. There are signs, too, of the development of stress among certain groups of people as a result of overcrowding. Further, economic and political implications are abundantly evident in many UDCs: appalling shortages of food, the inability of many countries to develop their economy, the resulting political turmoil that often leads to internecine wars. These and related issues will be examined in subsequent articles in this section.

We are really asking a crucial question: How many people can the earth support? This is unanswerable, unless we can set standards for the quality of human existence and also predict the potential for technological innovation. Certainly in some regions of the world—the very ones that are at present growing most rapidly—conditions are such that overpopulation already exists. However, we shall leave the question of regional disparity and the problems of the UDCs for the time being and consider (i) world population growth in terms of numbers and space, and (ii) the absolute limits imposed by our physical environment.

At the present time, assuming a total population of 3.6 billion, there are just under 10 acres of land surface for every human being. By the year 2000, according to United Nations' projections, this will have been reduced to just under 5 acres; by 2100, with a projected population of 48 billion, it will then have been further reduced to about 0.7 acres. When we consider the distribution and characteristics of the ecumene and non-ecumene and the existing densities of population, a figure of 0.7 acres of land surface per person—and this includes deserts, mountains, and ice caps—suggests that the population pressures in the more favoured areas of the world will be very great indeed.

Could such a situation actually come about? From a purely *physical* point of view, 48 billion would hardly present any problem at all, according to the following article by Fremlin. His examination of the ultimate physical limits of human population is based on the assumption that present rates of growth will be maintained, and that there will be world co-operation in the development and use of all resources.

Whether any of us would wish to live in the world that Fremlin describes, even in his Stage 1, is a question. Perhaps it is best to regard this article as an ingenious—and entertaining—speculation and not as a serious statement about possibilities that man may be actually called upon to face. (See Taylor's comments on this article on page 192.)

HOW MANY PEOPLE CAN THE WORLD SUPPORT?*

J. H. Fremlin

[1964]

STAGE 1: UP TO 400,000 MILLION IN 260 YEARS' TIME

Using existing crop plants and methods it may not be practicable to produce adequate food for more than four doublings of the world population, though the complete elimination of all land wildlife, the agricultural use of roofs over cities and roads, the elimination of meat-eating and the efficient harvesting of sea food might allow two or three further doublings—say seven in all. That would give us, with the present doubling time of 37 years, 260 years to develop less conventional methods, and would allow the population of the world to increase to about 130 times its present size, or about 400,000 million.

STAGE 2: UP TO 3 MILLION MILLION IN 370 YEARS' TIME

The area of ice-free sea is some three times that of land. Photosynthesis by single-celled marine organisms may be more efficient than that of the best land plants. If organisms could be found capable of the theoretical maximum efficiency (8 per cent of total solar radiation, according to A. A. Niciporovic) we should gain a factor of three in yield. We could then double our numbers a further three more times if all the wildlife in the sea, too, was removed and replaced by the most useful organisms growing under controlled conditions, with the optimum concentration of carbonates, nitrates, and minerals. (Of course a reserve of specimens of potentially useful species could be preserved, perhaps in a dormant state.) Again, for maximum efficiency we must harvest and consume directly the primary photosynthesizing organisms, rather than allow the loss of efficiency involved in the food-chains leading to such secondary organisms as zooplankton or fish.

By this stage, we should have had ten doublings, which at the present rate would take some 370 years, with a final world population of 3 million million. Since the world's surface (land and sea) is 500 million million square metres, each person would have a little over 160 square metres for his maintenance—about a thirtieth of an acre—which does not seem unreasonable by more than a factor of two, so long as

*This article was first published in *New Scientist*, the weekly news magazine of science and technology, London, No. 415, 1964.

no important human activity other than food production takes place on the surface.

No serious shortages of important elements need be envisaged so far, though extensive mining operations for phosphates might be needed, and we have not yet approached any real limit.

STAGE 3: UP TO 15 MILLION MILLION IN 450 YEARS' TIME

At first sight, it seems that a very big leap forward could be taken if we use sources of power other than sunlight for photosynthesis. The solar power received at the earth's surface is only about 1 kilowatt per square metre at the equator at midday, and the average value over the day and night sides of the globe is a quarter of this. Over half of it is in the regions of the spectrum of no use for photosynthesis.

About one kilowatt-year per square metre could be produced by the complete fission of the uranium and thorium in about 3 cm depth of the earth's crust or by fusion of the deuterium in about 3 mm depth of seawater, so that adequate power should be available for some time. It is, however, difficult to see how the overall thermal efficiency from fuel to the light actually used for photosynthesis could be even as good as the ratio of useful to non-useful solar radiation (about 40 per cent).

It would, therefore, be better to use large satellite reflectors in orbit to give extra sunlight to the poles and to the night side of the earth. A large number of mirrors could be maintained in quasi-stable orbits about 1.5 million kilometres outside the earth's orbit, any deviations being controlled by movable 'sails' using the pressure of sunlight. To double our total radiation income would require a total area of about 100 million square kilometres of mirror which, in aluminium a tenth of a micron thick, would weigh about 30 million tons. With plenty of people to design and make the equipment it should not be difficult by the time it would be required, and it would bring the whole earth to equatorial conditions, melting the polar ice and allowing one further doubling of population.

A second doubling of radiation income would give the whole earth midday equatorial conditions round the clock, which would be exceedingly difficult to cope with without serious overheating. The overall efficiency of local power sources for photosynthesis is likely to be less than that of sunlight, so that no real gain in ultimate population size can be expected from their use, without an even more serious overheating of the entire globe.

If, however, the mirrors outside the earth's orbit were made of selectively reflecting material, reflecting only the most useful part of the spectrum, and if a further satellite filter were used, inside the earth's orbit, to deflect the useless 60 per cent of direct solar radiation, a further gain of a factor of 2.5 should easily be possible without creating thermally impossible conditions, at the cost only of perhaps a 10-100 times increase of weight of mirror plus filter—not difficult for the larger population with an extra 50 years of technical development. We should then have attained a world population of 15 million million about 450 years from now.

STAGE 4: UP TO 1,000 MILLION MILLION IN 680 YEARS' TIME

A considerably larger gain is in principle obtainable if the essential bulk foods: fats, carbohydrates, amino acids and so on, could be directly synthesized. Biological methods might still be permitted for a few special trace compounds. The direct rate of energy production resulting from the conversion of our food into our waste products is only about 100 watts per person and, if high-temperature energy from nuclear fuel (or sunlight) could be efficiently used, waste products could in principle be changed back into food compounds with the absorption of little more energy. Cadavers could be homogenised and would not, at least for physical reasons, need to be chemically treated at all. The fresh mineral material which would have to be processed to allow for population growth would be much less than 1 per cent of the turnover, and its energy requirements can be neglected.

If we suppose that the overall efficiency could not be increased beyond 50 per cent, a further 100 watts per person would be dissipated as heat in the process of feeding him. We have some hundreds of years to work up the efficiency to this value, so at least this ought to be possible. Some further power would be needed for light, operation of circulation machinery, communications etc., but 50 watts per person should suffice.

As we have seen, the long-term average heat income of the earth's surface is at present about 250 watts per square metre, and this could be doubled without raising the temperature above the normal equatorial value. (The initial rate of rise would be low till the polar ice had gone, which might take 100 years.) We thus have 500 watts per head, which could support 1,000 million million people altogether. The population density would be two per square metre, averaged over the entire land and sea surface of the earth.

STAGE 4a: UP TO 12,000 MILLION MILLION IN 800 YEARS' TIME. DEAD END.

Above two people per square metre, severe refrigeration problems occur. If the oceans were used as a heat sink, their mean temperature would have to rise about $1°c$ per year to absorb 500 watts per square metre. This would be all right for the doubling time of 37 years, at the end of which we should have four people per square metre. Half another doubling time could be gained if efficient heat pumps (which, for reasons of thermal efficiency, would require primary energy sources of very high temperature) could be used to bring the ocean to the boil.

Two more doublings would be permitted if the oceans were converted into steam, though that would create an atmospheric pressure comparable to the mean ocean bottom pressure at present. Since the resulting steam blanket would also be effectively opaque to all radiation, no further heat sink could be organized and this procedure would therefore seem to lead to a dead end.

STAGE 5: UP TO 60,000 MILLION MILLION IN 890 YEARS' TIME

A preferable scheme would be the opposite one of roofing in the ocean to stop evaporation (this would, in any case, probably have been done long before, for housing) and hermetically sealing the outer surface of the planet. All of the atmosphere not required for ventilation of the living spaces could then be pumped into compression tanks, for which no great strength would be needed if they were located on ocean bottoms. Heat pumps could then be used to transfer heat to the solid outer skin, from which, in the absence of air, it would be radiated directly into space. The energy radiated from a black body goes up as T^4, where T is the absolute temperature ($°K$), but for a *fixed rate* of heat extraction from the living space, at a fixed temperature (say, $30°c$ or $303°K$), the heat-power *radiated* must for thermodynamic reasons be proportional to T even if the refrigeration equipment is perfectly efficient (see any good textbook on the principles of refrigeration). Hence the rate of heat extraction will go up no faster than T^3 where T is the outer surface temperature.

All the same, this gives more promising results than would the use of the ocean as a temporary heat sink. An outer skin temperature of $300°c$ would give a heat extraction of 3 kw per square metre and $1,000°c$ would give an extraction ten times greater. If heat removal were the sole limitation, then we could manage about 120 persons per square metre for an outer skin temperature of $1,000°c$—which represents nearly six further doublings of population after the end of Stage 4, with a world population of 60,000 million million in 890 years' time. $1,000°c$ may be a rather modest figure for the technology of A.D. 2854 and the population could, as far as heat is concerned, be able to double again for each rise of absolute skin temperature of $\sqrt[3]{2}$ or 26 per cent. The difficulties in raising it much further while keeping all thermodynamic efficiencies high would, however, seem to be formidable. A rise to $2,000°c$ would give us less than three further doublings.

We seem, therefore, to have found one possible absolute limit to human population, due to the heat problem, which at the present rate would be reached 800-1,000 years from now, with a world population of 10^{16}-10^{18}.

I have not considered emigration to other planets because it seems to me unlikely that our technical capacity to do so will catch up with the population expansion. To keep world-population level we would have to be sending out 60 million people per annum *now*. It is so much cheaper to feed them here that this will not be done.

If, however, it were possible to export population on the scale required it would not make a great difference. Venus is much the same size as the earth, so (assuming that it has all the raw materials needed) an extra 37 years would bring it to the same population density as the earth. Mercury, Mars, and the moon together give half the same area, so that Venus and the earth together would take them up to the same population density in a further 10 years. The moons of Jupiter and Saturn could give us another 2 years or so. It is not clear that normal human beings could live on Jupiter and Saturn themselves and impound their extensive atmospheres, and the outer planets would take a long time to reach; if all these extraordinary problems could be solved, nearly 200 years might be gained.

Other possible limitations than heat will doubtless have occurred to readers, but these do not seem to be absolute. The most obvious is perhaps the housing problem for 120 persons per square metre. We can safely assume, however, that in 900 years' time the construction of continuous 2,000-storey buildings over land and sea alike should be quite easy. That would give 7.5 square metres of floor space for each person in 1,000 storeys (though wiring, piping, ducting, and lifts would take up to half of that) and leave the other 1,000 storeys for the food-producing and refrigerating machinery. It is clear that, even at much lower population densities, very little horizontal circulation of persons, heat, or supplies could be tolerated and each area of a few kilometres square, with a population about equal to the present world population, would have to be nearly self-sufficient. Food would all be piped in liquid form and, of course, clothes would be unnecessary.

Raw materials should not be a problem. The whole of the oceans and at least the top 10 kilometres of the earth's crust would be available, giving a wide choice of building, plumbing, and machine-building materials. Even with 8 tons of people per square metre (reckoning 15 people to the ton) all the necessary elements of life could be obtained; some from air and sea (C, H, O, N, Na, Cl, Ca, K, and some trace elements) and some from the top 100 metres of solid crust (Fe, S, P, I, and remaining trace elements). Only after a further hundredfold increase in population would it be needful to go below the top 10 km of crust for some elements (N, S, P, I). Such an increase would need an outer skin temperature of 5,000°c (comparable with the surface of the Sun) to radiate away the body heat, which would seem to be well beyond the possible limits.

A question of obvious importance which is not easy to answer is whether people could in fact live the nearly sessile lives, with food and air piped in and wastes piped out, which would be essential. Occasional vertical and random horizontal low speed vehicular or moving-belt travel over a few hundred metres would be permissible, however, so that each individual could choose his friends out of some ten million people, giving adequate social variety, and of course communication by video-phone would be possible with anyone on the planet. One could expect some ten million Shakespeares and rather more Beatles to be alive at any one time, so that a good range of television entertainment should be available. Little heat-producing exercise could be tolerated. The extrapolation from the present life of a car-owning, flat-dwelling office worker to such an existence might well be less than from that of the neolithic hunter to that of the aforesaid office worker. Much more should be known about social conditioning in a few hundred years' time and, though it is difficult to be quite certain, one could expect most people to be able to live and reproduce in the conditions considered.

Many readers will doubtless feel that something unconsidered must turn up to prevent us from reaching the limiting conditions I have supposed. One point of this study is however to suggest that, apart from the ultimate problem of heat, we are now, or soon will be, able to cope with *anything* that might turn up. Anything which limits population growth in the future will, therefore, be something that we can avoid if we wish. It would be perfectly possible to choose not to eliminate some major killing disease or to neglect the world food problem and let famine do its work, but this would have to be a positive decision; it can no longer happen by mistake.

Consequently all methods of limitation of population growth will, from now on, be artificial in the sense that they are consciously planned for, whether or not the plan is carried out by individuals for themselves. We are, collectively, free to choose at what population density we want to call a halt, somewhere between the 0.000006 per square metre of the present and the 120 per square metre of the heat limit; if we do not choose, eventually we shall reach that limit.

POPULATION LIMITS IN TERMS OF ENERGY AND OTHER RESOURCES*

Paul R. Ehrlich and Anne H. Erhlich

[1970]

A British physicist, J. H. Fremlin, has calculated an ultimate terrestrial population density of some 100 persons per square yard of the earth's surface. At that point a 'heat limit' would be reached. People themselves, as well as their activities, convert other forms of energy into heat, which must be dissipated. Indeed, whenever energy is put to work, heat is produced. This is a basic law of the universe, one of the Laws of Thermodynamics. According to Fremlin, at about the density described, the outer surface of the planet (by that time an artificial 'world roof' covering the entire planet) would have to be kept around the melting point of iron to radiate away the excess heat.

Fremlin, however, made a series of extremely unlikely assumptions to permit the population to build to the 60,000,000,000,000,000 people of his limit. He assumed, for instance, that all social, political, and technological problems of crowding people into a 2,000-storey building, converting the entire surface of the earth, would be solved. It is more likely that a different sort of heat limit would prevail long before any such astronomical population size is reached. Meteorologists caution that world climates could be drastically altered if the additional heat that man dissipates in his global environment reaches about one per cent of the solar energy absorbed and re-radiated at the earth's surface. Since

*From *Population, Resources, Environment: Issues in Human Ecology* by Paul R. Ehrlich and Anne H. Ehrlich. W. H. Freeman and Company. Copyright © 1970. Reprinted by permission.

energy consumption is at present increasing at about 5 per cent per year, such a climatological heat limit could be reached in less than a century.

In *all* aspects of population, resources, and environment, the restrictions imposed by the laws of thermodynamics can be critical. Many futuristic proposals for expanding energy supplies, utilizing new resources, and increasing food production lose their lustre in the cold perspective of the efficiencies to which these laws restrict us.

ENERGY

Will the availability of energy impose a limit on human population growth? The energy situation is uncertain and complex, but it can be summarized as follows: we are not yet running out of energy, but we are being forced to use the resources that produce it faster than is probably healthy. Our supplies of fossil fuels—coal, petroleum, and natural gas—are finite and will probably be consumed within a few hundred years, possibly much sooner. Coal will probably be the last to go, perhaps 300-400 years from now. Petroleum (including that in oil shales) will go much sooner. The most recent and thorough estimate, by geologist M. King Hubbert, gives us about a century before our petroleum reserves (including recent Alaskan discoveries) are depleted. Already we are being forced to consider more expensive mining techniques to permit utilization of the oil shales. We are living beyond our means, 'spending our capital,' depleting what are essentially nonrenewable resources. Furthermore, some organic chemists consider the burning of fossil fuels for energy production to be one of the least desirable uses for these large organic molecules. Petroleum and coal have many other uses in areas as diverse as lubrication and the production of plastics.

The world's potential production of hydro-electric power is roughly equivalent to the amount of power now produced by fossil fuels. There are, however, serious problems in utilizing it to the utmost. Much of the potential lies in UDCs, where the power could not be used unless those countries become industrialized, and global ecological factors and shortages of resources will prevent industrialization in most of them. Furthermore, hydro-electric power depends on dams, which under present conditions of technology are temporary structures. In a few hundred years, sometimes much less, their reservoirs fill with silt and become useless. Finally, there is an aesthetic question. Do we wish to impound and control all of the wild rivers of the earth?

For many years men have speculated about the sun as a source of non-depletable power, but large-scale utilization of solar energy presents serious technological problems, especially in a crowded world. Sunlight must be gathered over large areas; the collecting device for an electric generating plant with a capacity of 1,000 megawatts (enough power to supply electricity to a city of perhaps 1.5 million people) would have to cover an area of about 16 square miles. Tidal power, also the subject of some speculation, does not have more than a minute fraction of the potential of water power, and will presumably never be of more than local importance. There is some dispute about the power potential of the heat of the earth's core (geothermal energy). This energy is nuclear in the sense that the heat is produced by radio-active decay. Some experts say that geothermal energy will never supply more than a very small fraction of the power used by man; others connected with companies attempting to harness this energy are much more optimistic. Some predict that towards the end of this century geothermal production of electricity will supply as much as one-half of America's electrical power.

Many people who are aware of the approaching end of our fossil fuel resources assume that uranium-based nuclear power will soon simply replace the fossil fuels. Unfortunately, the continued availability of high-grade uranium ore reserves is not proven, nor are the direct or environmental costs of nuclear power well established. Contrary to a widely held misconception, nuclear power is not now 'dirt cheap', and does not represent a power panacea for either DCs or UDCs. The largest nuclear generating stations now in operation are, even with their massive hidden subsidies, just competitive with or marginally superior to modern coal-fired plants of comparable size (in areas where coal is not scarce). At best, both produce power for approximately 4 or 5 mills (one mill = one-tenth of a cent) per kilowatt-hour. Smaller nuclear plants are less economical than small plants that operate on fossil fuels. In this connection it is important to note that UDCs rarely can use the outputs of large power plants. There are simply not enough industries, lightbulbs, appliances, neon signs, electric trains, buses, streetcars, and so on to utilize that much electricity. Significantly, the cost of the modernization and industrialization required to utilize the electrical power exceeds the cost of the power itself by several orders of magnitude. For example, economist E. S. Mason has calculated that the output of capital necessary to consume the output of a relatively small (70,000 kilowatt) plant—about 1.2 million dollars worth of electricity per year at 40 per cent utilization and 5 mills/kwh—would be 111 million dollars per year if the power were consumed by metals industries, and 270 million dollars per year if it were consumed by petroleum products industries. All things considered, only those UDCs that are now short of fossil fuels or have problems in transporting them would have reason to choose nuclear power.

Prospects for major reductions in the cost of nuclear power in the future hinge on the possibility that safe and economical 'breeder' reactors can be developed, and on the more remote possibility that a successful thermonuclear (fusion) reactor can be produced. The time scale for availability and the ultimate cost of energy are uncertain for both possibilities. The breeder reactor would convert more nonfissionable uranium and thorium to plutonium that it would consume as fuel for itself. Although breeder reactors would effectively extend our fissionable fuel supply by a factor of approximately 400, they are not expected to become economically competitive with conventional reactors until the 1980s. Whenever they do, there is no guarantee that the cost per unit energy beyond that time can be reduced, because of their probable continued high cost and the probable increase in the cost of the ore that the breeders will convert to fuel. In the latter regard, although crushing granite for its few parts per million of uranium and thorium has been suggested as a source of nuclear fuel, and is possible in theory, the problems and cost of doing so are far from resolved. Not the least of these problems is what to do with the leftover granite! It is too soon to predict the costs associated with fusion reactors, but few scientists active in the field of plasma physics today are willing to predict whether such a device can be developed to generate *useful* power within the next 25 years—and it is plasma physicists who must solve the critical problems. One guess puts the unit energy cost at more than one-half that for coal or a fission power station of comparable size, but this is pure speculation. Possibly the major benefit of controlled fusion will be to extend the energy supply rather than to cheapen it.

A second common misconception about nuclear power is that it can reduce our dependence upon fossil fuels to zero as soon as that becomes necessary or desirable. In fact, nuclear power plants produce only electrical energy; and electrical energy constituted only 19 per cent of the total energy consumed in the United States in 1960. Thus the length of time that nuclear fuels can postpone the exhaustion of our coal and oil depends on how much the use of electrical energy can be increased. The task is immense and revolutionary! It will require a conversion from engines fueled by petroleum products to electric or fuel-cell-powered transportation, conversion from coal and oil to electric heating, and conversion to electrically powered industries. All such conversions will take time and will be extremely expensive.

Nuclear energy, then, is a panacea neither for the DCs nor the UDCs. It may relieve, but not remove, the pressure on fossil fuel supplies, and may provide reasonably priced power in certain parts of the world where these fuels are not abundant. It has substantial, if expensive, potential applications in increasing food production.

It is clear that mankind, if it survives for another century or so, will witness drastic changes in the use of energy sources. It does not appear, however, that availability of energy itself will place a limit on population growth, although difficulties accompanying the transition from one source to another might well do so. The ultimate limits to the use of energy (assuming radioactive pollution and other safety problems associated with nuclear energy can be solved) come not from its shortage, but from the problem of dissipating the heat to which all useful energy is ultimately degraded.

NONRENEWABLE MINERAL RESOURCES

Geologist T. S. Lovering wrote in 1968 for the *Texas Quarterly*: 'Surprisingly enough, many men unfamiliar with the mineral industry believe that the beneficent gods of technology are about to open the cornucopia of granite and sea, flooding industry with any and all metals desired'. Lovering was responding to the outpouring of propaganda from technological optimists who discount the problems posed by the unprecedented consumption of nonrenewable resources and by their sporadic distribution. How well fixed is mankind for the fossil fuels, the metals, and the other minerals he extracts from the earth? Should we believe the technological optimists, who hold that science and technology can solve resource problems? Or should we listen to those who argue that mineral resources, whether they be extracted from undiscovered rich deposits or from such common rocks as granite, are exhaustible and irreplaceable? The answer goes something like this: for the next 30 years, the DCs will probably not fare too badly, since most of the UDCs will be unable to industrialize on any more than a modest scale. For approximately a century after that, mankind in general will do rather poorly, especially if any of several current trends continue. Beyond that time, the costs of energy required to extract whatever resources remain will tax far more than man's ingenuity.

The resources of the earth's crust are very unevenly distributed—a result of the uneven distribution of the processes that led to their deposition and concentration. The distribution of coal, for instance, presumably represents the pattern of distribution of certain types of swamp plant communities that existed several million years ago. Some minerals have been formed by sedimentation; others have been deposited in fractures in the earth's crust. The concentration of some minerals varies more or less continuously from very high-grade ores to below the average abundance of the element in the crust of the earth. Certain types of copper ores exhibit such a pattern of deposition, as do the ores of other important metals, such as iron and aluminum. Many others, including ores of lead, zinc, tin, nickel, tungsten, mercury, manganese, cobalt, precious metals, and molybdenum do not. They show sharp discontinuities in concentration.

This frequent discontinuous distribution, as well as other factors, makes untenable the views of certain economists who think that only economic considerations determine the availability of mineral resources. They have the idea that as demand increases, mining will simply move to poorer and poorer ores, which are assumed to be progressively more and more abundant. These economists have misinterpreted a principle called the 'arithmetic-geometric ratio' (A/G ratio)—a principle that geologists developed for application to certain types of ore deposits within certain limits. It is valid only for those ores (such as porphyry copper deposits) and only within those limits. The idea is that as the grade of ore decreases arithmetically, its abundance will increase geometrically until the average abundance in the earth's crust is reached. It is further assumed that the additional cost of mining the low-grade ores can easily be absorbed, since the dollar value of mineral resources is at present only a small part of the gross national product. But, as noted above, the geological facts of mineral distribution do not support the simplistic views of the cornucopians any more than the physical and biological facts of life support their views about the imagined panacea of unlimited power from atomic energy. Although some ores approximate a distribution where the A/G ratio may be applied, most do not.

Our present level of affluence depends on much more than the availability of relatively common substances, such as iron, aluminum, zinc, phosphate rock, coal, and oil. Also necessary are such 'mineral vitamins' as vanadium, tantalum, tungsten, molybdenum, and helium. Although these are little known to the layman, they are critically important to

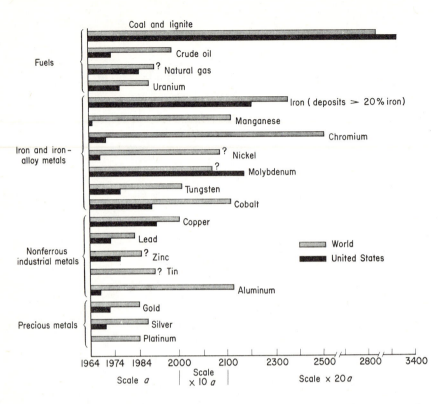

FIGURE 24 Lifetimes of estimated recoverable reserves of mineral resources. Reserves are those that are of high enough grade to be mined with today's techniques. Increasing population and consumption rates, unknown deposits, and future use of presently submarginal ores are not considered. (After Preston E. Cloud, *Realities of Mineral Distribution*, 1968.)

industrial processes. Like the familiar vitamins in our diets, these minerals are often required only in small amounts, but they are indispensable, which by analogy gives them the 'vitamin' label.

Figure 24 gives estimated time spans for depletion of various mineral reserves. Implicit in the chart are certain assumptions: these are that the population will remain constant at 3.3 billion, that consumption will not increase above 1965 rates, that no ore now uneconomical to mine will be exploited, and that there will be no discovery of presently unknown reserves. These assumptions, of course, had to be made to reduce variables; otherwise the chart could not have been made up.

Population and consumption have obviously both grown since 1965. Some low-grade ores have become economically competitive, and perhaps more will. Nor is there any doubt that new reserves of at least some of the minerals will be found. But how future developments will interact (or counteract) is totally unknown, so the chart is probably as good an estimate of today's reserves as is possible.

Clearly, these estimates hardly give us reason for optimism. A considerable amount of substitution and extraction from low-quality ores will be necessary well before the end of this century. Unless oil exploration is extraordinarily successful we will be well into our reserves of oil shale, and we may even need to convert coal to liquid fuels. There has been a rather gradual rise in [U.S.] domestic oil production from 318,535 metric tons in 1953 to 409,170 metric tons in 1966. In the same period, world oil production more than doubled—from 657,800 metric tons to 1,641,400 metric tons. At present the United States produces about one-fourth of the world's oil, but consumes about eight times the per-capita figure for the 'free world'—about 900 gallons per year for every man, woman, and child in this nation. Nuclear energy will possibly relieve some of the demand on oil reserves, but even so, in 1967 Charles F. Jones of the Humble Oil Company estimated that during the thirteen years between 1967 and 1980 the consumption of oil in the United States would be more than twice the amount of our known reserves. We will of course continue trying to supplement these reserves by importing oil. Unfortunately, however, we have already experienced some trouble in making trade agreements for oil and minerals with foreign countries.

By 1961 we were importing more than 90 per cent of our nickel and 30 per cent of our copper. In general, the United States is highly dependent on foreign sources for most of its basic industrial raw materials, except bituminous coal (for instance, in 1966 we mined 52,209,000 metric tons of iron ore, but we consumed 131,314,000 metric tons of steel). At the same time, our industrial production and affluence have reached unprecedented levels, far beyond the highest levels theoretically possible for the UDCs. Our national per-capita income is some 33 times that of India, and both our per-capita gross national product and our per-capita steel production are more than 50 times that of India. Our per-capita steel *consumption* (production plus imports minus exports) is some 667 times that of Indonesia, 133 times that of Pakistan, 83 times that of Ceylon, 23 times that of Colombia, 10 times that of Mexico, 2 times that of France and Switzerland, 1.8 times that of Japan, 1.7 times that of the United Kingdom and Russia, and marginally (3 per cent) higher than that of our nearest rival, Sweden. The United States in 1966 accounted for well over a third of the world's tin consumption, well over a fourth of its phosphate, potash, and nitrogenous fertilizer consumption and half of its newsprint and synthetic rubber (produced from a variety of resources), more than a fourth of its steel, and about a fifth of its cotton. Estimates of the total American utilization of raw materials currently run as high as 50 per cent of the world's consumption, with a projection of current trends to about 80 per cent around 1980. Probably 30 per cent and 50 per cent would be more realistic figures, but in any event our consumption is far beyond our 'share' on a basis of population. We number less than 6 per cent of the world's people!

The availability of critical resources has a considerable bearing on the possibilities of industrialization in the UDCs. Even if world population growth stopped in 1970, world iron production would have to be increased about sixfold, copper production almost sixfold, and lead production about eightfold to bring global per-capita consumption to the current American level. And these figures neglect the enormous amounts of these metals already mined, refined, and in use in the railroads, automobiles, girders, electrical wiring, and so on in the United States. To raise all of the 3.6 billion people of the world of 1970 to the American standard of living would require the extraction of almost 30 billion tons of iron, more than 500 million tons of copper and lead, more than 300 million tons of zinc, about 50 million tons of tin, as well as enormous quantities of other minerals. That means the extraction of some 75 times as much iron as is now extracted annually, 100 times as much copper, 200 times as much lead, 75 times as much zinc, and 250 times as much tin. The needed iron is theoretically available, and might be extracted by tremendous efforts over a long period of time, but a serious limit could be imposed by a shortage of molybdenum, which is needed to convert iron to steel. Needed quantities of the other materials far exceed *all* known or inferred reserves. Of course, to raise the standard of living of the projected world population of the year 2000 to today's American standard would require doubling all of the above figures. But, far from concentrating on ways to help UDCs while making a maximum effort to husband limited resources, economists in the DCs want to *increase* the rate of domestic consumption of nonrenewable resources far above that of 1970, while population growth continues. Our environment cannot stand 'world industrialization', partly because of the thermal limits mentioned earlier; but even if it could, the problem of supplying the raw materials alone staggers the imagination.

It is questionable whether the DCs will be able to obtain the steadily increasing amounts of critical resources that are projected as future 'needs'. In the short term, say until the end of this century, the United States *might* do all right by increasing its imports, assuming that the UDCs will continue to let us exploit their mineral resources, and by developing substitutes. Maintaining imports will be especially important. In common with almost all industrial nations, with the possible exception of the U.S.S.R., we are already net importers of most of the metals and ores we use (Figure 25). Obviously, should any unforeseen events limit our access to imports, we would be in trouble immediately. Unfortunately, such 'unforeseen events' are likely in our future. . . .

The long-run solution to world shortages of most mineral resources is seen by technological optimists to be in extracting them from such common rock as granite and from sea water, where 63 out of 92 naturally occurring elements have been found (although the important metals dissolved in sea water are present only in extraordinarily low concentrations). They further assume that in an era of cheap energy this will be feasible, but they are apparently unaware of the problems of thermal pollution and other ecological consequences of such a program. Both the geological and the economic facts of life make it probable that, as one knowledgeable geologist put it, 'average rock will never be mined'.

It is unlikely that cheap nuclear energy can greatly reduce the cost of mining, mainly because most mining will presumably continue to be subterranean; there are definite limits to the feasible depth of open-pit mining. Most plans call for underground nuclear blasts to fragment the rock, followed by hydrometallurgical or chemical mining. These techniques present enormous problems. Rocks must be fractured to the proper particle size, and then brought into contact with special solvents (which must also be derived from natural resources). Ways must be found to contain the solvents and to prevent them from being consumed by dissolving unwanted materials. In attempting to extract low concentrations underground, electrolysis also seems very unpromising, as are biologically catalyzed metallurgical reactions. If extraction below ground is successful, then the reagent and the dissolved material must be pumped to the surface, both possibly hot and extremely radioactive. After the separation both the waste rock and the solvent must be disposed of.

In reality, labour costs would probably remain quite high in any futuristic programs to extract desired minerals from low-grade deposits.

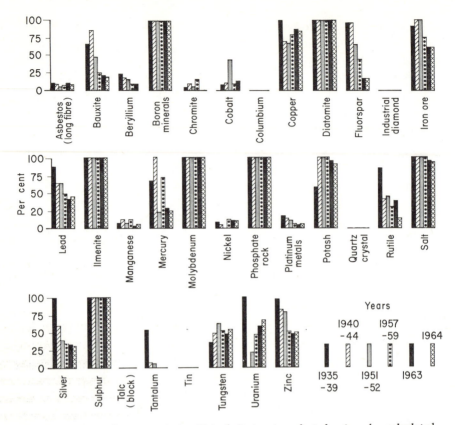

FIGURE 25 Self-sufficiency of the United States in selected minerals, calculated as the percentage of primary consumption mined in the country. (Data from the U.S. Department of the Interior, Bureau of Mines, Division of Minerals, 1965.)

It seems likely that it will remain much cheaper to search out mineral concentrations well above the average than to mine average rock, even if it means keeping human miners with picks at the mining face. As geologist Preston Cloud has observed: 'The reality is that even the achievement of a breeder reactor offers no guarantee of unlimited mineral resources in the face of geologic limitations and expanding populations with increased per-capita demands, even over the middle term. To assume such for the long term would be sheer folly.'

WATER

'Water is the best of all things', said the Greek poet Pindar. It is also, in the broad sense, a renewable resource. It circulates on the earth in a complex series of pathways known collectively as the hydrologic cycle.

The oceans serve as the principal reservoir, from which an estimated 875 cubic kilometres (ck) evaporate per day. About 775 ck return to the ocean through condensation and precipitation, there being a net wind-borne transfer of some 100 ck from the seas to the land. About 260 ck daily fall upon the land, 100 ck of which are blown in from the sea and 160 ck have been previously evaporated from the land. The cycle is balanced by about 100 ck of daily runoff from land to sea via the streams, rivers, and flow of groundwater. But even though it circulates, the finite supply of fresh water still places limits on the numbers of people that can be supported, both in specific locations and on the earth as a whole.

Water is needed in prodigious quantities just to produce food. Plants are constantly absorbing water from the soil and evaporating it from their leaves, which is the basic reason for the extreme water requirements of vegetable food production and the even greater requirements of meat production. A single corn plant may take from the soil, and evaporate, as much as 200 quarts of water in a growing season. The water needed for the production of one pound of meat includes that necessary for growing about 10 pounds of forage plants, plus the water required by the animal directly for drinking, and further water for meat processing. To produce a pound of dry wheat requires some 60 gallons of water; a pound of rice, 200-250 gallons; a pound of meat, 2,500-6,000 gallons; and a quart of milk, about 1,000 gallons Industrial processes are even more water greedy. Directly and indirectly, it takes an estimated 100,000 gallons of water to produce a single automobile. Each American's share of all the water disposed of in the United States in 1900 was about 525 gallons daily. This increased to almost 1,500 gallons per capita in 1960, and is expected to reach almost 2,000 gallons by 1980. These figures do not include the use of rainwater by crops, but roughly 50 per cent of the consumption given here is for irrigation.

Some 97 per cent of the world's water is salt water, stored in the ocean basins. Of the remaining 3 per cent, which is fresh water, almost 98 per cent is tied up in the ice caps, principally of Antarctica and Greenland. Since freeing all of this water would raise the sea level some 200 feet, inundating many of our cities and much of our crop land, it would seem best to leave most of that water tied up as it is, even if it were feasible to free it. Some of the water in the hydrological cycle is subject to re-use; in fact, the water in some river systems of the DCs is re-used up to 50 times. But the huge amounts of water required by living plants are returned to the cycle directly and cannot be re-used by man immediately.

The rather small total supply of fresh water is now being reduced. Man is removing fresh water from the continents faster than the hydrologic cycle replaces it. Michigan State's Georg Borgstrom [see page 176], an authority on food production, estimates that the people of Europe extract three times what the cycle returns to accessible reserves, and that North Americans take out about twice what is returned. Groundwater reserves, our 'water capital', have been depleted at a shocking rate. The groundwater supply will soon be below that necessary to meet withdrawal demands, and the water bank will fail. Projected American water requirements in 1980 will be about 700 billion gallons. Even on the basis of the most optimistic technological and economic assumptions, only an estimated 650 billion gallons can be made available. Similar shortages will occur in many areas of the world, especially in connection with the immense water needs related to agriculture. For instance, India, in her desperate struggle to grow more food, has greatly increased her tapping of groundwater. Between July 1968 and June 1969 the government drove 2,000 new tube wells, and private enterprise drove 76,000. In addition, 246,000 new pumps were installed. It is no wonder that scientists with such diverse interests as agriculturalist Borgstrom and Stanford geologist Richard Jahns feel that the world faces an extremely grave water crisis.

4 | The Biological Implications of Population Growth

Whether we consider the physical limits of population growth on the basis of Fremlin's conclusions or the much more narrow limits imposed by man's presently known consumption and reserves of basic resources, it is reasonable to assume that we possess, or will possess, the capability of developing a technology sufficient to support a larger population than exists on earth at present. However, the limits of population growth are not only physical; there are biological considerations too. This section examines two aspects of the biological implications of continued population growth: the influences of a crowding environment on mankind, and the effects of man's misuse of his natural environment.

STRESS IN HUMAN POPULATIONS*

George M. Carstairs

All of us are affected in one way or another by emotionally or mentally disquieting influences that we call stress. Overcrowding is a prime cause of stress. We do not have to look further than certain districts of large North American cities to find examples of this. In mere everyday terms, crowded stores, traffic jams, and the effect of noise causing loss of sleep also produce stress. As population increases so do the conditions that can lead to stress. This is a concern not only in the rapidly growing underdeveloped countries but also in crowded cities the world over. While it is extremely difficult to assess the effects of stress, there can be little doubt that if it isn't already a serious condition due to congestion and overpopulation it may soon become one. Consequently it is important to consider, in general terms at least, how this condition manifests itself.

Most of the work in connection with this particular subject has involved

*From 'Overpopulation and Mental Health' by George M. Carstairs in Henry Regier and J. Bruce Falls (eds.), *Exploding Humanity: The Crisis of Numbers*, House of Anansi Press Limited. Copyright © 1969, International Forum Foundation.

animals and clearly indicates that under crowded conditions they are adversely affected by stress. Symptoms of stress include ulcers, hypertension, impotence, and glandular upsets, as well as withdrawal from the family or group, desertion of the young, and different forms of aggressive behaviour. These are generally thought to occur when the adrenal cortex (which pumps out the hormones that control most body functions) becomes over-stimulated. Although it has not been proved that human beings react to stress in the same way that animals do, many scientists say that when people are forced to exist in crowded areas such as the slums of large cities, both physiological and psychological disorders result. These in turn may contribute to a breakdown in the mechanisms of social order and ultimately lead to unrest, violence, and crime.

In the following extract the author is concerned with a particular aspect of this whole question: What are the consequences of continued population growth on mental health?

[1969]

As yet, the science of human behaviour is not sufficiently developed to be able to answer this question with precision, or even with confidence. Nevertheless it is possible to learn from studies of animals, both in their natural environment and under experimental conditions, and to note certain regularly occurring consequences of severe overcrowding: with due caution, one can infer some similar repercussions of overcrowding in man. There are also a number of direct observations, in human populations, of the interrelationships between overcrowding and certain indices of mental health, from which we can predict with greater confidence the likely consequences of overcrowding on a still larger scale.

STUDIES OF ANIMAL BEHAVIOUR

At first sight, it might seem that much could be learned from observations on species such as lemmings, or voles, which are subject to periodic fluctuations in population size. There is still a good deal of controversy among naturalists as to whether these fluctuations are essentially determined by rather gross environmental factors of food supply or infection, or whether social interactions also play an important role. In recent years the work of ethologists has taught us a great deal about the interaction of innate, biological propensities and *learning experiences,* in many animal species. At a relatively crude level, this can be shown in the modification of the animal's adrenal size and activity. The adrenals play an essential role in an animal's response to stress, whether by fighting or by taking flight. There is a conspicuous difference between the size of the adrenals in wild rats and in rats which have been bred for generations in captivity, the latter having much smaller adrenal glands. When wild rats are caged, and allowed to breed, a diminution in adrenal size becomes apparent in a few generations.

In colonies in which there is a great deal of fighting the mean size of the rats' adrenals increases by up to 30 per cent—and this is true both of the aggressors and the victims. Observations in nature have shown marked diminution in adrenal size when rat populations are depleted; similar findings have been reported on an overcrowded herd of deer.

Adrenal activity is stimulated by social interaction especially by the challenge of attack and the need for counter-attack in self-defence. It is an interesting finding that the quality of the stress response takes on a different character for the animal which is victorious in the contest. Such an animal can go from strength to strength, able to fight one battle after another and in the intervals of fighting its sexual potency is also at a high level. In contrast, an animal which undergoes a series of defeats becomes debilitated, even although suffering no obvious physical injury, and is sexually less active. The biologist, S. A. Barnett has shown that prolonged exposure to even moderate hostility leads to weakness and death; he has epitomized this reaction as follows: 'evidently the bodily response to humiliation resembles, in some ways, that to danger to life or limb'. Usually the loser in such contests is able to survive by escaping from the scene of battle and thereafter refraining from challenging its victor; but there are situations both in the wild and in the captive state where animals are unable to escape, and are repeatedly confronted by the threat of a contest in which they are doomed to defeat. Observing such caged rats, Barnett reported that quite often when a rat had been engaged in combat and got the worst of it, that rat would drop dead. Sometimes this happened within hours of when it had been introduced into this threatening environment. Sometimes it happened some days later after prolonged exposure to a succession of threats. Barnett performed post-mortems on the dead rats and found that there was no gross injury, no loss of blood or wounding to account for the sudden death. He did histological studies of their adrenal glands and established to his satisfaction that it was in the first instance due to a massive over-secretion of the medulla of the adrenal gland. In the second instance, it was due to an exhaustion of the cortical cells of the adrenal gland. It seems that exposure to humiliation and defeat can be as physiologically wounding in its way as actual physical trauma.

An analogy may be found in observations on the toxicity of amphetamine drugs, whose action is similar to that of adrenaline, the secretion of the medulla of the adrenal gland. A relatively small dose of amphetamine will prove fatal to a rat which is confined in a cage with many other rats, whereas a rat which is kept in isolation can survive doses of amphetamine up to four times greater. It is presumed that the effect of the drug is greatly enhanced, in the former situation, by the numerous stressful interactions with the other rats, each of which stimulates the output of more adrenaline until complete exhaustion supervenes.

These, of course, represent extremes of overstimulation. Many species of animals and birds have evolved self-protective behaviour patterns to ensure that such extremes will not occur. Typical of these behaviour patterns is the 'peck order' or status hierarchy, by virtue of which a group of animals who meet each other regularly first fight each other, and then mutually agree on a rank-order of ascendancy after which the animal of inferior status invariably concedes in the face of a challenge from those above him in rank. More detailed studies have shown that status hierarchies can be either *absolute*, where every member of a group of animals invariably remains in the same position in relation to each of his fellows, or *relative* in which, under different circumstance of time or place, the individual's respective degrees of ascendancy over each other may change. Absolute status hierarchy is most likely to be found where all the animals in a group share the same living-space, and it becomes most clearly defined when that space is a restricted one. Under such circumstances, Barnett has shown that adrenal size becomes inversely correlated with height in the social hierarchy.

Relative dominance is seen most clearly in animals which have individual territories. When on their home ground, they are often able to vanquish an intruder and compel him to retreat, whereas if they are challenged by the same individual on *his* home territory they in turn will admit defeat. It seems that not only birds, but most mammals (including man) exhibit this kind of territorial behaviour. Not only football teams, but all of us, tend to perform best on our home ground—mental as well as physical—and to resist anyone who ventures to challenge us there. Naturalists have recognized in territorial behaviour, and in the varying degrees of dominance associated with the centre and the periphery of the territory, a self-regulating mechanism which ensures an optimal degree of dispersion of the species. It has also been noted that if several rats are introduced at the same time into a strange environment they co-exist amicably; but if strangers are subsequently added they fight the stranger.

When animals such as domestic cats, which customarily enjoy quite a wide range of movement, are crowded together in a limited space there tends to emerge one particularly tyrannical 'despot' who holds all the others in fear, and also one or more whom Leyhausen[1] terms 'pariahs', at the bottom of the status hierarchy. These unfortunate creatures, he observes, are 'driven to frenzy and all kinds of neurotic behaviour by continuous and pitiless attack by all the others'. Although these 'pariahs' bear the severest brunt, the whole community of cats held in such close confinement is seen to suffer. These cats 'seldom relax, they never look at ease, and there is continuous hissing, growling, and even fighting. Play stops altogether, and locomotion and exercise are reduced to a minimum.'

This clearly represents a pathological social situation, in which overcrowding and confinement conspire to accentuate disturbing confrontations between individuals. In Hamburg some years ago the rats became a plague to such a point that a special campaign had to be mounted in the sewers of the city. Biologists took advantage of this experiment of nature to study the rats before and after the extermination campaign. The campaign actually reduced their numbers to something like one-tenth of what they had been at the height of the plague. It was noticed that weight for weight there was a very significant reduction in the size of the adrenal glands when the numbers of the rat population were diminished by the extermination program. A precisely similar finding was reported by another naturalist who studied a herd of deer which increased in numbers till it was overpopulating its territory and then had to be artificially reduced. Again there was an increase in the size of the adrenal with the increase in population, and a diminution when the numbers in the territory were reduced.

A comparative psychologist, John Calhoun, studying the behaviour of colonies of rats under different degrees of overpopulation, observed similar changes in their customary interrelationships. Where overcrowding was most marked, the enforced social interactions were seen to interfere with the satisfaction of quite basic biological needs such as feeding, nest-building, and the care of their young. Normally mother rats whose nest is disturbed will carry their young one by one to a place of safety, but in overcrowded pens this behaviour pattern was lost, and the rat's maternal care became so faulty that in one experiment

[1] P. Leyhausen, 'The Sane Community—A Density Problem?', *Discovery*, September 1965.

80 per cent and in another 96 per cent of all the young died before reaching maturity. Among the males, some became ascendant over their fellows but others showed a number of disturbances of behaviour, of which two patterns were particularly striking; some males appeared to opt out of sexual and social interaction altogether, skulking alone on the periphery of the group, while others became morbidly hypersexual, mounting female rats, whether receptive or not, whenever they could do so without being attacked by one of the ascendant males. The latter type of action is very unusual among wild mammals. These hyperactive rats contravened many of the norms of behaviour of their group, even becoming cannibal towards the young of their own kind. Christian, observing mice, showed that with overcrowding the reproduction rate is lowered: there are stillbirths and failure of lactation, and hence infant deaths. There is also a delayed effect; the next generation shows faulty maternal behaviour.

These observations on rats and cats must be regarded as having only marginal relevance to human experience and human behaviour. We come a little nearer the human when we read of studies carried out by biologists on primates. For many years, in fact from 1932 till almost 1965, an old text of Zuckerman's[1] was the chief authority on primate behaviour. It was the report of very careful observations on primate behaviour carried out in a succession of extended visits to zoos in South Africa where he observed baboons and chimpanzees in captivity. He pictured their behaviour as being dominated by competition, particularly competition for sexual dominance within the little group, and fighting. It is only in quite recent years that Schaller, Washburn, De Vore, Jane Goodall, and other ethologists have reported on how these species behave in their natural wild state. We now realize that accurate though Zuckerman's observations were, they reflected a totally distorted picture of the natural behaviour of these apes. It was a picture of the behaviour of apes confined in a space much more crowded than their natural habitat. Even gorillas seem to engage in very few combats and relatively few threatening behaviourisms in their natural state. On the other hand observations on packs of monkeys in India which inhabit the fringe of jungles near human villages indicate an increase in the frequency of combative encounters as the packs increase in size.

OBSERVATIONS ON HUMANS

What about human behaviour in confined conditions? We do have some

[1] P. G. Zuckerman, *The Social Life of Monkeys and Apes*, Kegan Paul, London, 1932.

direct reports from survivors of concentration camps among whom are the outstanding psychologist Bettelheim of Chicago, and the psychiatrist Eitinger of Norway. Their candid reports of what it is like to be in a concentration camp with an extreme improbability of coming out alive make rather bitter reading because they show how even the most upright and courageous people tended to show a deterioration in their usual humanitarian values. It was exceptionally rare for anyone to be able to maintain his standards under these extreme conditions.

Others have described conditions of life in the slightly less rigorous but still very crowded and confined conditions of prisoner-of-war camps. Two biologists who have shown a special interest in this field have been Paul Leyhausen[1] and Konrad Lorenz, both of whom endured several years of internment in prisoner-of-war camps. Lorenz, who writes with such marvellous eloquence, has described his own experiences in a Russian prisoner-of-war camp. He tells very candidly how, after a longish confinement, he found the slightest mannerisms of his companions in the officers' huts to be unendurably irritating. However, he had the presence of mind to recognize the irrationality of his bad temper and when he found himself seething he would leave the company of his companions, walk to the barbed wire and look out across the acres of snow and empty land until his temperature subsided and he was fit to rejoin his fellows. The experiences of Leyhausen and Lorenz have been corroborated by other medical and psychiatric witnesses.

These too, like the observations on caged cats and rats, were instances of extreme conditions, and yet one has to realize that there are many impoverished groups in the world whose conditions of life today are scarcely better. In theory, of course, they can escape from their surroundings, but in practice the 'culture of poverty' can induce a sense of despair of ever being able to escape.[2] One is tempted to draw an analogy between the rat which is subjected to a series of physical defeats, or the 'pariahs' in an overcrowded colony of cats, and the members of problem families in our city slums who display a seeming inability to make a successful social adaptation. It appears that social institutions and transmitted value systems can create a sense of confinement no less demoralizing than the bars of a cage. People can be confined just as effectively by growing up in an impoverished social milieu

---

[1] P. Leyhausen, 'The Sane Community—A Density Problem?', Discovery, September 1965.
[2] Oscar Lewis, Five Families: Mexican Case Studies in the Culture of Poverty, Basic Books, New York, 1959.

as they can by iron bars. There is a sense of incapability to escape when one has been denied the opportunity to develop one's intellectual faculties, to develop the imagination, to develop skills or capacities which would enable one to break away from these belittling surroundings.

Many years ago, Faris and Dunham[1] drew attention to the ecological concentration of certain forms of mental illness in those parts of a large city where both overcrowding and social disorganization—or *anomie* as Durkheim[2] had earlier described it—were most marked. Subsequent research has challenged Dunham's specific contention that schizophrenia is generated by the conditions of life in a socially disorganized community, but many other studies have confirmed his demonstration that alcoholism, illegitimacy, divorce, delinquency, and numerous other forms of social pathology are most prevalent in such areas.

There remains, however, an interesting contrast, in the social correlates of two particular manifestations of social pathology, namely *suicide* and *attempted suicide,* at least as they are observed in cities of the Western world. Suicide rates are highest in areas where many people live in a state of *social isolation,* bereft of the support family, or of any other primary group. On the other hand studies of attempted suicide have shown that the most important social correlate is *overcrowding.* Typically, the person who makes a non-fatal suicidal gesture has been harassed beyond endurance by recurrent friction within the domestic group, in cramped and overcrowded premises. Here too, as in the instance of rats' dose-resistance to amphetamine, one can see the mutual reinforcement of multiple factors. A majority of those who attempt suicide are relatively young men and women, who often have had a bad start in life with unstable or absent parent-figures. These patients tend to experience great difficulty in their turn, in forming stable interpersonal relationships; they are often at the same time demanding and inconsiderate towards others, and yet themselves emotionally immature and dependent. Their deficiencies prompt them to seek out partners from whom they hope to derive support, but all too often the partner whom they select is handicapped in much the same way; so far from meeting each other's dependency needs, these unfortunates only succeed in making each other's state even worse than before. Often, too, they turn to drink or drugs to allay their need for dependence and this

[1] R. E. L. Faris and H. W. Dunham, *Mental Disorders in Urban Areas,* Chicago University Press, 1939.
[2] E. Durkheim, *Le Suicide,* Paris, 1897.

in turn further impoverishes their ability to form rewarding personal relationships.[1] During recent years many countries have been obliged to take stock of increasing rates of alcoholism, delinquency, and attempted suicide, indicating that an increasing number of citizens in our large cities feel alienated from the goals and the rewards to which their fellow citizens aspire, and alienated so profoundly that they despair of ever being able to get back into the mainstream of humanity.

Alienation and despair are the product of extreme situations, such as those, as I have noted, that were realized in the grotesque, doomed societies of the Nazi concentration camps. Many, if not most, of the inmates of such camps found themselves surrendering their customary standards of behaviour and their values, becoming completely disoriented by the inhuman conditions under which they were forced to live.

There have been crises, in the course of human history, when quite large sectors of mankind experienced this sense of alienation from participation in the life of their fellow-countrymen. Sometimes after prolonged deprivation their discontents have exploded in outbreaks of revolution, as a result of which a new social order has been created; but at other times leaderless masses of the dispossessed have shown themselves only too ready to become the dupes of mentally unstable yet charismatic demagogues, who promised them a magical deliverance from their miseries. As Norman Cohn[2] shows, they become the leaders of millennial cults, promising the dawn of a golden age. An interesting thing about these millennial cults, which have recurred over and over again in European history, is that they begin with a preaching of brotherhood, generosity, sharing, saying that the riches of the earth are going to be shared among us all. It is a naive Utopian optimism. They waited for a magical answer to all their problems, and of course the magical answer was denied, the dream remained unfulfilled.

Indeed, quite soon the authorities, the Establishment of the day, began to take repressive measures against the dupes of these demagogic leaders, and then came a clash. The repressive forces were seen as hostile, threatening, demoniacal, and the movement which began with brotherhood, peace, and charity, inevitably ended in bloodshed, and sometimes in extremely violent bloodshed. One sees this story repeated over and over again.

[1] W. I. N. Kessel and J. W. McCulloch, 'Repeated Acts of Self-Poisoning and Self-Injury', *Proceedings of the Royal Society of Medicine*, Vol. 59, No. 2 (February 1966), p. 89.
[2] N. Cohn, *The Pursuit of the Millennium*, Secker and Warburg, London, 1957.

Such an incident, though in a new guise, occurred after the Second World War. 'Cargo cults' emerged in the islands of Polynesia and Indonesia. Cargo cults are rather like the millennial movements of the Middle Ages in Europe. There was a preaching of a magical solution to the problems of the poor and underprivileged. The name derived from the belief that a cargo airplane was going to land and pour out a cornucopia of all the things that they had witnessed with the sudden intrusion of Western troops. Jeeps, radios, washing machines were going to be delivered in abundance. These cults began with kindliness, naive hopes, and innocent expectations, and ended with frustration, anger, and bloodshed.

A similar phenomenon has occurred repeatedly in modern times, when the pace of political change has outstripped a society's capacity to meet the newly aroused expectations of its members. When, because of increasing overpopulation, the standards of living actually decline at the very time when people's aspirations have been raised, the stage is set for further outbreaks of collective irrationality and violence.[1] This is the predicament of many developing areas today: India, Indonesia, South America, West Africa.

Now, going back to the beginning of my talk, I remind you that many of the movements of student protest in recent years have also begun generously, with concepts of brotherhood and concern for their fellow men. And this is still true of large elements in them. It is true of the work that many American students have done to further the cause of integration. It is true of the impulse that led them to protest against the war in Vietnam. For quite a time it was maintained in this style. They talked of flower power and love-ins, feeling that this generous spirit would prevail and would be recognized and accepted. There is just a hint now, perhaps especially since the unhappy events of the Chicago Convention, that there has been a turn in this millennial movement. I notice, consulting the student newspaper from Edinburgh, that in certain quarters the slogan of 'Flower Power' is being replaced by a new ugly slogan, 'Kill the pig'. You can see the sequence. The repressive forces, the men in blue with truncheons, have appeared and are now being portrayed by some as the forces of evil, an exaggerated, demoniacal, bad object whom it is permitted to hate. And I think we have to be on our guard against this.

It is not numbers only, it is in addition the crash of high expectations frustrated. This gives rise to anger and, if we don't look out, to violence

[1] P. Worsley, *The Trumpet Shall Sound*, MacGibbon and Kee, London, 1957.

and bloodshed. In that sequence, I suggest, is the real threat of uncontrolled overpopulation to mental health. It is imperative that we recognize the gravity of this threat, because mankind today possesses weapons of such destructive power that the world cannot afford to risk outbreaks of mass violence; and yet the lesson of history points to just such a disaster, unless population control can be achieved before vast human communities degenerate into the semblance of concentration camp inmates, if not to that of Zuckerman's pathologically belligerent apes.

OUR MAN-MADE ENVIRONMENTAL CRISIS*

Lamont C. Cole

[1969]

Ecologists represent a small group of persons who try to anticipate the effects of environmental changes before we make these changes. Unfortunately, these changes are often subtle and slow, and most of mankind is impatient to get on with changing the world whether by physical and chemical means or by dispersing exotic plants and animals. Man has created most of his problems. . . .

Man has been changing his environment almost from the beginning. Neolithic man probably used fire as a tool first to drive game and later to clear forests for grazing. By an incredible stroke of luck the grasslands which were created by fire and maintained by fire and grazing developed soils that eventually made them among the world's most valuable agricultural lands. In large part our North American prairies fall in this category, as do large grassland and savannah areas of Africa.

Of course smoke polluted the atmosphere, but man had already seen this happen from natural fires. The burning of vegetation on slopes led to erosion that polluted streams and sometimes blocked them, producing swamps and marshes.

Later, man began his serious agricultural efforts on the flood plains of rivers where the land was well watered and easy to work with simple tools. As populations grew he felt the need for more land and year-round cultivation. He built dams and canals for irrigation and established great civilizations. But he often failed to provide for adequate drainage, with the result that water moved upward through the soil, evaporated there and deposited dissolved salts on the surface, thus

*From Henry Regier and J. Bruce Falls (eds.), *Exploding Humanity: The Crisis of Numbers*, House of Anansi Press Limited. Copyright © 1969, International Forum Foundation.

destroying fertility. Burning, cultivation, and the grazing of slopes caused erosion so that the irrigation works filled with silt and the civilizations collapsed. Modern Iraq could not feed the once great Babylonian Empire, nor could modern Iran, without its income from oil, support the Persian Empire of Darius I.

Man's earliest industrial efforts created unrecognized pollution problems; similar practices still are carried on, yet many people refuse to acknowledge the problems. The Romans mined lead in Britain and smelted it there, and it is said that the sites of those old smelting operations are still recognizable from the impoverished vegetation growing on the poisoned soil. In Rome the lead went into paints and water pipes and to line the vessels in which wine was stored. Recent studies of Roman bones have shown concentrations of lead that indicate that many members of the upper classes must have suffered from lead poisoning—it has been suggested that this may have contributed to the decline of the Empire. But we refuse to learn. Modern industry and the burning of ethyl gasoline are putting tremendous quantities of lead into our environment. A recent study of old elm trees showed a rapidly increasing concentration of lead in the wood produced since about 1937, and a study of snow near the North Pole has shown a 300 per cent increase in lead content since about 1940.

When man started contaminating the world his impact went unnoticed, but by the twelfth century we find contemporary accounts of severe air and water pollution, for example the 'poisonous vapours' of Rome and the 'lethal waters' of the river Rhine (a name incidentally supposedly derived from the German word for 'clear'). But man created a new dimension of environmental deterioration when he began serious exploitation of the fossil fuels, peat, coal, natural gas, and, more recently, petroleum.

It is recorded that in the year 1306 a citizen of London was tried and executed for burning coal in the city. But three centuries later this was the way of life and London had a smog problem.[1] The profession of chimney sweeping was born and along with it one of the earliest and most striking examples of severe industrial pathology; cancer of the scrotum induced by exposure to soot. It is interesting to note that Los Angeles has recently banned the burning of coal in the city, so man has in a sense come full circle on this one problem.

We are now so dependent on fossil fuels that surveys have found

---

[1] The situation in London has been substantially improved since the passing of the Clean Air Act in 1956. (ed.)

farmers expending more calories running their machinery than are removed from their land in crops. Industrial plants, transportation, especially by automobile, and the heating requirements of an expanding world population have brought the combustion of fossil fuels to the point where we are actually causing measurable changes in the composition of the earth's atmosphere. And, as we shall see, we are risking much more serious changes in the atmosphere than anything noted so far.

And never before has man been able to spread particular pollutants over the entire surface of the earth. DDT is a case in point; it has been found in the fat of Antarctic seals and penguins, in the fatty tissues of fish all over the world, and in the ice of Alaskan glaciers. We have simply been incredibly lucky that DDT has not turned out to be a more noxious pollutant than it is because, if it had happened to possess certain properties that no one would have known about until it was too late, it could have brought an end to life on earth.

If you find it comforting that DDT is not as bad as it might have been, reflect on the fact that the U.S. Food and Drug Administration estimates that we are now exposing ourselves to over a half-million different chemicals all of which must eventually be imposed on the earth's environment, and the number is estimated to be increasing by from 400 to 500 per year.

Consider the completely novel types of materials we have asked the environment to assimilate just since World War II: synthetic pesticides, plastics, antibiotics, radio-isotopes, detergents. The detergents provide an instructive case. A few years ago people could see this pollution and they were agonizing because suds were coming out of their faucets. The answer was to turn to the so-called 'biodegradable' detergents, and the public relaxed, considering the problem solved. They don't realize that the new detergents are more toxic than the old visible ones to many forms of aquatic life, or that these detergents are phosphorus compounds, and that phosphorus is one of our most significant water pollutants.

We are at most a few generations away from running out of the fossil fuels on which our economy, including agriculture, now depends. Current thinking holds that our next source of energy will be nuclear fuel, but this raises some very disturbing thoughts. Before the controlled release of atomic energy the total amount of radioactive material under human control consisted of about 10 grams of radium, or 10 curies of radioactivity. Probably a billion times this amount of radioactivity has already been disseminated into the environment, and we are not really yet into the atomic age. A plant of modest size (by present dreams) is being constructed on the shores of Lake Ontario near Oswego, New York, that will, by the Company's own estimate, release to the atmosphere 130 curies per day. Knowing that exposure to radioactivity shortens life, causes malignancies, and can produce genetic effects that can damage future generations, have we cause for complacency?

Few people apparently realize that our atmosphere is a biological product that has probably remained essentially unchanged in composition for at least 300 million years, right up until the present century. Neglecting contaminants, the atmosphere at sea level consists of about 78 per cent nitrogen by volume, 21 per cent oxygen, and 0.03 per cent carbon dioxide plus minor amounts of other gases I shall not consider here.

Nitrogen is actually a scarce element on earth. Eighteen elements account for 99.9 per cent of the mass of all known terrestrial matter, and nitrogen is not among the 18. What is so much of it doing in the atmosphere? Oxygen is the most abundant of all the chemical elements but it is a highly reactive chemical which, aside from the atmosphere, almost never exists in the uncombined form. What is so much free oxygen doing in the atmosphere? The answers to both questions are biological.

Certain bacteria and algae take nitrogen from the atmosphere and convert it into ammonia, which is quite a toxic substance. If the story stopped at this stage we should all be fatally poisoned when we breathe. Two additional kinds of micro-organisms in soil and water are responsible for converting the ammonia to nitrate, and green plants absorb the nitrate and use its nitrogen in building plant proteins. Animals, including ourselves, and virtually the entire world of micro-organisms, obtain the raw materials for building their own proteins directly or indirectly from the proteins of plants. When plants and animals die, the decomposer organisms, again primarily micro-organisms, break down the proteins, mostly to ammonia, and this little cycle—ammonia to nitrate, nitrate to protein, protein to ammonia—can repeat. If the story stopped at this stage the atmosphere would long ago have run out of nitrogen. Fortunately, there are still additional types of micro-organisms that can convert nitrate to molecular nitrogen and so maintain the composition of the atmosphere.

So we can see that quite a variety of micro-organisms involved in the nitrogen cycle are essential for the continuation of life. But what thought does industrialized man give to the welfare of these forms? With reckless abandon he dumps his half-million chemicals into soil, water, and air, not knowing whether or not one of these chemicals or some combination of them might be a deadly poison for one of the steps in the nitrogen cycle and so cause the extinction of life on earth. In fact I have heard serious suggestions from chemically sophisticated but ecologically ignorant persons for deliberately blocking two of the steps in the nitrogen cycle. How long can our luck continue?

There is oxygen in our atmosphere only because green plants keep putting it there. The plants take in carbon dioxide and give off oxygen, and animals and micro-organisms take in oxygen and give off carbon dioxide. So do our factories, our furnaces, and our automobiles. Seventy per cent of the free oxygen produced each year comes from planktonic diatoms in the oceans. But what thought does man give to the diatoms when he disposes of his wastes? When he wants a new highway, factory, housing project, or strip mine he is not even solicitous of the green plants growing on land. The fate of Lake Erie and many lesser bodies of water has shown us that man is indeed capable of blocking the oxygen cycle by sheer carelessness.

If this leaves you complacent, let me mention just a few more of the details. The deciduous forests of the eastern United States appear to produce about 1,000 times as much oxygen per unit area as the average cover of the earth's surface. Yet forests seem to be the things that modern man is willing to dispense with first. Tropical rain forests, unlike our deciduous forests, carry on photosynthesis of oxygen throughout the year and so are probably considerably more productive. But several times each year I read of schemes for industrializing or otherwise 'developing' the tropical regions of Latin America, Africa, and Asia. I recently read a statement by the President of Brazil to the effect that we must get on with developing the Amazon basin.

Tropical soils are typically low in mineral nutrients and such minerals as are present leach from the soil quickly if the vegetation is unable to trap them and recycle them. Hence, when a tropical forest is destroyed, the change may be irreversible. I don't think any educated and responsible person would advocate applying defoliants and herbicides to a tropical forest without first making a careful survey of the nutrient status of the soil and vegetation. But ecological understanding is not a prerequiste for policy making!

In the United States today the military is taking 100 per cent of the production of the so-called weed killer 2,4,5T; they are taking about one-third of the production of 2,4D and they are taking the entire production of a newer and much deadlier weed killer known as Picloram. Picloram is awful stuff. When you spray it on vegetation, typically nothing grows for two years. We have a case in Vermont where mules fed on vegetation that had been sprayed by Picloram; a year later when manure from these mules was used as fertilizer, it killed all the plants it was put on. Now our government is negotiating to build new plants to step up the production of this stuff. What are they going to do with it? They are going to put it in tankers and ship it to Vietnam to defoliate the rain forest so that they can see the Viet Cong easier and also, they hope, kill rice.

Similarly, in the seas, estuaries tend to be much more productive than either the land adjacent to them or most of the open ocean. In Georgia we actually have figures that the estuaries and salt marshes are two or three times as productive of life as the best agricultural land in the state. They not only produce oxygen but also serve as the nursery grounds for the immature stages of species we harvest for seafood. Yet estuaries are where coastal man is likely to dump his refuse, and they are the places where commercial developers are constantly undertaking land fill and dredging operations. They are also among the places where it is proposed to locate huge electrical generating plants which would raise the temperature of the water and, in some cases, pollute it with radio-isotopes. But who is thinking of the welfare of the green plants, or the organisms involved in the nitrogen cycle, or of other types of organisms essential for man's survival?

As a corollary of our rapid use of oxygen and our threats to the species that produce it, we are adding carbon dioxide to the atmosphere more rapidly than the oceans can assimilate it. This has serious implications for changing the climate of the earth, but since the details are still so uncertain and controversial I shall not go into them here. But one point I do wish to put in the form of a question: Would any rational creature go on changing his environment like this without understanding the possible effects, and at the same time argue that it is necessary to keep the destructive process expanding each year? What is now popularly known as 'progress' begins to look very much like the path to extinction.

I have attempted some quantitative calculations on the oxygen cycle in order to see where we stand. For the forty-eight coterminous states of the U.S., I took the figures for the production and imports of fossil fuels for the year 1966, corrected the figures for exports and for non-combustible residues, and calculated the amount of oxygen consumed in their combustion. Then I made what I believe is the best possible estimate of the amount of oxygen produced in the forty-eight states that year through green plant photosynthesis. The estimate of oxygen produced turned out to be not quite 60 per cent of the oxygen consumed. I have no doubt that one would reach similar conclusions for other heavily industrialized nations.

The implication is clear; we are absolutely dependent upon atmospheric circulation patterns to bring in oxygen produced outside our borders, probably mostly in the Pacific Ocean. If we should inadvertently kill enough of the diatoms in the Pacific we would start running out of oxygen to breathe. Think again about those tankers carrying Picloram to Vietnam. I don't know what Picloram does to marine diatoms, probably nobody has considered it worth looking into, but from what it does to vegetation on land I take a very pessimistic view of it. If a few of those tankers should be sunk in the Pacific we might have an instant crisis. If we should seriously attempt to industrialize all of the nations of the earth after our own pattern, I think we would all perish for lack of oxygen before the transition was nearly complete.

I've been discussing the atmosphere without unnatural contaminants. I'm sure you all know the true situation—that over 3,000 foreign chemicals have been chemically identified in our atmosphere—that, in our cities, particulate matter, soot, fly ash and, perhaps more importantly particles of rubber and asbestos, pose a serious public health problem—that carbon monoxide, sulphur dioxide, and the various nitrogen oxides pose more problems. Our intense agricultural efforts are themselves causing some ironic difficulties. A few years ago there was an amusing debate running in an Iowa paper. It involved a law case in which the defendant was claiming that 2,4D should be considered a normal constituent of the Iowa atmosphere during summer. Similarly phosphorus is in such short supply and so badly needed for fertilizer that we permit severe damage to the environment by plants that process phosphate rock into phosphate fertilizer. In Florida and in several of the western states the fluorine which is produced as a by-product of this process has killed vegetation for long distances around the plant and has killed stock animals eating the plants. In Florida there was a law suit asking the company to put higher stacks on the plant. This of course would not reduce the pollution but would spread it a little more widely. The company argued that this was not practicable because fluorine is so corrosive that the taller stacks would corrode too rapidly. So human lungs are being asked to take what mortar and concrete can't.

Underlying all of our other problems is the problem of unrestrained population growth. During the first million years or so of man's existence his population doubled perhaps once every fifty thousand years. Sometime during the summer of 1968, the human population of the earth passed the 3.5 billion mark, and if present trends could continue the population would double every thirty-five years.

There is no possibility that the earth can continue to support such growth. In fact I doubt that the earth can support on a sustained basis a population as large as the present one. In the last quarter century man's impact on the earth has grown to the point where there is a real possibility that he can destroy its ability to support life.

A NATURALIST LOOKS AT OVERPOPULATION*

Joseph Wood Krutch

[1962]

One of the many indications that the population explosion poses the most desperate problem of our day is the fact that it inevitably arises in connection with every approach to the analysis of our civilization and its prospects. To the critic of culture it is a part of our emphasis on quantity rather than quality. To the economist it raises the question of economic stability. To the political scientist it evokes the spectre of wars for Lebensraum; to the conservationist the equally terrifying spectre of universal starvation.

To the specialists in their various fields I leave the discussions appropriate to them and say only something about the situation as it appears to a naturalist; to one who is, of course, aware of its other aspects but tends to think first of man's place in nature and the consequences of modern man's refusal to accept the fact that he is indeed part of a scheme which he can to some extent modify but which he cannot supersede by a scheme of his own making.

It is true, of course, that man became man rather than simply a member of the animal kingdom when he ceased merely to accept and submit to the conditions of the natural world. But it is also true that for

*From *Our Crowded Planet*, edited by Fairfield Osborn. Copyright © 1962 by Fairfield Osborn. Reprinted by permission of Doubleday & Company, Inc., New York, and George Allen & Unwin Ltd., London.

many thousands of years his resistance to the laws of animal nature and his modifications of his environment were so minor that they did not seriously interfere with natural law and required no such elaborate management of compensating adjustments as became necessary as soon as his intentions, desires, and will became effective enough to interfere with the scheme of nature.

It was not until well into the nineteenth century that his interferences did become extensive enough to force a dawning realization of the fact that you cannot 'control nature' at one point without taking steps to readjust at another the balance which has been upset. Improved methods of agriculture exhaust the soil unless artificial steps are taken to conserve and renew it. You cannot destroy all the vermin without risking the destruction of useful animals. You cannot, as we are just discovering, poison noxious insects without risking the extinction of birds who are an even more effective control. It is not that we should not interfere with nature, but that we must face the consequences of this interference and counteract or ameliorate them by other interferences. You dare not, to put it as simply as possible, attempt to manage at one point and to let nature take her course at another.

Considered in connection with this fact the population explosion becomes merely a special (and especially ominous) example of a phenomenon characteristic of civilized man's peculiar place in nature, where he is the only creature capable of effectively interfering with her operations while he remains at the same time not wise enough always to foresee the unwanted consequences of his interference. To reduce it again to the simplest possible terms, he has interfered with nature by preserving individual lives far more successfully than nature had ever been able to preserve them; at the same time he has allowed nature to take her course so far as propagation is concerned. As a consequence either one of two things must happen. Either he must control birth as well as death or nature will step in and by her own rough but effective methods —starvation, disease, or the brutal death struggle for food and living room—eliminate the excess, which failure to manage the consequences of his management has produced. No matter what fantastic increases technology may bring in the number of men the earth is able to support, the limit must be reached sooner or later. . . .

Many sociologists and political scientists recognize the fact that the question is not simply how many people the earth could possible support, but what is the optimum number from the standpoint of the possibility of a good life. Just as it is foolish to ask what is the largest number of children a family could possibly consist of rather than how many constitute an ideal family unit, so it is foolish to ask how many could be crowded onto our globe rather than what number can live happily there. Men need not only food and a place to sleep but also room to move about in. It is at least possible to believe that cities are already too big and that life would become almost intolerable if they were both more densely crowded and so merged one with another that there was no escaping from them.

Of this the naturalist is often more acutely aware than either the sociologist or the political scientist because he is more completely convinced than they sometimes are that the best life for the human being is one which is led, partly at least, in the context of nature rather than in a context which consists exclusively of the man-made environment. For a large part of the existing human race in the centres of civilization, contact with the natural world is tending to diminish almost to the vanishing point while he has little experience with anything except bricks, steel, and concrete on the one hand and mechanical contrivances on the other. As the cities spread and the country shrinks he is more and more imprisoned with his fellows in a world that has ceased to be even aware of many of the things of which he was once an intimate part. Already he has pushed into extinction many of the creatures with which he once shared the earth.

Those who feel that he has already begun to suffer from this fact talk about recreational areas, about nature education, about national parks, and even about wilderness areas. To some extent they can still meet the objections of those who say that we cannot afford to forego the use of any of our forests, or mountains, or deserts. But if our population continues to grow at its present rate, it will soon become evident that we do indeed need every available acre of possibly usable land either for agriculture or for building lots. Much of what is called conservation today is no more than a useful delaying action. The time may soon come when it will no longer be possible to protest against the despoliation of this or that park, or forest, or river. Hence the conservationist also must face the fact that behind almost every problem of today lies the problem of population. Unless that problem is solved, none of the others can be.

Let us suppose for a moment that those are in the right who say that the context of nature has ceased to be the most desirable context for civilized life, that man can live in a wholly man-made world and that he will in time forget all that he once drew from his contemplation of that world of which he has ceased to be a part. Let us suppose further that his increase in numbers stopped before space itself gave out, and that he has reached what some seem to think of as the ideal state, i.e., living in cities which are almost co-extensive with the surface of the earth, nourishing himself on products of laboratories rather than farms, and dealing only with either other men or the machines they have created.

What will he then have become? Will he not have become a creature whose whole being has ceased to resemble Homo sapiens as we in our history have known him? He will have ceased to be consciously a part of that nature from which he sprang. He will no longer have, as he now does, the companionship of other creatures who share with him the mysterious privilege of being alive. The emotions which have inspired a large part of all our literature, music, and art will no longer be meaningful to him. No flower will suggest thoughts too deep for tears. No bird song will remind him of the kind of joy he no longer knows. Will the human race have then become men-like-gods, or only men-like-ants?

To this question the naturalist has his own answer just as he has his own answer to the question why population continues to grow so rapidly in a world already at least beginning to be aware that this growth is a threat. His approach may seem to others somewhat oblique, even distorted by his special interests. But at least his conclusions are the same as those to which many other approaches no less inevitably lead.

5 | The Economic and Political Implications of Population Growth

From a consideration of the physical and biological aspects of population growth, we turn to what must certainly be regarded as the most critical part of any study of population: the conditions of deprivation under which a substantial portion of the world's population now lives. While it may be both physically and biologically possible for the world to support a considerably larger population, we must remember that, even with our present population, conditions of poverty, hunger, and illiteracy afflict millions. Overpopulation is one of the major factors responsible for inhibiting economic and social development in underdeveloped regions. Unless the rate of population growth is curtailed, not only will overall development be severely restricted, but within the next few decades severe, widespread, and continuous famine will be a distinct possibility.

The issue is basically one of deprivation. While stark poverty does exist in certain groups in the DCs, it is seen most clearly in the UDCs, where huge numbers of people lack the basic necessities of life and cannot hope to satisfy normal human aspirations. The important question, then, is not so much whether the earth is capable of providing food and the other necessary raw materials, but whether the present rate of population increase in most underdeveloped regions is preventing the economic and social advances that will be required to improve the overall quality of life in the UDCs.

MEASURES OF POVERTY

The term 'underdeveloped country (UDC), which is used throughout this book, refers to the state of a country's development in relation to the level of development in the industrial countries of North America and western Europe. The UDCs, therefore, are for the most part countries where the per-capita income is very low in relation to such wealthy nations as the United States and Canada and most of the countries of western Europe. The fact that an area is underdeveloped does not necessarily mean that living conditions are hopelessly bad: there are many

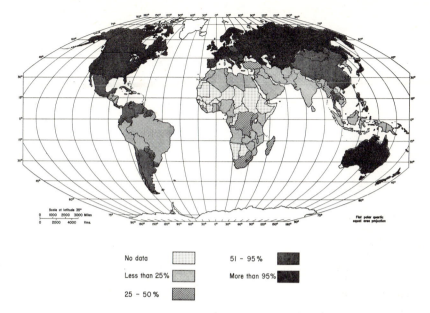

No data

Less than 25%

25 - 50 %

51 - 95%

More than 95%

FIGURE 26   Percentage of literate people fifteen years old and over.

people living in underdeveloped countries or regions who, while lacking the material comforts found in the developed countries (DCs), are healthy and well fed and live reasonably comfortable lives. Unfortunately, however, within these countries or regions there are millions of people living in conditions of abject poverty.

On the following pages some of the essential issues of poverty are discussed and illustrated. What is poverty and where is it located? Is rapid population growth a cause of poverty, or is poverty a cause of rapid growth? What is the relationship between population growth and economic development?

Poverty is a condition in which people are deprived of the basic necessities of life. One measure of poverty in a country is the per-capita national income. It is a crude indicator, however, because it is based on a general assessment of the national level of output of goods and services. Perhaps the principal weakness of this measurement is that it does not allow for the fact that people in different countries put different values on similar goods and services. Thus, while an average Canadian may spend five to ten times more than the average Pakistani on food and clothing, this does not mean Canadians are five to ten times better off. However, we can regard per-capita national income as a useful basis for *approximating* differences among countries in the availability of the basic needs to sustain a reasonable existence.

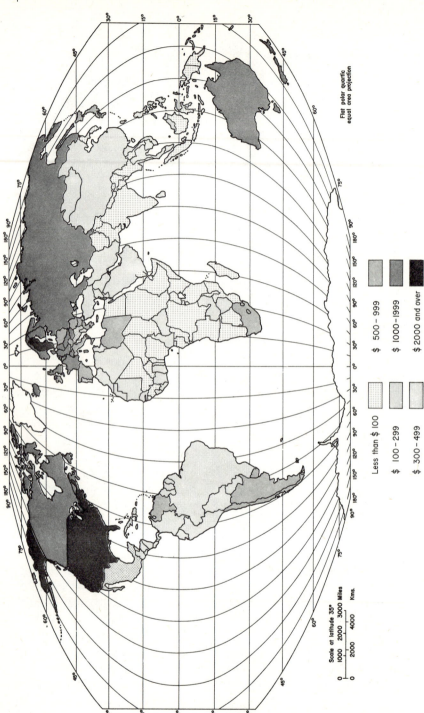

Less than $ 100

$ 100 - 299

$ 300 - 499

$ 500 - 999

$ 1000 - 1999

$ 2000 and over

Scale at latitude 35°

FIGURE 27   Per-capita national income (in U.S. dollars).

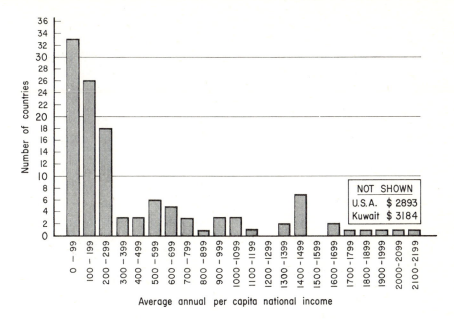

FIGURE 28   The distribution of nations according to per-capita national income (in U.S. dollars).

Figure 27 illustrates the variation in the average annual per-capita national income for most of the countries of the world. While it would be unrealistic to suggest any specific amount as indicating a cut-off point below which a country would be described as underdeveloped or poor, the highly-skewed (asymmetrical) distribution shown on Figure 28 does indicate that there are seventy-seven countries with a per-capita income below $300, while there are only forty-six above. (The figure of $300 is well below the usually quoted poverty line in the DCs, where the minimum per-capita income is several times greater.) In general then we can reasonably assume that a large segment of the population in those countries with an average per-capita income of under $300 do not possess the minimum requirements for a reasonable existence.

Per-capita national income is only one measure of poverty. To locate and measure the extent of poverty in the world we must also consider such matters as the availability of food, shelter, clothing, and medical and educational facilities. Unfortunately, information on such indicators for the world as a whole is limited, particularly in the case of the poorest countries, where the information is most needed. The materials on the following pages are concerned with just two measures of poverty: disease and the availability of food.

The incidence of disease is generally regarded as a good indicator of poverty because it is so closely related to such factors as the availability of medical facilities, the type and quantity of food available, and the presence or absence of measures of public health. While we do know that such general diseases as trachoma, hookworm, malaria, tuberculosis, typhoid, dysentery, and the deficiency diseases (marasmus, kwashiorkor, beri-beri, anemia, rickets) are very common in UDCs, it is almost impossible to obtain an accurate measure of their incidence. Experts usually refer instead to the infant and child mortality rates as the best available indication of a nation's general state of health. Table 15 illustrates some of the variations in child mortality rates; that is, for children in the 1- to 4-year-old category in various countries, which is one of the most susceptible segments of the population (even more so than the group under 1 year, which is protected through nursing from many diseases). (Estimates of the 1970 infant mortality rates are included in the Appendix.)

Hunger is usually considered to be the most basic measure of poverty. It reduces an individual's ability to work and makes him more susceptible to disease. And a hungry man is a social liability: he not only cannot live a normal existence himself but he is an inhibiting force on the economic and social growth of his country.

Table 15
CHILD MORTALITY RATES 1-4 YEARS, 1960-1962 (AVERAGE ANNUAL)

Continent and country	Rate per 1,000 children (ages 1-4) per Year	Continent and country	Rate per 1,000 children (ages 1-4) per Year
AFRICA		EUROPE	
Mauritius	8.7	Austria	1.3
Réunion	9.6	Belgium	1.0
United Arab Republic	37.9	Bulgaria	2.4
NORTH AND CENTRAL AMERICA		Czechoslovakia	1.2
Barbados	3.7	Denmark	0.9
Canada	1.1	Finland	1.1
Costa Rica	7.2	France	1.0
Dominican Republic	10.8	Germany, East	1.6
Guatemala	32.7	Germany, West	1.3
Mexico	13.8	Greece	1.9
Puerto Rico	2.9	Hungary	1.6
Trinidad and Tobago	2.5	Ireland	1.2
United States	1.0	Italy	1.9
SOUTH AMERICA		Netherlands	1.1
Argentina	4.2	Norway	1.0
Chile	8.0	Poland	1.6
Colombia	17.4	Portugal	8.0
Ecuador	22.1	Spain	2.0
Peru	17.4	Sweden	0.8
Venezuela	5.9	Switzerland	1.2
ASIA		United Kingdom—England, and Wales	0.9
Ceylon	8.8	Yugoslavia	5.2
China (Taiwan)	7.2	OCEANIA	
Hong Kong	4.4	Australia	1.1
Israel	1.8	Fiji Islands	3.7
Japan	2.2	New Zealand	1.2
Kuwait	3.6		
Philippines	8.4		
Syria	8.3		
Thailand	9.1		

SOURCE: United Nations, *Statistical Series*, K/3, 1967.

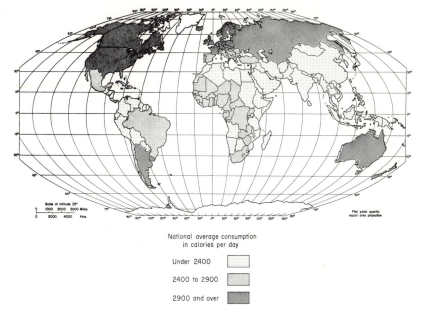

National average consumption
in calories per day

Under 2400

2400 to 2900

2900 and over

FIGURE 29   Levels of food consumption.

The terms *undernutrition* and *malnutrition* are commonly used to describe conditions associated with hunger. The former means an insufficient intake of calories as a result of an inadequate quantity of food. It is
a very general measure and makes no distinction between calories derived
from carbohydrates, fats, and proteins. Undernutrition causes loss of
body weight (or retards growth in children) and reduces a person's ability to perform a normal amount of physical activity. The world map (Figure
29) showing daily intake of calories indicates those countries where the
daily per-capita caloric intake is below that of the Western world.

Malnutrition refers to the *quality* of the diet. The quantity of food may
be sufficient, but in many areas the diet is unbalanced because it is

Table 16

PROPORTION IN THE DIET OF CALORIES FROM ANIMAL PRODUCTS, AND FROM CEREALS,
STARCH ROOTS, AND SUGAR[1]

	% Animal Products	% Cereals, Starch Roots and Sugar	% Other	% of World's Population	% of World's Food Supplies
North America	35	40	25	6.6	21.8
Europe	20	63	17	21.6	34.2
Latin America	16	64	20	6.9	6.4
Near East	8	72	20	4.4	4.2
Africa	7	74	19	7.1	4.3
Far East	6	80	14	53.4	29.1

[1] Food and Agriculture Organization, 1966.

largely composed of cereals and starchy foods and lacks an adequate supply of proteins, essential minerals, and vitamins (see Table 16). Malnutrition impairs health and can lead to a variety of deficiency diseases. It also reduces resistance to other diseases, is a major factor in child mortality, and generally results in a shorter life span. (The United Nations has estimated that 20 per cent of the population in the UDCs is undernourished while 60 per cent is malnourished.)

The article that follows, 'The Dual Challenge of Health and Hunger', is concerned principally with disease (or health) and the availability of food. In the article by Barbara Ward, 'Population Growth and Economic Development', the larger question of the relationship between population growth and economic development is briefly considered. While the process of cause and effect in this relationship is not easily sorted out, it is essential that the various factors involved be fully discussed in light of the information in this section and the pertinent statistics included in the Appendix.

THE DUAL CHALLENGE OF HEALTH AND HUNGER— A GLOBAL CRISIS*

Dr Georg A. Borgstrom

[1970]

If all the food in the world were equally distributed and each human received identical quantities, we would *all* be malnourished. If the entire world's food supply were parcelled out at the U.S. dietary level, it would feed only about one-third of the human race. The world as a global household knows of no surpluses, merely enormous deficits. Yet there is in the well-fed nations a great deal of nonsensical talk about abundance.

Already short of food, the world is adding 70 million people to its feeding burden each year—the equivalent of an entire United States every three years. The annual increase is itself growing at a rapid pace; it is outstripping the gains in world food production despite all the triumphs of agriculture and fisheries since World War II.

*From *Population Reference Bureau, Selection No. 31.* Copyright © 1970, Population Reference Bureau, Inc. Reprinted by permission.

THE HUNGER GAP

It is not enough to talk about absolute deficits, however, for the world's food resources are distributed with great unevenness. Over 2 billion of the world's 3.5 billion people live lives dominated by extreme shortages of food and water, and by inadequate resources in soils and forests. These billions lack satisfactory shelter, clothing, education, and medical care. In sharp contrast to their misery, a Luxury Club of at most 400 million people enjoys a rich and steadily more abundant diet as well as a high standard of living in most other respects. Between these two extremes are hundreds of millions of people who may be designated as fence-straddlers. They manage well enough despite numerous handicaps and limited resources, but their diet, although barely adequate, is monotonous and their life, in general, parsimonious.

The richly endowed are found in the United States and Canada, parts of western Europe, Australia, New Zealand, and the La Plata countries of Latin America. The Russians, East Europeans, and Japanese belong to the in-between group. Asia, Africa, and most of Latin America, with a combined population of more than 2 billion, are the most critical hunger areas. Their human numbers are increasing more than twice as fast (in per cent) as those of the well-fed world.

The widening hunger gap is an ominous feature of our days. It poses the greatest challenge mankind has ever faced, overshadowing atom bombs, continental missiles, microbial toxins and nerve gases.

Despite courageous efforts by devoted groups, this crisis has not yet received the attention it desperately needs. Timid bureaucracies are caught in a striking discrepancy between thought and action. Although mankind is 'hitting the ceiling'—reaching the limit in its use of the vital resources of soils, water, and forests—it is quite obvious that nowhere in our population control measures have we moved beyond the very limited tactic of family planning. True population control in the sense of a deliberate effort to bring down birth rates has hardly anywhere been adopted. Limiting our efforts to averting 'unwanted' children, however, is wholly inadequate. Studies show that even if successful, such a policy would have only marginal effects on world population growth by the year 2000.

The most disquieting aspect of the food issue is the fact that, with few exceptions, the scientific and technical community has been signaling a green light to mankind when a stop sign would have been far more appropriate. Recent statements by leading Western scientists in almost all disciplines reveal a shocking disregard for the abject conditions which enclose almost three-fifths of the human race.

It is indeed macabre to witness the present game of calculating how many people the world *could* nourish—*if*. The figures soar beyond 7 billion to 10 billion and even more. Yet, scandalously, the world has failed to provide satisfactorily for even half the 3.5 billion people alive *now*. To give our current population a minimally sound diet would require the immediate doubling of world food production. Thus, whatever else happens and whatever urgent measures are taken, food is going to be the overriding issue of the next 30 years.

THE GREAT LAND GRAB

Few undertakings in human history have had a greater impact than the enormous, prolonged effort to Europeanize the world. The psychological investment in this drive may explain both the West's lofty promises of abundance for all men and its complete misjudgement of mankind's true situation. In truth, the white man's experience has been misleading. No group of individuals ever seized a greater booty than did the Europeans who took possession of the vast forests and rich prairie soils of the North American continent. Unassuaged, the white man also grabbed the fertile pampas and most other good soils in Central and South America, the South African veld, and the rich highland plateaus of interior Africa. He managed to gain control of an entire continent, Australia, with its valuable satellite, New Zealand. In addition, he secured strongholds all over Asia where he monopolized trade and to a considerable degree controlled agricultural production, making India British and the East Indies Dutch.

The Second World War ostensibly brought an end to this era in geopolitical relations. But as late as 1939, shipload after shipload of groundnuts left starving India to fatten the cows of the British Isles. Hundreds of millions of people in Asia and Africa have since attained independence. Superficially, world food markets have adjusted to this fact. More than 25 million tons of grain are now moving from wealthy areas to feed the hungry—as against the latter part of the 1930s when 11 million tons of cereal grains were dispatched from the hungry world to provide for the well fed.

The monopoly of the European tribe, however, is still strong in the economic field. While public attention is focused on grain, let us direct the searchlight to other commodities and especially to proteins. Here the West finds no cause for self-congratulations. The almost 3 million tons of grain protein recently contributed to the poor nations by the rich and well fed have been more than counterbalanced by a flow to the Western world of no less than 4 million tons of *superior* proteins in the form of soybeans, oilseed cakes and fish meal. The West is benefiting from a most deceptive exchange.

CROPS FOR CASH VERSUS CROPS FOR FOOD

Thus, although it has far greater per-capita soil and water resources than the hungry world, the West is tenaciously intruding on the latter's struggle for subsistence. Hundreds of millions of people in the tropics must limit their harvests for domestic consumption in order to raise export crops (groundnuts, cotton, coffee, tea, and cacao, etc.) for foreign currency. This situation is further aggravated by the fact that the cash crops now enjoy a high priority with regard to credit, fertilizers, and irrigation. Their fortunes in the world market, however, are declining. Since 1952 the developing nations have been delivering about 33 per cent more tonnage in cash crops while registering only a 4 per cent gain in income. Prices, of course, are largely controlled by the West. These sombre facts help explain the collapse of two UNCTAD[1] conferences, both of which ended in solemn pledges by the rich countries to devote a mere one per cent of their Gross National Product to the dire circumstances of the needy. Not only have most industrialized countries failed to live up to this meagre commitment, but the percentage of GNP which the United States parcels out as 'aid' has actually been declining.

The great good luck of Western man in the lottery of history underlies his profound belief that technology will bestow a universal abundance. Good luck has also made him complacent. He imagines that he is more capable than the poor and the hungry. He blames them for listlessness, apathy, laziness, inefficiency, lethargy, resistance to change, notorious backwardness, and wavering creativity. In his self-deception he forgets that the ancestors of today's poor and hungry peoples created a host of great civilizations which, with an improvidence much like his own, wore out their soils and forests.

In his imagined superiority, Western man chooses to label this hungry world 'underdeveloped'. If it were not for his historical oversight, he would find 'overdeveloped' a more appropriate term. The overwhelming majority of the underfed live in countries where the soil has been over-

---

[1] United Nations Conference on Trade and Development. (ed.)

cultivated for thousands of years, where forests have been pulled down in the erroneous belief that this act would best provide for ever-growing populations, and where water reserves have been exploited to the utmost.

We should not underrate the ingenuity of Asian, African, and Latin American societies which not only survive but slowly advance under these conditions. With the meagre resources available to them, many farmers in India and other parts of the so-called 'underdeveloped' world display outstanding efficiency. Throughout Asia and Latin America, one can find an astonishingly thorough use being made of available land.

Hundreds of millions of hungry people live in the tropics, where farm acreages are exceedingly small and constantly fragmented through inheritance. Often it is possible to see original two- to four-acre holdings which have been subdivided into five or more plots. Though large-scale increases in production are difficult even on the poor world's *latifundia*, we naively expect the 'mini-plot' farmers of Asia, Africa, and Latin America to triple or quadruple their production within three decades— something the Western world has never been able to do with all its immense resources of enriched soil and ample land.

The soils from which the poor nations must feed their people are often far inferior to those of the West's 'marginal' lands, which are now being abandoned by agriculture. Water is also a scarce commodity in most regions of the hungry world, and agriculture is subject to many more vagaries of climate than in the temperate regions. Moreover, the farmer in a poor nation usually lacks capital for expanded irrigation, for fertilizers, for better sprays against insects and fungi. The handicaps he faces are so severe that any comparison with farmers in the West is absurd.

HEALTH AND HUNGER

I could delve at great length into the human consequences of this situation but will limit myself to a few remarks about the relationship between health and hunger. A great many people in this world are hungry or malnourished all of the time or part of the time. How is their working capacity affected? And what does an insufficient diet do to their overall health?

The prime global deficiency is that of protein. Until recently this fact was grossly neglected by experts who measured tonnages and profits but who limited their nutritional considerations to calories. Indeed, 10 to 15 per cent of the world *is* short of calories, or 'undernourished'.

But vastly more people—perhaps 1.5 billion—suffer from the calamity of inadequate nutrients, or 'malnutrition'. A shortage of protein is the number-one problem everywhere in the hungry world. Many other deficiencies related to shortage of fat, minerals (calcium, iodine, etc.), and vitamins (B1, B6, folic acid, vitamin A, etc.) are also quite common, and as the hunger problem broadens, these and other dietary shortcomings will greatly assert themselves.

Today a wealth of documentation confirms the existence of a nutritional crisis. Detailed dietary and health surveys have been made in numerous countries in tropical Africa, Latin America, the Caribbean, and other regions of the world. Many medical experts believe the situation is even more grave than these studies indicate, since victims of undernourishment who are already thoroughly sick or dead are seldom taken into account. For each case of malnutrition treated in the hospitals, many others never come under care. It is clear that the nutritional crisis has far greater dimensions than have so far been mapped out.

SOME TELLING EXAMPLES

Vitamin-A deficiency frequently results in blindness, curtailing productivity. In India alone there are at least one million cases of such blindness. In East Pakistan 50,000 children every year are threatened with a possible lifetime of blindness due to their precariously low vitamin-A intake. The blind have limited opportunities to contribute to society and often become a drain on it. Yet, for a few pennies a year, such blindness could easily be prevented.

Deficiency diseases are extremely insidious in that they often sap vitality without causing other easily noticed symptoms; they thus frequently belong to the category of 'hidden hunger'. Hundreds of millions of people are now short of proteins, minerals, and vitamins—not to the degree of manifesting precise symptoms but short enough to suffer from lowered efficiency, alertness, endurance, and creativity.

One of the most significant findings of modern nutritional research is that protein hunger may cause devastating brain damage in infants. Since the damage is irreversible, it can lead to a lifetime of mental retardation or to other mental and physical aberrations. Similar effects are traceable to prenatal malnutrition. These findings should be a cause for overwhelming global concern. The recognition that malnourished children may emerge from childhood without the ability to reach their full intellectual potential injects a new and frightening element into development theorizing.

The implications are ominous. For many years we have assumed that, given educational opportunities and environmental advantages, even children born to poverty have every prospect of growing up to be bright and productive. It is now suggested that malnourished children may become permanently retarded. The significance of this can be appreciated when we recognize that as many as two-thirds of the children of most developing countries are now suffering from some degree of malnutrition.

Much earlier it became evident that malnutrition profoundly retards physical growth—and this, too, in a frequently nonreversible way. In many developing countries the average twelve-year-old has the physical stature of an eight-year-old in western Europe and North America. Indian nutritionists report that four out of every five pre-school children in certain areas suffer from malnutrition-caused dwarfism. During the months of breast feeding, children from the poorest areas grow at a rate comparable to the best-nourished children elsewhere. Usually, after six months of age, when breast milk is no longer a sufficient source of protein, growth is progressively retarded.

The relationship of malnutrition to mental growth dramatizes the issue, but the insidious drain of malnutrition on natural development takes other even more harsh forms. Half the deaths in the developing countries occur among children under six years of age. In parts of Southeast Asia, 40 per cent of the children die of disease in their first four years. This is a proportion of deaths not cumulatively reached in the Western world until the age of sixty.

Most of these childhood deaths are commonly attributed to infectious diseases. Yet such diseases would be of relatively minor consequence in the West. Among children in poor countries, we now know, the cause of death is often not the infection alone but a combination of the infection and malnutrition. In other words, malnutrition debilitates the body to such a degree that it is incapable of resisting what otherwise would be a passing infection. In a country like Ecuador, child deaths ostensibly due to measles are more than 300 times more frequent (per thousand of population per year) than in North America. Whooping cough is still a major killer in much of the world. Similarly, chicken pox is often fatal because of poor nutrition. Diarrheas cause more deaths than any other infectious diseases through the operation of a vicious spiral: the diarrhea is keenly aggravated or even invited by malnutrition, and the malnutrition is exacerbated by diarrhea.

The world has close to one billion children below the age of fourteen.

A very large number of these children will never reach adulthood. They will die prematurely, largely because of malnutrition. This is the tragedy of hunger in its grimmest perspective. To hundreds of millions of children life is very little more than a vigil of death; it is certainly no banquet.

The true economic costs to the poor world of nutritionally induced disease, inefficiency, and death have never been calculated. They must run into many billions of dollars per year. Yet one can still encounter innumerable experts who would give health and dietary measures a very low priority in development programs. We face a gigantic educational task right in our own midst, thanks to a series of false notions and to the fact that most of our technology and much of our agriculture and medicine have lost sight of the ecological dimension.

The bulldozer and the miracle drugs may be chosen as symbols of Western man's simplistic faith that he has become the master of his destiny. Only gradually and painfully is he learning that he cannot go on working *against* nature if he is to endure.

The groundnut fiasco in Tanzania, the collapse of Gambia's big poultry project, the persistent spread of schistosomiasis in China, Egypt, and tropical Africa, the resurgence of rodents in Europe and malaria in Southeast Asia, the firm hold of malaria and sleeping sickness in tropical Africa—all are examples of man's ecological malfeasance.

But far more serious is another shortcoming. We of the rich, well-fed world are subject to a gigantic self-deception. There is, for instance, nothing wrong with our impressive dairy development, but we conveniently fail to realize that its high level of performance depends on the influx *from the hungry world* of millions of tons of proteins, partly of high quality. And so with other aspects of Western food production. Europe, for instance, receives through the back door over ten million tons of feed protein and close to one million tons of fish protein. In the postwar period there has been a massive exploitation of the oceans, but only to a very limited extent does its bounty reach the poor. Japan and the Soviet Union have expanded their large-scale catching operations into all oceans—primarily to procure food to fill their own needs. They have been followed in highsea fishing by eastern and western Europe. It is true that the most spectacular gains in ocean fishing have been made by a poor country, Peru. The result, however, has been to create a majestic feeding bastion not for Peru or Latin America but for the wealthy world, to which are annually delivered more than one million tons of fishmeal. Postwar developments have therefore seen a steadily growing percentage of ocean catches being earmarked to feed the chickens and hogs of the United States and Europe and to provide cheap margarine for the industrialized populations of western Europe. The underfed millions remain . . . underfed.

One-third of the world, in short, is disposing of two-thirds of the harvests both from the lands and the seas. The West's glib talk of a Green Revolution therefore has implications quite different from those its propagandists like to talk about.

BACK TO REALITY

Facing the world food issue, it is high time we abandoned simplistic notions and came to grips with the complexities. Despite innumerable projects and an almost hypertrophic bureaucracy within WHO, FAO, UNESCO, and other specialized agencies, the joint efforts of governmental and international organizations have yet to reflect the magnitude of this issue. There is little awareness that, to avert catastrophe, mankind must mobilize all its available resources in money, material, and brainpower.

The most serious fallacy connected with the world food issue is the idea that man's globe is limitless, when it should be evident to everyone that our planet is clearly restricted in its resources of soils and water. Over the centuries, biologically useful forests and pastures have lost far too much ground to the plough; this implement has been pushed by mankind's growing millions into places where it has no business. Despite ingenious irrigation accomplishments, it has helped man convert far larger acreages into deserts than he has managed to transform into productive farmlands.

The self-destructive process continues. One-third of the irrigation water of the Nile is already used to remove salt left largely by previous irrigation. Man is fighting a desperate struggle with salt, and he has rarely managed to turn this battle from a losing to a winning one. Soil erosion is furthermore taking a frightful toll. In critical areas where land should be reverted to forests and grasslands or where grazing pressures should at least be reduced—all with the urgent aim of saving the topsoil—the old hell-for-broke exploitation continues. We here touch upon the basic ecological requirements for life.

Instead of protecting our land at high productivity for future generations, we have contented ourselves with busy-work. Much of this busy-work reflects an almost religious faith in gadgets. We naively seem to assume that by willing the means we attain the goals. If someone in a fire station got the idea that silencing the alarm clock would be a good way of handling fires, we would classify him as a mental case. Yet this is the way we act as a human family in facing malnutrition.

We talk about giving the world adequate amounts of fertilizer, forgetting to analyse water as the major limiting factor. Only one-tenth of all fertilizer is currently used by the hungry world and, absurdly enough, not for food but for cash crops. Many times more fertilizer is needed for adequate harvests today and still more to feed the additional billions of people we will have at the end of the century. But is there water enough to accommodate such a massive chemical assault on the soils? Presumably not.

Today we talk about high-yielding strains of wheat and rice, forgetting that their productive capabilities have to be honoured with much more water, much more fertilizer, more insecticides and fungicides, greatly expanded storage and processing facilities, and vastly increased amounts of capital. Even assuming all this is possible, we have yet to face up to the ecological consequences. Only in very few instances do we know these new strains will stand up in entirely new environments and under bombardment from insects and fungi to which they are not adapted. Simply by hoping for the best, we will not attain our goals. What is required is a sophisticated strategy and very large-scale measures.

GLOBAL PLANNING REQUIRED

Despite the euphoria over various new high-protein foods now emerging from laboratories—spun soybean protein, fish and grain protein concentrates, and so forth—their impact on human nutrition has been insignificant. There is no sign that they will be distributed to the hungry on a massive scale in the foreseeable future. Meanwhile, as the talk goes on and as the gap between words and action grows and grows, the ranks of the hungry increase by millions each year. It is not sufficient, in this crisis, to provide free or low-cost school lunches, to cure infants suffering from kwashiorkor, to help an occasional Indian village, to ship food relief to Colombian *campesinos* or Polynesian islanders, and to set up soup kitchens in the slums of Lima and São Paolo. These are all commendable acts, but the world has long ago passed the point where charity sufficed.

In conclusion, I would argue that the hunger crisis reflects man's inability to imagine what he already knows. We are participating in a grand-scale evasion of reality which bears all the signs of insanity. In order to bring health and restore vitality to the whole human species, nothing less is required than a global *will* to act, simple justice, true population control, worldwide food planning, effective execution by the scientists, engineers, and public leaders of states and regions—and a massive commitment of funds. Furthermore, the resources of lands and seas must reach the larders of all mankind, not just the wealthy. It is time the West kept faith with the Atlantic Charter, which proclaims that all peoples should have equal access to the harvests of the world.

POPULATION GROWTH AND ECONOMIC DEVELOPMENT*

Barbara Ward

[1961]

The increase in population in such areas as Latin America or the Indian subcontinent is such that new mouths threaten to gobble up the margin of fresh savings which alone permits enough capital accumulation for sustained development to become possible. The dilemma is very real. The whole of our modern economy depends upon saving, upon not consuming. But if year after year the population goes on increasing, the number of new mouths coming in to consume can quickly eat up the fresh savings which should have been available for the transformation of the economy. So the question can be restated: Is the rate of population growth so great that in fact economic development cannot take place?

So far, the answers of history are ambiguous. In Western countries where modernization and rising population went hand in hand, the enormous spurt in population in fact spurred expansion by producing sufficient workers for the new industries and a mass market without which the output of the economy would certainly have been checked.

On the other hand, in tribal or traditional society—for instance, in the great traditional civilization of China—the opposite tendency has been at work. As we have seen, in times of peace the trend is that population climbs to the limits of production. These cannot be further expanded, for science and technology have not yet brought about such

---

*From *The Rich Nations and the Poor Nations* by Barbara Ward. CBC Massey Lectures. Copyright Barbara Ward 1961. CBC Publications, Toronto. Reprinted by permission of W. W. Norton & Company, Inc., New York, and Hamish Hamilton, London. Copyright © 1962 by Barbara Ward.

astonishing phenomena as the American farmer constantly producing more food from a smaller acreage. At this point, therefore, a melancholy cycle sets in: rising births first eat up the means of living; then starvation and its accompanying disorders set in motion a downward trend. Once population is again below the possible levels of production, there is a restoration of peace and stability which, unhappily for humanity, also brings the return of rising population. This vast, hopeless alternation between the fat years, and the lean years can be all too fully documented from the records of Chinese history.

In our own day, which of these two patterns is likely to prevail? One has to remember that the new technology is based on saving. The means of ending the disproportion between people and resources is to apply capital massively to the resources. The difficulty is to secure this massive saving when rising population forces up the levels of consumption. If the rate of increase is two per cent a year—as it is in India, or even three per cent as in parts of Latin America—can people really save on anything like an adequate scale?

By a rough rule of thumb, economists reckon that to secure one unit of income you have to invest three times as much capital. So, even to keep pace with a three-per-cent increase in population, a nation has, roughly speaking, to invest nine per cent of its national income each year. This is well beyond the four to five per cent of traditional society. To get *ahead* of such a birth rate, the rate ought to go up to between twelve and fifteen per cent of national income devoted to productive capital. This is thought to be the central point in achieving a breakthrough to sustained growth. But can you push savings up to that level, given the original poverty of society? And can you have any hope of doing so if the tide of babies rises faster still?

Communist societies hope to do so by the iron discipline of forced saving. Russia undoubtedly achieved its break-through by this rule; but Russia had no excess population in relation to resources. Scarcity of manpower was the trouble in the early days. China claims to have reached a level of saving in excess of twenty per cent of national income. But we do not yet know whether it has moved decisively ahead. In democratic India, where people are being asked for the first time in history to vote themselves through the tough period of primitive accumulation, savings are lower. Domestic saving is probably not yet ten per cent of national income, although it is rising. But outside capital assistance has raised the proportion to over thirteen per cent. As a result, in spite of a two-per-cent increase in population, India is just keeping ahead. Savings are growing, consumption is a little higher, the vast majority of the people can work and eat. Clearly, however, material progress might have been more rapid if some eighty million more people had not been added to India in the last decade. It is for this reason that Asian governments tend to put increasing emphasis on birth control as one of the pre-conditions of development.

However, here we have something of a 'hen-and-egg' puzzle. It seems to be a historical fact that nations tend to have the birth rates they want. For example, in the nineteenth century the French, confronted by new laws on the inheritance of property, opted for smaller families. The Japanese first went through a cycle of very rapid expansion of their population. Now, however, as a result of both personal choice and government legislation, the expansion has ceased and the population seems to be stabilizing. We have to stress the point of choice because we are certainly not suggesting, I take it, that governments should decree what size of families people should have. Their choice will be decisive. And in this context of choice one thing seems clear: that it is when people see more opportunities for better education that they begin to consider whether a smaller family might not be better for themselves and for their children. In other words, I doubt whether one can disentangle the issues of economic development and rising population by any flat argument that stabilization of the population must come first. Lower births are more likely to be a consequence than a cause of economic expansion. It is above all by the thrust of development and literacy in the modernizing economy that conditions can be achieved in which parents begin to choose smaller families. Governments may assist the choice by encouraging family planning. There will doubtless continue to be considerable moral debate upon the means of limitation. But the decisive point is what millions of parents choose to do; and here, I think, history suggests strongly that a certain amount of modernization must occur before smaller families seem desirable.

This leaves unsolved the problem of securing the original thrust of investment. The Communist answer remains that of forced saving. The answer in the free world should, I believe, be a sustained and imaginative strategy of economic aid by the wealthy to the poor. This we shall discuss later. Here the point need only be stressed that modernization does appear to bring with it a corrective influence on high rates of expansion in the population. If, for instance, in the next twenty years there is a very large increase in the momentum of economic growth in India, there is nothing to suggest that the Japanese rhythm of expansion followed by stabilization may not occur. The basic point remains that without the thrust of growth there is no particular reason why people should want smaller families. Children may not die; they cannot be educated; meanwhile they work. A certain fatalism prevails. It is only when hope and expansion begin that the choice of a smaller family makes sense. So the revolution of scientific and capitalist change probably decides the biological revolution as well.

6 | The Concept of Optimum Population

We have been concerned in Part 2 with identifying the causes of the existing population crisis as well as those criteria that enable us to assess the implications of the present size and rate of growth of the world's population. The information that has been presented leaves little doubt that the carrying capacity of the earth is being strained and that in some regions at least a condition of overpopulation exists. If man is to consider seriously the problem of controlling growth, then it follows that he must also be concerned with trying to determine, not the maximum number the earth can support, but what an *optimum* population might be.

The principal concern of our discussion thus far has been overpopulation. We have noted its relationship to such criteria as the reserves of mineral and other resources, the quality of the environment, the availability of food, and the effects of crowding. It is necessary to point out also that a condition of underpopulation can exist, and this would be related to such factors as the numbers required for an adequate division of labour and the provision of basic facilities and materials essential for accepted minimum standards of existence. The concept of optimum population refers to some middle ground where in economic terms there is full employment, a satisfactory level of life, adequate daily intake of food, and where resources are being exploited in a rational fashion. There are other psychological and cultural factors as well that are involved in determining an optimum: these can be summarized under the general concepts of 'the quality of life' and 'the pursuit of happiness'.

While we can understand the concept of optimum population as a general idea and appreciate its usefulness as a part of the whole issue of population control, it has never been precisely defined. This is because it is an extremely complex concept, involving a vast number of factors, many of which are extremely difficult to assess objectively. And the factors involved are changing all the time as a result of technological developments and cultural evolution, further compounding the problem. The following article considers the subject of optimum population in general terms.

OPTIMUM POPULATIONS*

Gordon Rattray Taylor

[1970]

Demographers are embarrassed when the question of optimum population is raised for it is notoriously difficult to avoid generalities; and when I ventured to raise it at the first Conference on Population called by the Interdisciplinary Communications Program, the New York Academy of Sciences and the Smithsonian Institution at Princeton in 1968, there was a shocked silence; after which the chairman ruled that that subject be postponed to the end of the meeting. It was never, in the end, discussed. Yet the fact that one cannot decide on a figure does not make the question an unreal one; and the fact that almost every member of a well-informed audience of over a hundred felt that Britain was not at the optimum, but decidedly over it, suggests that it is possible to evolve a social policy. After all, it is possible to advise the driver of a car that he is going too fast for safety even if one cannot name the exact speed at which he should be going.

To be sure, the optimum population of a country cannot be expressed merely as a figure expressing the total number of inhabitants. How they are distributed is vitally important. Parts of the U.S. today are certainly underpopulated, just as parts are certainly overpopulated. Redistribution is the immediate problem; when this has been done (if it ever is) it will be easier to see whether there are too many or too few. What each of us is interested in is the area we normally move about in, say a radius of 50-100 miles from our home, or something of that order. If that area is dense, the presence of wilderness fifty miles off is of limited value; if it is too lonely, the existence of a town two hours away will only make it slightly less so.

With this caveat, I believe we can detect three main kinds of criterion for defining an optimum. The commonest criterion is the economic, which tends to favour a relatively high density. A bigger population provides a bigger market, supports a richer social and cultural life, and so on. Thus Professor Victor R. Fuchs points out that the economies of scale make hospitals of at least 200 beds desirable, and may even operate up to 500 beds. This implies the existence of a population of 100,000 to 200,000 within driving distance. It has even been suggested

*From *The Doomsday Book* by Gordon Rattray Taylor. Reprinted by permission of the World Publishing Company, New York, and Thames and Hudson Co. Ltd., London. Copyright © 1970 by Gordon Rattray Taylor.

that larger populations means better local government but I suspect this is chiefly a matter of setting reasonable sizes for administrative units.

The economist only recognizes a limit when pollution, traffic congestion and other economically measurable factors begin to undermine the economic benefits. Motor-accident mortality is inversely correlated with population density across the United States. In point of fact the car, by bringing people into contact more often, has the same effect as an increase in population. The pressure in a gas rises, and the molecules collide more often, when it is heated, or when more gas is introduced into the vessel; if both are done at once, the pressure rises proportionately to the product of both factors. Analogously, mankind has both added more units and more energy to the situation. The proper course, when the car became generally available, was a reduction in population. Instead we increased it.

At the opposite pole from the economic, is the biological set of criteria, according to which the land should not carry more people than it can support without the consumption of irreplaceable resources, such as fossil fuel.

No one appears to have calculated just what this would mean in practice. This, too, is an economic criterion, but based on a much longer view than that of the dry-as-dust economist.

Between the economic and the biological criteria lie the psycho-social criteria which I have attempted to discuss: the need to avoid loneliness on the one hand, and lack of neighbourly support, feeling 'hemmed in' on the other. These I think call for levels of population intermediate between the economic and the biological.

On an even longer view, the rate at which all irreplaceable resources are being consumed—not merely fuel—is a limiting factor. In this context, a special committee of the National Research Council has concluded, after a three-year study, that there are already too many people on earth. Irreplaceable natural resources are simply not sufficient to meet future demands. Says the Resources Committee, headed by Professor Preston E. Cloud, Jr, of Santa Barbara: 'A population less than the present one could offer the best hope for comfortable living for our descendants, long duration for the species and the preservation of environmental quality.'

Professor J. H. Fremlin, a physicist at Birmingham University, has discussed the extreme cases of a population for Britain of 1,000 million (20 times the present figure) and of 30 million. At 30 million, he points out, everyone could own a car without undue congestion, food could be grown without battery methods, housing standards would rise and change of abode would be easier, while more people could enjoy country recreations. At 1,000 million in contrast there would be a better chance for far-out writers and artists to find an audience, more cultural facilities, and 'several Newtons and Shakespeares'. But everyone 'would have to want to stay under cover nearly all the time.' There would be space to roam outside the cities 'provided only one in a thousand wanted to spend more than a few hours in it a year.' He is not disturbed by this prospect and says: 'I doubt very much whether this would be a difficult state to achieve in a generation or two. Many animals become dangerously disturbed when heavily overcrowded, but we can learn to accept enormous numbers of social contacts if we don't have to take any notice of most of them and if we each have our own in-group with whom we feel secure.'

Frankly, this is the sort of outlandish nonsense you get when physicists move out of their sphere and start laying down the law in social fields, where their knowledge is quite superficial. Ethologists, like Leyhausen, know better.

Professor Joseph Hutchinson has proposed as a realistic long-term aim to reduce the population of Britain to 40 million, a process which he thinks might have to be spread over 200 years. For the U.S., Professor Kingsley Davis would like to aim even lower: 20 million.

With so many kinds of criterion there are naturally many definitions of an optimum population. For the agriculturalist it is the level at which the land can be farmed without deterioration. Characteristically, Professor Fuchs, as an economist, offers this definition: 'We can define the optimum as that size where the amount that people in the society would be willing to pay to have the population reduced by (say) 10 per cent is exactly equal to the amount other people in the society would be willing to pay to have it increased by that amount.' But this would depend on the way incomes were distributed, and assumes that people are wholly rational in such judgements, which everyone knows is not the case. I prefer the definition of a biologist, Professor Southwood: 'The optimum population of man is the maximum that can be maintained indefinitely without detriment to the health of the individuals from pollution or from social or nutritional stress.'

Over and above all this, there are in addition some political implications of large populations. Montesquieu said that democracy was only possible in a country appropriately small in size, a thought expressed two thousand years earlier by Plato. It is possible that expansion of population leads to greater centralization of control; the demand for decentralization may be only a form of protest against the inevitable. Paul Leyhausen is one who has pointed out that the sacrifices which the individual must make for the common good grow greater as population density rises—a point I also made twenty years ago in *Conditions of Happiness*. If you live in a forest, you can keep pigs or even let your house burn down without offending your neighbours, for you have none. In a city, you are forbidden to do either, and cannot even play the radio loudly at night! As populations rise, you cannot leave your car where you will, or build a house without approval. Eventually the whole ownership of real-estate may have to be abandoned. Such restrictions become increasingly onerous, and must be weighed against the advantages to which the economists draw attention.

Finally be it noted that, even if we decide that the world, or any large part of it, has not yet reached an optimum population density, there is still the question of how rapidy it is sensible to move towards that level. Too rapid growth creates strains, as we have seen, and I conclude, with Professor Athelstan Spilhaus: 'When we can treat all existing persons as human, it will be time enough to think about having more.'

part three

the population problem

---

towards
a
solution

Introduction

The current rate at which the population of the world is increasing (approximately 2%) and the predicted consequences of this increase clearly indicate the need of control: that is, the reduction of birth rates. However, equally important to the solution of the population problem is the alleviation of poverty and human misery—especially through international efforts to improve economic conditions in underdeveloped countries. Such efforts are necessary for humanitarian reasons alone, but there is another reason for improving economic conditions in underdeveloped countries: it has been quite clearly demonstrated that economic growth and the resulting improvement in living conditions are the most effective means of reducing births. In fact the two issues of reduction of birth rates and economic development, as Barbara Ward has indicated (see pages 186 to 189), are so closely linked that it is difficult to say which should have priority. Thus, though most countries agree that action must be taken, there is legitimate disagreement about whether policies associated with population growth or with economic growth will most likely secure the general welfare.

The purpose of Part 3 is, first, to examine the various measures of population control and to comment on both their present use and practicability. Consideration is given to some of the moral issues inherent in the subject of birth control, seen largely in terms of the attitudes of the world's major religions. Then, under the heading 'Solutions—Economic and Political', a number of articles discuss the problems of economic development in the poor nations. The main purpose of these articles is to provide a basis for examining two very critical questions: What are the various means that are being used, or have been proposed, to tackle the problems posed by overpopulation and inadequate economic growth? What are the responsibilities of the DCs in helping the UDCs to better themselves?

PLAYING GOD*

Robert C. Cook

[1968]

What anthropologist Ralph Linton called 'The Age of Faith and Epidemics' suddenly began to end when Jenner[1] discovered vaccination in 1800. A half-million years of terror-impelled and fruitless efforts to deal with death by prayer, incantation, incense, and magic went into the rubbish heap as the genius of the human mind began to be applied to fundamental life processes. In less than a century, this application changed utterly the pattern of man's dying.

The 'vital revolution' had begun. It was not enthusiastically received. Clerics were understandably dismayed at what to them seemed blasphemous arrogance—a sacrilegious tinkering with God's plan of survival. Since Eden, the Lord had given and the Lord had taken away. The giving and the taking were the perquisite of Deity. No wonder men asked who these bumptious nobodies were, and how they dared to meddle with the divine plan.

The preachers were not alone in their dismay. Law, medicine, and the press rallied to the defence of tradition. But times were changing. The burning of heretics was out of fashion, and opposition to Jenner lacked sales appeal. If a child could be spared smallpox by a scratch on the arm, what were these worthies fussing about, thought the mothers. Then, in 1801 the king and queen of England had themselves vaccinated, and the first round went overwhelmingly to Jenner. In 1805 the number of deaths from smallpox in London dropped from over 2,000 to about 600.

The first phase of the vital revolution was over. A generation passed before Parliament enacted a compulsory vaccination law in England. Jenner's discovery was only the beginning. Why vaccination worked he did not know; it was Pasteur who established that infections were caused by 'tiny beasties'. Thereafter, the causes and the timing of death were removed from the exclusive purview of divine Providence and turned over to the Bureau of Public Health.

At the other end of the equation of life, matters arranged themselves differently. Throughout all those millennia of the age of faith and

*Reprinted by permission from *World Population—The View Ahead*, edited by Richard N. Farmer, John D. Long, and George J. Stolnitz (Bloomington, Ind.: Bureau of Business Research, Indiana University, 1968). Copyright © 1968 by the Foundation for the School of Business.
[1] Edward Jenner, an English physician (1749-1823). (ed.)

epidemics, very high levels of fertility were essential to survival. Pre-Jenner existence was a horrendous gamble against a multitude of killers whose special target was the young. If half of the babies born in any particular year managed to survive to have children of their own, it was a veritable miracle. In some years, half of the babies born did not even live to celebrate a first birthday. The consequence of this ghastly slaughter of the innocents by the microscopic Herods of the bacterial and viral worlds was that human fertility had to be sustanied at flood level if the human species was to have any hope of surviving. Mores and superstitions intended to guarantee an abundant human harvest were legion, a part of every culture everywhere on earth. Any society that took a casual attitude toward the necessity to 'be fruitful and multiply' had long since disappeared. Those fertility imperatives were backed by the most august sanctions; they were essential to survival of the human race during the vast reaches of time before the pre-Jenner era.

The next step does not require the genius of an Einstein to figure out. The modest intricacies of human population dynamics were foreign to practically the entire human species. Hence, nobody had any inkling that Jenner and those who followed him were initiating one of the great cultural revolutions of all time.

As long as man was at the mercy of an apparently blind and indifferent Providence, he could only fight back by trying frantically to outbreed the ravening regiments of the apocalyptic cavalry: war, famine, and pestilence. Jenner changed all that, but nobody had any idea that winning at long last a round with death could be anything but a blessing. It never occurred to anyone that, in upsetting a fundamental demographic balance, humankind was off on a numbers game that today threatens the most dire consequences.

Put in its simplest terms, Jenner's momentous discovery opened up a frightening new era in which it became necessary to review some fundamental morals, taken for granted, and to engage in a most difficult game of truth and consequences. Man, having to a great extent elbowed Providence out of the timing of life's end, had opened up a veritable Pandora's box of most difficult formulations and decisions; he must forsooth apply all his wit, will, and wisdom to the basic facts of human arithmetic. Compassion, too, would be required. The arduous task of dealing with this power to prolong life has until very recently been shunned. In the game of truth and consequences a fantastic and disastrous dichotomy developed. Man disposed of disease and death to the best of his rapidly growing powers, and thus postponed the ravages of the Grim Reaper. Divine Providence, with the co-operation of that rather moronic bird, the stork, continued to be looked upon as the arbiter of who was born, when, where, and to whom.

This, in a nutshell, presents the background of the ethical problem man must face in the mushrooming population crisis. The preachers, physcians, and other defenders of the *status quo* were right in 1880. Jenner was definitely upsetting the vital applecart. The opposition sensed that Jenner's arrogant meddling with age-old patterns of survival was dangerous, but the nature and scope of the danger escaped them.

With the opening of the vital revolution, man took the first steps towards becoming the master of his own destiny. Charles Darwin had shown how, over the ages, blind forces could create forms so varied, so beautiful, and yet so admirably adapted that they could function in many environmental contexts. Out of this process of natural selection had grown the human mind. And this mind had the power to probe the mysteries of entwined matter and energy, to plumb the depths of space, and to unlock the secrets of life and death.

In a real and challenging sense, the increasing power to control mortality and the timing of births puts mankind in the position of playing God, of facing the frightening reality that he must—or else.

The coin of life has two sides, birth and death. It may be—though it is not likely—that those who opposed Jenner recognized that mankind lacked the wisdom, the insight, the compassion, and the guts to play God all across the board. To purchase progress with only one side of the coin of life is to buy a ticket to disaster, as we are finding out today. The oft-repeated story engraved on rocks and fossils tells us that many species have reached their highest levels of specialization just before they were cast into the evolutionary rubbish heap. The human experiment centring around the emergence of mind has reached the point where we human beings must face both our potential for power and our responsibility for using it wisely. Ultimately, the alternative is extinction.

Do we have the intelligence, and with it the humility, to make the vital revolution work? Can we become the architects of our own evolution? Indeed, dare we do any less? That is the challenge of this particular and unique age of man in which we find ourselves. The possibilities are limitless, and the difficulties, complexities, and dangers terrifying.

If we dare—and we can hardly not dare and still survive—the problem that confronts us is basically ethical. Heretofore, ethics have always been abstracts and reconstructs from tradition, revelation, and experience. Today, in the era of the vital revolution, there are fundamental ethical challenges for which the past can give no answers. The Jennerian dilemma is an example. Superficially viewed, the power to avert death could only be conceived as an absolute good. Yet, given an equation wherein time is a co-ordinate, the vital imbalance can prove in the end to be a prelude to disaster.

The population crisis is a case in point. Annual rates of population increase of 3.5 or even 4.0 per cent a year are even now pushing vast areas and many hundreds of millions of human beings to the verge of famine—and beyond. Such rates of population growth are due to human action. In the end they are bound to be destructive to the very lives that Jenner and those who followed him hoped to save. The correction of man-induced changes that are catastrophic in their implications is obviously and basically a moral imperative.

The ethical considerations involved are complex enough to tax the wisdom and the conscience of man. Since the issues are related to sex with its high emotional octane, solutions will be difficult. Fundamental consideration of evolutionary serendipity will also loom large. A classic example of this principle is illustrated, as Dr F. Frazer Darling has pointed out, in the evolution of feathers, which started out as an adaptive expedient to make possible a high and stabilized body temperature. With the passage of ages, feathers became an essential component of organs of flight. In the fantastic plumage and colouring of some genera of birds, feathers also came to have an important sexual function. These benefits accrued over a long and zig-zag course as they amplified the original function of merely keeping the creature warm.

Sex itself has been enriched by a comparable evolutionary change. Initially, the function of sex was reproduction. This became specialized in various ways with the passage of evolutionary time. Modern science recognizes that sex contributes abundantly to the fundamental emotional components of personality. The spectrum of this complex chain reaction is much too long to catalogue here. Nevertheless, with the technology of fertility control becoming highly developed, the tangled emotive functions of sex can be—and indeed are being—divorced from the reproductive.

This whole area of human experience demands searching ethical re-evaluation. The current wide-ranging revolt against assumedly divinely ordained moral codes and traditional standards of conduct is not un-related to the revolt that Jenner innocently set off over a century and a half ago. Events since that time underline the far-ranging conse-quences of upsetting an ecological balance. Humankind can never go back to the imposed absolutes of the past. But mere revolt against the dead hand of the past is not enough. In this new kind of world, the elaboration of a code tailored to this time of crisis demands the orches-trating of many skills and insights and more than a tincture of genius. The challenge is tremendous and the prospect is disturbing.

Sex is a powerful creative force, and at its best one of the great sacramental experiences of life. Albert Ellis recently described the American attitude toward sex as 'addled, straddled and spraddled'. This is hardly a state of mind likely to apprehend and to deal effectively with the extremely varied and complex moral and ethical issues involved.

An ethical code for the age of the vital revolution must centre around three major objectives. It must do a better job of enabling human beings to pursue happiness in an atmosphere of adventure than our present moral assumptions and imperatives permit. Beyond that, it must ensure that man recognize the responsibility entailed in the ultimate game of truth and consequences as it is now beginning to be revealed. Finally, a moral code for tomorrow must challenge the best in man to accept with courage and compassion the great undertaking of becoming master of his own evolutionary fate.

No other species has ever had the opportunity of thus mastering and guiding its destiny. The king of the hominids has the intelligence to write the necessary new rules, but has he the wisdom as well? 'And Jehovah God said: Behold man is become as one of us, to know good and evil.' The fellowship with the Deity which this knowledge con-ferred, as recorded in Genesis, can no longer be evaded. Nothing more difficult has ever challenged the mind, the finest aspirations, and the genius of man.

1 | The Means of Controlling Births

BIRTH CONTROL

Birth control refers to the various methods that are used to prevent conception. Although the history of birth control is very old, it has only been in recent years that the subject has been discussed with any freedom. This is not to suggest that there is universal agreement about the desirability or acceptability of the various measures that might be included under this heading, but it can be said that many people today advocate the need for planned parenthood or controlling the growth of population, and this presupposes the adoption of some birth-control measures.

There are a great variety of different birth-control methods, and a description of these is available from any of a number of sources (see Bibliography). What requires emphasis here is that, assuming general agreement on the need for controlling the growth of population, there is no single method of birth control that combines the qualities of simplicity, complete effectiveness, and low cost. These characteristics are absolutely essential if control is to be effective, particularly in UDCs.

When discussing methods of birth control, it is important to recognize that, demographically speaking, both sterilization and abortion must be taken into account. Sterilization (particularly of males) has become much more widespread in recent years. It is a relatively simple operation (vasectomy) and is usually completely effective. However, such an operation requires skilled medical personnel, and it is doubtful whether there are sufficient qualified people and clinics—particularly in the UDCs—to perform enough operations to have an appreciable effect on population numbers. Another difficulty is that many men hesitate to undergo this operation; first, because it *is* an operation and second because the result can be irreversible. The sterilization of the female (salpingectomy) is also becoming a more common operation, but it is more complex than that for the male and, consequently, is much less likely to gain widespread acceptance.

Historically abortion has been a taboo subject in almost all societies. Until fairly recently it was an illegal operation in most countries, and

202

today, even in countries where the law has been changed, an abortion can still be difficult to obtain. Without going into the arguments for and against abortion—and there are many on both sides—the following material provides some information on its effects in different areas.

In general it is only in certain nations—Britain, the Scandinavian countries, Japan, China, and many of the countries of eastern Europe as well as Canada and the United States—that abortion laws have been made more permissive; that is, abortions are allowed on broad medical, humanitarian, and eugenic grounds. In some cases they are permitted simply at the request of a pregnant woman. What has been the effect of these liberal laws?

Not surprisingly, where the abortions laws are as permissive as they are in eastern Europe, the number of legal abortions has risen sharply. In Hungary, for example, the increase has been so great that the number of legal abortions now exceeds the number of births. In 1967 there were 187,500 legal abortions in that country as against 148,900 live births. The contrasting curves, showing that as the abortion rate has gone up the birth rate has gone down, suggest that for many women in Hungary abortion has replaced contraception as the means of birth control. Similarly, the statistics in Czechoslovakia indicate that legalized abortion has reduced the birth rate, although it is still considerably higher than the abortion rate.

The drop in the birth rate has caused two countries of eastern Europe to revise their abortion laws. In October 1966, Romania substituted a restrictive statute for one allowing abortion on request. Abortions on medical grounds are permitted now only if the pregnancy threatens the woman's life, and the other acceptable indications are limited to cases in which the woman is over forty-five years of age, or has four or more children, or may give birth to a malformed child, or has become pregnant as a result of rape or incest. Following the enactment of the new Romanian law the birth rate rose from 13.7 (per 1,000 of population) in the fourth quarter of 1966 to 38.4 in the third quarter of 1967. This rise indicates that before the repeal of the permissive law the annual rate of legal abortions in Romania had been at least 24.7 per 1,000 of population, which is considerably higher than the high rate of 18.4 that was reported for Hungary in 1967.

In 1968 Bulgaria also imposed restrictions—somewhat less drastic—on abortion. Women with three or more children may still have an abortion on request, but those with one or two children must apply to a board that 'shall explain the harmfulness and dangers of abortion, the need to take the pregnancy to full term, the financial support the family will receive after the birth of a child and, in general, shall make every effort to dissuade every woman who expresses the desire to have her pregnancy interrupted from doing so. If, nevertheless, the woman concerned persists in asking for her pregnancy to be interrupted, the board shall give its approval to this effect.' Childless women may be aborted on medical grounds only.

In Japan the Eugenic Protection Law authorizes abortion if the pregnancy will seriously affect the woman's health 'from the physical or economic viewpoint'. This provision has been interpreted so broadly that any Japanese woman can have a legal abortion on request. The number of legal abortions reported in Japan rose from 246,000 in 1949, the year after passage of the law, to 1,170,000 in 1955. After that year the reported number declined, and by 1967 it had fallen to 748,000. There are reasons to believe, however, that the reports may understate the actual number of legal abortions by several hundred thousand. It is said that many Japanese physicians, in order to minimize their income taxes, do not report all the abortions they perform. Curiously, the number of reported abortions continued to decline instead of rising when the birth rate dropped precipitately in 1966, the 'Year of the Fiery Horse'. (According to tradition, girls born during such a year grow up to be bad-natured and hence difficult to marry off.) Since it is doubtful that the sharp drop in births can be attributed mainly to a surge in the effective use of contraception by the most tradition-bound segment of Japanese society, one can surmise that the number of abortions must actually have risen, rather than declined in 1966.[1]

Of course another aspect of the problem that is of great concern is the matter of illegal abortions. While figures are not available, the number in the United States is estimated to be in the hundreds of thousands each year. In western Europe the estimated figures are even higher, with some authorities suggesting (but not proving) that in some countries the abortion rate exceeds the birth rate.

It would be wrong to assume that all the evils associated with illegal abortions, particularly the high death rates, disappear when abortion laws are liberalized. Experience has shown that, for various reasons, illegal abortions still occur in such countries, although they do so on a greatly reduced scale.

FAMILY PLANNING

Family planning may be carried out by both government and non-government agencies that have as their objective the regulation of human population. In general terms family planning involves counselling and the dissemination of information on birth control with the object of making it possible for parents to decide how many children they wish to

---

[1] From Christopher Tietze and Sarah Lewit, 'Abortion', *Scientific American*, January 1969. Copyright © 1969 by Scientific American, Inc. All rights reserved.

Table 17
FAMILY PLANNING IN THE UNDERDEVELOPED COUNTRIES

Size of population (in millions)	Have an official family planning policy and/or program, or major governmental involvement	Are doing something official in family planning, or limited governmental involvement	Are doing nothing official in family planning
400 & more	China (1962?) India (1952, reorganized 1965)		
100-400	Pakistan (1960, reorganized 1965)	Indonesia	
50-100			Nigeria Brazil
25-50	Turkey (1965) United Arab Republic (1966) South Korea (1961)	Mexico Philippines Thailand	Burma
15-25	Iran (1967) Colombia (1967) North Vietnam (1964)		Ethiopia Congo South Vietnam Afghanistan
10-15	Morocco (1966) Taiwan (1964) Ceylon (1967)	Peru Nepal	Sudan Algeria Tanzania North Korea
Less than 10	Malaysia (1966) Kenya (1966) Chile (1966) Tunisia (1966) Hong Kong (c1960) Dominican Republic (1967) Honduras (1965) Singapore (1966) Jamaica (1966) Trinidad & Tobago (1967) Mauritius (1965)	Venezuela Cuba Nicaragua Costa Rica Barbados	Africa - 31 countries Asia - 12 countries Latin America - 9 countries

SOURCE: Berelson, *Studies in Family Planning No. 39*, (supp.). The Population Council, 1969.

have. The primary concern of the family planning movement has been to stress the welfare of the family and the advantages of well-spaced and limited numbers of children.

Early attempts at family planning began in the nineteenth century and in both Great Britain and the United States resulted in government suppression. In the United States the Comstock Law of 1873 forbade the use of the mails for birth-control information, classifying this as obscene literature. (The last vestiges of this law were not repealed until 1966.) One of the more famous of the early advocates of family planning was Margaret Sanger, whose efforts to establish a birth-control clinic in the United States in 1916 led to a prison term. Despite the difficulties encountered by pioneers of this movement in North America and Europe, the importance of their efforts cannot be overestimated. While the effect of family planning on birth rates in North America and Europe is difficult to assess, what is not arguable is its influence on the removal of restrictive laws, the development of medical and religious support, the free circulation of birth-control information, and the development of a social climate in which family planning has come to be regarded by many as a legitimate and necessary aspect of marriage and parenthood.

The family planning movement did not become established in the UDCs until the 1950s. In 1952 Mrs Sanger and others founded the International Planned Parenthood Federation, which by 1968 had organizations in 36 countries. It was joined by many other agencies, such as the Ford Foundation and the Population Council in the United States. Most of them were private (although some were sponsored by governments), and almost all of them were supported by the official policy of the government in whose country their work was being carried out. (See Table 17.)

POPULATION CONTROL

Family planning is not population control, although it constitutes an important element of it. Population control refers to the efforts of society, usually through government, to regulate the rate of population growth. It includes all those measures that the government might take to slow the growth rates. Although a number of countries do have a policy of family planning, and some have adopted a number of measures that might be described as a form of population control, many other countries (as shown in Table 17) do not have any kind of policy.

In their book on population, Ehrlich and Ehrlich[1] emphasize the need for population control and propose three approaches that together would constitute an effective policy. These and related matters are summarized below. In this summary there is no mention of the 'optimum population' that these measures should be directed towards. This is an understandable omission, since the first objective of any population policy is to achieve control over growth rates. When this has been accomplished it will be time to consider what an optimum population should be.

1. FAMILY PLANNING

As family-planning policies assume freedom of choice, any attempt by a state to regulate growth by this means alone may well be unsuccessful. While such methods will likely achieve a reduction in the birth rate, this may not be great enough in the long run to produce the population level desired by a particular country. Thus most population experts, while advocating the rapid expansion of family-planning programs, are also adamant in their belief that additional programs will be essential if control over population growth in the underdeveloped countries is to be achieved.

2. SOCIO-ECONOMIC MEASURES

The principal object of this approach is to reduce births by influencing

[1] Paul R. Ehrlich and Anne H. Ehrlich, *Population, Resources, Environment: Issues in Human Ecology,* W. H. Freeman and Company, San Francisco, 1970.

people's motives or attitudes. This can be done in various ways. In countries where people are affluent enough to pay taxes, tax laws could be so designed to provide inducements for people to have small families. For example, a substantial tax deduction would be given for the first two children, and nothing for those that follow. Much the same kind of effect could be achieved through family allowances by instituting a sliding scale that results in the payment of large allowances for the first two children and progressively smaller ones for those that follow.

Many other socio-economic measures have been suggested that might assist a government to achieve some degree of control over the rate of population growth. These include limiting the amount of free education available to any family, paying the cost of abortions, paying bonuses to childless couples, encouraging and simplifying adoption procedures, and making it easier for women to work, particularly through the provision of proper day-care centres. Obviously some of these proposals would be considered unsuitable in some societies, but the principle behind this form of population control should be fairly clear.

In any deliberate effort to control the birth rate along these lines, a government has two powerful instruments—its command over economic planning, and its authority (real or potential) over education. The first determines (as far as policy can) the economic conditions and circumstances affecting the lives of all citizens; the second provides the knowledge and attitudes necessary to implement the plans. The economic system largely determines who shall work, what can be bought, what rearing children will cost, how much individuals can spend. The schools define family roles and develop vocational and recreational interests; they could, if it were desired, redefine the sex roles, develop interests that transcend the home, and transmit realistic (as opposed to moralistic) knowledge concerning marriage, sexual behaviour, and population problems. When the problem is viewed in this light, it is clear that the ministries of economics and education, not the ministry of health, should be the source of population policy.[1]

3. INVOLUNTARY MEASURES

In such matters as the use of drugs, weapons, natural resources, and public and private property, the need for regulation by society is generally recognized. But in the sphere of human reproduction most people would balk at the suggestion that the state should control the number of children a couple can have. A great number of involuntary measures have

[1] From Kingsley Davis, 'Population Policy: Will Current Programs Succeed?', *Science*, Vol. 158, November 10, 1967, pp. 730-9. Copyright © 1967 by the American Association for the Advancement of Science.

been suggested as a means to control growth if voluntary measures do not succeed. These include the compulsory sterilization of males or females after a certain number of children have been born, the development of a sterilizing capsule which could be implanted under a woman's skin at puberty or after the birth of her first child and removed only when pregnancy is desired, or the use of marketable licences entitling women to a certain number of children. It has even been suggested that it might be possible to develop a sterilant that could be added to water or foods as a means of controlling population growth. These controls are repugnant to many, principally because the element of choice would no longer exist. However, they are in many ways less repressive than the socio-economic ones and, by not discriminating against the poor, are certainly much fairer.

The Ehrlichs conclude their book by emphasizing not only the necessity for control, but also the importance of changing human attitudes. While agreeing with the need for immediate and effective population-control policies, they point out that once people are convinced that it is in their interest to control the size of their family, they will find the ways and means of doing this.

No form of population control, even the most coercive and repressive, will succeed for long unless individuals understand the need for it and accept the idea that humanity must limit its numbers.

Therefore, the ultimate key to population control lies in changing human attitudes concerning reproductive behaviour and goals in all societies. Achieving this throughout the world would be a gigantic task even if it became the world's first-priority goal, as many believe it should be.

But human survival seems certain to require population-control programs, at least in some places, even before the necessary changes in attitudes can be brought about in the population. In fact, the establishment of such programs might in itself help to convince people of the seriousness of the population problem.

Most of the control measures discussed here have never been tried; we know only that their *potential* effectiveness may be great. The socio-economic proposals are based on knowledge of the sort of social conditions that have been associated in the past with low birth rates. We need to know more about all people's attitudes towards human reproduction; we need to know how these attitudes are affected by various living conditions, including some that seem virtually intolerable to us. Even more, we need to know what influences and conditions will lead to changes in these attitudes in favour of smaller families. How can we convince a poor Pakistani villager or a middle-class

American that the number of children his wife bears is of crucial importance not just to himself and his family but also to his society? How can we make everyone care?[1]

[1] From *Population, Resources, Environment: Issues in Human Ecology* by Paul R. Ehrlich and Anne H. Ehrlich. W. H. Freeman and Company. Copyright © 1970.

2 | Birth Control/ Population Control: A Controversy

The problems of instituting comprehensive population-control schemes in the UDCs are made especially difficult by lack of money and education, by poor communications, and by the widespread inertia that can only be described as a general human resistance to change. Other factors are also involved. Among the developed countries are some that oppose in principle the provision of assistance for population control or disagree on the methods of providing it. In addition, where aid has been made available for such schemes, it has been too small in some cases to be of any real help to the recipient countries. While most UDCs are willing to accept, and indeed request, assistance in setting up family-planning programs, there are some that regard any form of birth control as part of a plot by the DCs to exercise control over, or even subjugate, their countries both economically and politically. Aid in the form of birth control is sometimes viewed in the UDCs as a new form of imperialism or a genocide plot. A more common belief is that greater numbers of people are essential for economic growth and as a basis for political power. This idea is much more difficult to dispel, particularly when those that uphold it can point to such developed countries as the United States, where rapid population growth has indeed been a major factor in the economic and political evolution of that nation.

All these problems are vexing ones, partly because they are difficult to measure and in some cases to substantiate. And some of them are controversial. But of more importance to the layman, because it receives by far the greatest amount of attention in the media, is the controversy that has been created in discussions of birth control by the differing views of morality and religion that exist throughout the world.

It is important to remember that the whole birth-control controversy is in large measure influenced by the fact that, until fairly recently—roughly over the last hundred years in the DCs, and in the last few decades in most UDCs—a high birth rate was essential to the preservation of the human species. Very high and variable death rates, particularly the infant- and child-mortality ones, long conditioned people to believe that it was vital to have as many children as possible. If this attitude had not existed, it is unlikely that the human species would have survived.

It is not the purpose of this book to be critical of, or comprehensive in examining, the role of religion in this controversy. Rather our aim is to provide sufficient information to acquaint the reader with several different points of view. (If the reader wishes to examine the whole matter in greater detail, he should refer to the sources listed in the Bibliography on pp. 329-38.) In examining the beliefs of different peoples, our purpose is to learn how they have developed and how they affect such matters as family development and the relationship of the family to the community. It is only in the light of this knowledge that the various policies of birth control, family planning, or population control can be assessed. Indeed, such knowledge is necessary if effective policies are to evolve.

In Part 2, Section 2 we learned that religion is only one of many factors that affect the fertility rate of a population. Certainly it would be wrong to place the blame for our present population crisis on religious opposition to birth control. For most of the period when the countries of western and northern Europe were passing through the demographic transition, none of their churches sanctioned birth control. However, it is important to emphasize that these countries had over a century in which to accomplish the change from high to low birth rates. This leads to the deduction that, over a sufficiently long period of time, and with improving economic and social conditions, the influence of religion in affecting birth rates is relatively minor. But today time is running out for many of the UDCs. Knowing how rapidly their populations are growing, and how slowly attitudes with deep cultural roots change, we cannot afford to ignore the influence of religion on fertility. For the UDCs to complete the transition in the next two or three decades, as most demographers believe they must, *every* factor that has a bearing on fertility has to be carefully examined.

THE CHRISTIAN CHURCHES

What are the attitudes of the Christian churches towards birth control and family planning? In times past, this question could be answered simply and unequivocally: the aim of marriage was the procreation of children, and any artificial interference with this natural process was contrary to the laws of God. Within the past fifty years most Protestant churches have changed their position, and that of the Roman Catholic Church has been modified. What has brought about these changes? Of course they represent much more than just a change in thinking within the churches themselves. The answer is a very complex one; it is to be found in the radical transformations that stem from the vast social, economic, and political developments of the twentieth century. The desire to control the number of births, as noted previously, is the result of a large number of interconnected factors, which include developments that have produced great improvements in living standards in many areas of the world, giant steps forward in medical science that have reduced infant- and child-mortality rates, widespread developments in all forms of communication, and—a very important factor—the gradually changing position of women in most modern societies.

The attitudes of the various Protestant denominations to birth control, family planning, and related matters do vary, but some generalizations can be made. Most of them approve the principle of voluntary family planning and responsible parenthood. Birth-control devices are acceptable if they contribute to the spiritual, emotional, and economic welfare of the family. One of the first statements permitting (with some qualifications) the use of birth control was made by the Bishops of the Anglican Church attending the Lambeth Conference of 1930. They stated that 'in those cases where there is such a clearly felt moral obligation to limit or avoid parenthood, and where there is a morally sound reason for avoiding complete abstinence, the Conference agrees that other methods may be used, provided that this is done in the light of the same Christian principles'. While this did not receive unanimous approval, it represented a significant shift in the attitude of the Anglican Church. Many other similar statements followed from different Protestant denominations in Canada, the United States, and western Europe. In 1931 the Committee on Marriage and Home of the U.S. Federal Council of Churches held that 'the careful and restrained use of contraceptives by married people is valid and normal'. In 1936 the General Council of the United Church of Canada supported the establishment of Voluntary Parenthood Clinics. In 1939 the Methodist Conference of Great Britain, while stressing the responsibilities and obligations of parenthood, stated that conception control should have as its aim 'the healthiest family in the healthiest sort of way'.

After the Second World War, statements on responsible parenthood increased in number and became more representative and comprehensive. It would serve little purpose to note these here.[1] However, one of the most important, and in many ways representative, Protestant statements was the clear and unequivocal support of family planning passed without dissent by the 1958 Lambeth Conference of the Church of England.

---

[1] A detailed examination of these developments and the whole question of religion and population is found in R. M. Fagley, *The Population Explosion and Christian Responsibility*, Oxford University Press, Inc., New York, 1960.

The Conference believes that the responsibility for deciding upon the number and frequency of children has been laid by God upon the consciences of parents everywhere: that this planning, in such ways as are mutually acceptable to husband and wife in Christian conscience, is a right and important factor in Christian family life and should be the result of positive choice before God. Such responsible parenthood, built on obedience to all the duties of marriage, requires a wise stewardship of the resources and abilities of the family as well as a thoughtful consideration of the varying population needs and problems of society and the claims of future generations.

The position of the Roman Catholic Church has also changed. Traditionally children were regarded as the supreme blessing of marriage and childless couples were rare. As late as 1930, in an encyclical issued by the Pope, this position of the Church was reiterated, and artificial contraception was described as 'intrinsically immoral'. It was just after this encyclical, however, that the work of two Japanese doctors gave validity to the 'safe-period' theory. It is based on the fact that there is only a certain time in the month when a woman can conceive, and if sexual abstinence is practised on these days then conception cannot occur. The practical application of this information led to the development of the 'rhythm method' of birth control and was sanctioned officially by the Roman Catholic Church as a method that could be legitimately used to limit the number of children in marriage. Unfortunately, however, this method requires some careful calculations, and even then it is not suitable for all women. For this and other reasons it is not generally regarded as an effective means of birth control.

Pressures for change continued, from within and without the Church. The development of the 'Pill' in the early 1960s gave new hope to many that this form of birth control would be acceptable. Certain statements during the papacy of John XXIII, in which he emphasized the primacy of the individual conscience, were interpreted by some as a licence to go beyond traditional thinking.

Early in the papacy of John's successor, Paul VI, a Papal Study Commission was appointed to consider the birth-control problem, and in 1966 made its report to the Pope. In essence the report contained a majority and a minority opinion, which indicated a division within the Church itself. The majority report stated:

The regulation of conception appears necessary to many couples who wish to achieve a responsible, open, and reasonable parenthood in today's circumstances. If they are to observe and cultivate all the essential values of marriage, married people need decent and human means for the regulation of conception. They should be able to expect the collaboration of all, especially from men of learning and science, in order that they can have at their disposal means agreeable and worthy of man in the fulfilling of his responsible parenthood.

The morality of sexual acts between married people takes its meaning first of all and specifically from the ordering of their actions in a fruitful married life, that is, one which is practised with responsible, generous, and prudent parenthood. It does not depend upon a direct fecundity of each and every particular act.

Included in the minority report were the following comments:

Contraception is understood by the Church as any use of the marriage right in the exercise of which the act is deprived of its natural power for the procreation of life through the industry of man. Contraceptive sterilization may be defined theologically as any physical intervention in a generative process (opus naturae) which, before or after the proper placing of generative acts (opus hominis), causes these acts to be deprived of their natural power for the procreation of life by the industry of man. . . . In every age it is clearly evident that contraception essentially offends against the negative precept 'one may not deprive the conjugal act of its natural power for the procreation of new life'. . . . The Church cannot change her answer *because this answer is true.* Whatever may pertain to a more perfect formulation of the teaching or its possible genuine development, the teaching itself cannot not be substantially true. It is true because the Catholic Church, instituted by Christ to show men a secure way to eternal life, could not have so wrongly erred during all those centuries of its history.

The report was followed two years later (1968) by an encyclical issued by the Pope entitled 'Humanae Vitae' ('Of Human Life'). This document, a portion of which follows, is an instruction that applies to all members of the Roman Catholic Church.

These acts, by which husband and wife are united in chaste intimacy and by means of which human life is transmitted, are, as the council recalled, 'noble and worthy', and they do not cease to be lawful if, for cause independent of the will of husband and wife, they are foreseen to be infecund, since they always remain ordained toward expressing and consolidating their union. In fact, as experience bears witness, not every conjugal act is followed by a new life. God has wisely disposed natural laws and rhythms of fecundity which, of themselves, cause a separation in the succession of births. Nonetheless the Church, calling men back to the observance of the norms of the natural law, as interpreted by her constant doctrine, teaches that each and every marriage act ('quilibet matrimonii usus') must remain open to the transmission of life.

We must once again declare that the direct interruption of the generative process already begun, and, above all, directly willed and procured abortion, even if for therapeutic reasons, are to be absolutely excluded as licit means of regulating birth.

Equally to be excluded, as the teaching authority of the Church has frequently declared, is direct sterilization, whether perpetual or temporary, whether of the man or of the woman. Similarly excluded is every action which, either in anticipation of the conjugal act or in its accomplishment, or in the development of its natural consequences, proposes, whether as an end or as a means, to render procreation impossible.

To justify conjugal acts made intentionally infecund, one cannot invoke as valid reasons the lesser evil, or the fact that such acts would constitute a whole together with the fecund acts already performed or to follow later, and hence would share in one and the same moral goodness. In truth, if it is sometimes licit to tolerate a lesser evil in order to avoid a greater evil or to promote a greater good, it is not licit, even for the gravest reasons, to do evil so that good may follow therefrom; that is, to make into the object of a positive act of the will something which is intrinsically disorder and hence unworthy of the human person, even when the intention is to safeguard or promote individual, family, or social well-being.

Consequently it is an error to think that a conjugal act which is deliberately made infecund and so is intrinsically dishonest could be made honest and right by the ensemble of a fecund conjugal life.

If . . . there are serious motives to space out births, which derive from the physical or psychological conditions of husband and wife, or from external conditions, the Church teaches that it is then licit to take into account the natural rhythms immanent in the generative functions, for the use of marriage in the infecund periods only, and this way to regulate birth without offending the moral principles which have been recalled earlier.

The Church is coherent with herself when she considers recourse to the infecund periods to be licit, while at the same time condemning, as being always illicit, the use of means directly contrary to fecundation, even if such use is inspired by reasons which may appear honest and serious. In reality, there are essential differences between the two cases: in the former, the married couple make legitimate use of a natural disposition; in the latter, they impede the development of natural processes. It is true that, in the one and the other case, the married couple are concordant in the positive will of avoiding children for plausible reasons, seeking the certainty that offspring will not arrive; but it is also true that only in the former case are they able to renounce the use of marriage in the fecund periods when, for just motives, procreation is not desirable, while making use of it during infecund periods to manifest their affection and to safeguard their mutual fidelity. By so doing, they give proof of a truly and integrally honest love.

PARENTHOOD AND OTHER WORLD RELIGIONS*

Richard M. Fagley

[1960]

Anything as fundamental, mysterious, and awesome as the birth of new life is inescapably related to man's religious instinct. The miracle of birth links the living with the dynamic, the creative in the universe. Fertility in the natural world is essential to individual survival, and human fertility is essential to social survival. Thus it is understandable that anthropologists should find fertility rites common in primitive religion in all parts of the world. The uncertainties of the flock and the harvest, and the uncertainties of high mortality surrounding the family, made propitiation of the fertility gods important for daily bread and progeny. In some societies ignorance of the physiology of generation made parenthood doubly mysterious, and where the relationship between sexual intercourse and procreation was dimly understood, there were still the baffling questions of successful pregnancy, of safe childbirth, of healthy babies, of sons. The fertility cult was a normal fact in primitive society.

Apparently, the major religions of today had to struggle in their infancy in varying degrees against such cults and the sex mores related to them. Hinduism, in its characteristic syncretistic fashion, absorbed a fertility cult in the worship of Shiva, who among other things is the god of reproduction. Buddhism is an ascetic revolt against the passions of this life, yet in the Buddhist literature can be found the imprint of older pro-fertility patterns. Judaism had a struggle to oust the local fertility gods, the *baals*. Early Christianity was concerned with the corrupting influence of Greco-Roman licence, in which the worship of Venus was a factor. And Islam came onto the scene in this field as a reform movement, elevating somewhat the low status of women and curbing somewhat the unrestricted polygamy in the Arab culture of the time.

At the same time the major religions, except perhaps Buddhism, preserved the nearly universal concern for fertility in their doctrines and practices, and Buddhism offered a compromise way for the married laity. In addition to Hindu syncretism, there is the strong fertility element in Judaism, which continued in the Old Testament heritage of Christianity. And the moral and marital reforms of Mohammed stopped far short of any hostility to fertility. The persistence of pro-fertility attitudes may represent to some extent the impact of the vanquished faiths, or the compromises contributing to victory. In either case, the mystery of new life is a basic question for all religion, and since for most of man's history the struggle for life has been waged against heavy natural odds, a generally strong pro-fertility emphasis in the major religious traditions is wholly comprehensible.

Our concern, however, is primarily the contemporary bearing of the main religions on the question of responsible parenthood, particularly as they affect attitudes and policies in the underdeveloped world, rather than the historical evolution of their teachings. . . .

HINDUISM

The attitude toward parenthood in Hinduism, which counts a total community of perhaps 300 million souls and is the predominant faith in the most densely populated large region on earth, is obviously important if a limitation of fertility is to restore a balance between population and available resources. Hinduism is such a conglomeration of different religious beliefs and folkways that the answer is complex. The amoral behaviour of the Hindu pantheon, reminiscent of the Greek deities, gives little or no ethical guidance, and the wide range of cults existing side by side offer quite divergent norms for conduct.

There are strong pro-fertility elements in Hinduism. . . . The male-centred view of life, combined with the belief in reincarnation, makes sons[1] important to pray for their ancestors and deliver them from hell, and tends to relegate woman chiefly to her childbearing function. The 'seed and soil' concept of procreation seems to be common in the Hindu tradition and, with the *ahimsa* or noninjury doctrine, would appear to indicate a predisposition against any form of contraception.

[1] The procreation of male offspring is an important part of Hindu tradition and unquestionably a factor contributing to high fertility. (ed.)

On the other hand, there is a strong ascetic element in Hinduism. Kenneth Saunders has pointed out in *The Ideals of East and West* that the early thinkers held out as 'the ideal man the *muni*, or wandering friar, who has "risen above the desire for sons, for wealth and for domination" '. Later the religious ideal is the *yogi*: 'aloof, benevolent, detached, severe in mystic contemplation'. This ideal was diluted for the layman in the favourite book of devotion, the *Bhagavad Gita*, but it offers some counterweight to the erotic and fertility elements in Hinduism. Probably more important, in regard to present-day issues of contraception, is the fact that the Hindu approach places more emphasis on spiritual attitudes than on ethical rules. The head of the Ramakrishna Mission in New Delhi wrote a friend in Chicago, stating that the Mission had 'no official opinion on social problems like birth control', having faith in enlightened social opinion:

> Swami Vivekananda held the view that social evils are like diseases in the body politic whose radical cure is through purifying and strengthening the life blood of the body through fundamental spiritual education of man; social reforms remove only the surface symptoms; this is also important and necessary; but he desired his movement to concentrate on the first while saying godspeed to all well-meaning social reformers.

The problem of special population pressures in India is comparatively recent.[1] One factor was high rates of infant mortality. Carr-Saunders in *World Population* points to three other factors. One was maternal mortality: the census of 1931 showed that the average Indian mother had four children born alive and slightly less than three survive; the partial explanation is that many mothers died before reaching the end of the reproductive period. A second factor was child marriages, with 181 per thousand married 'women' under the age of fifteen in 1931. Carr-Saunders points out that intercourse shortly after puberty is 'inimical both to health and fecundity'. The third factor was the Hindu ban on the remarriage of widows. The health programs have since reduced infant and maternal mortality and the reform spirit of modern India has reduced the number of child marriages and relaxed the prohibition on remarriage. Another antifertility factor was the various and numerous

[1] 'Prior to 1921 the growth of population and cultivation were nearly in balance. Population increase was fitful and slow, and increase in cultivation managed to keep pace with it. After 1921, however, population growth has been rapid and uninterrupted, while increase in cultivation, even where it has occurred, has been small and proportionately much less than the increase in population'—*Census of India*, 1951, Vol. I, Part IB, p. 1.

ritual restrictions on sexual intercourse. It seems probable that this factor, too, has been modified in the growth of secularism in the new India.

Thus both the natural and unintended religious and social restrictions on fertility have been reduced during the past generation, inexorably raising the question of other means to keep the birth rate in check. I say 'inexorably', though it is evident that Gandhi's opposition to birth control, apart from complete abstinence, considerably delayed a more realistic approach to the problem. Gandhi regarded contraception as morally equivalent to prostitution, and, as Father de Lestapis has recorded, told Mrs Sanger that he regarded periodic continence in the same category. But his successors have felt compelled to initiate birth-control measures, starting rather gingerly with the promotion of contraception in the First Five Year Plan, and stressing more energetically both contraception and sterilization in the Second. At the Third All India Conference on Family Planning in January 1957, a government spokesman declared the intention to equip 2,000 rural planned parenthood clinics. The desperate character of the situation is indicated by the fact that in at least one state bounties are now offered to parents who undertake sterilization after the third or fourth child.

While the statement that 'all the great Hindu social reformers' in recent years have been in favour of family limitation may give too optimistic a picture, it seems true that Hinduism presents no sharply defined doctrinal obstacle to curbs on parenthood. The fundamental doctrine is on a different level. Moreover, Indian opinion is moving toward support of family limitation. A poll in several communities in the states of Mysore and Uttar Pradesh indicated that from 60 to 78 per cent of the parents expressed the desire to limit progeny. Yet this does not mean that the cultural obstacles, partly rooted in religious belief and custom, are no longer formidable. Nor does it mean, especially in view of the lack of suitable and readily available methods of contraception, that social inertia is not still a major obstacle to India's most critical problem.

BUDDHISM

Buddhism like Hinduism . . . appears rather 'passive' in regard to efforts to control fertility. 'Passive' seems particularly appropriate for the faith that counts from 300 to 350 million Asians, for Buddhism appears to have very little doctrine of parenthood in the sense used in this review. The whole point of view seems calculated to discourage fertility.

A central tenet of Buddhist doctrine is that the origin of suffering is desire. In his final words under the *sala* tree, the Buddha said:

> Consider your body; think of its impurity; how can you indulge its cravings as you see that both its pain and its delight are alike causes of suffering? . . . You must break the bonds of worldly passions and get rid of them as you would a viper.

Buddhist literature abounds with references to renunciation of earthly love for the free mind and spirit. A man, for example, sees his fair wife approaching, his son upon her arm; but he sees in her 'a subtle snare'—such bonds have lost their hold, because his mind is free.[1] Passions accumulate the *karma* or just reward of further troubles in later reincarnations. This asceticism applies to love of children as well. In the tale of Prince Wessantara, whose vow of self-abnegation is tested, the Prince gives his children away 'that I may have perfect insight', whereupon legions of gods exclaim: 'Wondrous is he whose mind is unshaken even at the loss of both his children!' The hierarchy of values is indicated in this teaching, the last point bringing us back to the primacy of individual salvation:

> One should forget himself for the sake of his family;
> one should forget his family for the sake of his village;
> one should forget his village for the sake of his country;
> one should forget all the world for the sake of enlightenment.

Under Buddhism, the married man is definitely a second-class citizen, tied down by worldly desires and cares, who may ultimately achieve enlightenment—by leaving his family to become a 'homeless brother'. In the meantime, he should learn to live with wife and child in harmony, train and provide for his children, and follow the rules of detachment so far as possible. The family should work as 'busy as bees' —partly to support the 'homeless brother', the ascetic beside whom the benedict is a 'common man'. In all this there is precious little sanction either for marital relations and procreation or against family limitation. Parenthood seems to begin after the children are born.

There is in Buddhism a strong compassion for all sentient life, one of the points in the 'noble eightfold path' being to harm no living creature. This presumably constitutes a ban on abortion as well as

---

[1] K. J. Saunders (ed.), *The Heart of Buddhism*, Association, Calcutta, 1915, p. 43. This works both ways: another verse describes how a wife is a 'liberated bride', freed from mortar, butter churn, and 'crooked hunch-back lord', and now 'freedom from birth and death's assured' (ibid.). There is considerable sexual equality in Buddhism.

infanticide.[1] ... Thus far I have found no evidence that the 'seed' is regarded as a living creature, and the legislative situation in predominantly Buddhist countries, mentioned below, supports the view that it is not so regarded.

From the point of view of actual practice, it appears that Buddhist belief gives a certain spiritual tone to the culture of its adherents, rather than any kind of detailed ethical system. Referring to the Buddhist ideal of compassion and awareness of common creaturehood, Professor Philip Ashby of Princeton wrote in an unpublished paper:

> While it cannot be denied that the precepts did succeed to some degree in furthering this ideal, yet the moral patterns which predominate among the masses of the people in Buddhist areas are more to be identified with the indigenous pre-Buddhist cultures and general custom morality of the specific area than with a system of ethics or morals which are peculiarly Buddhist.

ISLAM

The followers of Mohammed, who constitute the largest religious group in the underdeveloped world, with a total of 350 to 400 million persons, form an obviously key sector not only in Asia but also in northern Africa. Two of the gravest population problems are found in Egypt and Indonesia, or, more accurately, Java. The Population Reference Bureau estimated in 1958, on the basis of admittedly inadequate statistics, that the population of the Middle East was growing at the rate of 2.5 to 3 per cent a year, a rate of growth exceeded only by that of tropical South America. While the Muslim world is not growing proportionately as rapidly as it did in those astounding decades of the seventh century, it is no doubt growing more rapidly today in terms of numbers. The cradle is proving more potent than the sword.

Islam has important roots in the Old Testament, but in regard to parenthood, they grow chiefly in the soil of patriarchal history. In contrast with the unrestricted marital opportunities for Arab males in his time, Mohammed limited his masculine followers to four wives at a time, an austerity tempered by permission to supplement the quota with such slaves as they could afford. Also wives that did not suit could be replaced at the cost of the *mahr* or marriage settlement.

---

[1] Thomas Burch, however, states that, in regard to Japan, 'neither Shinto nor Buddhism, the two largest creeds in Japan, categorically oppose abortion'. Thomas K. Burch, 'Induced Abortion in Japan', *Eugenics Quarterly*, Vol. 2, No. 3, September 1955.

'Consecutive polygamy' consequently has been a common pattern.[1] One of the conveniences of the Mohammedan heaven is that a righteous man may have his favourite wives with him, or opt for the 'large-eyed maidens' if he did not fare too well on earth.

Actually, this is not the full picture. Mohammed recognized some reciprocal marriage rights and urged men to 'admonish your wives with kindness, because women were created from the crooked bone of the side'. He tolerated rather than approved divorce: 'the thing which is lawful but is disliked by God is divorce'. Also, impartial treatment of wives was a moral obligation: 'When a man has two wives and does not treat them equally he will come on the day of resurrection with half of his body fallen off'. Contemporary Muslim reformers argue from this that the Prophet was basically opposed to polygamy, since it is obviously impossible for a man to treat two wives equally.[2]

In regard to parenthood, the ethos of Islam might be generally described as procreation unlimited. The Koran echoes Genesis 1:28 in the injunction, 'marry and generate', and 'marry a woman who holds her husband extremely dear, and who is richly fruitful'. The description of family conditions in Egypt appended to the Warren Report, *The Family in Contemporary Society* indicates some additional pro-fertility factors that operate and have operated in the past in other Muslim countries as well as in Egypt. Children are employed on the land at an early age, and hence are economically useful. Muslim (as well as Christian) opinion attaches high prestige to the parents of large families. Further encouragement to the large family is given by the Muslim law of inheritance.

With the explosive population pressures of the past decades, Islamic scholars have been making a fresh search of their traditions to find clues favourable to a doctrine of voluntary family limitation. They find a reference by a companion of the Prophet to the need to watch out for too many children; they are difficult to raise. Another reference suggests that birth control may be permitted when a woman is too feeble, a man too poor, or a woman fears the loss of her beauty. Such

[1] 'It has probably always been true that by far the largest part of Muslim men have had but one wife at a time.' George Foot Moore, *History of Religions*, Scribner's, New York, 1932, II, p. 492.
[2] In one place the Koran appears to regard monogamy as a means to family limitation. If a man fears he may not be fair, he is to take one wife—not counting slaves—'that is more likely to secure that ye be not over-burdened with children' (4:3). This phrase is an alternate reading for 'that ye be not partial'. *The Qur'an*, trans. by Richard Bell, Clark, Edinburgh, 1939.

arguments are supplemented by demographic and nationalistic reasons. In March 1953, the Fatwa Committee of Azhar University in Cairo, an influential group of scholars on Muslim 'canon law', stated in response to a query:

> The use of medicine to prevent pregnancy temporarily is not forbidden by religion, especially if repeated pregnancies weaken the woman due to insufficient intervals for her to rest and regain her health. The Koran says, 'Allah desireth for you ease; He desireth not hardship for you' (2/185); 'And hath not laid upon you in religion any hardship' (22/78). But the use of medicine to prevent pregnancy absolutely and permanently is forbidden by religion.

This statement indicates, I think, that there is little specific sanction for contraception in the tradition of Islam, and also that the contemporary leaders are determined not to let that fact impede the current efforts for voluntary family planning. The Minister of Social Services in Egypt spoke of birth control as a social necessity. The Minister of Food and Agriculture in Pakistan said: 'The senseless race between increase of food and increase of population must not continue any longer'. The governments of both countries have established a number of family-planning clinics. Despite the pro-fertility elements in Islamic culture, the leaders of some Muslim countries, at least, do not find serious doctrinal obstacles in the way of a necessary population policy.

JUDAISM

The pro-fertility orientation of the Old Testament is continued in Judaism. 'Be fruitful and multiply' is the first of the 613 *Mitzvoth*—precepts or commandments. ... The *Jewish Encyclopedia*, however, indicates that as Judaism became urbanized the injunction regarding procreation was modified. Two children might meet the requirements of the *mitzvah*. Rabbi Kertzer gives a summary formula: 'According to Jewish law, every man and wife have a solemn obligation to bring at least two children into the world'.

On the obligation to marry and procreate, Judaism is agreed. Celibacy, says Rabbi Hertz, is 'contrary to nature'. The differences come in regard to limiting the size of families, the Orthodox tending to restrict severely both the reasons and the means, the Reformed and Conservative taking a less strict position. There is also considerable variety of interpretation among the Talmudic teachers. ...

The composite picture is one of a tradition which permits, if it does not encourage, certain measures of family limitation at least after the second child. From the Orthodox viewpoint, according to Willy Hofmann, 'Jewish tradition and viewpoint cannot consider planned parenthood for social or economic reasons'. The Conservative and Reformed Rabbis do consider such reasons. The resolutions of 1929 and 1930 of the Central Conference of American Rabbis, the Reformed group in the United States, 'urge the recognition of the importance of the control of parenthood as one of the methods of coping with social problems', and support 'intelligent birth regulation'. 'We are aware', said the Conference, 'of the many serious evils caused by the lack of birth control'. The Rabbinical Assembly, the Conservative body in the United States, stated in 1935:

> Careful study and observation have convinced us that birth control is a valuable method for overcoming some of the obstacles that prevent the proper functioning of the family under present conditions. . . . Proper education in contraception and birth control will not destroy, but rather enhance, the spiritual values inherent in the family and will make for the advancement of human happiness and welfare.

It should be added that the practice of the Jewish laity has outstripped the debate among the Rabbis. As Moses Jung has stated in *Judaism in a Changing World* (ed. Leo Jung), 'the practice of birth control seems to have become almost universal among the Jews'. This is borne out by census statistics, indicating the low birth rate of Jewish groups in Western countries. One is reminded of the fact that polygamy was not finally outlawed until the eleventh century although monogamy, favoured in the oral tradition, had established itself as the norm much earlier.

We find in Judaism, despite the legalism which has played such a large part in Jewish thought, the continuing ferment produced by the leaven of the 'one flesh' concept. 'Named "covenant" in the Bible', writes Professor Jung in the symposium cited, 'marriage became in the Talmud *"kiddushin"*, sanctification—the hallowing of two human beings to life's noblest purpose.' A similar concept is expressed by Sidney Goldstein in *The Meaning of Marriage and Foundations of the Family*: 'The sanctity of marriage does not depend upon conception or contraception but upon the spirit of consecration with which men and women enter the marriage bond'. A good conclusion is provided by Rabbi Eugene Mihaly in *Marriage and Family Life* (ed. A. B. Shoulson):

Procreation is undoubtedly a fulfillment in marriage, but the love and companionship is no less a primary purpose. Eve was created to be a 'helpmate' to Adam since 'it is not good for man to be alone' and only later were they commanded 'to be fruitful and multiply'.

FAMILY PLANNING IN COLOMBIA: A CASE STUDY*

Clyde Sanger

The following extract from Clyde Sanger's book *Half a Loaf* illustrates some of the problems of birth control and family planning as they exist in the South American country of Colombia. Faced with rapid population growth, both government and privately sponsored efforts in promoting birth control have encountered a vast array of difficulties in which politics, economics, and religion are all involved. The second part of the article deals with the question of international aid for family planning and briefly examines such questions as How much? By whom? and Why so little?

[1969]

There was every reason for Lleras Restrepo[1] to have campaigned in favour of birth-control programs in 1966. The results of the July 1964 census had recently been published, showing a terrifying population explosion. Since the previous census thirteen years earlier, the population had leapt up by almost six million youngsters to 17,482,000. As many babies were being born—and were surviving through infancy—as in France, a Catholic country with three times Colombia's total population. There were predictions that by the end of the century Colombia's numbers could swell to seventy million people.

And the balance had tipped heavily towards the cities. For in 1951 about 60 per cent of all Colombians still lived in the countryside, while by 1964 there was nearly that proportion crowding into the towns, filling the hillside *barrios* and creating new slum suburbs. All sorts of strains were obvious. A drastic shortage of urban housing, and of drinking-water amenities. Nearly half a million children without hope of finding places in a primary school—and anyway only one-quarter of the primary teachers had professional training. Finally, because such a large proportion of the population was under fifteen, each Colombian of productive age was having to support on average three other people. It was a melancholy picture, especially since Colombia is far from the

*Reprinted from *Half a Loaf* by Clyde Sanger (The Ryerson Press), by permission of McGraw-Hill Company of Canada Limited.
[1] Carlos Lleras Restrepo was elected President of Colombia in 1966. (ed.)

poorest of Latin American countries, and in several respects is among the most progressive. When the census was published, one Bogota newspaper editor wrote, 'Our long nightmare has now become reality'. And the Conservative president of the day, Guillermo Leon Valencia, worried particularly about the influx into the cities. 'Our population is now dangerously maldistributed, and efforts should be made to get people to return to the countryside.'

That was the presidential solution of the day: get people back to the land, return to olden-time standards and perhaps some of the problems of today will disappear. It has been no more successful in Colombia than in other industrializing countries. INCORA, the government land reform institute, set out manfully on a program of purchase or expropriation much larger than the British began in the 'White Highlands' of Kenya. With an annual budget of twenty-five million dollars, INCORA started taking over five million acres and giving the land to thousands of campesino families. But a survey by the institute showed that the land of Colombia couldn't support more than one million families, and there were already eight hundred thousand extra families trying to subsist in the countryside; a figure that would be doubled in ten years if families didn't move to the towns—or if there wasn't a vigorous family-planning campaign. I remember how in 1965 the INCORA director, Dr Peñalosa (who is now Agriculture Minister), surveyed some of the institute's achievements for my benefit and then added: 'But they're all marginal. The main solution to our problem is birth control.'

The solutions which ordinary Colombian women were finding to their problems were pathetic: abandonment of their children, abortion, even murder. For the richer and better educated it was easy, as by then about 150,000 women were taking the pill. It was easy, too, for the men—who simply wandered away from their growing responsibilities and set up another establishment elsewhere. But the poorer mothers found themselves acting against all traditional behaviour, for Colombian women are well known for the care they will take of children, the way they will see them adequately fed even if it means starving themselves. A few statistics reveal the desperation of the poorer women. One-third of the twenty-five thousand cases admitted annually to the San Juan de Dios maternity hospital in Bogota are the sequel to botched abortions, while at the University Hospital in Cali one woman in every twelve who dies between the ages of fifteen and thirty-four is the victim of a septic abortion. A 'special rehabilitation commission' in 1959 estimated that there were thirty thousand children abandoned in Bogota and four times that figure in the surrounding department. As for child-murder, homicide ranks unusually high (eighth) among the causes of death in the five-to-fourteen age-group; and, beyond such clear cases, doctors will explain to you how many suspicious times they have known a mother bring to them a child in its final stage of sickness when no treatment could save it.

Not surprisingly, the initiative for a family-planning program came from a few doctors who had had these insights into the misery of so many Colombians.

The initiative has had two main thrusts. The Association of Medical Faculties (ASCOFAM) has concentrated on research, on educational booklets, and on training doctors in family planning. The Association began as a body to help standardize training and check the titles of those setting up medical practice; but it created a Population Division when some leading doctors realized the size of the social problem. The other thrust has come from a group of privately financed doctors who are concerned with the most immediate form of action. La Asociacion Pro-Bienestar de la Familia Colombiana (ProFamilia) began with a single clinic in the office of Dr Francisco Tamayo, a Bogota obstetrician who could count many of the capital's wealthiest women among his patients. By 1969 ProFamilia was running on a budget of nine hundred thousand dollars, mainly provided by the International Planned Parenthood Federation (IPPF). The previous year, with thirty-five doctors working part-time in sixteen urban clinics, ProFamilia helped eighty-one thousand Colombian women with advice and contraceptives.

[Despite the seriousness of the situation] the ASCOFAM educational teams found it hard to get a campaign moving. It was even difficult to convince obstetricians that they would not be out of a job if the campaign succeeded. As for the doctors who staffed the 370 government health centres, few of them had ever had any training in contraceptive methods, for these were not taught in medical schools until a few years ago. Through ASCOFAM some twelve hundred doctors were given short courses, on government funds, in family planning. So were social workers and nurses, and even policemen. But a lot of this training failed to produce early returns in terms of an active campaign through a network of rural clinics.

Dr Martin now thinks a mistake was made by paying too little heed to male attitudes in the early days. The discovery that his wife had been to a clinic and been fitted with an IUD offended a man's sense of *machismo*. She tells of a man, father of six children already, who came to her office holding a pistol and threatening the life of a Pro-Familia doctor; it took her two hours to mollify and educate him. After that, she began a round of talks to factory groups in Bogota. With feminine flattery she played on the fact that they were *machos*, the masters in their houses, and presumably wanted to have children of which they could be proud, so why have so many? Dr Gonzalo Echeverry, the director of ProFamilia, thinks male attitudes are important, but not the key factor in a campaign's success. The difficulty is to get to them as a group, for few would return to a factory for a meeting held after working hours. But he admits there has been male opposition strong enough to bring about the closing of one of their clinics, at Santa Marta, twice after experimental periods. In the coastal areas, where Colombia's more Negro population is concerned to show the most visible proof of masculinity, the ProFamilia campaign has yet to win ground.

Statistics are notoriously suspect in Colombia, but there seem to be reasons for cheering a recent trend. Official government figures suggest the birth rate has been reduced from 40.14 to 34.79 per thousand during the ten years to 1967, and by far the larger drop—of 3.8 per thousand —took place during the years after 1963. Several reasons are behind this change, Dr Echeverry thinks, besides the ProFamilia campaign: publicity about the whole controversy on birth control has helped, abortions have increased but, perhaps most important, education levels are being raised.

Yet even with this decline in the birth rate, the absolute number of babies born in 1967 was about a hundred thousand more than in 1957. Colombia had only just begun to tackle its population problem when Pope Paul announced on 29 July 1968 that

> . . . it is an error to think that a conjugal act which is deliberately made infecund and so is intrinsically dishonest could be made honest and right by the ensemble of a fecund conjugal life.

The encyclical launched a period in Colombia in which it was hard for the leaders, in public statements as much as in private acts, not to be dishonest. But by mid-1969 it was clear they had done what was right.

By mid-1969 any momentum in family-planning programs that had been lost because of the encyclical and the Pope's visit, seemed to have been regained. The government had placated conservative groups in the Church and elsewhere with its laws against erring fathers,[1] and in April it turned round to sign an agreement with the Pan-American Health Organization for a large program through the maternal- and child-welfare clinics. The Colombia Government had to provide 40 per cent of the funds, which meant that it was back to its 1967 position of actively promoting birth control. It also agreed with the ProFamilia doctors to allow their teams into the maternity wards of the social security clinics; since the Bogota clinic has beds for sixteen hundred mothers, the opportunity of reaching a great number of women just after childbirth to offer them the means of spacing out future babies was most welcome to ProFamilia. Finally, a new program of teaching family planning to INCORA's social workers offered the Population Division a broad avenue by which to reach the campesino women.

For, in the end, success or failure of the family planning campaign will depend on the reaction in rural areas. Sophistication is spreading swiftly through the cities of Colombia. There are plenty of symbols to illustrate this change: the planetarium being built beside the bull-ring in Bogota; the girls with granny glasses or a Joan Baez hairstyle far outnumbering the ragged Indian women who hawk lottery tickets; the barrios themselves feeding off the central city like piglets off a sow, imbibing new ideas in the daily flow of people and goods. But take a country bus from Popayan over the Andes, and it is a different, older world. An exquisitely beautiful world of deep green valleys along the San José river, the little white colonial towns far below you looking like pools of some milky libation. In the bus a portrait of the Pope dangling like a benediction over the driver's head as he pulls round the steepest bends; a relay of passengers with great brimmed hats and gaucho moustaches or humorously curved Mayan-like noses. Young boys stride up the bus clutching heavy machetes. A girl begins her journey in a town called Hobo by devoutly crossing herself. To what extent in these parts is manliness, with all its ancient prerogatives, still the supreme standard? How unquestioning is religious devotion?

The rural health promoters from the Health Ministry, the INCORA social workers, are the teams which can reach the campesino women with a message in a way they will understand. The ProFamilia doctors admit their work is limited to the towns. There is a great deal more to

---

[1] In 1969 the president, with the very active collaboration of his wife Doña Cecilia de la Fuente, enacted a bill under the 'Responsible Parenthood' title that prescribed penalties for men who default on maintenance payments to their wives or the children they have sired. The law also requires for the first time that the father's name be put on every birth registration form. (ed.)

be done in the towns before the deadline the doctors have set themselves of August 1970 when, under the pact that established the National Front in 1958, a Conservative president must take over. The task is to make it so patently clear that Colombian women want a vigorous family-planning program that no Conservative administration, however pushed by elder churchmen, will attempt to cut off the funds and divert the personnel. ProFamilia has a target to reach of having established by then thirty-five clinics.

Although Colombia in 1969 was receiving two million dollars in international aid for family-planning projects, it was clearly only a tiny segment of the world picture. Even the whole of Latin America, with the prospect by 1980 of numbering three hundred and fifty million people (or eighty million more than all of North America), is only one awkward part of a massive problem. So many world population projections have been wide of the mark that any set of figures becomes suspect. But a distinguished American panel, headed by David Rockefeller of the Population Council and George Woods, the former World Bank president, put broad aims in May 1969 when it appealed to U Thant to help establish a vigorous UN program, with a powerful Population Commissioner and an annual fund of one hundred million dollars. This panel hoped that a world program could succeed in limiting the population in the year A.D. 2000 to about five billion people, instead of the seven billion there will be if the present rate of growth from today's figure of 3.5 billion is not checked.

Robert McNamara, in his speech to the World Bank board of governors in September 1968, put the 'terrifying statistics' of population growth and its 'crippling effect' on economic development in a succinct way. He pointed out that world population totaled only 250 million in the first century A.D., took 1650 years to add another quarter billion; it then added one billion in the next two hundred years, a second billion in the following century and a third billion in the next thirty years. 'It is now expected to add three more billion by the end of the century. By then, at present rates, it will be increasing by one billion each eight years.'

To show the crippling effect, McNamara cited two typical developing countries with similar standards of living and each with a birth rate of 40 per thousand—which he explained was the actual rate in India and Mexico. If one of those countries, he said, managed to halve its birth rate over a perior of twenty-five years (and a rate of 20 per thousand is still well above that in Europe) while the other remained static, the first country would raise its standard of living 40 per cent above the other country in a single generation. McNamara added: 'In terms of the gap between rich countries and poor, these studies show that more than anything else it is the population explosion which, by holding back the advancement of the poor, is blowing apart the rich and the poor and widening the already dangerous gap between them'.

What are the rich countries doing about it? What is the United Nations, the World Bank, and governments like those of Britain and Canada doing to help clear this largest obstacle to the economic advancement of most countries? The answer is: very little. Sweden is an exception, for it is now putting 12 per cent of its foreign aid to family planning. The government of Canada has done nothing at all so far, for it considered itself shackled until mid-1969 by the ancient provisions of the Criminal Code forbidding the domestic sale of contraceptives. As Maurice Strong[1] explained to the Commons standing committee on External Affairs in April 1969, 'It has not been government policy to do outside of Canada what it is not feasible to do in Canada'.

The United States Government is now doing a great deal. From small beginnings in 1965, when AID[2] spent only about two million dollars, American assistance has grown to a figure of eighty million dollars in 1969-70. In many countries where the government has no inhibitions about promoting family planning, the American aid goes directly to central funds. But in Catholic countries the aid is often channelled through private organizations, such as the IPPF, or a regional body such as the Pan-American Health Organization. As the Rockefeller-Woods panel pointed out in its brief to U Thant, assistance in family-planning programs is '. . . a delicate subject. Many governments would find it more desirable to work through the United Nations than bilaterally with the United States.'

The problem at the United Nations has been to win the votes of Catholic governments for policy decisions. For years the forty-five-nation executive board of UNICEF hesitated on the brink of approving some active participation in family planning, and the only help it gave was in supplying vehicles to medical teams in India and Pakistan; but just before the encyclical was issued the board took its courage up and declared outright support of such programs. A UN population

[1] Mr Strong was Head of the Canadian International Development Agency until late 1970, when he became United Nations Undersecretary-General with responsibility for Environmental Affairs. (ed.)
[2] Agency for International Development, Washington, D.C. (ed.)

division with a 1.5 million dollar fund, whose main contributors have been the U.S. and Scandinavia, has made a modest start by training a dozen demographic advisers to work with governments in programming. But the Rockefeller-Woods panel criticized the UN agencies as 'reluctant as a whole to make a more impressive commitment'; the argument about whose mandate covered this new work—whether UNICEF or the World Health Organization or FAO—they termed a 'classic delaying tactic' being used by reluctant men. Hence their plea for an autonomous new post of Population Commissioner, who would work directly with Paul Hoffman, the UN Development Program's co-administrator.

A few groups in Canada, who are not tied by the government's inhibitions, have ventured some paces into this field of aid. CUSO in India has had a few volunteers working with the Christian Medical Association of India's teams that tour hospitals and clinics to teach nurses and health assistants. Canadian doctors working abroad under several different sponsorships, such as COMA (Canadian Overseas Medical Association), have played a more direct part in the programs. In St Lucia the Manitobans have given strong support to the single active program on that Catholic island, and have provided Mr Louisy with a mobile cinema unit so that he can travel to, and educate, men as well as women in the remoter villages. And Oxfam of Canada has made a special decision to allocate around 15 per cent of its welfare and development funds (which could mean as much as two hundred thousand dollars a year) as grants to family-planning programs, and to put half of it to projects in the Caribbean and Latin America.

There is no doubt some programs are meeting with encouraging success. And success is usually linked with educational levels. Barbados, for example, can claim good school facilities; it has also achieved the lowest birth rate in the Caribbean and Latin America, having dropped from 26 per thousand in 1965 to 22 per thousand only 3 years later.

But there are obviously many problems ahead. The population explosion has occurred because better health services have drastically cut mortality rates. In Lord Ritchie-Calder's words, 'Let us be quite clear: there is not an orgy of procreation going on. Parents in the developing countries are not having more children. More children are surviving. . . . This is the picture I have seen all over the world—an avalanche of children smothering every effort at progress in the developing countries.' The infant mortality rate in many countries is clearly going to decline further, before it approaches the rate in industrialized countries: Jamaica, a comparatively advanced country, has a rate still 50 per cent higher than that of Canada. And this continued drop in deaths of course means the family planners have a rising population figure to contend with.

In Latin America and other Catholic countries some methods of birth control will remain officially taboo. While a main drive in the Indian campaign has been for male sterilization through vasectomy, this is unthinkable today in Colombia: ProFamilia workers shook heads vigorously when I mentioned it. And cheap, legal abortions, a system which has been so effective in Japan that its birth rate is now down to 9 per thousand (or half that of Canada), are also an unlikely innovation for Latin America.

India has its own massive problems in this sphere. After a huge campaign has run for years, its leaders can claim only that about 11 per cent of the couples of child-bearing age were using some effective form of contraception. The momentum behind the vasectomy drive, which was launched in 1967, is apparently faltering, to judge from figures in the progressive Maharashtra state. In any case, the compilation of statistics must be suspect in a country where rural records of births and deaths depend often on reports from illiterate village watchmen. The post-independence cut in deaths from such diseases as cholera, smallpox, and malaria has doubled the life expectancy of an Indian infant to more than fifty years. But this welcome human change has been a major developmental headache to the planners and politicians.

Now that the Criminal Code's provisions against the domestic sale of contraceptives have been amended, the least the Canadian government can do is to make up for lost time in giving international aid to family-planning programs. It should advertise widely the fact that the law has been altered, and that Canada is ready to receive requests. To the Commons committee Mr Strong declared Canada had never had 'any official requests' for such aid; he is no doubt right, but some countries (including Tunisia) have in the past made preliminary inquiries about aid and been firmly told about the Code's prohibitions. The initiative is now with Ottawa, to seek out these—and other—governments, and tell them Canada is actively interested in helping their programs. Mr Strong went some distance to acknowledging this obligation, when he told the MPs: 'We just cannot ignore the whole field of population growth and family planning if [we] are going to be seriously interested in the development field'.

It is equally important for Canada now to play an active role in gathering support for a large UN population program. It is clear that such a program is not vulnerable to the sort of objections or suspicions which can threaten a bilateral agreement: people in Peru are not going to say a UN program is a plot to keep their population small, their international standing inferior, while they might say something of the sort these days to Washington. With the Maldive Islands casting as weighty a vote in the General Assembly as the United States, there is no premium on being big there. A population program launched through the UN would focus clearly on development, and avoid any Big Brother associations which direct aid from the industrialized states can generate. Such a large new venture would require a formal vote of approval, after considerable debate, in either the Second or Human Rights Committee and then the plenary Assembly. Some African states, not yet feeling the weight of population, may waver and several Catholic governments may join in opposition during such a debate. The question still unanswered is whether Pope Paul through his encyclical has blocked this United Nations avenue to the progress of peoples.

3 | Solutions—Economic and Political

The overriding and long-term goal of all schemes to reduce population growth and bring about economic development must be to enable all peoples to achieve sufficient control over their immediate environment to obtain adequate housing, education, and health facilities, necessary goods and services, opportunities for recreation and leisure, and to offer every person a reasonable chance of following a particular vocation or pursuit in life. We must be concerned then, with improving the quality of life. Success in achieving this goal must be measured not in terms of how many people the earth can support but of the numbers that can lead healthy, productive, and happy lives.

The role of economic development in attaining these ends has already been stressed. Not only will such development cause living standards to rise; but experience has proven that it is also the most effective way of lowering birth rates. This is not to say that other measures of population control should be suspended until major economic advances have been achieved in the underdeveloped countries, but rather that the whole challenge of population control will be dealt with more effectively if ways and means can be found to improve the material well-being of the people.

The following articles consider the problems of economic development in the UDCs. What is being done and what can be done to promote economic growth in the UDCs to alleviate poverty and improve the quality of life for their peoples? Many different plans, goals, and recommendations are described in the following pages, but in general they include measures that involve the migration of peoples, speeding the pace of industrialization, increasing the production and availability of food, improving transportation, stimulating international co-operation and trade, and providing development grants and loans.

The world has always had 'have' and 'have-not' nations, but we are now faced with a number of relatively new considerations. First, as Harrison Brown points out in the following article, the tremendous economic gap between the 'haves' and the 'have-nots' is widening.

Second, the 'global village' or 'instant communication' aspect of civilization in the 1970s has made the deprived of the world more aware than ever before of the extent of their deprivation, giving rise to what has been described as 'the revolution of rising expectations'. Third, the first two factors tend to result in instability in the UDCs, with possibly dangerous political and military repercussions not only for the UDCs themselves but for all of mankind. We are in a race with time. If we are to maintain our own way of life, we must extend—very quickly—to other people and other countries the advantages we have won for ourselves.

THE WIDENING GAP*

Harrison Brown

[1967]

The United States Government has now been in the business of providing technical and economic assistance to a number of the poorer nations of the world for about twenty years. It seems likely that had we not become involved with assistance programs, certain countries would be worse off economically than they actually are. And the Agency for International Development points with pride to Taiwan as an example of a country in which our efforts have been so successful that it is no longer necessary for us to continue them. Yet when we look at the plight of the poorer countries today we find that from certain points of view they are worse off today than they were twenty years ago. In particular during the last ten years the situation has been deteriorating at an alarming rate.

Although the economies of both the richer and poorer countries have grown at about the same rate during the past decade—about 4 per cent per year, the economic well-being of the average individual in the poorer countries has not improved very much. The reason for this is the relative rates of population growth. Although rates of population growth in the richer countries have dropped to an average of about 1.1 per cent per year, those in the poorer countries have risen to an average of about 2.5 per cent per year and are still growing. Indeed, in some regions rates of population growth are approaching 4 per cent annually. Thus, while on the average the economic well-being of persons in the richer countries is improving at the rate of nearly 3 per cent per year, that of persons in the poorer countries improves at a rate of but 1.5 per cent per year—a rate too small to raise the hope of the

*From Harrison Brown, 'The Combustibility of Humans', *Saturday Review*, June 24, 1967. Copyright © 1967 Saturday Review, Inc. Reprinted by permission.

individual. The ratio of annual per-capita incomes in the richer countries to those in the poorer ones, which stands at about 15 to 1 today, is increasing at the rate of about 1.5 per cent annually, giving rise to what Patrick Blackett, the president of the Royal Society, calls 'the ever-widening gap'. . . .

Unfortunately, our knowledge of how to develop a poor country into a less-poor one is not very good. We can learn some basic lessons by examining the economic, social, and political histories of countries which have recently made the transition, such as the United States, the U.S.S.R., and Japan. We can learn more by examining success and failure in countries which are now attempting to transform themselves. From these experiences we know that large quantities of capital are required. There must be a resource base which can be utilized. There must be a transfer of technology enabling effective utilization of the resource base. There must be education, the development of technical and administrative skills, the evolution of technical, economic, and social 'problem-solving capacities' (i.e., local research and development capabilities). And ever-present is the question of social organizations—old ones must be changed and new ones must be created.

No one today knows enough about the development process to say just what the most effective 'mix' of these ingredients should be for a given country. But certain conclusions can be drawn.

First, a great deal of time is required for the transition. Thus far, at least, there is no such thing as 'instant development'. We must think in terms of many decades rather than of years.

Second, most of the poorer countries appear to have reached the point where they simply cannot, without help, extricate themselves from the vicious circle in which they now find themselves. Population growth rates have grown too high, per-capita food production has fallen too low, and the crushing problems of urbanization and industrialization have become too great. Certainly few, if any, of the poorer countries are in a position to develop by themselves at rates which are sufficiently rapid so that the economic and social well-being of the average individual improves visibly during his lifetime.

It seems clear that in the absence of truly substantial help from the outside, the poorer nations are headed squarely toward famine, pestilence, revolution, and bloodshed on a massive scale—with consequences for the rest of the world which are difficult to foresee. But in addition to being substantial the help must be sustained. And if it is to be effective it must be balanced. Thus far, development efforts in the world have not been large enough, nor have been sustained, nor have they been adequately balanced.

CAN INTERNATIONAL MIGRATION EASE POPULATION PRESSURES TODAY?*

W. S. Thompson and D. T. Lewis

[1965]

This question has been much mooted in recent years and deserves much more extended consideration than is possible here. Perhaps about 65 to 70 per cent of the people in the world today live in underdeveloped countries. In these countries the birth rates are high—averaging about 40 per 1,000 or higher—and in most of them death rates have already fallen substantially below what they were 15 to 20 years ago. As a consequence, most of these people are now increasing rapidly, from 1.5 to 3 per cent per year, averaging in the neighbourhood of 2 per cent per year, a rate which will double their numbers in about 35 years. Of this approximate 2 billion of people living in underdeveloped countries, about 1,200 to 1,300 million live in Asian countries where population is already dense and where there is little new land that can be tilled without costly reclamation. This is about eight times the population of Europe in 1800 (not including the U.S.S.R.). This 1,200 million to 1,300 million does not include the populations of Burma, Indonesia, the Philippines, Thailand, and other countries of Southeast Asia—total population a little over 200 million—because these countries still have considerable amounts of unused but tillable lands. Indonesia is especially favoured in this respect. It will be assumed that these peoples are not yet much interested in emigration, and it will also be assumed that the same holds for the peoples of Africa and Latin America at the present time.

The question in which we are most interested here may be phrased thus: Is it reasonable to expect that the population pressures building up in these densely settled but underdeveloped lands can be substantially relieved by emigration? This is another of those questions regarding the effects of migration to which no very satisfactory answer can be given. However, several aspects of this question can be usefully explored a little further.

1. In the first place, it is obvious that the unsettled tillable lands in the world today bear an entirely different ratio to the population that might want to emigrate to them than was the case in 1800 when European migration to the New World was already well established. The combined population of the Americas in 1800 is estimated at about 25 million. They now have a population about 16 times as large—400 million or more. Africa had an estimated population of 90 million in 1800 and now has over 250 million. Most of the countries of East, South, and Southeast Asia now have far larger populations than in 1800, and the population of Oceania, though not yet large, has grown to many times its size in 1800. Clearly, in 1960 there are vastly more people needing outlets and far fewer outlets open to them than in 1800.

2. From 1800 to about 1914 there was little restraint on European emigration by either the sending or receiving countries. But when Asiatics began to enter any of the predominantly European settlements in significant numbers, barriers were soon raised. Today, restrictions on international migration are in effect in most countries. None of the countries of Southeast Asia, including Indonesia, want Chinese immigrants, and it is reasonably certain that if Indians and Pakistanis started to migrate into them in appreciable numbers, they also would be barred. The days of relatively free immigration into all countries are past. Moreover, practically all authoritarian states permit little if any emigration or immigration.

3. Under the strong political nationalism prevailing in the world at present, any substantial migration from the densely settled countries of Asia would almost certainly depend upon the prior conquest of new territory by the country desiring to send out emigrants. Indonesia, which of all Asian countries has the largest area of thinly settled lands, will oppose to the limit of its ability any immigration of Chinese, Japanese, or Indians. The political obstacles to substantial international migration probably cannot be changed in the next few decades except by conquest.

4. In order to give somewhat more precision to our thinking about the feasibility of international migration as a means of relieving population pressures today, we may well ask some specific questions: (*a*) How many Chinese, or Indians, or Japanese, or Pakistanis would need to migrate each year in order to ease the pressures on the necessities of life for the populations remaining in these countries? (*b*) How could the lands needed by these emigrants be acquired? (*c*) How could this migration be financed and managed?

Although none of these questions can be answered with assurance, attention may be directed to a few pertinent facts. If we accept the figure of 583 million given by the Communist census of 1953 as the population of Mainland China and if the rate of growth is 2 per cent per year (the minimum figure claimed by China's leaders), by the middle of 1963 the population of Communist China would already have increased to about 710 million. If 10 million had emigrated each year since 1953 and if this had reduced the calculated 1963 figure for the mainland by the full amount of 100 million, it would still have left China a net gain of about 28 million in this 10-year period.

Moreover, the living conditions within Communist China are still so rigorous that any substantial improvement in the per-capita consumption of the necessities of life would almost certainly have decreased the death rate at an even faster pace than has yet been attained. Hence the rate of natural increase might very well have risen from the minimum figure used by the leaders of China—2 per cent per year— to 2.5 per cent, for there is as yet no evidence of any significant decline in the birth rate. Such a rate (2.5 per cent) is frequently used by the Communist leaders in recent years.

Assuming that improvements in living conditions resulted from this large emigration and that better health services raised the rate of natural increase to 2.5 per cent annually during the last 5 years of the 10-year period 1953 to 1963, we can estimate that the total increase within the boundaries of Mainland China during these 10 years, assuming a net emigration of 100 million, would be about 45 million. Certainly this smaller average annual increase, about 4.5 million per year, as compared with an average annual increase of 12 to 13 million with no emigration, should be favourable to a somewhat faster improvement in living conditions. But, of course, what would actually take place depends upon simultaneous and complementary changes in so many other factors affecting production and its distribution that one cannot assert with any confidence that an improvement would take place. Nevertheless, it seems reasonable to assume that such a vast emigration from Mainland China might at least be of substantial assistance in getting a more efficient economy started and thereby making possible some slight improvement in the living conditions of the mass of the people, if the cost of supporting such an emigration did not seriously interfere with the accumulation of capital for development at home.

But we should not forget that the other densely settled countries in

Asia mentioned above have a combined population almost as large as China and need any relief that might result from large-scale emigration just as badly as China. Elsewhere,[1] the senior author has discussed briefly some of the most outstanding problems, political, economic, and logistic, involved in the migration of 10 million people annually from all of these densely settled Asian countries as a group. He arrived at the conclusion from the political standpoint that 'no country in South and East Asia can start large-scale emigration without acquiring actual political control of the area to be colonized, and such control can be achieved only by conquest'.

In the second place, assuming that political control has been established over an area of sufficient size to make possible large-scale emigration for some years, we think it highly improbable that China (or any other country or group of underdeveloped countries) would have the economic means to undertake large-scale emigration at once. It is much more likely that it would take a decade or even two decades to establish a steady outflow large enough to assure the migration of even 3 or 4 million annually. Meanwhile, population would be accumulating at home about as at present, and the areas receiving such emigrants would be filling up at a surprising rate if the experience in European colonization during the eighteenth and nineteenth centuries is any guide as to what would happen in the Far East.

In the third place, the mere logistic problems involved in transferring 10 million persons any considerable distance overseas and supplying them with the necessities of life until they could become self-supporting are tremendous but probably would not be insuperable if the economic capacity of the home country were increasing at a very rapid rate—a far more rapid rate than any Western country ever achieved during its early decades of economic modernization.

By way of illustrating the magnitude of this logistics operation, we may give a few hypothetical figures. If this were an overseas operation, as it must be, and if each ship could carry 2,000 emigrants and their necessary household goods and agricultural equipment on each trip, and if this ship could make 12 round trips per year, it would require the services of about 425 ships making a total of over 5,000 round trips to do this job. This would mean the loading and unloading of approximately 14 ships every day of the year. In addition, vast quantities of materials would have to be transported each year for several

---

[1] Warren S. Thompson, *Population and Progress in the Far East*, The University of Chicago Press, Chicago, 1959, pp. 391-7.

years to establish temporary quarters for the arriving immigrants, to carry the machinery needed to build roads and prepare land for cultivation, and to build the villages needed by the new immigrants arriving daily—somewhat over 27,000 every day.

The organization required at each end of such an operation to carry it out successfully staggers the imagination both by its intricacy and its cost. Moreover, if only 10 million emigrants were moved annually from all of these densely settled Asian countries combined, this would constitute considerably less than one-half of their present annual increase. Quite aside from the practical impossibility of achieving such a large migration for a decade or two, the increase within these countries would thus still be such as to require a steady and very rapid economic development at home merely to keep up with population growth, to say nothing of making possible a modest improvement in food and other goods essential to decent living and in the services such as education and health. The broad conclusion regarding the effectiveness of migration in relieving the pressure of population in the more densely settled countries of Asia based on the best information now available can be summed up in the simple statement:

Emigration can do very little within the next three or four decades to relieve population pressure in these Asian countries, which now contain about 40 per cent of the population of the world and over 60 per cent of the population in all the underdeveloped countries.

INDUSTRIALIZATION—THE PANACEA?*

Alan B. Mountjoy

[1966]

The most noticeable effect of development which the underdeveloped lands can see in the wealthy lands is the mass of manufacturing industry from which the wealth, power, and poise of the developed world appears to emanate. Consequently it is not surprising that the introduction of manufacturing industry should be regarded uncritically as a panacea by many members of the have-not nations. Fortunately, major industrial and development schemes nowadays nearly all come under the close scrutiny of international experts, particularly if interna-

*From Alan B. Mountjoy, *Industrialization and Underdeveloped Countries*, Hutchinson University Library. Copyright © 1966, Hutchinson Publishing Group Ltd., London.•Reprinted by permission.

tional capital is sought for them, and this acts as a check on wilder promotions that might have little prospect of success. It should be made clear that the switching of a large mass of humanity to industrial pursuits is in itself no answer to the world's population problem. We have still not reached the state when we can synthesize food from inanimate matter in our factories, and new industrial populations still need to be fed. It is, of course, in the prospect of greater returns accruing from manufacturing industry making possible the purchase of food from food-surplus countries, as is done in much of northwest Europe, that the hopes of the poorer lands lie. It must be noticed, however, that this state of affairs does not occur overnight, and initially indigenous supplies of food need to be increased, if at all possible, to feed the growing urban-industrial population and thus preserve capital for re-investment rather than spend it on imported foodstuffs. It follows that developments in agriculture must not be neglected and should continue with industrial development, a situation frequently to be mentioned in the following chapters, although our prime concern is with industry.

OCCUPATIONAL STRUCTURES

As we have seen, it is possible to classify the cycle of population development into stages; in turn it is thought that the cycle of economic development is susceptible to a similar analysis and that stages of economic development may be discovered and classified. Foremost in this field is the work of W. W. Rostow, in whose view an economy moves from a traditional stage through a take-off period to sustained growth, maturity, and a stage of high mass-consumption.[1] Development implies changing emphases within an economy, and this is evidenced in the shifting distribution of labour among the major kinds of activity. Colin Clark in his book *The Conditions of Economic Progress* makes a now widely accepted simple division of production into primary, secondary, and tertiary groups.[2] The primary activities include farming, fishing, and forestry; secondary production includes mining, manufacturing, and public utilities such as gas and electricity production; and tertiary production includes all other activities, such as transport, distribution, public administration, entertainment, etc.

[1] W. W. Rostow, *The Stages of Economic Growth*, Cambridge University Press, 1960, pp. 4-16.
[2] C. Clark, *The Conditions of Economic Progress*, London, 1951, p. 401.

From the beginning of time primary activities have been basic to man's existence, and development signifies a movement whereby primary activities continue, but with increasing efficiency so that labour is released for other work involving more application of science, invention, and capital. Thus we shall expect the underdeveloped countries to have an overwhelming proportion of their working population engaged in agriculture with quite small proportions in secondary and tertiary occupations, while fully developed lands might show an opposite pattern. In fact, underdeveloped lands have around 60-70 per cent of their labour force engaged in primary production, whereas developed countries that have entered the stage of maturity generally have less than 25 per cent thus engaged.

Throughout the world agricultural incomes per head tend to be less than non-agricultural incomes. Sometimes, as in Australia, the differences are not great but, for example, in Indonesia non-agricultural income per head is five times higher than agricultural income. Such a discrepancy is a measure of underdevelopment and, given the opportunity, spurs labour away to other sectors of the economy. A developed economy gives a high per-capita income since it is associated with a more varied economic structure whereby science and capital play an increasing part, and agriculture, using a smaller proportion of the labour force, functions with higher efficiency.

These features are demonstrated in Table 18, where it will be seen that in the case of Britain only 4 per cent of our working population is engaged in primary activities, the lowest proportion for any country, whereas nearly half are engaged in secondary activities, the highest for any country. The special character of our mercantile economy is reflected here, but it should be remembered that the small agricultural labour force produces nearly half the food these crowded islands need. Agricultural efficiency is steadily improving; an increase of capital invested allows each farm worker to cultivate an increasing number of acres while a greater application of science raises productivity per acre. In 1957 one British farm worker produced enough food for twenty people, the Australian farm worker enough for thirty-two people, and the New Zealander for sixty-two people. The development of the United States may be interpreted from her changing occupational structure. The proportions for 1958 are quoted in Table 18, but in 1870 the three groups of activity claimed respectively 53 per cent, 23 per cent and 24 per cent of the labour force. During these eighty years the numbers of workers in the agricultural sector fell from a maximum of

Table 18
OCCUPATIONAL STRUCTURES OF SELECTED COUNTRIES 1958-62[1]

Country	Per cent of total active labour force		
	Primary activities	Secondary activities	Tertiary activities
United Kingdom	4	47	49
Belgium	8	44	48
France	22	38	40
Western Germany	16	46	38
Sweden	20	41	39
Switzerland	16	46	38
Italy	27	39	34
U.S.S.R.	41	32	27
U.S.A.	8	32	59
Brazil	58	17	25
Egypt	57	8	35
Algeria (European & Muslim)	72	12	16
Japan	29	30	41
India	70	10	20
Turkey	80	10	10
Australia	14	38	48
New Zealand	14	36	50

[1] The figures refer to the latest year available between 1958 and 1962.
SOURCE: *Yearbook of Labour Statistics*, International Labour Office, Geneva (various years).

11.6 to 6.7 million, but the volume of agricultural production increased two and a half times.

From a comparison of the more advanced and less advanced countries in the table it may be deduced that as the primary (mainly agricultural) proportion of the working population declines that engaged in secondary (manufacturing) production increases: a further indicator of economic growth. The demand for foodstuffs is relatively inelastic and as real incomes rise a lesser proportion of the increase is spent on food, thus stimulating the demand for manufactured goods and services. The reasons for the growing proportions engaged in tertiary activities are not always fully understood nor the reasons why, in the eyes of some, the higher the proportion thus engaged the further the stage of economic development. Tertiary activities include a wide range of occupations, some such as 'pop-singers' and 'beauticians' virtually unproductive in the strict economic sense and others such as dockers and truck drivers clearly vital to a modern economy. The most numerous members of this group are the shopkeepers and their assistants, then comes transport, public administration, domestic service, sport and entertainment. To claim that the greater the proportion of these strange bedfellows in an economy the more developed it is may seem odd, but it should be remembered that also in this group are clerks, accountants, directors, bankers, underwriters, teachers, inventors, and the professional classes who, by and large, smooth, direct, and control the economy.

THE DISABILITIES OF AGRICULTURE

The fact that throughout the world agriculture is reaching or entering the stage of decreasing returns whereas industry, in the main, goes on under conditions of increasing returns raises the question of the differences between the two activities, and in particular the disadvantages of agriculture *vis-à-vis* manufacturing industry. The fundamental disadvantage under which agriculture labours is that the farmer has virtually no control over the natural forces of the physical environment which he utilizes. His crops depend upon sunshine, water, air, and mineral salts and while locally farmers may irrigate or drain, add fertilizer or trace elements to their soils, by and large it is the environment that calls the tune. From this stem a number of other disadvantages, not least being that yields vary from year to year according to the ravages of weather, disease, and pests. Consequently farmers cannot foretell accurately the volume of their production each year. Further, production is generally slower than in manufacturing industry, requiring farmers to look ahead and estimate the character of the market at least a year in advance. Crops and animals take months to mature and slow down farmers' reactions to changes in demand, for once crops are in the ground and animals fattening most farmers prefer to reap their crops, shear their sheep, pick their cocoa beans and so on despite glut conditions and falling prices. These factors all help to account for the considerable price fluctuations, alternating with gluts and shortages, notable in primary production and of serious consequences to steady economic development in underdeveloped lands. The seasonal character of farming operations in many parts of the world may well impose uneconomic use of labour and certainly of machinery. Farming machinery is costly and is generally of a specialized character and may only be in use for a few weeks each year, a great contrast to most factory machinery which may be in almost continual operation.

For the relative inflexibility of agriculture there are a number of reasons, not all of them economic. In many parts of the world the traditional conservatism of the peasantry may present a formidable bulwark to progress, especially where the agricultural way of life has become intimately interwoven into the fabric of society, and where changes in agriculture might presage deep repercussions on social groupings and ways of life. This is exemplified in many parts of Africa where the white man's concept of the individual ownership of land has conflicted severely with the natives' concept of tribal ownership and use. Similarly the threat of far-reaching changes in their way of life reinforced peasant opposition to the Soviet and East European attempts at collectivization. Agriculture is also at some disadvantage when there is a preponderance of agrarian population, for the onset of decreasing returns comes more swiftly than with industry. Much of the poverty in many underdeveloped lands is attributable to this: pressure of population with no alternative employment forcing far too many into agriculture. Labour is applied beyond the point of decreasing returns with consequent inefficiency and low productivity per head.

A further serious drawback lies in the relative inelasticity of demand for agricultural products. The bulk of the products of agriculture are foodstuffs and, being vital to life, are already consumed in great quantities; consequently relatively little extra food is bought if prices fall. Equally, if incomes rise, a less than proportionate extra amount is spent on food: instead, the sale of manufactured goods is stimulated. This suggests that as the developed lands have become richer the primary producers selling them their agricultural produce have received a less than proportionate share in the increased wealth. From this it would seem that international trade in primary products does not really produce the equalizing tendencies often claimed for it, but tends to work in favour of the industrialized nations. Even the fruits of greater efficiency of production may not be passed on to the primary producers. Surplus rural populations offering a mass of unskilled labour at the lowest of wages all too often act as a disincentive to greater efficiency and resist innovation. However, where improvements take place and exports are produced more cheaply, the inelasticity of demand prevents the enlargement of the market, which might bring the response of greater productivity and employment, instead the advantages of the cheaper production accrue to the importing country. . . .

THE RELATIVE ADVANTAGES
OF MANUFACTURING INDUSTRY

On the other side of the coin, the advantages that manufacturing industry holds over primary production might be considered as distinct from the disadvantages of primary production. First it must be recognized that manufacturing industry is far more flexible in methods, competition, and output than agriculture. While decreasing returns may be expected in industry as in agriculture they are, in fact, usually postponed by continual improvements in techniques, by the frequent introduction of new inventions and improved machinery (far less typical in agriculture), and by increasing specialization and division of labour raising the efficiency and productivity of the labour force. The character and scale of operation are also more favourable: it is possible to control production much more closely than with farming, and supply—of a standard quality—can be trimmed more closely to demand, making for greater price stability.

It will be realized that the farmer may have to brief his labour force daily, their tasks depending on the weather, but in a factory it is possible to manage a far larger labour force because their activities are specialized and regular and generally entirely insulated from vagaries of weather. Consequently advantages of scale lie with manufacturing industry, which by its organization and specialism aims at mass production through increasing efficiency and the application of power. It is, of course, basically through the application of inanimate energy that manufacturing industry offers greater productivity per worker than agriculture, and the amount of power available to each worker is sometimes taken as an indicator of economic stature.

Another advantage to industry but disadvantage to the farmer lies in the proportion of operating costs to fixed costs. A very high proportion of farm costs are in fixed charges and, relatively, the cost of seed, labour, etc., is small. This is a further factor in explaining the sluggish response to adverse conditions, for contraction of a farmer's output in times of difficulty saves relatively less than contraction of a factory's output. In the factory a far higher proportion of costs is in raw materials, labour, and services, and these can be more readily cut down. It is the operation and interplay of such factors that help to account for the present state of affairs where so much of world agriculture operates under decreasing returns, whereas manufacturing industry yet shows increasing returns.

EFFECTS OF AGRARIAN OVERPOPULATION

In most development the two major goals are the provision of work for growing populations, and the raising of standards of living. The degree to which these aims may be realized seems to depend primarily on the demographic situation in each country. Countries with population problems are faced with the double task, those without such a problem have a much more straightforward path to raising standards of living. It is, of course, possible to envisage populations (e.g. in the British West Indies) too heavy for their agricultural resources but insufficient to sustain large scale industrial development. As has been discussed, the capacity to support population depends upon the character of the economy: an industrial economy can carry a higher population before the onset of diminishing returns than an agricultural one. If population increases over the years and the economy stagnates—possibly as a result of restricted ownership of land or social conditions where equal division of property between the heirs (as in some Muslim countries) leads to a state of chronic and uneconomic fragmentation—then a situation may well be reached when a country's agricultural output will not increase with a further increase of agricultural population. This state of affairs indicates an extreme form of overpopulation, a stage beyond that occurring with the onset of diminishing returns (where increase of population brings a less than proportionate increase of production). Not many countries have reached the extreme state, although a number are generally considered to be on the brink, among them Java, Egypt, and Barbados.

Overpopulation, then, should always be thought of as relative to a country's economy. As we have seen, not all underdeveloped agricultural lands are overpopulated although many in Asia are, to which may be added Egypt and the British West Indies. In many underdeveloped lands the poverty of the masses may be related sometimes to land tenure systems whereby there is an institutional monopoly of land and therefore of capital (as in many states of Latin America), sometimes to poor farming reinforced by social and religious taboos exhausting the soil (as in India), sometimes to naturally poor soils, leached or waterlogged, where the application of considerable capital for irrigation or drainage is necessary in order to raise yields. There is, in fact, a wide range of immediate causes of poverty and underdevelopment. It is in the heavily populated underdeveloped lands that prevailing conditions constitute the greatest spur to development since they build up to increasing unrest, or even anarchy or revolution.

It must not be thought that in overpopulated agrarian countries there are necessarily vast masses of unemployed. The onset of overpopulation is slow and insidious and demonstrates itself rather by growing poverty and increasing under-employment. Excessive numbers are to be found in domestic service, casual employment, and agriculture; one notices a proliferation of newsvendors, boot-blacks, porters, and petty traders—all doing little business and earning barely enough for subsistence. Similarly in agriculture more and more labour finds employment on the land until the marginal productivity of labour is zero, or even negative. This situation may well lead to a loss of soil fertility by the reduction of fallow periods, lack of manuring, and over-cropping. This results in falling output per acre and not merely falling output per head. The term 'disguised unemployment' is sometimes used to describe an element of the working population that can be regarded as surplus in the sense that if it was removed from the land the volume of production would not fall. It is in this context that the massive population of Southeast Asia, with 70-80 per cent of the workers toiling on the land, should be viewed. . . .

The demographic element has further important effects of both geographical and economic significance. As population pressure mounts so do farming character and technique respond. As more and more labour becomes applied, so more labour-intensive methods become adopted (e.g. removing spade-excavated earth from new canals in Egypt by baskets on camels and in India by human porterage) and more labour-intensive crops become grown. Quality and variety of crops are sacrificed to quantity: where subsistence farming predominates the most labour-demanding and highest food-yielding plants oust all others and virtual monoculture appears, as in the case of rice in the delta lands of Southeast Asia. On large properties where commercial crops are grown, cotton becomes favoured as one of the most labour-intensive of the industrial crops; it is also liked by absentee 'gentlemen farmers' because an impoverished peasantry cannot eat it. In short, it is true to say that farming and tenure systems mould themselves to growing populations, absorbing more and more labour but under in-creasingly unfavourable conditions as the law of diminishing returns comes into play.

This chain of human misery is incomplete without recognition of the additional and concomitant social consequences. Under such condi-tions the power and wealth of the landowning classes expand while the mass of the peasantry grows poorer, creating in these agrarian societies a deep gulf between the governing class and the bulk of the population, for a middle or professional and commercial class is too small to span the gap. Money becomes concentrated into the hands of a very few while the mass of the population lives at a level of poverty not readily comprehended in the West. This means that there is virtually no saving and thus a very low rate of capital accumulation and re-investment. To the wealthy, land is the principal source of wealth and has first claim on further investment, otherwise much tends to be spent on ostentatious living.

We now see that a root cause of the abysmal conditions of the mass of the peasantry in many lands is the excess of hands at work and mouths to be fed—the 'surplus' element in the agrarian population which also provides a disincentive to agricultural improvement. This situation is characteristic of many countries extending from south-eastern Europe through Southeast Asia to China and is also found in the Caribbean area. It is not common in Africa and South America but is probably beginning in parts of Central America. Obviously it is not possible to estimate closely the proportion of the surplus element in these populations. Estimates in the 1930s for some southeast European countries were as high as 25-30 per cent of the agricultural labour force, the proportion in Egypt is probably rather higher, while for India an estimate of at least a quarter has been made (representing 25-30 million people). By their presence these millions drag down the general level of living and, in the sense that if their labour were removed the volume of production would not suffer, they contribute nothing to productivity. The magnitude of the problem is becoming greatly increased with the impact of the medical revolution leading to improvements in the health of the peasantry.

As these conditions move from bad to worse unrest frequently increases. Landowners tend to become more obstinate and reactionary in their resistance to change. Reforms often wait upon crisis and even anarchy (southern Italy, 1950); upon political revolution (Mexico, Egypt); or follow the upheavals of war (Bulgaria, 1880; Yugoslavia, 1918 and 1945). The redistribution of land at the expense of the great landlords is an early reform and under certain conditions can have a number of beneficial effects. However, the main problem of too many people on too little land remains, no matter how the ownership is juggled with, and acts as the most powerful incentive to an introduction or expansion of an industrial sector in the economy.

Thus the most weighty factor in the movement for development lies in the abysmal and worsening conditions that can occur under a combination of primary production, population pressure, and mal-distributed land ownership and tenure. The theory of greater returns and higher living standards from manufacturing industry is easy to grasp and in practice even where industry is only in its infancy begins to make itself felt. For example, whereas the annual income of the Egyptian fellah was estimated at £E8 in 1944 the annual income of the Egyptian industrial worker was around £E50, while in India in 1931 the income per head in industry was estimated at five times the income per head in agriculture. These comparisons may not be pressed too far, for it is not easy to be precise in valuing the self-sufficient element of the farmer, while industrial workers generally live under urban conditions where living costs are much higher.

THE SOCIAL AND DEMOGRAPHIC
EFFECTS OF INDUSTRIALIZATION

Particularly in its early stage, manufacturing industry is related to the urban centres where market, labour, and a range of public utilities are available. Some writers suggest that the ideal industrial development in underdeveloped countries should be one of dispersal among rural areas where so much surplus labour is available. This is very much of an idealized solution and for many reasons is not practicable, especially in early stages. Furthermore, such developments are less likely to capitalize a range of social opportunities and advantages that the development of urban communities makes possible. The agglomeration of people makes it easier and cheaper to provide social, educational, police, sanitary, and health facilities, as well as to install such services as piped water, main drainage, gas, and electricity. A far higher scale of creature comforts become possible and attainable than in the village. Imported goods in the shops give glimpses and knowledge both of a wider world and a high standard of attainment, and desires are raised that become the spur to betterment. Education and training are seen as the keys to better living, and these are more readily available in the towns. However, in the long run it is of transcendental importance that with education and increased standards of living the size of family will be reduced by a fall in birth rates, as has happened in the West.

It has already been stressed that the only real and ultimate solution to the world's population problem is a reduction of birth rates broadly commensurate with the fast-dropping death rate. Development to be completely successful should not only raise living standards and give more employment but should create conditions that eventually bring birth rates down; industrialization alone will not solve the economic problems of such countries as India, Java, China, and Egypt. Despite much study, the mechanism by which this has happened in the developed countries of Europe and their overseas offshoots can only be postulated in rather general terms. It is certain that industrialization in itself does not explain the reduction in the size of families, for whereas Britain certainly was industrialized the overseas Dominions were still heavily agricultural when their birth rates began to fall; moreover in their cases neither could the spur of population pressure be cited. Carr-Saunders [a noted demographer, see Bibliography] has pointed out that these countries and western Europe (and rather later eastern and southern Europe) shared a similar mode of life, food, clothes, social fashions and conventions. The practice of family limitation spread among these closely associated countries much as any new habits and novel ideas spread. In other words, attitudes gradually changed as a result of changing social and economic conditions, and not, for example, through any sudden new knowledge of birth-control methods.

Development, embracing urbanization and education, takes a large share in the establishment of the conditions for such changing of social conventions and attitudes. Pure water supplies, improved sanitation, and medical facilities in towns reduced the toll on young children and made it unnecessary for eight children to be born in order to rear four. Parents come to realize that the smaller the family the greater the opportunities they can offer their children and the easier their own passage up the social ladder. Much of this social evolution is closely bound up with the position of women. Towns offer women far more opportunities of education and emancipation than the village, and with a lifetime no longer devoted to producing and rearing numerous children employment outside the home becomes possible. All this takes time: two and possibly three generations in the developed lands. Whether the pattern will be both followed and speeded in the present underdeveloped lands are crucial questions. In that it represents social development fructifying from economic development we might regard it as logical and inevitable. Whether a speeding up is possible remains doubtful, for these tendencies evolve, they cannot be imposed. Religious and governmental sanction might do much to clear the path, as also the spread of education and the emergence of a middle class from a newly created or enlarged proletariat; the development of social and cultural standards cannot be accomplished overnight.

It is clear that a wide range of social and economic factors and emotions are involved in accounting for the fall in birth rate that seems to be an early attendant upon a developing urban way of life. One feature deserving of mention is that for a time in underdeveloped countries urban birth rates may appear higher than rural rates, but investigation shows that this is usually due to more complete registration. In rural areas the births of a substantial number of babies may never be registered. The more difficult question, to which it would not seem possible to give a definite answer, is whether, in fact, economic

Table 19

RATES OF BIRTHS, DEATHS AND NATURAL INCREASE FOR SELECTED COUNTRIES (AVERAGE 1960-4)

	Crude birth rate %	Crude death rate %	Natural increase %
United Kingdom	18.2	11.7	0.6
United States	22.5	9.4	1.2
Canada	25.3	7.7	1.8
Australia	21.9	8.8	1.3
New Zealand	25.9	9.0	1.7
Ceylon	35.0	8.5	2.7
China (1957)	34.0	11.0	2.3
India	40.0	17.8	2.3
Japan	17.2	7.8	0.9
British Guiana	43.7	8.9	3.5
Guatemala	48.7	17.1	3.2
Chile	34.9	12.3	2.3
Ghana (1956-60)	52.4	21.7	3.1

SOURCE: United Nations, *Demographic Yearbook, 1964.*

and social developments in the underdeveloped lands will elicit a similar demographic response to that during the past century in the Western world. It would be wrong to assume automatically that the same values will be set upon social position, upon the use of leisure, and upon women's emancipation. To our eyes many of the taboos (religious and social) of a number of Asian societies seem odd and anachronistic. In a similar manner it is possible that the response to development by these people may not follow the lines of the Western logic.

In this context attention must be paid to the post-war demographic situation in some of the wealthiest of the developed lands, all in the fourth (low fluctuating) stage of the population cycle. We find that the high immediate post-war birth rates have been maintained (Table 19). This is surprising and we may well consider whether the thesis of industrialization and urbanization damping down birth rates is really valid after all, although allowance must be made for net immigration into the United States, Canada, Australia, and New Zealand of people mainly young. It may yet be early to advance explanations, but one suspects that the population wheel is turning full circle in these countries. All of them have for some time been in the high mass-consumption stage of economic growth. Their populations have previously experienced the slowing down of growth as towns grew and their economies developed, but they are now enjoying the fruits of development: their living standards are higher than ever before and the mother's and housewife's tasks eased by mechanical aids, so that having a family need no longer mean drudgery and the complete sacrifice of leisure. To this change in the material situation may be added a changing attitude of mind. The day of the one and two children per family is passing: it is becoming fashionable to have more children. Other supporting arguments may be advanced; it is enough here to suggest that with growing prosperity in the developed lands their level of births in the fourth stage of the population cycle will become distinctly higher than when the stage was first entered. With economic development in many underdeveloped countries a reduction of rate of population increase to the 1.5 per cent of, say, New Zealand would offer little amelioration; rates of increase far below this must be reached. Japan, which has reduced its rate of natural increase in the last fifteen years from 1.8 per cent to 0.9 per cent, is the example here.

THE NEED FOR BALANCED DEVELOPMENT

It is not always appreciated that attempts to foster and expand manufacturing industry must be paralleled with development and expansion of the agricultural sector of the economy. There is no simple choice between developing either industry or agriculture; the two sectors are intimately related. Put at its simplest, the farmer should produce more in order to feed the growing population engaged in secondary and tertiary activities and he should be able to do this with a reducing labour force, for successful industrial development necessarily attracts labour from agriculture. This has been the pattern of development in Western countries and it is worth noting that the world's most efficient and productive farming is to be found in those countries, whether the criterion be output per acre or per man employed. However, in that the kind of farming tends to be wasteful of land (considerable emphasis on meat and milk and therefore 'two-stage' agriculture) the supporting power or carrying capacity per acre is exceeded by certain countries such as Japan and Egypt, with their double and treble cropping and emphasis upon 'one-stage' cereal crops.

If agriculture fails to provide food for growing industrial and urban populations, then much-needed capital will have to be spent on importing foodstuffs and development will be retarded. Conversely if agriculture can increase its production for export of primary raw materials, then more foreign exchange is available to aid development of the whole economy. It is of course easy to make such suggestions, but for a host of varied reasons (land tenure systems, surplus agricultural population, institutional monopoly of capital) far more difficult for them to be carried out. However, a more prosperous agricultural sector is also needed to provide a market for the products of the new industries. At the moment the poverty of agriculturists and therefore the smallness of the available market for manufactured goods is probably the greatest hindrance to development. Any enlargement of purchasing power of the peasantry should act as a stimulus to industrial development—one factor cited in favour of land reform.

Hence the successful launching of programs of industrialization depend upon improvements in agriculture, and the degree to which the improvements can be attained can either provide a curb or act as an incentive to the success of the new ventures. From this it follows that systematic improvement (and therefore investment) in agriculture must be a foremost task of the underdeveloped lands. The aim should be mutual self-support between these two sectors of the economy, whereby agriculture's surplus population may be siphoned off into industry as agriculture under the stimulus of greater demand becomes more efficient, and industry in turn raises the market for agricultural produce. This theory underlies planned development in Communist countries and is the basis of the Commonwealth's Colombo Plan. Agriculture is one of the major existing sources of wealth in underdeveloped lands; from it they must expect to obtain a substantial proportion of the capital needed for development. Thus profits from both the ownership and the working of land need to be made available for productive investment, not only to establish new industries but particularly to sustain and nourish them during the lengthy period when they are struggling to gather momentum.

THE GREEN REVOLUTION

Agricultural developments over the past few years have caused many experts to become optimistic about food production in the UDCs. While optimism is difficult to justify when you consider that famine and malnutrition exist in many parts of the world, there have been some encouraging advances. These have emerged as a result of what may be a new agricultural revolution—a series of events described by some observers as a 'green revolution'.

This had its beginnings after the Second World War with the development over a number of years, through the process of artificially induced mutations, of dozens of different plants, of which 'high-response' varieties of wheat and rice have been the most important.[1] They are referred to

---

[1] Dr Norman E. Borlaug, an American, was awarded the 1970 Nobel Prize for Peace for his work in developing new strains of wheat. Dr Borlaug carried out his work over the past twenty years in Mexico at the Rockefeller Foundation's International Wheat and Maize Improvement Center.

as 'high-response' varieties because they will give two or three times the yield of the old varieties, though only if provided with sufficient soil moisture, ample fertilizer, and protection by pesticides. For example, where the new wheat varieties have been planted in Mexico, yields per acre have more than quadrupled since 1950; and the introduction of new rice strains has made former rice-importing countries such as Japan and the Philippines virtually self-supporting. In India in 1968 the wheat crop was 35 per cent above the previous record, and that same year a wheat yield was recorded in Pakistan that was 37 per cent greater than any previous year. Largely as a result of these new grains, India's food supply is currently gaining at the rate of 4 per cent a year, with 5 per cent well within grasp. (Though this is impressive in terms of India's agricultural production, the population is increasing at the rate of 2.5 per cent per year.) Whether or not such improvements will be sufficient to solve the food crisis in the long run will almost certainly depend upon the extent by which the present rate of population growth can be reduced. Probably the most important contribution of the green revolution is that more time has been made available—perhaps an additional ten to fifteen years—in which to stabilize population growth.

While the new high-yielding crop varieties, together with the new farming practices they require, may bring great benefits to mankind, they have also spotlighted a whole second generation of problems. In the first place, to realize the full benefit of the new so-called miracle seeds, farm practices have to be revised; this entails a greater use of fertilizers, insecticides, machinery, electric power, and irrigation works, all of which are costly and difficult for the UDCs to manufacture. However, even if the production of such materials can be expanded sufficiently in the UDCs, the purchase of these goods is beyond the capability of the average farmer. This and other agricultural problems can be attributed in part to the fact that most farmers in the UDCs work very small landholdings that are often fragmented and inefficient. The consolidation and enlargement of these holdings is essential if the full effects of the green revolution are to be realized. This particular reform, however, means the reduction of the number of people living off agriculture. Its beneficial effects, then, must be weighed against the adverse consequences of adding to the already large surplus rural population. Today, millions of displaced rural people, who are culturally and vocationally unsuited to urban life, are being forced into cities and towns, where the economic base is insufficiently developed to provide them with employment.

The UDCs are further hampered by inadequate and outdated systems for the transportation, storage, and distribution of foodstuffs, and also by international trade practices that in many cases work against them. Not only is it difficult in some UDCs to move food within a country, but it is equally difficult—when, for instance, natural hazards (drought or flood) reduce a country's harvest and necessitate food imports—to move foodstuffs from a UDC with a surplus to another with a shortage. A further aspect of this problem will emerge if more UDCs begin producing exportable food surpluses, as some experts predict will soon be possible. In order for these countries to take advantage of surplus situations, they will have to overhaul radically their marketing and distribution systems and, more important, find new markets not only in the UDCs but in developed countries as well. In a world already burdened with agricultural surpluses, this may be very difficult, as Ester Boserup points out in her article 'Surpluses in the Third World—Who Wants Them?', beginning on p. 282.

There is yet another problem. The new grain varieties themselves have been developed very quickly—some think with insufficient testing— and as a result not enough is known, for example, about their resistance to disease and pests. As more and more land is planted with these grains, the risks and consequences of a widespread disaster in any crop year become greater. A related factor is the danger of serious environmental pollution as a result of substantially greater use of fertilizers and insecticides.

Finally, it has been said that the hungriest people in the world have also some of the most conservative tastes in food. Because the new grain varieties taste a little different from the ones they are replacing, considerable resistance to them has developed in some areas. While it is difficult to imagine, some people, even when they are hungry, will resist or reject foodstuffs that for one reason or another they find unappealing.

It is generally accepted by most authorities that the driving force behind any substantial improvement must be supplied largely through the efforts of the UDCs themselves. Nevertheless some of the problems associated with the green revolution, like most of those concerned with overpopulation and economic growth, must also be viewed as international ones. The DCs have accepted in principle, if not sufficiently in practice, the need to provide assistance to the UDCs in the form of food, raw materials, and financial and technological aid. It is especially important for the DCs to assist in the process of agricultural development in every way possible, particularly by adapting their trade regulations so that the UDCs can find markets for whatever surpluses they are capable of producing. Only in this way can the UDCs bring about substantial economic improvements by raising rural incomes and, through the accumulation of foreign exchange, finding the means to develop other sectors of their economies.

THE INDICATIVE WORLD PLAN FOR
AGRICULTURAL DEVELOPMENT—FAO*

United Nations

In 1963 the Food and Agriculture Organization (FAO) of the United Nations was asked by its member states to prepare a plan for agricultural and trade development, emphasizing the measures needed to reduce the imbalance between food and population that exists in the world. This plan, known as the Indicative World Plan for Agricultural Development, was submitted in 1969. The following is extracted from a pamphlet prepared by the FAO to summarize the principal findings of the study.

[1970]

Nearly seven out of every ten persons in developing countries depend directly upon agriculture for their living. In monetary terms, by industrialized countries' standards, it is not much of a living. At the bottom is the rural African with an average annual income of the equivalent of $43, followed closely by his Asian counterpart with the equivalent of $46. The rural Latin American is at the top with $138, while the man on the land in the Near East and northwest Africa averages an annual income of only $73.

Agriculture accounts for almost one-third of the developing countries' total domestic output of goods and services, or gross domestic product (GDP).

And for most developing countries agriculture provides 80 to 90 per cent of their exports. The figure is 40 per cent if the relatively few oil and mineral exporting countries in the group are included.

Since agriculture plays such an obviously prominent role in the Third World, it is surprising that its importance has been widely recognized only rather recently. Now, however, developing countries themselves, international development agencies like the United Nations Development Programme (UNDP) and the World Bank, and industrialized countries involved in helping the poor countries all agree that agriculture must provide the foundation for a healthy economy in the developing regions.

How can this be accomplished, given the primitive state of agriculture in much of the Third World and a projected expansion of its population by 1,000 million persons by 1985 compared with 1965? (This is exclusive of Mainland China which had a population estimated at

*From the Food and Agriculture Organization of the United Nations, *A Strategy for Plenty: The Indicative World Plan for Agricultural Development*, Rome, 1970.

between 700 and 800 million in 1965, while the population of the rest of the developing regions totalled 1,500 million.)

What are some of the dimensions of the challenge?

Providing the future food supply of developing countries, with population growing at 2.5 to 3 per cent a year, will continue to be the main role that agriculture must fill, in the view of the Indicative World Plan.

'Should this challenge not be met, it would almost certainly lead to grave crises in economic and human terms, with incalculable political consequences', IWP asserts.[1]

By 1985 the developing countries will require nearly 2.5 times as much food as they did in 1962*.[2] About two-thirds of this will result simply from the multiplication of mouths to be fed, while only about one-third will be due to higher individual purchasing power.

If the developing world continues to produce food at the rate it has in recent years, the amount produced and retained for consumption by 1985 would be 84 per cent above the 1962* level, but the projected demand would be 142 per cent higher. To fill the gap would require food imports in 1985 costing the low-income countries more than $40,000 million (at constant 1962 prices) compared with their outlay of somewhat more than $3,000 million in food imports in 1962*. But prospects of their being able to pay for the huge imports projected for 1985 in this hypothetical example are unrealistic. Unless there is a much more rapid rise in production of food retained for consumption in the developing countries, they will be faced not only with increasing dependence upon food imports from high-income countries but also with an upward pressure on prices and great hardship on people with low and medium incomes and much lower rates of economic growth than promised by IWP.

The challenge is not only to produce huge additional quantities of staple food to banish hunger. There must also be more and different kinds of protein-rich foods to reduce, if not eliminate, malnutrition. The problem is not only to cope with the demands of rapidly rising population but to adjust production to changing patterns in demand for food which come with rising incomes. This is illustrated by the prospective situation in Asia where demand for cereals for human consump-

---

[1] Unless otherwise indicated, all quotations are taken from the full *Provisional Indicative World Plan for Agricultural Development*, FAO, Rome, 1969.
[2] Where an asterisk is used beside 1962 it means the average of the three years 1961-3.

tion is expected to double by 1985. By contrast, demand for meat, fish, and eggs (taken as a group) is projected to increase by 250 per cent and that for milk by 230 per cent. The respective annual rates of increase in demand are 3.1 per cent for cereals and 5.6 per cent for meat, fish, and eggs. This shows the pressures toward a change in production patterns and is a continuing theme of the Plan.

It also shows that even rapid rates of agricultural growth may leave serious distortions in the economy if the pattern of production cannot be changed fast enough. In particular the feasibility of meeting projected demand for livestock products and fish, and the rates at which growth in these sectors can be accelerated in practice, already emerge as key issues of IWP.

A significant change already well under way in the developing world is the growth of urban centres which will create an ever growing market demand for agricultural products. This obviously cannot be met by the subsistence agriculture which characterizes much of the developing regions—where a large part of the food is consumed by the farmers who produce it.

The major factor in rapid growth in production for the market by 1985, according to IWP, will be the increase in the nonagricultural population. It is expected to grow by between 3.6 per cent and 4.9 per cent between 1962 and 1985, depending on the region. The nonagricultural population of all developing countries is estimated to increase over this period from 460 million to over 1,100 million. The real challenge on the production and distribution front, therefore, is to secure an increase of around 5 to 6 per cent a year in marketed farm output.

In most countries the domestic market is going to take over from the export market, which will in any case be weaker than in the past, as the main driving force toward modernization, greater productivity of land and labour, and higher farm incomes.

IWP believes that the pull of the domestic market will play a principal role in future in most developing countries, in laying the foundations for economies which are self-generating.

The resulting rise in incomes in rural areas would increase the demand for industrial products, so helping to ensure that the momentum of industrial expansion is maintained. . . .

Most developing countries still depend mainly on agricultural products for earning foreign exchange. They need these earnings to pay for imports, many of them for development purposes. Countries which cannot earn large sums from oil and other mineral resources or tourism will have to keep their agricultural economies in a position to take advantage of whatever market opportunities for agricultural (including forestry and fishery) products there will be over the next 15 years to 1985.

However, prospects for most agricultural exports from the developing to the advanced countries are 'very unsatisfactory'. The exceptions are primarily beef and veal, fish meal, and processed products from tropical timbers.

In the light of this conclusion, the Plan raises questions as to what changes the industrialized countries, including those with centrally planned economies, might make in their production and trade policies to enable the poor countries to expand their export earnings. It also discusses actions the poor countries should take towards the same end.

Agriculture is, or could be, of great importance to developing countries in other ways. Potentially it could provide a part of the raw material base as well as vast markets for domestic industries. It could also generate savings for investment in and outside of agriculture.

A 'problem of stunning dimensions' is how agriculture will be able to absorb the more than 400 million persons expected to be added to the rural population between 1962 and 1985.

'The problem of employment looms as far more intractable than that of food supply. With it can come not only human misery, but social unrest and political instability. In fact it may be that the greatest threat to the technological revolution which could solve the food problem

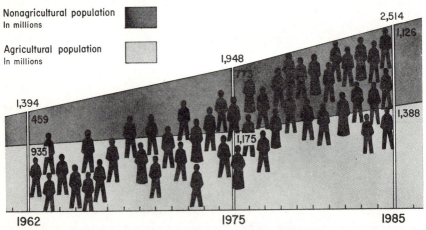

FIGURE 30 Present and projected population for the developing countries [UDCs] 1962-1985 (all developing countries excluding the People's Republic of China).

—at least for the foreseeable future—lies in the social disorganization which could result from the ever-increasing millions dependent on a living from the agricultural economy.'

It will be a gigantic job to reshape and improve agriculture in the developing countries so that it will satisfy their needs in the 1970s and early 1980s, the remaining period of the Indicative World Plan. The Plan concludes, however, that 'the main problems of hunger and mal-nutrition could be overcome, trade flows could be improved, and a substantial contribution made to providing additional employment'. But this optimistic vision could become reality only if technical, in-stitutional, and economic measures such as those proposed by IWP are adopted and carried out.

In very broad terms, IWP's strategy is built around five key objec-tives:

1. Securing the staple food supplies, with population growing at 2.5 to 3 per cent per year. For most countries this means achieving a faster growth of cereal production.

2. Improving the quality of the diet. This calls for adjusting to the changes in the composition of the diet that accompany rising incomes and urbanization, and to the specific requirements in food policy which emerge from the analysis of the main dietary deficiencies. Here the supply of protein, particularly animal protein, is the crucial problem.

3. Earning and saving the foreign exchange that is crucial to financing overall development. Emphasis must be upon both boosting exports of agricultural products and reducing imports through economic substitution.

4. Providing a large part of the additional employment that will be needed over the period up to 1985, and at the same time helping to create opportunities for jobs in industries related to agriculture.

5. Increasing productivity through intensified use of the basic physical resources of land and water, including forests, oceans, and inland waters.

On the basis of the provisional regional studies, the farm value of agricultural production at constant prices in the 64 countries studied under the IWP is estimated to have been about $55,000 million in 1962*. If the production objectives recommended in the regional studies were achieved, the value would increase to about $122,000 million by 1985. The compound annual growth rate would be 3.5 per cent compared with the projected population growth for the same countries of 2.6 per cent per year. This would be a significant improvement over the rate at which agricultural production has grown in the developing countries over the last decade or so, when it barely kept pace with population growth.

It is suggested in the world study that the gap in meat supplies apparent from the regional studies could largely be bridged by using some 20 million tons of potentially surplus grain to achieve a faster growth in poultry and pork production. This would raise the annual overall production growth rate to about 3.7 per cent.

Table 20 shows the proposed breakdown of the gross value of production at constant prices by major categories of products. It highlights the shift of emphasis toward livestock production, which would have the fastest rate of growth of all subsectors of agriculture. The rate would be 4.1 per cent under the proposal to accelerate poultry and pork production, compared with 3.8 per cent for fisheries, 3.6 per cent for crops, and 3.5 per cent for forestry.

The conclusion of the Plan is that, if its various proposed policies are adopted, an average annual increase in growth of gross value of production of 3.7 per cent is feasible. That it will nevertheless be a 'very tough task' is indicated by the fact that the annual rate of growth for a recent decade—1955-7 to 1965-7—was only 2.7 per cent.

Because priorities need to change over a period of time, IWP says that its strategy should be applied in two stages. In the first stage, top priority must be given to a major breakthrough in yields per hectare of the basic food crops. Carefully planned programs to spread or intensify the use of high-yielding varieties of wheat and rice, where ecological conditions permit, should spearhead the drive.

'Only in this way can dangers of famine be avoided, can the agricultural economy do its part to sustain a good rate of progress in the economy as a whole and resources be released within the agricultural sector for a more diversified pattern of production and consumption.' Recent progress in Asia, particularly in India and Pakistan, in exploiting high-yielding cereal varieties is encouraging. But these varieties 'have not yet made much impact in the majority of developing countries where only about 5 per cent of total area is at present planted with them'.

Simultaneously, priority should be given to pushing up the production of animal products where very quick progress is possible. Essentially this means poultry, meat, eggs and (where acceptable) pork. Increasing

Table 20

COMPOSITION OF GROSS VALUE OF AGRICULTURAL PRODUCTION 1962[1] AND 1985, BY REGIONS[2]

	Africa south of Sahara		Asia and Far East		Latin America		Near East and northwest Africa		Zone C (study countries)	
	1962[1]	1985	1962[1]	1985	1962[1]	1985	1962[1]	1985	1962[1]	1985
	Thousand million dollars									
Crops	5.44	11.06	22.12	52.96	8.89	17.71	3.62	8.08	40.06	89.81
Livestock	0.82	2.53	3.55	9.64	5.19	12.26	1.84	4.36	11.39	28.80
Crops and livestock	6.25	13.59	25.67	62.60	14.08	29.97	5.45	12.44	51.45	118.60
Fisheries	0.12	0.38	1.12	2.60	0.24	0.54	0.09	0.16	1.56	3.67
Forestry	0.46	0.83	0.50	1.25	0.85	1.98	0.08	0.16	1.89	4.22
Total Agriculture	6.83	14.80	27.28	66.45	15.17	32.48	5.62	12.76	54.90	126.49
	Growth rates 1962[1] to 1985 (per cent per year)									
Crops	3.1		3.9		3.0		3.6		3.6	
Livestock	5.0		4.4		3.8		3.8		4.1	
Crops and livestock	3.4		3.9		3.3		3.7		3.7	
Fisheries	5.3		3.7		3.6		2.8		3.8	
Forestry	2.6		4.1		3.7		2.9		3.5	
Total Agriculture	3.4		3.9		3.4		3.6		3.7	

[1] 1961-3 average.
[2] Totals and growth rates calculated from unrounded figures.

production of milk, beef, veal and other meat is urged, but is inevitably slow because the biological cycle of cattle and other ruminants is so long.

If poultry and pig production are not stepped up immediately, production of all foods of animal origin is almost certain to fall below effective demand, prices are likely to rise sharply and protein malnutrition could grow worse in those groups where it is now most serious.

If the developing countries meet the proposed targets for cereals production, emphasis in food aid over the next decade or so (apart from emergency action and special projects) should be shifted from grains to processed milk, to help cover their prospective inevitable milk deficit.

Research is urgently needed to develop and multiply high-yielding varieties of pulses, oilseeds, fruits and vegetables, fodders, and raw material crops. Thus, as the cereal programs succeed and land can be released for other crops, there will be varieties available that are sufficiently profitable to compete with cereals.

Finally, in stage one, the numbers of cattle and other ruminants must be built up to ensure a more rapid increase in the production of milk, beef, and veal in later years.

In the second stage several important changes should occur.

Production of cereals for direct human consumption should expand less rapidly as calorie supplies become adequate and other foods are able to provide a bigger proportion of them. This should accelerate the release of land for other crops and for livestock breeding.

An increasing proportion of cereals will be needed to feed livestock. This, over a period of time, would stimulate greater production of coarse grains such as maize.

Crop production must become more varied as high-yielding varieties for crops other than cereals become available. This would permit more variety and better balance in the diet.

A change in the composition of foods of animal origin should gradually become possible. Poultry, meat, eggs, and pork would no longer have to bear the brunt of the battle to provide more animal protein. Beef and veal would probably regain a part of the share of the meat supply, although this need not mean an absolute decrease in poultry and pork production. Fresh milk must gradually take over the vital role that processed milk from developed countries will have to play during the transitional period.

Agriculture can then shift toward multiple cropping and mixed farming, which would have the important side benefit of providing more jobs.

The transition between one stage and another would of course be gradual. The timing would vary for different aspects even within the same country because of local conditions.

'The important thing is that the general order of precedence be built into agricultural and food policies and that the years immediately ahead be used to lay the foundation for the second stage, particularly in respect of research.'

THE TASK AHEAD IN WORLD AGRICULTURE*

Subcommittee on Foreign Aid Expenditures, United States Senate

The following is part of a report presented to the Subcommittee on Foreign Aid Expenditures of the United States Senate in 1968. The panel referred to included seventeen authorities in such fields as agriculture, medicine, food science, and demography, as well as representatives from a variety of public and private organizations in the United States. The report is concerned with the growing problem of food shortages, its

*From a publication entitled *Population Crisis*, containing an account of the Hearings before the Subcommittee on Foreign Aid Expenditures of the Committee on Government Operations, United States Senate, Ninetieth Congress, U.S. Government Printing Office, Washington, 1968.

relationship to the population crisis, and the roles that must be played by all nations if this problem is to be solved. Of course the emphasis is put on the responsibilities of the United States, but it should be quite clear that these apply to all the developed countries.

[1968]

THE GENERAL PROBLEM

We have been unable to devise any new or original statement of the world food problem. The subject has been treated so thoroughly in orations and editorials during the past two decades that both its size and significance tend to be obscured by rhetorical overkill. All has been said before and said extremely well; all has been repeated, reiterated, and rephrased. The stark misery of hunger, the ravages of malnutrition, the threats of civil strife, social unrest, and political upheaval posed by food shortages, and the shadow cast by impending famine have all been portrayed in urgent and compelling terms. The need for the United States, other developed nations, international agencies, and voluntary institutions to help the hungry nations has been pointed out time after time. Insofar as the citizens of the developed countries of the West are concerned, this obligation to aid the less fortunate of the earth has been accepted without argument and they seem to assume that they are already supporting effective programs which will finally alleviate the problem. So repetitively has the problem been brought to the attention of the American public during the past several years that they seem almost to have lost the ability to respond to the stimulus; they are aware of the existence of the problem, they converse about it from time to time, but there is no longer any depth of understanding or concern. The situation has been aptly put:

> A nation conditioned by affluence might possibly be suffering from compassion fatigue, or from conscience sickness, the peril of narrowing our field of vision to leave out the unpleasant view of life disfigured by hunger.[1]

Despite expenditures of billions of dollars for foreign aid; despite donations and concessional sales of millions of tons of food to developing nations; despite herculean efforts by numerous voluntary groups; despite examples of highly productive technical assistance programs by foundations; and despite years of activity by international organi-

[1] Norman Cousins, *Saturday Review*, March 25, 1961.

zations such as International Bank for Reconstruction and Development (IBRD), Food and Agriculture Organization (FAO), World Health Organization (WHO), United Nations Educational, Scientific, and Cultural Organization (UNESCO), and United Nations International Children's Emergency Fund (UNICEF), there are more hungry mouths in the world today than ever before in history.

Throughout our deliberations and our efforts to respond to the President's directive, we have continually asked ourselves, 'Why is the race between food and population being lost?'

Several factors have contributed:

1. The overall problem of the world food supply is so large and so extremely complex that it is almost impossible for the casual or even the moderately concerned observer to comprehend its true dimensions or to grasp its intricate interrelationships with the many other aspects of economic growth and development.

2. Despite its true complexity, the problem, at first glance, seems deceptively straightforward and is, therefore, unusually susceptible to oversimplification. Because eating and even farming seem readily understandable to the average citizen in a developed country such as the United States, the temptation to act on the basis of superficial or incomplete information is almost irresistible. This leads to seizure and overemphasis upon panaceas and piecemeal 'solutions' which are inapplicable, ineffectual, or inadequate. The cumulative delays engendered by false starts and stop gap measures mask the requirement for broad and effective programs, tailored to the demands and dimensions of the overall problem.

3. The details of the task involved in increasing food production to meet world needs have never been charted with the clarity and exactness that the available information will permit. The problem has been treated dramatically but incompletely—usually to incite short-term action for humanitarian reasons. A wholehearted response to an *incomplete proposal*, however, lulls the participants into an unjustified feeling of security that the problem is coming under control.

4. Food shortage and rapid population growth are separate but interrelated problems. The solutions, likewise, are separate but related. The choice is not to solve one or the other; to solve both is an absolute necessity. The current tendency to think of food production and fertility control as alternative solutions to a common problem is dangerously misleading.

5. The twin problems of food and population imbalance have one

feature in common that adds immeasurably to the difficulties of achieving control. Their eventual solution is crucially dependent upon success in convincing millions of citizens in the developing nations to take *individual* action. Fertility control cannot be achieved by declarations of government policy or by executive decree although adoption of a policy and the provision of information, instruction, and materials are obviously needed and are helpful. Similarly, political declarations concerning agricultural productivity are ineffective unless individual farmers can be convinced to adopt the necessary improved practices. The provision of these personal incentives is a task that encompasses a vast array of social, economic, and political considerations which differ between countries and within countries. Indeed, the very fabric of traditional societies must be rewoven if the situation is to change permanently.

6. The eventual alleviation of world hunger will require many years. It is dependent on far-reaching social reforms and long-range programs of hard work which offer no promises of quick and dramatic results of the type so helpful in maintaining enthusiasm for a concerted, difficult undertaking. The results cannot be seen as a dedication of new buildings, as a successful launching into space, or as other spectacular, 'newsworthy' events to punctuate the year in and year out toil.

7. The problem of food production is but one part, albeit a very important part of the enormous problem of economic development in the poor nations. As the years have passed, the great expectations which ushered in our foreign assistance programs, fresh on the heels of the heady successes of the Marshall Plan, have not been realized. Domestic political constraints have so eroded the program and the agency responsible for it that there remains virtually no possibility of commitment to long-range, co-ordinated action, dedicated to the systematic solution of a series of interrelated problems, none of which can be solved in isolation from its fellows. The original emphasis upon technical assistance has been so diluted that it is almost correct to say that this form of aid, indispensible to the accomplishment of increases in food production, now receives little more than lip service. Despite chronic reiterations of the need to involve private industry in economic assistance, no significant progress in engaging this rich reservoir of resources and skills can be reported at this time.

PRINCIPAL FINDINGS AND CONCLUSIONS

This report defines and directs attention to a threatening problem of the global environment in which the United States and all nations must dwell together—the declining condition of more than two-thirds of the human race.

The Panel's detailed analysis of the world food problem has led to four basic conclusions:

1. The scale, severity, and duration of the world food problem are so great that a massive, long-range, innovative effort unprecedented in human history will be required to master it.

2. The solution of the problem that will exist after about 1985 *demands* that programs of population control be initiated now. For the immediate future, the food supply is critical.

3. Food supply is directly related to agricultural development and, in turn, agricultural development and overall economic development are critically interdependent in the hungry countries.

4. A strategy for attacking the world food problem will, of necessity, encompass the entire foreign economic assistance effort of the United States in concert with other developed countries, voluntary institutions, and international organizations.

THE NATURE OF THE WORLD FOOD PROBLEM

The world's increasingly serious nutritional problem arises from the *uneven distribution* of the food supply among countries, within countries, and among families with different levels of income. Global statistical surveys, based upon total food produced per person, suggest that there is no world-wide shortage of food in terms of quantity (calories) or quality (protein) at the moment. But in the developing countries, where two-thirds of the world's population live, there is overwhelming clinical evidence of undernutrition (too few calories) and malnutrition (particularly, lack of protein) among the people. Clearly, millions of individuals are *not* receiving the amounts of food suggested by average figures.

Many South-Asian and Latin-American countries, for example, have average diets which are nutritionally inadequate according to minimum standards of the United Nations Food and Agriculture Organization (FAO). In these regions, surveys show that the poorest 25 per cent of the people consume diets with caloric and protein contents that are only about three-fourths of the country average and fall far below calculated nutritional requirements. It is in these low income groups that overt malnutrition is found, particularly among the most susceptible groups: infants and pre-school children, pregnant women, and nursing mothers.

POPULATION GROWTH AND FOOD NEEDS

If the world population continues to increase at 1965 rates, 52 per cent more calories will be required in 1985. This estimate is based on calories actually consumed and does not consider production, losses, quality, and wastage of food. If, as a result of family-planning programs during 1965-85, one optimistically assumes a progressive decrease to 30 per cent in the probability that a woman of given age will bear a child (fertility rate[1]), the caloric requirements will still be 43 per cent higher by 1985.

These projections of *world* food requirements, however, fail to depict the plight of the developing countries. India, at her present population growth rate, will require 108 per cent more calories by 1985; with a 30 per cent reduction in fertility, the increased nutritional requirement will be 88 per cent. The corresponding figures for Pakistan's increased caloric needs in 1985, allowing for the same reduction in fertility, are 146 per cent and 118 per cent, and for Brazil, 104 per cent and 91 per cent.

These estimates portray two of the most crucial aspects of the relationship between population growth and food needs:

1. Population and food problems centre directly in the already poor, already diet-deficient countries where food production is low and population growth rates are high. In these developing nations, under the best of circumstances, food needs will at least double within the next two decades.

2. The disproportionate additional need for food in the developing countries cannot be solved by successful programs of family planning alone during the next twenty years. This mathematically demonstrable fact of demography *must not* be interpreted to indicate that population-control measures are inherently ineffective or in any way secondary in importance to increasing food production. On the contrary, the Panel's

---

[1] Assumptions concerning future effectiveness of family planning were not made on the basis of an estimated reduction in *birth rate* (births per 1,000 total population). Rather, a reduction in the *age-specific fertility rate* was assumed. Age-specific fertility is a more accurate reflection of success in family planning than is birth rate alone.

estimates simply show that the impact of successful family planning is cumulative and makes itself felt in the size of the next generation.

For example, the difference in our high and low estimates for world population in 1985 is only 385 million (5.03 billion and 4.65 billion). The difference is greater in later decades and is 1.15 billion in the year 2000 (7.15 billion and 6.0 billion).

To avoid a continued worsening of the population-food situation during the years beyond 1985, that may even reach an economically or ecologically irreversible state of imbalance, *it is imperative to institute intensive programs of family planning now.*

The Panel is unanimous in supporting and urging, in the strongest terms, continuing and increasing emphasis upon research, technical assistance, and capital funding in family planning. Only by such continuing emphasis and effort can the outpacing of food production by population growth be avoided as a problem that might continue well into the next century. The long lag-period that necessarily precedes the main effect of programs of family planning adds to the urgency of the need for action now.

The world food problem is not a future threat. It is here now and it must be solved within the next two decades. If it is solved during this time, it will be manageable for the years thereafter.

This report, then, is addressed to the grim reality of the food shortage that will occur during the next 20 years (actually 1965/66 to 1985/86) before programs of family planning can be expected to bring about long-term amelioration of the problem by reducing world population growth.

NUTRITION, INFANT MORTALITY, AND FAMILY PLANNING

That reduction of population growth is essential to achieving a balance between food supply and food need is an obvious, easily understood, and widely appreciated fact.

There is, however, another more complex, less well-known, and crucially important relationship between nutritional needs and family planning. Surveys of the attitudes of married couples in developing countries show that the numbers of children desired are higher than in the developed nations. Furthermore, the average number of live births per woman in the developing countries is 30 per cent greater than the desired number of children.

Emphasis on the desire for heirs leads to large families. Only one son may be needed for ritual or economic purposes but it is common to want two sons to insure against the death or incapacity of one. Couples must average four children to obtain two sons.

Availability and efficacy of pills, intra-uterine devices and other technical means for birth control are largely irrelevant until couples have secured the desired number of living children.

If we assume the necessary preconditons for reducing fertility rates in the developing countries are low infant and child mortality and a public awareness that mortality is low, then *we have the apparent paradox that a reduction in childhood mortality will reduce rather than raise the rate of population growth.*

In the United States, approximately 25 of every 1,000 liveborn infants fail to survive to the age of one year and most of the deaths result from prematurity or congenital defects. In the poor countries of Asia, Africa, and Latin America, published infant mortality rates range from 100 to nearly 200 per 1,000 live births. *Much of the higher death rate is the direct or indirect result of protein-calorie malnutrition.*

Protein-calorie deficiency, in the form of a disease called kwashiorkor, is a great killer. Acute diarrhea can be a dangerous illness for a well-nourished American baby; in the malnourished infants of the developing countries, it has an appalling mortality. Common childhood diseases are catastrophic in protein-deficient children. In 1960, for example, the fatality rate from ordinary measles was more than 100 times greater in Chile than in the United States.

If lowered infant and child mortality is a precondition to acceptance of family planning, and the major underlying cause of excessive childhood deaths in the developing nations is malnutrition, it follows that an increase in both quantity and quality of food in these countries is essential to achieving stability of population growth.

Viewed in this light, alleviation of the world food problem must be accorded the highest priority in planning for the developing nations.

SUBSISTENCE FARMING AND COMMERCIAL AGRICULTURE

In countries where, for centuries, farming has been traditionally at a *subsistence* level, intended to produce food and fibre only for family or local needs, the urgent problem of converting individual farmers to a *commercial* system in which production is primarily for markets at a distance from the farming area has been superimposed upon the other demands of modernization. The cornerstone of economic progress of any nation is the development of its natural resources and manpower. Many of the developing nations must concentrate on agricultural resources as the foundation for building self-sustaining, productive national economies. Conversely, the growth of the entire national economy will be essential in the future to increase agricultural production, which will depend critically on the farmer's ability to purchase fertilizers, tools, high-yielding seeds, pest controls, and irrigation water. To be able to purchase the required materials, farmers will need to sell a major portion of their harvests, which means that there must be increasingly prosperous customers who can buy farm products.

To persuade farmers to accept the techniques and methods of modern agriculture is a formidable and complex undertaking. Farmers in traditional subsistence economies are understandably wary of assuming new risks because they are so close to the margin of survival. If a farmer is to invest in the modern inputs of improved seeds, fertilizers, and pesticides that are essential to increasing the output of his land, these resources must be easily available to him, a system of farm credit must be established so that he can afford to purchase them, he must be instructed in the proper and economic utilization of these materials, he must be reassured that he will be compensated for possible losses incurred in the process of innovation, and, above all, he must be shown that the potential payoff is worth the risk. Land tenure policies should not be such that his landlord will profit and he will not. Government pricing policies should not favour the consumer at the expense of the producer.

All of these factors enter into the vital matter of providing incentives to the farmer to increase production for the market. Fundamentally, it appears that many nations are under-utilizing the power of the market economy. Needed inputs for modern agricultural production are scarce, unreliable in availability, and expensive in relation to the prices of farm products. For example, a bushel of rice will pay for four times as much fertilizer in the United States as it will in Egypt and more than twice as much as it will in Thailand or India.

Both producers *and* consumers are responsive to prices and to income if governments will recognize and use the market mechanism. The Mexican government has recognized this fact in pricing policies and this is a major reason for the growing promise of the Mexican agricultural development program.

To induce farmers to change, the potential payoff must be high—not 5 to 10 per cent but 50 to 100 per cent. Adoption of deep wells for supplemental irrigation in West Pakistan is an example. In five years, nearly 32 thousand private 'tube' wells were installed, at a cost of $1,000 to $2,500 each, on farms no larger than 25 acres in the cotton and rice regions of the former Punjab. A private investment of $50 million was made by traditional farmers without government subsidy. Why? The wells typically paid for themselves in two years. If the payoff is large enough, farmers will change.

THE EFFECTS OF URBANIZATION

The enormous increase in nonfarm population in the diet-deficient countries has aggravated the food problem further by making it necessary to develop distribution systems to move more and more food into the cities from the producing areas. This requires the establishment of transportation, storage, processing, and marketing facilities on an unprecedented scale in economies which are already stretched to their limits.

The growth of large cities is a well-recognized characteristic of developed nations but it is not generally realized that the trend towards urbanization is fully as strong in the developing countries. As early as 1950, more than one-third of the world's cities with populations exceeding 100 thousand were in Asia and the exodus from rural areas has accelerated each year since.

The shift of people from farms to cities in the United States and western Europe has resulted primarily from the reduction in rural labour requirements brought about by advances in modern agricultural technology and increased labour requirements of industry. In the developing countries population growth alone has heightened the frequency with which families leave the overcrowded, poverty-stricken countryside, hoping to find a livelihood in the city. The results in most developing nations have been growing slums and unemployment since unskilled labour is overabundant in both rural and urban areas.

FOOD CUSTOMS AND TABOOS

Dietary habits are established early in life and, in the highly traditional cultures of the developing countries, food selection and diet more often reflect religious and social beliefs than they do the principles of human nutrition. During the past several years, there have been many commercial programs intended to make unfamiliar new food products available to low-income groups in the developing countries. It has become abundantly clear that it is extremely difficult to change fixed food habits. Market research and feasibility studies must give proper attention both to family income and to existing habits and taboos. It has been demonstrated that dietary customs *can* be changed (e.g., people whose dietary staple has been rice have been persuaded to accept wheat as a supplement or substitute) but success in any such undertaking requires time and a carefully prepared program of consumer education. In summary, *any program to remedy malnutrition which involves changing traditional food habits is highly likely to be ineffective in the short-run and even a long-range plan must be carefully programed for the specific local situation.*

MEETING THE NEED FOR MORE FOOD

For the next several years, any major expansion of the world food supply will be dependent on increased production from conventional sources and upon more efficient utilization of available foodstuffs through reduction of waste and spoilage. *The vast majority of the increased production must take place within the developing countries themselves.*

Periodically, the news media draw attention to ongoing research on systems which offer possibilities as new sources of human food. Because there is a strong tendency to portray these as possible 'solutions' to the world food problem and because the public is drawn understandably to such panaceas, this publicity undoubtedly lessens concern about the seriousness of the food supply in the developing nations.

The Panel has examined carefully and in detail the several new processes which are under current study. 'Single-cell protein' derived from fermentation by yeasts or bacteria of carbohydrates, hydrocarbons, or cellulose is particularly promising. A great advantage of single-cell protein is that it can be produced independently of agriculture or climatic conditions. However, there are major unsolved problems of scale of production, processing characteristics, nutritive quality, consumer acceptance, and cost which remain to be worked out. It will be several years, *at least,* before even a decision concerning the possible usefulness of such materials in the food supply can be made.

Methods for extraction of protein directly from green leaves have been devised and deserve careful consideration and further research, since the materials utilized are frequently wasted or are fed to animals. Again, many problems of nutritive quality, scale, cost, and acceptability must be solved before evaluation of the usefulness of this material will be possible.

Investigations of the processing of algae as human food have been unrewarding thus far because of the excessive cost of deriving a product that is safe for human consumption. It now appears that the usefulness of algal materials economically derived as a by-product of reclaiming sewage and other waste waters will be as a feed for livestock.

In summary, some nonconventional sources of food appear to offer great potential for the long-term but in the judgement of the Panel none of these can be expected to lessen the problem of increasing food production from conventional sources during the next two decades.

Furthermore, the magnitude of the world's food problem is so great that nonconventional sources, when and if they become available, may be needed to supplement rather than supplant modernized agriculture. The problem will be with us for so long, however, that every effort must be made now to invent new processes and develop known ones to produce novel foodstuffs. In order to provide a reasonable probability that the long-range potential of unconventional food sources may be realized within two decades, we must accelerate research on these methods now.

There are good opportunities for improved production of livestock and increased utilization of fishery resources, including fish farming (aquiculture), in the developing countries. These deserve emphasis and exploitation because animals are capable of converting to food different types of by-products and forages that cannot be consumed directly by people, and for the significant contribution that they can make to improving the quality of protein in diets and earning foreign exchange. A process of producing fish protein concentrate (FPC) appears to hold promise for the future although major problems of scale, technologies for different species, and consumer acceptability must be solved before its usefulness can be evaluated.

It is, therefore, evident that the *bulk of the increase in food supply must come from increased production of farm crops.* There are two ways in which agricultural production can be increased: by bringing more land under cultivation or by increasing yields of land under cultivation.

Until the present time, most of the increase in food production in the developing countries has been achieved by extending traditional farming methods over a larger area of cropland. Substantial opportunities remain to bring additional land under cultivation in the less densely populated areas of Latin America and of Africa, but the vast majority of arable land in Asia is already in use. While there are marginal possibilities for using small additional areas, it is clear that as the population continues to grow, the amount of cropland per person in the Asian countries will diminish progressively.

In Asia, a shift to increasing crop production by intensifying agriculture and using modern methods to improve annual yields on land under cultivation will be mandatory. Even in Latin America and Africa, the increasing cost of clearing additional land may well make it more economical in many regions to concentrate on elevating yields rather than expanding cultivated areas.

To increase yields, a major expansion of irrigation facilities will be necessary to make multiple cropping possible independent of wide variations in seasonal rainfall. It also will be necessary to develop and utilize new, high-yielding varieties of plants, to develop and utilize plants with a higher quality of protein, to increase the use of fertilizers and pesticides, and to employ improved farm machinery. Increased capital investments and increased expenditure on the part of farmers will be required to make these tools of modern agricultural technology available. These are the techniques that have been employed so successfully in the developed countries to transform farming into a *business.*

The transition from traditional farming to modern agriculture will be difficult and expensive for the hungry nations but it is absolutely essential if their food needs are to be met. There is no alternative.

THE NEED FOR TECHNICAL ASSISTANCE

The modernization of agriculture in the developing countries will involve capital investment, provision of inputs in the form of seeds, fertilizers, pesticides, water, and machinery, organization of distribution and marketing systems, education of agricultural specialists and extension workers, provision of production incentives for individual farmers in the form of land-reform and pricing policies, and other changes in social and economic structures.

Critical to the success of all of these measures, however, is the necessity for adaptive research needed to gain an understanding of the principles governing plant and animal production under the conditions, soils, and climates existing in the developing countries.

Modern scientific agriculture has been brought to flower in the temperate regions of the developed world. In the tropical climates where the bulk of the world's low-income people live, scientific agricultural efforts have been concentrated on the traditional tropical export crops: sugar, tea, coffee, cocoa, bananas, and rubber. Only recently have food crops received serious attention.

The products of technology and 'know-how' cannot be transferred directly to the developing nations. Many plant varieties transferred to different climates fail to flower or set seed if, indeed, they survive at all. Livestock may become non-productive or die. Adaptive research must be accomplished within the developing countries. A blueprint for a bicycle or a steel mill can be shipped overseas and utilized without alteration but the blueprints and architecture for a food crop must be developed overseas. There, as in the United States, new plant varieties, each better than the last, must be produced frequently to increase plant resistance to insects and disease.

There is an urgent need to carry out this adaptive research, to establish strong indigenous institutions, and develop the manpower that will enable the poor, food-deficit nations to carry out the self-sustaining, continuing programs of research and development that are essential to modern food production.

Increasingly, United States foreign assistance should take the form of knowledge, technical aid, adaptive research, education, and institution building.

The scarcest and most needed resource in the developing countries is the scientific, technical, and managerial skill needed for systematic, orderly decision-making and implementation. Through technical assistance programs, the United States should emphasize guidance, education, and the development of indigenous capabilities—for the long term—because the task in the developing nations has only just begun and will continue for many decades to come.

In recent years, United States programs of technical assistance have largely given way to capital assistance and the purpose and value of each has become blurred. The important distinction between these two instrumentalities of aid should be recognized and each should be employed sharply and effectively to reinforce the other in helping those developing countries that are willing to make the effort to solve the complex problems of feeding their people and improving the quality of their lives.

NUTRITIONAL NEED AND ECONOMIC DEMAND

The Panel's approach to the world food problem has been almost the opposite of that employed by economists. It costs money to produce food, however, and someone must pay the bill. Therefore, no matter what the physiological *need* may be, the production of food is controlled by effective market *demand*.

Economists tend to relate income and food demand in a causal fashion. The Panel, of necessity, has quite literally reversed the usual economic approach by first estimating the food shortage and setting a future goal for food production. The next step was to calculate the rate of change in income that will be required to generate the effective market demand for the targeted nutritional needs.

There are certain relationships between the demand for foodstuffs and the overall demand for goods and services in any economy. In order for 'effective demand' for food to exist, the means of buying the food—purchasing power—must be available. In other words, aggregate income must grow at a rate which permits consumers to purchase the projected food requirements.

Likewise, on the production or supply side, there are relationships which link agricultural food production to overall production. The production of food crops requires manufactured inputs such as fertilizers, pesticides, and machinery which must be imported or produced domestically. If they are imported, the overall economy must generate sufficient exports or must rely on a net inflow of foreign assistance or private capital to pay for the imports. If these inputs are to be produced domestically, or paid for by industrial exports, the non-agricultural sectors must expand at rates consistent with the need of the agricultural sector. Similarly, various nonagricultural sectors are dependent on agricultural raw materials and, in some cases, food products.

Because of the interdependence which exists among food need, food demand, overall income, agricultural (food) output, and total output (GNP), *it is meaningless to consider a nation's demand and supply of foodstuffs independently from overall economic growth.*

The Panel's analysis of the overall problem indicates that the required compound annual growth rates (1965/66–1985/86) for the developing countries in aggregate will be:

Per cent

Increase in food demand 4.0
Increase in food production 4.0
Increase in gross national income 5.5

The achievement of such growth rates will require massive efforts which must be more successful than history has recorded in any previous 20-year period. Now the developing countries, in aggregate, are increasing their compound annual growth rates approximately as follows:

	Per cent
Increase in food demand	3.0
Increase in food production	2.7
Increase in gross national income	4.5

Only countries such as Mexico and Taiwan are achieving growth rates of the order deemed necessary.

Additional investments for acceleration of agricultural output in the developing countries as a whole have been analysed but not verified by detailed country studies. The direct capital requirement for fertilizers, seeds, mechanization, and pesticides for a 4.0 per cent growth rate in agricultural output approximates $300 million annually in the early years, increasing to almost $4 billion per year by 1985. This estimate does not include direct investments in land and water resources nor does it include the necessary direct 'infrastructure' investments in power, transportation, marketing, credit, food processing, storage, and distribution. It is estimated that *to achieve a 4.0 per cent annual growth rate in food demand and supply, capital investments will have to increase from the current 15 per cent to 19 per cent of the gross national products of the developing countries. This would be equivalent to a $12 billion increase in investment above the 1965 base. To achieve such a feat will require capital and technical involvement of developed and developing nations alike on a scale unparalleled in the peacetime history of man.*

The Panel is convinced from its study of the world food problem that food shortages and high rates of population growth in the developing countries are not primary problems. Rather, they are manifestations of a more fundamental difficulty, *lagging economic development in the hungry countries.* We find the prospects for the future both sobering and alarming.

SURPLUSES IN THE THIRD WORLD—WHO WANTS THEM?*

Ester Boserup

[1968]

Propaganda addressed to a broad audience is most effective if it can avoid complicated issues and can stick to a small number of very simple ideas. One such simple idea is to explain rural poverty, malnutrition, and famine in developing countries as the result of rural overpopulation.

This idea has been widely propagated as a means of obtaining popular support for birth-control programs and for programs of food aid. But a public which has been taught to accept this explanation of rural misery is ill equipped to understand the needs of those developing countries which are saddled with problems of surplus agricultural production for which they are unable to find remunerative outlets. It is necessary to abandon such oversimplified ideas in public discussion of agricultural problems and in trying to explain why it is necessary not only to help the developing countries to produce more food, but also to help them find outlets for food surpluses.

The first step towards a more complete view of the agricultural problems of developing countries than the simplistic identification of rural misery with rural overpopulation is to distinguish two possible causes of rural poverty: one is low labour productivity which reflects the use of unsuitable farming systems, primitive techniques, and lack of capital; the other, an excessive number of people engaged in the cultivation of a given land area.

It is true that the rural population in some developing countries with a high population density suffers from chronic malnutrition, and that famines may occur in years of bad harvest.

But these phenomena are by no means restricted to the densely populated countries; they are found in many developing countries which must be characterized as underpopulated. In fact, droughts seem to be the most frequent cause of famine, and droughts do far more serious damage to harvests in underpopulated countries, where only rain-fed land is used for cultivation, than in countries where heavy population pressure has brought most of the agricultural land under artificial irrigation. Thus, in cases where population pressure on land promotes the application of artificial irrigation it may serve to forestall famines rather than to foster them.

*Reprinted by permission from *CERES*, the FAO Review, September-October 1968, Vol. I, No. 5, p. 19.

This is not to deny that, in some cases, population pressure can be identified as the chief cause of the lowness of rural incomes in developing countries. But it is important to remember that population pressure is a highly elusive concept. Its existence and degree cannot be gauged simply by a consideration of the ratio of rural population to existing land resources, without regard to the prevailing agricultural system.

In a very sparsely populated country, the increase of population may depress rural standards of living if the rural population is unwilling to give up the traditional system of shifting cultivation. But in other cases, when the increase of population density leads to more extensive provision and use of irrigation facilities, the result of the demographic expansion may well be to raise per-capita rural income. And since multi-cropping of irrigated land requires several times more labour than extensive dry farming of the same amount of land, even with an increase in population there may still be a shortage of labour.

Thus, land improvements, such as irrigation or the draining of swamps, may change a region which was held to be overpopulated into a region of scarcity of labour. Indeed, in regions where major schemes for land improvement are undertaken, decades may pass before the population has grown sufficiently, by natural increase and immigration, to ensure the proper use of all the improved land.

The basic cause of rural poverty in developing countries is low investment in agriculture and little use of industrial and other purchased inputs per worker. This is true of densely as well as sparsely populated countries, and it is the main feature which distinguishes agriculture in developing countries from that in industrialized countries. The gap in agricultural labour productivity and rural incomes as between developing and industrialized countries has become wider still in recent decades because the industrialized countries have increased the use of capital and of modern procedures at a rate which the developing countries have been unable to emulate.

Many industrialized countries—among them the United States, France, and the Netherlands—which face the problem of disposing of burdensome surpluses of food, have reached their high level of agricultural production by means of large public investments in land improvement in the past. Owing to the long time lag from the decision to execute major works of this kind to the time they come into full use, the fruits of these investments have often ripened at a time when it was impossible to dispose of the additional output at remunerative prices. Many developing countries now have large-scale schemes for land improvement in the offing and it is possible that some of them will run into similar difficulties in disposing of the increased output in their home markets. Their access to export markets will then be crucially important.

Generally speaking, the aim of agricultural policy in developing countries should not be seen as that of feeding increasing numbers of subsistence producers, but rather as that of improving rural incomes by higher per-capita output in agriculture. This implies that investment in land improvement so as to create employment and subsistence for increasing numbers of producers must be supplemented by investment in improved equipment, seeds, livestock, fertilizer, etc.; i.e. by the type of investment which raises output not only per unit of land, but also per worker.

If a developing country succeeds in such an investment policy, by its own financial efforts or by loans and grants from abroad, its farmers will produce an increasing surplus of agricultural products over and above their own needs, and outlets for this surplus must be found either by sales to the urban sector or by exports.

EXPORT OUTLETS URGENTLY NEEDED

In many developing countries at a relatively advanced economic stage and with a fairly large urban sector, the disposal of a steadily growing marketable surplus of agricultural produce may create few problems and be a great help in improving urban living standards, or providing the food basis for an expansion of nonagricultural employment, and/or reducing food imports.

But in developing countries at the early stages of economic development, where the urban sector is tiny compared to the large numbers of rural subsistence producers, it is impossible to find sufficient consumers in the country itself for a surplus large enough to permit a significant increase in rural incomes. In such countries, average output and incomes of farmers cannot be improved significantly unless a large share of the additional agricultural output is exported.

Even those least developed countries which can provide the necessary foreign exchange for expansion of the urban sector by exports of minerals, forest products or services, need to sell increasing agricultural surpluses in export markets if the average output and income of the agricultural sector is to be improved, since the absorptive capacity for food in the urban sector is very limited, and since a rapid large-scale transfer of agriculturists to nonagricultural employment cannot be envisaged.

Thus, in the least developed countries, the hope of improving average rural incomes, and thus of reducing the incidence of rural malnutrition and famine, depends upon the development of exports of food and other agricultural products to other developing countries, or to industrialized countries.

HIGH-YIELDING VARIETIES MAY PRODUCE SURPLUSES

It is frequently stated in books on economic development that developing countries may be well advised to limit their efforts to expand agricultural exports and, instead, to speed up industrialization with a view to exporting manufactures. This may be sound advice in the case of some economically advanced developing countries where further expansion of agriculture would require heavy investment, but it is wholly irrelevant as a recommendation to developing countries at the early stage of economic development, where a great majority of the population will for a long time continue to be engaged in agricultural pursuits. In the latter countries neither birth control nor food aid will provide the solution to rural poverty. The only efficient assistance to the rural population in such countries is to help them produce larger marketable surpluses and to help them dispose of those surpluses at a fair price.

Recently, some important scientific improvements, notably the development of high-yielding varieties of wheat and rice, have become available for producers in developing countries. It has thereby become possible with quite moderate increases of inputs to achieve spectacular increases in output both per hectare and per worker. One probable result of this is that in the near future many more of the poorest countries will develop surpluses which must be exported in competition with the surplus disposal of industrialized countries.

Here, then, seems to be a problem that should be tackled forthwith at an international level with a view to finding politically acceptable solutions of an expansive kind. Otherwise, it is only too likely that solutions of a restrictive kind will be imposed when the problem becomes acute. It is also urgent that the public be informed about the true nature of agricultural problems of countries at different stages of development and with different degrees of population pressure. In other words, we must get rid of the oversimplified picture of the overpopulated poor world depending on the food surpluses of the rich countries.

We have now made a distinction between one group of countries, which must raise production in order to get food enough for domestic consumption, and another group of countries, where the income of the rural population must be raised by the production of food and other agricultural goods for export. But this is only the first step towards a better understanding of the agricultural problems of developing countries. A further important distinction must be made between countries which have temporary surpluses of food in years of good harvest, but are dependent upon food imports in other years, and those countries which normally produce surpluses. This distinction is important because the two types of surpluses call for different kinds of policy.

Just now, in 1968, the problems of a temporary surplus are highlighted by events in India. From one year to another that country moved from near-famine conditions in certain areas to being a surplus producer. This is not solely the result of climatic conditions, but also of the rapid spread of the use of improved seeds and of investment and other economic initiatives in response to the increase, long overdue, in agricultural prices which came about during the years of scarcity. The present situation is in some ways similar to the temporary surplus production in Indian agriculture which occurred after a very good harvest year at the beginning of the nineteen fifties. At that time, the temporary surplus caused a collapse of agricultural prices which seems to have had a deterrent effect upon the agriculturists who had contributed to the increase of production investment in the preceding years. It is much to be hoped that, this time, the program of government purchases of cereals for stocking will prevent similar unfortunate effects of the abundant harvest. It is generally agreed that for half a decade or more India must continue to be a deficit country in years of average harvest, so that any Indian surplus can be disposed of by stocking and by an appropriate reduction of imports. Therefore, barring the particular problems of certain crops, the need to find export markets does not arise.

SOLUTIONS NEEDED BEFORE PRICES COLLAPSE

In view of the rapid increase of output now made possible by high-yielding varieties, we may expect, in years of good climatic conditions, to see other developing countries in the unaccustomed role of surplus producer. It is important to foster awareness of this possibility among technical advisers and national civil servants in such countries, so that administrative and political preparations can be made for meeting this problem when and where it arises. Otherwise, a collapse of prices attendant on an unexpected surplus may discourage the agriculturists from their efforts to modernize and expand food production.

In addition, some developing countries already produce a surplus in all normal harvest years, and with the new agricultural techniques more countries may be expected to join that group in a near future. In such countries, programs of stocking of course provide no solution to the surplus problem and room must be made in the world market for regularly forthcoming exports from these countries.

The Indicative World Plan of FAO may make an important contribution to the solution of this problem because it will throw light on the prospective pattern of deficits and surpluses of food in both developing and industrialized countries.

To be sure, in a world market already burdened by agricultural surpluses it will be no easy task to provide such regular outlets for exports from developing countries. The crucial preconditions are: (1) that food-importing industrialized countries show willingness to buy from other than their traditional suppliers, within or outside their own regional groups, and (2) that developing and industrialized countries with favourable possibilities for expansion in other fields than agriculture show willingness to refrain from pursuing policies of self-sufficiency in food, so that they may instead purchase food from, and sell manufactures to, those developing countries which must base their development policy upon the earnings from exports of agricultural surpluses.

For such policies to be acceptable, however, world opinion must be enlightened by realistic analysis instead of being misled by propaganda that describes all developing countries as 'hungry' countries which need food imports, and only industrialized countries as needing to get rid of food surpluses.

THE IMPORTANCE OF TRANSPORTATION*

Subcommittee on Foreign Aid Expenditures, United States Senate

[1968]

Four facts define the crucial importance of transportation facilities in a program for increasing agricultural production.

1. Agricultural production uses solar energy, through photosynthesis in plants. This solar energy is widely distributed over the surface of the earth and must be utilized where it hits the earth. Farms, therefore, must be located wherever conditions of soil, moisture, and micro-climates are or can be made favourable and many intensive growing areas are likely to be remote from centres of consumption.

2. Only in a stagnant, wholly subsistence agriculture, do farmers limit themselves to the use of resources that are found 'naturally' on their farms: the existing chemical properties of the soil, tools and equipment that can be made by the farmers out of materials produced on the farm, sources of power that can be sustained by products of the farm, and the labour of the farm family. As agriculture progresses it *must* use more and more inputs purchased from other parts of the economy. In a progressive agriculture, farms are only the 'assembly lines' utilizing fertilizers, pesticides, tools and equipment, construction materials, and sources of power transported to the farm from factories, oil refineries, seed multiplication farms, and other suppliers of the inputs of progressive farming.

3. If farmers are to utilize purchased inputs, they must sell farm products. These farm products must be transported to processors and ultimate consumers scores, hundreds, or thousands of miles away.

4. If farm families are to have incentives to increase production in excess of their own needs, there must be not only a market demand for their products but there must also be available, in each rural locality, desirable consumer goods that farm families would like to be able to purchase. These industrial products come largely from urban centres and must be transported to widely dispersed rural markets, within easy access of farm families, if they are to provide incentives for increasing agricultural production.

Transport *alone* is not sufficient to increase the supply of food, but it

*From a publication entitled *Population Crisis*, containing an account of the Hearings before the Subcommittee on Foreign Aid Expenditures of the Committee on Government Operations, United States Senate, Ninetieth Congress, U.S. Government Printing Office, Washington, 1968.

is one of the essentials to agricultural progress and its neglect can nullify all other measures designed to increase farm productivity. Current plans for increasing the output of food tend to focus on fertilizers and other farm inputs, without considering the need to deliver the inputs to the farm and to distribute outputs to consumers. In regions where the food problem is most critical, the transport capacity is often least able to move the required tonnage of farm inputs and the facilities needed to move foods to markets are lacking, are too costly, or are too slow.

Most of the developing countries are allocating a very large proportion of development resources to transportation. The percentage typically ranges from 20 to 40 per cent of expenditures in the public sector. But planners usually have failed to relate rural transport investments to the specific needs of agriculture. The major effort usually has been on the more obvious need for inter-city movement of industrial traffic.

The relation between transportation and the ability to grow and market food has been demonstrated in many parts of the world. In Thailand, partially used jungle land was transformed into highly productive, prosperous farms along the hundred-mile course of the Friendship Highway. Travel time was reduced from eleven hours on the old road to three on the new. The production of sugar cane, vegetables, bananas, and other fruits more than tripled in three years and Thailand began to export corn to Japan.[1]

In Bolivia, the highway from Cochabamba to Santa Cruz reduced travel time in the rainy season from several weeks to fifteen hours and provided a link between the country's food supplies and its consumers. Until then, the price of Bolivian rice was 50 per cent higher than imported rice simply because the cost of domestic transport was high. The highway has largely eliminated the need for imports.

In Costa Rica, before the Inter-American Highway was constructed, driving beef cattle from grazing lands to San José customarily resulted in a 40 per cent loss of weight, and imports were necessary to satisfy domestic market demand for beef. With an all-weather highway, it became possible to deliver cattle by truck-trailer units overnight and Costa Rica has become self-sufficient in meat.[2]

---

[1] Wisit Kasiraksa, *Economic Effects of the Friendship Highway*, SEATO Graduate School of Engineering, Bangkok, 1963.
[2] U.S. Department of Commerce, *Motor Transport in Middle America*, World Trade Information Service, 4, No. 55-13.

Where transport has been included in a program containing the other ingredients needed for increasing agricultural productivity, the results have been uniformly rewarding. There are many examples, however, where lack of transport has frustrated well-intentioned efforts to produce more food. In many agricultural areas, intensification of cultivation is inhibited mainly by the poor quality and high cost of rural mobility. Where access roads become impassable for several months of the year, input costs are high, marketing possibilities are uncertain, and incentives to accelerate production are low. It has never been possible to change traditional methods of cultivation and patterns of production until transport is adequate, because transport is a means of moving ideas and information as well as goods.

Farmers in regions lacking transport are prevented from specializing in crops that offer the best return. In such areas each farmer, forced to meet all the needs of his family and livestock, tends to retain more food than he actually requires, knowing that if supplies run short they will be difficult to replenish from other sources. Inaccessibility means that operations such as fertilization and application of pesticides are at the mercy of unreliable delivery schedules. Agricultural extension workers find it too time-consuming to visit the farms that are not on a hard-surfaced route.[1] Fruits, vegetables, and other foods that spoil readily cannot be produced because they require rapid transportation to markets.

Some idea of the magnitude of the transportation task in a modern agricultural system is illustrated by the estimate that in 1964-65 94 million tons of farm supplies and equipment were moved into the commercial farms of the United States[2] and 324 million tons of farm products moved from these farms to markets.

Storage and processing facilities may enhance marketing to a greater extent than can be accomplished by transport alone. The development planner must weigh transport along with all of the significant factors and combinations of factors capable of increasing agricultural output.

---

[1] A study in the Philippines revealed that visits by extension workers and personnel of other government agencies increased by 400 per cent to 1,000 per cent to barrios after motorable roads reached these villages.

[2] Information supplied by Mr James Vermier, Economic Research Service, U.S. Department of Agriculture. Of the 94 million tons of supplies and equipment 5.8 per cent was machinery, 28.1 per cent was limestone, 33.2 per cent was fertilizer, 25.4 per cent was fuel and lubricants, 2.1 per cent was pesticides, and 5.4 per cent was building materials. The total tonnage of farm supplies and equipment represented an average of about 2,600 pounds per crop acre.

This type of 'systems approach' to agricultural development is essential if the problem of feeding the world's people is to be solved.

THE TRANSPORTATION 'SYSTEM'

The critical dependence of a country's food supply upon the availability and efficiency of transport makes it important to define what is meant by a 'transportation system' and the special requirements that agriculture imposes on such a system.

A transportation system is any feasible combination of transport methods that provides an adequate and continuous flow of goods between producers and consumers. In an agrarian economy, therefore, the concern, in a very real sense, is with a system of physical communications to and from each individual farm-family unit—a network that includes the interconnection of population centres but one that is far more complex and extensive.

A transportation system has three general features: (1) a fine-mesh network of low-capacity routes blanketing each food-producing and food-consuming area; (2) a scattering of focal points within each of these networks that serve as collection and distribution centres; and (3) a loose network of high-capacity routes that connects the collection-distribution centres with major cities and seaports (Figure 31). Each of these is an essential ingredient of any national transportation system, and the effectiveness is no greater than the system's weakest link.

The critical importance of a fine-mesh transport grid is universally recognized for the population-dense, food-consuming areas but is almost completely ignored for the rural, food-producing areas. The objectives in each type of region are the same—equal convenience in marketing or acquiring products, whether it be the commuter going to work to sell his services, or the farmer taking his produce to market and picking up his supplies. In rural or urban settings, productivity will increase with efficiency of transport—the more the individual is isolated in a time sense, the less will be his incentive to produce or to purchase more than his minimum needs.

It is this fact that makes the rural transport network of such fundamental importance in the food supply problem. Farm operations are, by their very nature, geographically widespread. Unless it is reasonably convenient for the farmer to exchange surplus crops for consumer goods, he lacks an important incentive to exploit the full potential of his land. The lack of an efficient rural transport net may be the real limiting factor in attempts to increase agricultural productivity.

Local collection and distribution centres in towns may be regarded as storage and transfer terminals whose basic function is to provide an efficient coupling between the rural transport network and the external urban network. The terminal, if practical, should be for *transfer* rather than storage because all primary food products are perishable through deterioration, contamination, or spoilage. Storage is necessary for seasonal carry-over of local products, to implement price stabilization schemes, or to hold imported goods until they are needed by local consumers.

The final link in a transportation system requirement serves to connect a country's regional economies and to link the nation with the avenues of world trade. In contrast to the rural network, which must consist predominantly of roads to accommodate a variety of low-density animal and vehicular traffic, the national network may consist of a relatively few routes with heavy enough traffic to justify the highly specialized equipment of modern highway, rail, air, and marine operations. There is a great tendency to view these sophisticated systems as the answers to all transport problems, with the result that developing countries often find themselves with an expensive and poorly utilized main transport network that falls far short of meeting the basic transportation requirements of a predominantly rural economy.

It is clear that the food transported on this primary national network will be no greater than that fraction of rural production which is marketed. The primitive state of rural transportation in most developing countries would make it impossible to market more than a small fraction of the production. Except for a few countries whose highly specialized economies are based on only one or two products which are exchanged for all other goods that are needed or wanted, the capacity of inter-city networks is not likely to limit agricultural productivity in the developing nations. The critical components of these networks is the efficiency of their extension into existing and prospective producing areas. Where this efficiency is low, it will not be possible to provide the incentive for farmers to adopt improved farming techniques and to exploit the productive potentials that are possible through modern practices.

For those highly developed regions where agricultural production is

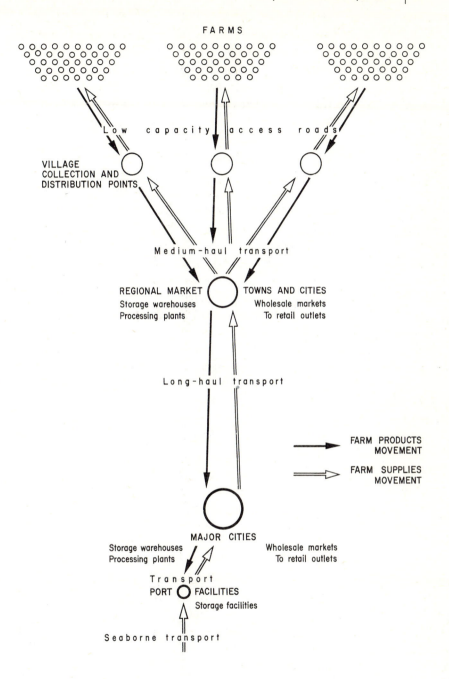

FARMS

Low capacity access roads

VILLAGE
COLLECTION AND
DISTRIBUTION POINTS

Medium-haul transport

REGIONAL MARKET   TOWNS AND CITIES
Storage warehouses   Wholesale markets
Processing plants   To retail outlets

Long-haul transport

FARM PRODUCTS
MOVEMENT

FARM SUPPLIES
MOVEMENT

MAJOR CITIES

Storage warehouses   Wholesale markets
Processing plants   To retail outlets

Transport
PORT FACILITIES
Storage facilities

Seaborne transport

FIGURE 31 Essential elements in transportation system serving agriculture.

characterized by a high degree of specialization, ocean transport is often a major and critical extension of the internal transportation system. In some cases, the whole economy of such a region may be based on sea lines of communication. It is clear, however, that this cannot be true within the context of the problem we are concerned with here. In the first place, our initial problem is how to increase the food supply within the developing countries. In the second place, the improvement of agricultural productivity within these developing countries is necessarily a two-phase process. Phase one, with which we are primarily concerned, is predicated on internal trade within the developing region—the generation and exchange of local farm surpluses for those agricultural inputs and consumer goods that make the surpluses possible and desirable. Phase two, the overseas export and import of related products, is generally a long-term result of highly successful phase-one operations under conditions where intensification and specialization have led to a fairly sophisticated agricultural economy.

Viewed in this light, our analysis of transportation in support of agricultural development need not be vitally concerned with overseas lines of communication. The initial dependence of any program on this type of logistics will be small and can be expected to be met by existing privately financed shipping operations. Furthermore, in any areas where an increasing need for ocean transportation begins to develop, the demand trend can be anticipated far enough in advance so that again private enterprise can be relied upon to furnish the required transport capability.

The foregoing conclusion does *not* imply that one can forget about the overseas logistics problem entirely. It does have its critical components, and one is the interface between the sea and land-lines of communication. Unless there is at least one good deep-water port facility that connects efficiently with the internal transportation network, a developing region is vulnerable to shortages of critical inputs no matter how much ship capacity might be available on the high seas. Vessel operators are reluctant to contract for calls that are likely to involve extensive delays; therefore, good port facilities are essential regardless of the volume of cargo to be handled.

The best way to assure a good port facility is to project shipping requirements on a continuous basis even though this means small tonnages per ship call. It is the long-term prospect of reasonably frequent *calls* that provides the business incentive necessary to attract capital and labour into port facilities and operations. There is no reason that this kind of scheduling should not be done as part of an agricultural development program. It would be much more efficient to partially subsidize regular vessel calls and thus stimulate port, terminal, and trade development than it would be to try to conduct sporadic supply operations on an as-needed basis through inadequate terminal facilities. This latter procedure is often responsible for the difficulties encountered in fixing spot charters for emergency shipments because vessel operators know their ships will have to spend an inordinate time in port. On the other hand, the economic opportunity presented by a regular schedule of reasonably frequent future calls creates an environment where adequate terminal facilities can develop naturally.

A final critical factor in overseas supply to developing countries relates to the form of the cargo. Distribution to the ultimate consumer is often frustrated because the cargo is not packaged in the manner and quantity in which finally it must be handled and used. For example, a ship-load of grain or fertilizer in bulk form would be an awesome thing if it were to appear suddenly in a port that had neither bulk handling and storage facilities nor bulk transporters for inland distribution. By the time the material could be hand-sacked and taken to individual farmers by whatever means available, its value in a physical or a time sense could well have disappeared.

Difficulties of this kind can be minimized by pre-packaging commodities in units that are compatible with the manner in which they must be transported during the final phase of the journey to the farmer's door. Whatever the characteristics of the rest of the transport system, the whole process breaks down if this ultimate requirement is not met. Containerized operations, where truck bodies can be hoisted on or off the truck to and from rail cars or ships, is an ideal method for accomplishing the desired purpose in those areas where the final road link can accommodate the operation. This method has the added virtue of eliminating much of the handling difficulty, cost, and delay usually associated with cargo transfer at the interface between different transport modes. Where the final transport link to the farmer's door is not suitable for containerization, many of the same benefits can still be realized by careful pre-selection of unit loads that are compatible with the final mode of transport, whether it be A-frame, burro, or ox-cart.

THE CONTRIBUTION OF THE HIGH-INCOME COUNTRIES
THROUGH TRADE LIBERALIZATION*

Committee for Economic Development

[1967]

The efforts of the low-income countries can be made much more effective with the help of an inflow of suitable goods and services, including technical assistance, from high-income countries. These may be financed by means of aid and private investment, or they may be paid for with money earned by the low-income countries' exports. Exports to high-income countries are by far the largest source of foreign exchange for low-income countries: $26 billion in 1965, or well over two-thirds of their total receipts from high-income countries. While it must be emphasized that aid and private capital are very important sources of finance for development, joint efforts by the high-income countries to facilitate a faster growth of imports from the low-income countries would greatly enhance the prospects for economic progress in the latter.

The low-income countries have two major trade problems, which any such joint action by the high-income countries must help to solve.

First, the growth in their export earnings in the past decade has been slow in relation to the need for imports to support reasonable development programs. More than four-fifths of their exports consist of primary products, the demand for which has tended to grow only very slowly. For example, the increase in the demand for tropical foods does not keep pace with the growth of income in the high-income countries, while the long-term trend in the demand for industrial raw materials is limited by economies in the use of such materials, and by the growth of synthetic substitutes. Policies of low-income countries— for example, the toleration of inflation and the over-inflation of currencies—have also in many cases inhibited the growth of exports. The sluggish growth of exports to high-income countries has been accompanied by an even slower growth in trade among low-income countries themselves due mainly to the lack of diversity in their exports and their generally high level of protection.

Second, low-income countries' exports are frequently subject to sharp fluctuations in prices and earnings. These fluctuations may arise

---

*From *Trade Policy Toward Low-Income Countries*, Committee for Economic Development, New York, June 1967, pp. 14-27. (Prepared in association with counterpart organizations in Britain, France, Germany, Italy, Japan, and Sweden.)

from causes affecting supply, such as variations in crops, or affecting demand, such as changes in the level of economic activity in the high-income countries. Export instability is accentuated by the fact that many low-income countries depend heavily on one or two products for their export earnings.

Although there are many differences in the economic condition of the low-income countries, these two trade problems have in the case of the great majority of them prevented their earnings from growing rapidly and regularly enough to finance a satisfactory pace of development.

These were the circumstances in which the GATT[1] agreed upon its Action Program in 1963, consisting of measures to increase access for low-income countries in the markets of high-income countries. While progress in carrying out these measures has been slow, the low-income countries are likely to derive significant benefit from tariff cuts and other measures resulting from the Kennedy Round, or stimulated by the negotiations. The low-income countries moreover pressed for the holding of the 1964 United Nations Conference on Trade and Development (UNCTAD) and for the establishment of the United Nations Trade and Development Board, to deal with their trade problems. The second UN Conference on Trade and Development will be held in 1968.

RECOMMENDATION 1. The high-income countries should now declare their intention to give priority to a special comprehensive program designed to provide the opportunities for low-income countries to increase their export earnings more rapidly. It would be appropriate that such a program should be launched at the second UN Conference on Trade and Development and that the subsequent negotiations should take place within the GATT.

TARIFFS AND OTHER BARRIERS TO TRADE

The conditions of trade and the types and extent of trade barriers differ widely from product to product and from country to country, but some generalizations can nevertheless be made about the liberalizing of trade in the major product-groups.

[1] The General Agreement on Tariffs and Trade. GATT was established in 1948 to organize the conduct of international trade. Membership includes 72 countries, with others participating under special arrangements. While most of the principal trading nations of the world are members, there are some notable exceptions, including the U.S.S.R. and the People's Republic of China. (ed.)

A. TROPICAL PRODUCTS

There is a range of the products of tropical agriculture, such as bananas, cocoa, coffee, and tea, which are not in competition with the production of high-income countries. Where import duties are imposed on these, they are necessarily either revenue duties or else duties that give a preference to certain countries such as the states associated with the European Economic Community (EEC) or the members of the British Commonwealth. The preferences are dealt with later. It has often been urged that the revenue duties on tropical products, whether they take the form of import duties or of consumption taxes, should be removed, and they have in fact been abolished by Norway and Sweden. Against this, two main arguments have been brought forward: first, that the responsiveness of demand and supply for these products to price changes is so small that removal of the duties would not provide a substantial gain for the exporter; and secondly, that in certain countries the revenue raised by the duties is so large that their sudden removal would lead to a budgetary problem and, to the extent that they were not immediately replaced by other sources of revenue, the possibility of inflationary pressures.

A gradual reduction of the duties on tropical products with a view to their eventual elimination would go far to meet both points: the first, because the response of demand and supply to price changes could be tested empirically as the reductions took place; the second, because the budgetary adjustment each year would be comparatively small. In order to strike at the root of the problem of world surpluses of these and other primary products, moreover, strong support should be given to redeployment into other types of production and to the search for new uses and markets for the products that are in surplus. We propose:

RECOMMENDATION 2. The high-income countries should reduce their import and consumption taxes on tropical products not produced in high-income countries, with a view to the progressive elimination of such taxes. High-income countries should also give strong support to low-income countries' efforts to reorient their economies away from products of which there is a world surplus, as well as to research directed to finding new uses and markets for such products.

B. OTHER PRIMARY PRODUCTS

The bulk of primary products exported by the low-income countries compete with the production of certain high-income countries. These include both raw materials (e.g., copper, cotton, iron ore, petroleum) and foodstuffs (e.g., cereals, fats and oils, meat, sugar).

In the high-income countries, the foodstuffs and natural fibres are generally subject to a managed market. The world balance of supply and demand for cereals and some other foods is such that high-income countries are now exporting them on a large scale to low-income countries. Indeed, surpluses of these products have for some years been distributed as a form of aid, as in the United States Food for Peace Program. For certain other products, such as fats and oils and sugar, it is less evident that the balance of supply and demand justifies the degree of support and protection that now exists in the high-income countries.

RECOMMENDATION 3. The high-income countries should make reductions in the level of their domestic subsidies and price supports for specific agricultural products when it appears likely that such reductions would be likely to lead to higher imports of those products from low-income countries.[1]

A number of raw materials or foodstuffs which are not subject to domestic managed markets in the high-income countries are nevertheless subject to import restrictions, generally in order to protect domestic producers. Examples are citrus fruit in the United States, frozen shrimp in the European Economic Community, and alumina in Britain.

RECOMMENDATION 4. Over a transitional period the high-income countries should eliminate their tariffs and quotas on those raw materials and foodstuffs that are not subject to domestic managed markets.

C. MANUFACTURES

Without in any way minimizing the importance of primary products, we must recognize that the establishment of an increasing range of manufacturing industry is an essential feature of economic development. For some low-income countries, not well endowed with natural resources, the export of manufactures is indeed the only way of expanding their earnings of foreign exchange enough to pay for the imports of goods and services that their economic growth requires and to pay for the servicing of their external debt. Given the slow growth of the world market for primary products, the expansion of their exports of manufactures is necessary for the exporters of primary products too, if they

---

[1] In the case of products where price support is achieved through import quotas (e.g., sugar in the United States) the quota should be liberalized or eliminated.

are in the long run to share in general prosperity and to pay their way in the world.

It is, moreover, not only in order to earn foreign exchange that the low-income countries must export manufactures: the size of their home markets is in many cases too small in a number of industries for the economic operation of a single plant, let alone of a number of plants in competition with each other. In these circumstances the export of manufactures is, for many countries and industries, an absolute condition for the maximizing of efficiency or even for the development of manufacturing on a reasonable economic basis.

One way in which the low-income countries can expand their markets for manufactures is, as suggested above, to reduce their own protection so as to increase their mutual trade. Their efforts in this direction, whether on a most-favoured-nation basis or by establishing regional common markets or free trade areas as is suggested below, should receive strong support. The results of such efforts, however, are not likely to be substantial for some time to come. Thus, the high-income countries should be ready to import manufactures from the low-income countries, and a policy seriously designed to help the growth of these countries must create the conditions for the expansion of such imports.

In the high-income countries the typical pattern of protection is one in which the more the basic material has been processed or fabricated the higher the tariff. Raw materials usually enter with a low level of restriction or none at all, processed materials encounter moderate tariffs, whereas final products, particularly consumer goods, encounter the highest degree of protection.[1] But even moderate tariffs on materials that have been through the early stage of processing often result in a high degree of effective protection for the processing industry itself. This is because the tariff is levied on the total value of the processed product but the value added in the processing industries is only a small percentage of this total value.[2] For some products the early stages of

---

[1] Thus the level of the common external tariff of the EEC, which [came] into force July 1, 1968, is set at zero for hides and skins and 10 per cent for most leather, whereas the duties on leather manufactures range between 14 and 19 per cent; and the tariff is 6.7 per cent on cocoa beans (reduced to 5.4 per cent until 1969), 20 per cent on cocoa butter, 25 per cent on cocoa paste, and 27 per cent on cocoa powder. There are many similar examples in the tariffs of other high-income countries such as Britain and the United States.

[2] For example, suppose that the world price of a certain type of leather is $100 and the cost of the hides to make the leather is $70. Then the 'value added' by the foreign producer is $30. Now assume that imports of hides into the EEC are

processing are the natural first steps for the entry of low-income countries into manufacturing and in such cases it is clearly important to reduce or eliminate even low tariffs on the processed product.

Recent studies have also shown that the effective protection of the manufacture of highly fabricated products is for similar reasons often substantially greater than the stated tariff.[1] The final stages of processing some products involve a great deal of hand labour and constitute precisely the kinds of manufacturing most suited to newly-developing countries. Thus a reduction in tariffs on manufactured products, even when they appear to have been fixed at moderate levels, can in certain cases be crucial for the export prospects of developing countries.

Further types of industrial activity that can be particularly appropriate for low-income countries are the assembly of parts produced in industrialized countries and the manufacture of parts for firms in the industrialized countries. In considering what trade barriers should be reduced, the governments of high-income countries should give full weight to such possibilities.

These are some general criteria that suggest the types of manufacture most likely to be successful in low-income countries and to become internationally competitive. For recommendations as to the precise products with respect to which the reduction of barriers would be most fruitful, governments might well seek advice from the staffs of appropriate international organizations such as the GATT, the United Nations Industrial Development Organization, and the World Bank, as well as from other experts with relevant experience. To this end we propose:

RECOMMENDATION 5. The high-income countries should adopt a program of reduction in barriers to the import of manufactures, concen-

duty-free, but that imports of leather are subject to a 10 per cent tariff. The tanner in the EEC is, therefore, in a position to charge $110 for the leather. But the $10 duty protects not the cost of producing hides, which can be imported free of duty, but only the 'value added' in tanning the hides which amounts to $30. Thus, a nominal tariff of 10 per cent on leather gives effective protection to the tanning industry equivalent to 33.3 per cent by permitting the domestic producer to incur higher costs to that extent on his processing operation.

[1] For example, in the United States the nominal tariff on shoes is 16.6 per cent but it has been calculated that the effective protection is 25.3 per cent. Likewise in the EEC the nominal tariff is 19.9 per cent and the effective protection 33.0 per cent; in Japan the nominal tariff is 29.5 per cent and the effective protection 45.1 per cent; in Britain the nominal tariff is 24.0 per cent and the effective protection 36.2 per cent. The source of these estimates is an article by Bela Balassa, 'Tariff Protection in Industrial Countries', Journal of Political Economy, Chicago, December 1965.

trated on those products offering the best opportunities for the development of exports from low-income countries. These products are likely to include those resulting from the early stages of processing of commodities and from labour-intensive manufacture, including assembly processes and the manufacture of parts.

It is desirable, in order to maintain a free and open world trading system as delineated in the GATT, that the reduction in barriers should take the form of tariff cuts on a most-favoured-nation basis and of the enlargement or abolition of quotas. In certain cases, however, preferential tariff reductions for low-income countries have been adopted or proposed, and this method of liberalizing trade is considered below in the section on 'Preferences'.

A further way of strengthening the ability of low-income countries to export manufactures is to encourage enterprises from the high-income countries to establish plants there or to adapt their home production to the increased use of processed materials and components imported from low-income countries. Such enterprises are particularly well placed to expand the low-income countries' exports of the products concerned, because of their knowledge of marketing techniques and their access to international channels of distribution.

PROVIDING FOR ADJUSTMENT ASSISTANCE

Our purpose in recommending reductions of trade barriers and other measures is to allow a steady increase in the low-income countries' exports of manufactures on a competitive basis. This can be achieved without causing substantial overall hardship in the high-income countries. The total imports of manufactures from low-income countries into the high-income countries are estimated to be only about 1 per cent of the total consumption of manufactures by the latter. Even big tariff cuts and quota enlargements would, therefore, cause little need for adjustment in the high-income countries' market for manufactures as a whole. But the impact would be substantial and might be crucial for a limited number of industries, particularly textiles, clothing, and light engineering, and for certain regions where such industries predominate. The extent and timing of the program of tariff cuts and quota enlargements in these industries should therefore be such as to allow a process of orderly change, which should moreover be eased by means of adjustment assistance.

Problems of adjustment would arise not only in manufacturing industries of high-income countries but also in their primary industries. Various methods of easing these processes of change have been adopted in a number of countries in recent years. Provision has been made for a transitional period during which trade barriers are regularly but gradually reduced, for example, five years in the case of the European Coal and Steel Community (ECSC) and the United States Trade Expansion Act and a maximum of fifteen years laid down in the Treaty establishing the European Economic Community. Financial and other help has been provided for those who have to redeploy as a result of competition arising from the program of liberalization, for example, the Social Fund in the EEC and adjustment assistance under the Trade Expansion Act. Other programs have also been provided for dealing with economic dislocation.

RECOMMENDATION 6. In order to ease the adjustment necessitated by trade liberalization, the program should be carried out over a transitional period. The high-income countries can[1] also provide for financial and other assistance to any of their citizens who have to redeploy as a result of the trade liberalization.

POSTPONEMENT OF RECIPROCITY BY LOW-INCOME COUNTRIES

The high-income countries' program of trade liberalization would not be conditional on reciprocity in the reduction of trade barriers by the low-income countries. It has already been agreed by the governments of high-income countries, formalized in a recent addition to the General Agreement on Tariffs and Trade, and implemented in the Kennedy Round negotiations, that the high-income countries do not expect such reciprocity. Unless, however, the low-income countries themselves adopt the right policies as suggested above, their exports are unlikely to increase satisfactorily merely because they have better access to the markets of high-income countries. Soundly based efforts by the low-income countries to help themselves are also required and will constitute a response of the most effective type, giving the high-income countries a strong incentive to adopt favourable trade and aid policies.

Conventional reciprocity by the low-income countries, in terms of liberalization of their own import policies, should also take place over time, when they have reached the stage where it would be consistent

---

[1] The British group participating in this statement would substitute the word 'should' for 'can'.

with their own development. Eventual liberalization is, indeed, in the interest of the low-income countries themselves, in view of the limitations imposed by highly protected home markets, particularly when these are very small. A special committee should be established within the GATT to establish procedures and formulate a program for ensuring that reciprocity is eventually realized.

RECOMMENDATION 7. The high-income countries should not expect the low-income countries to reciprocate the program of trade liberalization by reducing their own protection until their industries have had reasonable time to become internationally competitive. A special GATT committee should, however, formulate a program for ensuring that reciprocity is eventually realized and should at regular intervals report to governments on the execution of this program.

THE PROBLEM OF TARIFF PREFERENCES

A large number of low-income countries benefit from tariff preferences and preferential import quotas in European markets. The Commonwealth countries of Africa, Asia, and the West Indies have preferential entry to the British market. The Overseas Associated States have the right of duty-free access for their exports to the European Economic Community. As part of these arrangements, the European countries concerned also enjoy reciprocally preferential access to the markets of certain low-income countries.

A number of objections have been made to these preferential systems. Insofar as they grant special advantages to particular high-income countries in the markets of some low-income countries, they work to the disadvantage not only of other high-income countries but also of other low-income countries that might hope to sell in the low-income countries bound by these arrangements. Insofar as they grant special advantages in European markets for the Commonwealth countries and the Overseas Associated States, they do so at the expense of almost the whole of Latin America and the Middle East, of major countries in Asia, and of a number of African countries. On the other hand, it may be argued that participation in the EEC's preferential area is open to other African countries, and that the sudden removal of preferences would cause severe damage to some of the low-income countries that now receive them.

The EEC has in recent years reduced the margin of preference granted to the associated states by means of important cuts in the common external tariff on certain tropical products; and the British government offered, at the first UN Conference on Trade and Development, to abandon Commonwealth preference should a system of generalized tariff preferences in favour of all low-income countries be adopted by the high-income countries. Further tariff cuts by the high-income countries proposed earlier, would in any case reduce preference margins.

We also propose:

RECOMMENDATION 8.[1] The countries granting preferences should agree to eliminate them progressively over a transitional period, during which the low-income countries now receiving preferences would have time to make the necessary adjustments. The high-income countries should in addition take action, preferably by means of further general tariff cuts or special financial aid, to avoid causing significant losses to the low-income countries now receiving the preferences, and to help them to become internationally competitive by the end of the transitional period.

The best ways of compensating low-income countries for the loss of preferences in those markets where they now enjoy them are general tariff cuts, or financial aid used for the development of new export industries such as has been provided by the European Development Fund. Any generalized tariff preferences granted concurrently by all high-income countries to all low-income countries would likewise facilitate adjustment to the loss of special preferences by the low-income countries that now benefit from them. If, however, the measures taken by high-income countries acting together were inadequate, the countries originally granting preferences could introduce certain tariff-free or tariff-reduced quotas for imports from countries originally receiving them.

The main preference issue that arose at UNCTAD in 1964 was, however, broader than the question of rectifying the discrimination as among low-income countries caused by existing Commonwealth and EEC preferences. The most insistent demand of the low-income countries was for all high-income countries to extend generalized preferences on manufactured products.

The basic case for generalized preferences rests on an extension into the export sphere of the infant industry argument for protection in the home market. It is claimed that if producers in low-income countries

---

[1] The French, German, and Italian groups participating in this statement 'believe that the present framework of association of overseas states with the EEC is justified and should therefore be maintained'.

are to compete in high-income markets with established exporters from other high-income countries, the low-income producers need some special advantage to offset the initial costs of penetrating these new markets. Unlike protection in the domestic market, which often insulates the domestic producer completely from foreign competition, generalized preferences for low-income countries would expose producers in those countries to competition on at least equal terms with domestic producers in the high-income countries and with exporters of other low-income countries. These competitive pressures should promote efficiency in manufacturing for export and should tend to orient government policy with respect to the manufacturing industry from narrow import substitution toward competitive export promotion.[1]

Despite the case which can be made for preferences on a number of manufactured products to be extended by all high-income countries to all low-income countries for a limited period, it is unlikely that such preferences would be granted in unlimited volume because of fears of market disruption. Recent proposals have suggested that a limit be established through tariff-reduced quotas, which might be enlarged year by year. But the administration of such quotas would involve all the administrative difficulties inherent in any quota system, in addition to the special problem of deciding when a given country ceases to be a low-income country and thus to qualify for a quota. We therefore consider that if such a system of preferences is to be established, it should be limited in duration and applied only to those products for which on careful examination international competitive ability seems clearly within the reach of certain low-income countries. One way of introducing such a preferential arrangement with the least departure from existing practice would be to grant developing countries the benefit of selected future tariff reductions as soon as they are negotiated, while staging the reduction for high-income countries over an extended transitional period.

A special committee, which might be the one proposed above to deal

---

[1] The Japanese group participating in this statement wishes to add: 'It is to be noted that, in the case of the exports of some labour-intensive manufactured products by the low-income countries which are already internationally competitive in price, small tariff reductions to be granted by generalized preferences would have only a very limited favourable effect on their exports to the high-income countries. A more effective way of increasing the exports of these internationally competitive manufactured products by the low-income countries would be to remove or reduce non-tariff barriers of the high-income countries such as import quotas. These non-tariff barriers are more formidable obstacles than the tariffs to increasing exports by the low-income countries.'

with the question of reciprocity, could advise upon the proper extent and duration of any such generalized preferences. One criterion for determining how far they were justified might be the degree to which low-income countries were themselves taking steps to increase their competitiveness, in particular by avoiding excessive measures of protection and by the establishment of regional common markets of free trade areas.

NOT BY BREAD ALONE*

Barbara Ward

The following extract is from the text of a series of radio lectures given by Barbara Ward in 1961 over the Canadian Broadcasting Corporation. Mrs Ward sets out in a clear and concise manner the major requirements of the modernizing process in the UDCs. Her principal ideas, particularly the emphasis on how countries in the Western world are totally unprepared (or in some cases unwilling) to provide assistance, are as relevant today as when her lectures were written.

The revolutions that are referred to in the first paragraph are those that introduced the changes that have so affected the Western world over the past century. They include the emergence of the concept of equality, the development of an economic and social system that now emphasizes the goods and opportunities of this world, the growth of population and its concentration in urban areas, and the application of science and capital to all the economic processes of life. Whether these revolutions have made us happier or more civilized is questionable, but they have made some of us much wealthier. The crucial point, however, is that these developments have affected only a part of the world, creating a complex and tragic division that is becoming more and more obvious. It is the task of bridging this gap that forms the subject of 'Not by Bread Alone'.

[1961]

All the great revolutions of our contemporary world had their origin round the North Atlantic. The revolution by which equality has become a driving force in political life, the new concern with material things, the absorption in scientific analysis, the spurt of growth in the world's

*From *The Rich Nations and the Poor Nations* by Barbara Ward. CBC Massey Lectures. Copyright Barbara Ward 1961. CBC Publications, Toronto. Reprinted by permission of W. W. Norton & Company, Inc., New York, and Hamish Hamilton, London. Copyright © 1962 by Barbara Ward.

population, the whole transformation of our economic system by the application of technology and capital: all these vast changes were launched in the North Atlantic arena. Yet if you look at these Atlantic nations today they make the strange impression of not being particularly concerned with the revolutions they have wrought. The changes have been unleashed on mankind. Blindly, blunderingly, with immense impact and immense confusion, they are remaking the face of the earth. But can one say that the Western powers follow their course with any intimate concern? Do they see them as direct projections of the Western way of life or accept responsibility for the fact that it was the Western colonial system that chiefly set in motion the present world-wide movement of revolutionary change?

I wonder why this is. After all, is it not strange to care so little for what we have launched; to lose interest in our inventions just when they are beginning to have their maximum impact? And if one asks why this is so, I suppose some of the answers are not entirely comfortable. It seems to be a law of life that when you become rich you tend to become complacent. What is the Biblical phrase? 'They sat down to eat and they rose up to play.' Since the post-war economic revival in the West, the feeling has become fairly general that things are not going too badly. Elections have been fought on the slogan: 'You never had it so good'; great nations have been lulled with the promise of 'peace and prosperity'. The once militant working class substitutes 'I'm all right, Jack' for 'Workers of the world, unite'. This mood of ease and complacency unsuitably limits our ability to understand the needs and hungers of the millions who have not yet found their way into the modern world. To be rich and to be complacent invites the nemesis of such a condition—which is by indifference and by a narrowing of the heart to lose contact with the urgent desires of the great mass of one's fellow men. This constriction of pity can happen to individual men and women. History has always shown it. Today perhaps we see a new phenomenon: rich communities succumbing to the same limitation of human understanding.

But there is another more subtle reason that helps to explain why we are not as interested as we might be in all the revolutions we have launched. We simply cannot, out of our own experience, measure their truly daunting difficulties. All of them happened in the Western world under the conditions of maximum convenience. The West was relatively underpopulated: it was immensely well endowed with the resources that are needed for the new kind of economy. Iron ore and coal were plentiful for the launching of industry. The great plains of North America and southern Russia quickly began to pour out food for the new industrial millions.

But perhaps the chief reason for our overconfidence is to be found in the mechanism by which, in the main, the Western break-through to sustained growth was accomplished. In the critical early stages of change, the profit motive proved to be an immensely powerful engine of growth. Its success implanted deeply in the minds of many of us the idea that the greatest good of the greatest number can be achieved provided each individual or company or even nation vigorously pursues its own self-interest. The strength of the case lies in the fact that, up to a point and under certain conditions, the premise may well be right. Competition in a free market has produced enormous gains in wealth and efficiency. In fact, we are living today through another such burst of growth as the tariff barriers go down inside the Common Market. But equally the conditions in western Europe between the wars showed that if each nation pursued its own self-interest by a wrong route—in this case by constantly increasing its protective tariffs—the end result was not the good of all but the ruin of each. Nor has the Common Market come about by the unguided pressure of local interests. On the contrary, it has been an act of high statesmanship, pursued by dedicated political leaders and purposefully formulated by planners associated with M. Jean Monnet—surely one of the most quietly and effectively revolutionary groups the world has ever known.

In other words, there are conditions in which the unchecked pursuit of self-interest is an excellent guide to socially desirable action. There are also conditions when it is not. But the West still has a certain bias towards believing in its general efficacy, without regard to the framework within which it is to act. We tend to have a Micawberish attitude towards life, a feeling that as long as we do not get too excited something is certain to turn up. Yet if we look back over history I do not think the experience of other generations teaches us precisely this lesson. On the contrary, it suggests that not the Micawbers, but those who will, and want, and work, are more likely to see their plans and visions realized. It is, therefore a disturbing reflection that in our own day the amount of effort, interest, preparation, and sheer slogging hard work which the Communists tend to put into the task of building *their* version of world order very greatly exceeds what we are ready to do or the sacrifices we are prepared to make. Even more obviously, their vision of a world brotherhood made one by Communism, outstrips the scale of our imagination. The West thinks only marginally in terms of the whole world, the whole family of man. Each group tends to concentrate on its own parochial interests. There is apparently no energy comparable to the world-wide ambitions that set the Communists to work from one end of our planet to the other.

If we are to face the vast gap between the rich nations and the poor, between the nations round the Atlantic area which have been through their modernizing revolutions and the searching nations all around the world who seek desperately to make the same transition, perhaps the first decision we have to make is to abandon the fallacy that, somewhere, somehow, everything is going to turn out all right. We have to be ready to be as foresighted, as determined, as ready to work and to go on working, as are our busy Communist comrades. We must be prepared to match them, policy for policy, vision for vision, ideal for ideal.

I must confess that I can see no inherent reason why such a re-dedication of ourselves to great tasks should be impossible. We have the resources available; we have more resources at our disposal than any group of nations in the history of man. And it is hard to believe that we have run out of the moral energy needed to make the change. Looking at our society I certainly do not feel that it already presents such an image of the good life that we can afford to say that we have contributed all that we can to the vision of a transfigured humanity. Our uncontrollably sprawling cities, our shapeless suburbia, our trivial pursuits—quiz shows, TV, the golf games—hardly add up to the final end of man. We can do better than this. We also have the means to do better. If we do not feel the need there is only one explanation. We no longer have the vital imagination for the task.

Let us suppose, however, that we slough off our innate complacency. What ought we to try to do? What should be our aim in the challenging testing-period that lies ahead when the aspirations of the poor nations are going to become more and more urgent? For let us have no doubt about this. So far we have been living through the more comfortable phase of transformation in the underdeveloped areas; we have seen them during a time when their concentrated effort to get rid of colonialism gave them political unity and a sense of national purpose which they may well lack now that independence is achieved. Now that they are running their own affairs, all the grim problems of life face them in the raw: their bounding birth rates, their lack of capital, their desperate poverty, and, above all, the rising expectations of their own people. Every leader who has led his nation to the overthrow of Western influence or colonial rule is now faced with the stark problem: 'What next?' . . . There are no evasions now, no blaming it on the West—though that temptation continues—no looking for outside scapegoats. So, by a paradox, the post-colonial period is more tense, dangerous, and uncertain than the colonial struggle itself.

What can we do? What sort of policies can help the developing nations in the crucial years that lie ahead? And if I give you something of a shorthand answer, it is because we have already discussed a number of the crucial changes that must be made. Let us be clear first of all over the general aim. During the next twenty to thirty years we hope to see a majority of the developing nations pass through the sound-barrier of sustained growth. Moreover, we want these societies to have political elbow-room with a measure of autonomy for different groups and political power organized on a plural basis. We do not specify institutions or ideologies, but we hope for open societies in an open world. How shall we set about it?

The first point to make is that some general strategy is needed. And strategy is inseparable from a sustained effort through time. The rhythm of growth is not the rhythm of annual budgeting appropriations. Unless the Western nations bring themselves to accept the need for five- and ten-year programs, they will even waste what they do spend, for it will not be geared into a genuine strategy of growth.

The next point is that the scale of aid must be adequate. Patchy development, a litte here, a little there, does not lead to sustained growth. In every developing economy, there comes a time when, for perhaps two decades, a 'big push' is needed to get the economy off the launching-pad and into orbit.

Not all nations come to that point at the same time. There seems to be a certain pattern of progress and expansion, and different economies are ranged at different points along the line. First there is a phase that one might call the 'pre-investment' phase. Nearly everything needed for a 'big push' in investment is still lacking. Educated people are not available, training is minimal, capital overheads or infrastructure—power, transport, harbours, housing—have still to be built. At this stage, the country must be prepared for a later plunge into investment and help with education and training, investment in infrastructure, surveys of resources, and some preliminary planning, are the great needs.

But at the next stage—where such countries as India or Brazil or

Mexico now stand—the big investments begin to pay off. The ground is laid, rapid growth can be secured. It is at this point that large-scale capital aid from abroad can offset local poverty and lack of capital, thereby sparing governments the cruel choice of using totalitarian methods to compel people to save. Of all the countries at this stage of growth, I would say that India is the most important. The framework of a functioning economy is already built. But its ambitious capital plans are gravely endangered by a critical shortage of foreign exchange. In any Western development-strategy for the next decade, I myself would hope to see something like a billion dollars a year reserved for India's foreign exchange bill. If India can achieve its breakthrough, it is not only a question of India's preparedness. Nearly half the people living in the underdeveloped areas will be on their way to the modern world. If one adds Pakistan, more than half the problem of under-development could be met there in the Indian sub-continent.

Given that we accept the philosophy of a 'big push' in aid and investment, once the pre-conditions of growth have been realized, where should the capital be directed? It is quite impossible to define a general strategy since each country varies so much in its capacities, in its endowment of resources, in the scale of its internal market, and its export prospects. But perhaps one or two general points are worth making here. The first is that investment in education must continue to receive strong emphasis. Recent studies suggest that between fifty and sixty per cent of the gains in productivity made in the West in the last half-century spring from better trained minds, from more research, and more systematic use of the economy's brain-power. At present, most of the developing economies are only in the very first stages of the needed advance in education. Africa is strewn with societies where not more than ten per cent of the people are literate, where perhaps only one per cent ever reach secondary levels of schooling. The final tragic consequence of these standards can be seen in the Congo which became independent with perhaps not more than a dozen people with university degrees. No modern economy can be built on this basis.

A second critical area is that of farming. Modernized agriculture is, as we have seen, indispensable to the creation of general momentum in the economy. There are two separate needs: to encourage the structural changes which modern agriculture demands—the land reforms, the consolidation of holdings, the building of an influential co-operative movement; and to ensure a sufficient flow of capital into farming. The great variety of modern techniques, new fertilizers, new seed, new methods in planting and tilling, are nearly all costly. So is the scale of credit needed to launch a successful co-operative system. So last of all are the agricultural extension systems without which the farmer cannot learn what new opportunities are open to him. In the past, agriculture has been all too often the last on the government's priority list. Modern experience suggests it should be moved to the top.

The third area of expansion—industry—shows such universal variety that most generalizations have little value. However, one or two comments have some validity. One can say that industrialization will proceed more rapidly if a mistaken sense of national prestige does not precipitate large and costly mistakes in planning, such as investing in an integrated steel-works where there is neither iron ore nor coking-coal. Programs will lead to a better use of resources if capital is recognized for what it is in all developing economies: extremely scarce. Its price should be high, even if this idea upsets the more usual concept that basic services should be kept cheap in order to stimulate growth.

Another aspect of the same problem is that since foreign exchange is the scarcest of all forms of capital, it may be necessary, by high import duties or by auctioning import licences, or by other measures, to ensure that the entrepreneur who gets his hands on foreign exchange pays for its full value. This approach may contradict another tendency —to overvalue a developing nation's currency so that its exports will buy a maximum amount of foreign supplies. But, then, the way to development is, as Professor Higgens once remarked, 'paved with vicious circles'.

A developing government should aim its policies at ensuring the quickest rate of capital accumulation. Profits should be strongly encouraged, in public as in private enterprise, and tax-systems arranged so that all the incentives are towards their reinvestment. This again does not always arouse much enthusiasm among planners brought up to believe in the inherent immorality of profits and ready to run essential public services on a 'no profit, no loss' basis. But profits are one of the chief means by which resources can be put at the disposal of the investors in society and, as we have seen, are a major source of investment in Soviet Russia.

When it comes to the actual content of industrial policy, it must fit local conditions. Most countries can begin to produce locally some of the goods they import, provided protection is given. The 'beer, boots, and bricks' stage of consumer industry only awaits a determined government and some local entrepreneurial talent. But large-scale industry depends upon the availability of crucial raw materials. And it depends, too, upon the scale of the internal market. Five large steel-plants in India, where over four hundred million people make up the market and where iron ore and coking-coal are available, make perfect sense. East Europe's proliferation of steel-mills after 1948 did not. Clearly, developing governments would be well advised to look round and see whether by customs unions or common markets with their neighbours they may not increase the size and efficiency of their industrial units without risk of overproduction.

To all these changes—in education, in farming, in industry—there are more than economic consequences. Investment in men, investment in new techniques, investment in new forms of activity, all widen and strengthen the managerial and professional class and increase the training and scope of the manual worker. That gradual extension of the middle class to cover more and more of the nation's citizens is set in motion. With it goes a brighter hope of rational politics and civil rights.

These, then, are some of the elements in a broad strategy of modernization. But I think we have to realize that we in the Western world are not now organized to accomplish anything of the kind. It may be true that for nearly a hundred years we have been a kind of interconnected economy, taking some seventy per cent of each other's foreign investment, engrossing nearly seventy per cent of world trade, and affecting each other radically by the shifts and changes in our economic policy. But here Mr Micawber has reigned; here, above all, we have assumed that if everybody pursues his own national interest to the limit the outcome will somehow be to the advantage of everybody else. But this is very far from being generally true. Everyone's decision in 1929—as the recession deepened—to cut imports and push exports reduced world trade by three-quarters in nine months. The recession itself had been in some measure sparked by the fact that between 1925 and 1929 Britain did not dare reflate its economy for fear of losing its foreign reserves and America dared not deflate its wild boom for fear of attracting even more of the world's gold. Now if we think that this unreconciled opposite pull between domestic and foreign interest is a thing of the past, let us remember that all through 1960 we saw comparable pressures between the German mark and the dollar. In short, we have not yet worked out the policies and institutions needed to overcome the conflicting interests in our interdependent Atlantic world. In fact, only once did we have such a policy: during the Marshall Plan when for a time, owing to America's generosity and leadership, the nations of the Atlantic area walked in step towards common goals.

Today, I believe we have to revive the Marshall spirit if we are to have any hope of dealing—and dealing in time—with the problem of our obligations to the underdeveloped areas. Once again, I can suggest only in shorthand terms some of the policies we should undertake if we were a genuine community of rich nations dedicated to the task of creating the prosperity and the well-being of the developing world. And perhaps I should add, in parenthesis, that in doing so we should expand our own well-being as well. To me, one of the most vivid proofs that there is a moral governance in the universe is the fact that when men or governments work intelligently and far-sightedly for the good of others, they achive their own prosperity too. . . . 'Honesty is the best policy' used to be said in Victorian times. I would go further. I would say that generosity is the best policy and that expansion of opportunity sought for the sake of others ends by bringing well-being and expansion to oneself. The dice are not hopelessly loaded against us. Our morals and our interests—seen in true perspective—do not pull apart. Only the narrowness of our own interests, whether personal or national, blinds us to this moral truth.

What then should we do? Our first step must be a commitment. All the wealthy nations must accept a common obligation to provide capital and technical assistance to the underdeveloped areas. Britain, Canada, Australia, western Europe: we must all begin to do our share. Let us be quite clear about one thing. The reason why there is trouble over the American balance of payments is nothing to do with the inherent strength of the American economy, which is vast. It is nothing to do with the American trade balance, which is favourable. It has something to do, admittedly, with the American export of capital. But, above all, it is created by the fact that America is carrying far more than its fair burden both of the defence of the free world and of aid to the developing nations. And before we can hope to have a functioning Atlantic economy the other member nations must play their part. A suggested one per cent of national income is a fair criterion; and, incidentally, I consider that Germany, so generously rebuilt after the war and so generously forgiven the enormous destruction which Hitler created, might be in the forefront of those who accept this obligation.

This commitment is, however, only the beginning of the matter. Such a common purpose needs the proper institutional form. I believe we should attempt to build up in our Atlantic world some of the institutions which make it possible for us to co-operate *within* the national community. I think we should have an Atlantic Reserve Bank. I think we should develop common strategies for development and investment both inside and outside the Atlantic arena. I think we should take a long, hard look, at our trade policies, particularly the prices we pay for primary products. At present they do not, as they once did, pull up the rest of the world behind us. On the contrary, they tend to widen the gap. And for all this I think we need to expand our present Atlantic Organization for Economic Development into as many institutions—banks, development funds, trade groups, common markets, statistical services, and, above all, common policy-making organs—which might be needed to knit our interdependent economy into an integrated whole.

If we did this, I think we should do more than simply provide ourselves with the means to work out a strategy for the developing world; we should be creating the economic pre-conditions of a functioning world order. After all, we know that inside our domestic society we cannot survive in peace without law and welfare. It is upon these two pivots that the health of a community depends. Is our narrow interdependent world so different? Should we not be trying to create in the world at large the basic pre-conditions of a peaceful society?

We recognize the principles more or less inside our own domestic community. We do not have private wars. The rich do indeed contribute to the advancement of the poor. And while I am not concerned here with the whole great issue of world law and of disarmament, I am deeply concerned with the second aspect of good order: the ability of the rich to recognize their obligations and to see that in an interdependent world—and Heaven knows our interedpendence cannot be denied when we all stand under the shadow of atomic destruction—the principles of the general welfare cannot stop at the limits of our frontiers. It has to go forward; it has to include the whole family of man.

And having said so much, I begin to wonder whether there are any forces inside our comfortable, cosy, complacent Western world that will make us accept this challenge and see that we now face thirty to forty years of world-building on a scale never known in human history, since all our forefathers lived without the community of science, the speed of transport, the whole inter-connectedness of the modern globe. What will spur us to face this kind of decision? Facts? The facts are there. We cannot wish away the great revolution of modernization that is sweeping round the world; we cannot say it would be easier or more pleasant if it had not happened. Perhaps so; but we started the revolution and we can hardly ignore the forces that we unleashed upon the world.

Should we be guided by fear? Fear can indeed be the beginning of wisdom. Those who can live comfortably and without perturbation under the hideous threat of atomic destruction do not seem to me to be very wise. But blind fear is not a constructive force. Fear will serve us only if it drives us on to find a way out of our fears. And there is only one: to leave behind our present community of potential annihilation and build a community of moral purpose in its place. In such a world public law would take the place of private violence and the genera! welfare would be accepted over and above the particular interests of particular communities; above all, mankind would discover, beneath the clash of ideology, some minimum standards of trust rooted in the fact that we are all men, that we all stand under the judgement of history, and that we all love and seek to live and know that we must die.

It is just because the task before us is the positive task of building a peaceful home for the human family that I doubt whether realism or fear is enough to set us to work. We need resources of faith and vision as well. Do we have them? Or have the revolutions of our day, while increasing our physical powers, damped down the ardours of our spirit?

I do not believe it. Every one of the revolutions we have discussed goes beyond our material concerns and offers a challenge to the quality of our mind and spirit. The equality of men which is such a driving force all round the world sprang originally from the Western sense that men, as souls of infinite metaphysical value, stand equal before the throne of God. And if we feel this equality of man as a profound, moral fact, can we really be content to see men hungry, to see men die, to see men continue in starvation and ill-health when we have the means to help them? Is this our concept of equality? If it is, do we not betray our faith?

What Can Be Done?

SUMMARY AND RECOMMENDATIONS*
Paul R. Ehrlich and Anne H. Ehrlich

More and more people are becoming aware of the problems of over-population and are asking questions both of themselves and of their government representatives. What responsibilities must we as individuals assume towards the problems that face all of mankind? If the under-privileged segments of our own society have a right to assistance, should not the same right apply to people in other countries? In a democratic society, how can pressure be exerted on government so that a greater effort will be made towards solving the problems that have been described in this book, problems that are in large measure related to the 'population explosion'? The answers to these questions can only come from each one of us.

The summary and recommendations presented below are from a book that has been referred to previously: *Population, Resources, Environment* by Paul and Anne Ehrlich. The Ehrlichs summarize the population problem in a brief but logical fashion and set out a series of recommendations that are far-reaching and provocative. Despite the fact that this was written principally for an American readership, there can be little doubt that the thoughts it contains are also applicable to the residents of most of the developed countries of the world. Of particular significance is the distinction the authors make in emphasizing not only the importance of determining *what* can be done but *how* it should be carried out.

[1970]

SUMMARY

To recapitulate, we would summarize the present world situation as follows:

1. Considering present technology and patterns of behaviour our planet is grossly overpopulated now.

*From *Population, Resources, Environment: Issues in Human Ecology* by Paul R. Ehrlich and Anne H. Ehrlich. W. H. Freeman and Company. Copyright © 1970. Reprinted by permission.

2. The large absolute number of people and the rate of population growth are major hindrances to solving human problems.

3. The limits of human capability to produce food by conventional means have very nearly been reached. Problems of supply and distribution already have resulted in roughly half of humanity being undernourished or malnourished. Some 10-20 million people are starving to death annually now.

4. Attempts to increase food production further will tend to accelerate the deterioration of our environment, which in turn will eventually *reduce* the capacity of the earth to produce food. It is not clear whether environmental decay has now gone so far as to be essentially irreversible; it is possible that the capacity of the planet to support human life has been permanently impaired. Such technological 'successes', as automobiles, pesticides, and inorganic nitrogen fertilizers are major causes of environmental deterioration.

5. There is reason to believe that population growth increases the probability of a lethal worldwide plague and of a thermonuclear war. Either could provide an undesirable 'death rate solution' to the population problem; each is potentially capable of destroying civilization and even of driving *Homo sapiens* to extinction.

6. There is no technological panacea for the complex of problems composing the population-food-environment crisis, although technology, properly applied in such areas as pollution abatement, communications, and fertility control can provide massive assistance. The basic solutions involve dramatic and rapid changes in human *attitudes*, especially those relating to reproductive behaviour, economic growth, technology, the environment, and conflict resolution.

RECOMMENDATIONS: A POSITIVE PROGRAM

Although our conclusions must seem rather pessimistic, we wish to emphasize our belief that the problems can be solved. Whether they *will* be solved is another question. A general course of action that we feel will have some chance of ameliorating the results of the current crisis is outlined below. Many of the suggestions will seem 'unrealistic', and indeed that is how we view them. But the system has been allowed to run downhill for so long that only relatively idealistic programs offer any hope of salvation.

1. Population control is absolutely essential if the problems now facing mankind are to be solved. *It is not, however, a panacea.* If population

growth were halted immediately, virtually all other human problems—poverty, racial tensions, urban blight, environmental decay, warfare—would remain. The situation is best summarized in the statement, 'whatever your cause, it's a lost cause without population control'.

2. Political pressure must be applied immediately to induce the United States government to assume its responsibility to halt the growth of the American population. Once growth is halted, the government should undertake to regulate the birth rate so that the population is reduced to an optimum size and maintained there. It is essential that a grass-roots political movement be generated to convince our legislators and the executive branch of the government that they must act rapidly.

3. A massive campaign must be launched to restore a quality environment in North America and to *de-develop the United States*. De-development means bringing our economic system (especially patterns of consumption) into line with the realities of ecology and the world resource situation. This campaign would be largely political, especially with regard to our over-exploitation of world resources, but the campaign should be strongly supplemented by legal and boycott action against polluters and others whose activities damage the environment. The need for de-development presents our economists with a major challenge. They must design a low-consumption economy of stability, and an economy in which there is a much more equitable distribution of wealth than in the present one. Marxists claim that capitalism is intrinsically expansionist and wasteful, and that it automatically produces a monied ruling class. Can our economists prove them wrong?

4. Once the United States has clearly started on the path of cleaning up its own mess it can then turn its attention to the problems of the de-development of the other DCs, population control, and ecologically feasible semi-development of the UDCs. It must use every peaceful means at its disposal to bring the Soviet Union and other DCs into the effort, in line with the general proposals of Lord Snow and Academician Sakharov.[1] Such action can be combined with attempts to achieve a general detente with the Soviets and the Chinese. Citizens, through the ballot, letter writing, and continued peaceful protest, must make clear to American leaders that they wish to move towards disarmament in spite of its possible risks. They must demand detailed appraisal of

[1] Dr A. D. Sakharov, a member of the Soviet Academy of Sciences, proposed among other things that the DCs (in particular the U.S.A. and the U.S.S.R.) should contribute 20 per cent of their national income over a 15-year period to the tasks of population control and economic development in the UDCs. This proposal was supported by Dr C. P. Snow, a British physicist and novelist. (ed.)

the risks of continuing the 'balance of terror' versus the risk that the other side might 'cheat' in a controlled disarmament situation. Americans should inform themselves of what is known about the causes and the psychology of conflict and about deterrence theory, and attempt to elect officials who are similarly informed.

5. It is unfortunate that at the time of the greatest crisis the United States and the world has ever faced, many Americans, especially the young, have given up hope that the government can be modernized and changed in direction through the functioning of the elective process. Their despair may have some foundation, but a partial attempt to institute a 'new politics' very nearly succeeded in 1968. In addition many members of Congress and other government leaders, both Democrats and Republicans, are very much aware of the problems outlined in this book and are determined to do something about them. Others are joining their ranks as the dangers before us daily become more apparent. These people need public support in order to be effective. The world cannot, in its present critical state, be saved by merely tearing down old institutions, even if rational plans existed for constructing better ones from the ruins. We simply do not have the time. Either we will succeed by bending old institutions or we will succumb to disaster. Considering the potential rewards and consequences we see no choice but to make an effort to modernize the system. It may be necessary to organize a new political party with an ecological outlook and national and international orientation to provide an alternative to the present parties with their local and parochial interests. The environmental issue may well provide the basis for this.

6. Perhaps the major necessary ingredient that has been missing from a solution to the problems of both the United States and the rest of the world is a goal, a vision of the kind of spaceship earth that ought to be and the kind of crew that should man her. Society has always had its visionaries who talked of love, beauty, peace, and plenty. But somehow the 'practical' men have always been there to praise the smog as a sign of progress, to preach 'just' wars, and to restrict love while giving hate free rein. It must be one of the greatest ironies of the history of *Homo sapiens* that the only salvation for the practical men now lies in what they think of as the dreams of idealists. The question now is: can the 'realists' be persuaded to face reality in time?

Appendix

1970 WORLD POPULATION STATISTICS

The following statistics have been provided by the Population Reference Bureau, Inc., Washington, D.C., and contain a great deal of data on 142 countries as estimated for 1970. These statistics are reproduced here because they constitute basic reference material that should be consulted in conjunction with various articles in this book. Second, they provide population information for all the major countries of the world, information that is not available in any single article in this book. Third, the statistics can be used as raw material for various kinds of research projects. For example, data can be mapped and analysed, or information can be graphed in order to create visual representations from which observations and conclusions can be made.

Note that there are a number of discrepancies among the population figures quoted in different parts of this book. In many instances this is because official data for a particular country do not exist and one must rely on several differing estimates that are available. (The population of the People's Republic of China is a good example.) Where a discrepancy of this kind occurs, it is advisable for the sake of conformity to use the statistics supplied by the Population Reference Bureau.

1970 WORLD POPULATION STATISTICS

Region or Country	Population Estimates Mid-1970 (Millions)†	Births per 1,000 population‡	Deaths per 1,000 population‡	Current Rate of Population Growth	Number of Years to Double Population □	Infant Mortality Rate (Deaths under one year per 1,000 live births)‡	Population under 15 Years (Per cent)◆	Population Projections to 1985 (Millions)†	Per Capita Gross National Product (U.S. $)§	Population Increase 1965-1970 (Millions)†
WORLD	3,632[1]	34	14	2.0	35		37	4,933		343
AFRICA	344[2]	47	20	2.6	27		44	530		41
NORTHERN AFRICA	87	47	16	3.1	23		45	140		12.1
Algeria	14.0	44	14	3.2	22		47	23.9	250	2.1
Libya	1.9			3.1	23		44	3.1	720	0.3
Morocco	15.7	46	15	3.3	21	149	46	26.2	190	2.4
Sudan	15.8	52	18	3.2	22		47	26.0	90	2.2
Tunisia	5.1	45	16	3.0	24		44	8.3	210	0.7
U.A.R.	33.9	43	15	2.8	25	117	43	52.3	160	4.4
WESTERN AFRICA	101	49	23	2.5	28		44	155		11.7
Dahomey	2.7	54	26	2.6	27	110	46	4.1	80	0.3
Gambia	0.4	39	21	1.9	37		38	0.5	90	0.03
Ghana	9.0	47	20	2.9	24	156	45	14.9	200	1.3
Guinea	3.9	49	26	2.3	31	216	44	5.7	90	0.4
Ivory Coast	4.3	50	25	2.4	29	138	43	6.4	230	0.5
Liberia	1.2	44	25	1.9	37	188	37	1.6	190	0.1
Mali	5.1	50	25	2.4	29	120	46	7.6	80	0.6
Mauritania	1.2	45	25	2.2	32	187		1.7	130	0.1
Niger	3.8	52	25	2.9	24	200	46	6.2	70	0.5
Nigeria	55.1	50	25	2.6	27		43	84.7	80	6.4
Senegal	3.9	46	22	2.4	29		42	5.8	190	0.4
Sierra Leone	2.6	44	22	2.3	31	136		3.9	140	0.3
Togo	1.9	50	24	2.6	27	127	48	2.8	100	0.2
Upper Volta	5.4	49	28	2.1	33	182	42	7.7	50	0.5
EASTERN AFRICA	98	47	21	2.6	27		44	149		11.4
Burundi	3.6	46	26	2.3	31	150	47	5.3	50	0.4
Ethiopia	25.0			2.1	33			35.7	60	2.4
Kenya	10.9	50	20	3.1	23		46	17.9	120	1.5
Madagascar	6.9	46	22	2.7	26	102	46	10.8	100	0.9
Malawi	4.4			2.5	28	148	45	6.8	60	0.5
Mauritius	0.9	31	9	2.5	28	70	44	1.2	220	0.1
Mozambique*	7.7	47		2.1	33			11.1	180	0.7
Reunion*	0.5	37	4	3.1	23	59		0.7	560	0.1
Rwanda	3.6	52	22	2.9	24	137		5.7	60	0.5
Somalia	2.8			2.4	29			4.2	50	0.3
Southern Rhodesia*	5.0	48	14	3.4	21	122	47	8.6	230	0.8
Tanzania	13.2	47	22	2.6	27	163	42	20.3	80	1.6

1970 WORLD POPULATION STATISTICS

Region or Country	Population Estimates Mid-1970 (Millions)†	Births per 1,000 population‡	Deaths per 1,000 population‡	Current Rate of Population Growth	Number of Years to Double Population □	Infant Mortality Rate (Deaths under one year per 1,000 live births)‡	Population under 15 Years (Per cent)◆	Population Projections to 1985 (Millions)†	Per Capita Gross National Product (U.S. $)§	Population Increase 1965-1970 (Millions)†
Uganda	8.6	43	18	2.6	27	160	41	13.1	100	1.0
Zambia	4.3	51	20	3.0	24	259	45	7.0	180	0.6
MIDDLE AFRICA	36	46	23	2.2	32		42	52		3.6
Angola*	5.7			2.1	33		42	8.1	190	0.5
Cameroon (West)	5.8	50	26	2.2	32	137	39	8.4	130	0.6
Central African Republic	1.5	48	25	2.2	32	190	42	2.2	120	0.2
Chad	3.7	45	23	2.4	29	160	46	5.5	70	0.4
Congo (Brazzaville)	0.9	41	24	2.2	32	180		1.4	190	0.1
Congo (Democratic Republic)	17.4	43	20	2.2	32	104	42	25.8	90	1.8
Equatorial Guinea	0.3			1.3	54			0.4	240	0.02
Gabon	0.5	35	25	0.9	78	229	36	0.6	410	0.02
SOUTHERN AFRICA	23	41	17	2.4	29		40	34		2.5
Botswana	0.6			2.2	32		43	0.9	90	0.1
Lesotho	1.0	40	23	1.8	39	181	43	1.4	60	0.1
South Africa	20.1	40	16	2.4	29		40	29.7	590	2.2
Southwest Africa (Namibia)*	0.6			2.0	35		40	0.9		0.1
Swaziland	0.4			3.0	24			0.7	280	0.1
ASIA	2,056²	38	15	2.3	31		40	2,874		223
SOUTHWEST ASIA	77	44	15	2.9	24		43	121		10.3
Cyprus	0.6	25	7	0.9	78	28	35	0.7	780	0.02
Iraq	9.7	48	15	3.4	21		45	16.7	230	1.5
Israel	2.9	26	7	2.4	29	26	33	4.0	1,200	0.3
Jordan	2.3	47	16	3.3	21		46	3.9	250	0.3
Kuwait	0.7	47	6	8.3	9	31	38	2.4	3,490	0.2
Lebanon	2.8			3.0	24			4.3	520	0.4
Saudi Arabia	7.7			2.8	25			12.2	350	1.0
Southern Yemen	1.3			2.8	25			2.0	130	0.2
Syria	6.2	47	15	3.3	21		46	10.5	180	0.9
Turkey	35.6	43	16	2.7	26	155	44	52.8	290	4.4
Yemen	5.7			2.8	25			9.1	70	0.7
MIDDLE SOUTH ASIA	762	44	16	2.7	26		43	1,137		96.9
Afghanistan	17.0			2.5	28			25.0	70	1.9
Bhutan	0.8			2.2	32			1.2	60	0.1
Ceylon	12.6	32	8	2.4	29	53	41	17.7	160	1.4
India	554.6	42	17	2.6	27	139	41	807.6	90	67.9
Iran	28.4	48	18	3.0	24		46	45.0	280	3.8
Nepal	11.2	41	21	2.2	32		40	15.8	70	1.2

1970 WORLD POPULATION STATISTICS

Region or Country	Population Estimates Mid-1970 (Millions)†	Births per 1,000 population‡	Deaths per 1,000 population‡	Current Rate of Population Growth	Number of Years to Double Population □	Infant Mortality Rate (Deaths under one year per 1,000 live births)‡	Population under 15 Years (Per cent)◆	Population Projections to 1985 (Millions)†	Per Capita Gross National Product (U.S. $)§	Population Increase 1965-1970 (Millions)†
Pakistan	136.9	50	18	3.3	21	142	45	224.2	90	20.6
SOUTHEAST ASIA	287	43	15	2.8	25		44	434		37.6
Burma	27.7			2.3	31		40	39.2	70	3.0
Cambodia	7.1	50	20	3.0	24	127	44	11.3	130	1.0
Indonesia	121.2	49	21	2.9	24	125	42	183.8	100	16.3
Laos	3.0	42	17	2.5	28			4.4	90	0.4
Malaysia (East and West)	10.8	35	8	2.8	25	48	44	16.4	290	1.4
Philippines	38.1	50		3.4	21	72	47	64.0	180	5.8
Singapore	2.1	25	6	2.4	29	25	43	3.0	600	0.2
Thailand	36.2	46	13	3.3	21		43	57.7	130	5.4
North Vietnam	21.2			2.1	33			28.2	100	2.2
South Vietnam	18.0			2.1	33			23.9	120	1.8
EAST ASIA	930	30	13	1.8	39		36	1,182		78.1
China (Mainland)	759.6	34	15	1.8	39			964.6	90	64.6
China (Taiwan)	14.0	29	6	2.3	31	21	44	19.4	250	1.6
Hong Kong*	4.2	21	5	2.5	28	23	40	6.0	620	0.5
Japan	103.5	19	7	1.1	63	15	25	121.3	1,000	5.5
Korea (North)	13.9	39	11	2.8	25			20.7	230	1.8
Korea (South)	32.1	36	11	2.5	28		42	45.9	160	3.7
Mongolia	1.3	40	10	3.1	23		44	2.0	410	0.2
Ryukyu Islands*	1.0	22	5	1.7	41		39	1.3	540	0.1
NORTHERN AMERICA	228[2]	18	9	1.1	63		30	280		13.2
Canada	21.4	17.7	7.4	1.7	41	22.0	33	27.3	2,380	1.8
United States[3]	205.2	17.6	9.6	1.0	70	21.2	30	241.7	3,670	11.4
LATIN AMERICA	283[2]	38	9	2.9	24		42	435		37
MIDDLE AMERICA	67	43	9	3.4	21		46	112		10.5
Costa Rica	1.8	45	8	3.8	19	70	48	3.2	410	0.3
El Salvador	3.4	48	13	3.4	21		45	5.9	270	0.5
Guatemala	5.1	46	16	2.9	24	89	46	7.9	310	0.7
Honduras	2.7	49	16	3.4	21		51	4.6	240	0.4
Mexico	50.7	44	10	3.4	21	64	46	84.4	490	8.0
Nicaragua	2.0	47	16	3.0	24		48	3.3	360	0.3
Panama	1.5	42	10	3.3	21	43	43	2.5	550	0.2
CARIBBEAN	26	35	11	2.2	32		40	36		2.7
Barbados	0.3	29	9	0.8	88	54	38	0.3	420	0.01
Cuba	8.4	28	8	1.9	37	38	37	11.0	330	0.8
Dominican Republic	4.3	48	15	3.4	21	73	47	7.3	260	0.7
Guadeloupe*	0.4	32	8	2.4	29		42	0.5	470	0.04

1970 WORLD POPULATION STATISTICS

Region or Country	Population Estimates Mid-1970 (Millions)†	Births per 1,000 population‡	Deaths per 1,000 population‡	Current Rate of Population Growth	Number of Years to Double Population □	Infant Mortality Rate (Deaths under one year per 1,000 live births)‡	Population under 15 Years (Per cent)◆	Population Projections to 1985 (Millions)†	Per Capita Gross National Product (U.S. $)§	Population Increase 1965-1970 (Millions)†
Haiti	5.2	45	20	2.5	28		42	7.9	70	0.6
Jamaica	2.0	39	8	2.1	33	30	41	2.6	460	0.2
Martinique*	0.4	30	7	2.0	35		42	0.5	540	0.03
Puerto Rico*	2.8	25	6	1.4	50	28	39	3.4	1,210	0.2
Trinidad and Tobago	1.1	30	8	1.8	39	42	43	1.3	790	0.1
TROPICAL SOUTH AMERICA	151	39	9	3.0	24		43	236		20.8
Bolivia	4.6	44	20	2.4	29		44	6.8	170	0.5
Brazil	93.0	39	11	2.8	25	170	43	142.6	250	12.3
Colombia	21.4	44	11	3.4	21	78	47	35.6	300	3.3
Ecuador	6.1	47	13	3.4	21	90	48	10.1	210	1.0
Guyana	0.7	40	10	2.9	24	40	46	1.1	330	0.1
Peru	13.6	44	12	3.1	23	62	45	21.6	350	1.9
Venezuela	10.8	46	10	3.4	21	46	46	17.4	880	1.6
TEMPERATE SOUTH AMERICA	39	26	9	1.8	39		33	51		3.4
Argentina	24.3	22	8	1.5	47	58	29	29.6	800	1.7
Chile	9.8	34	11	2.3	31	100	40	13.6	470	1.1
Paraguay	2.4	45	12	3.4	21	52	45	4.1	220	0.4
Uruguay	2.9	24	9	1.2	58	43	28	3.4	550	0.2
EUROPE	**462²**	**18**	**10**	**0.8**	**88**		**25**	**515**		**18**
NORTHERN EUROPE	81	18	11	0.6	117		24	90		2.3
Denmark	4.9	16.8	9.7	0.8	88	15.8	24	5.5	1,950	0.2
Finland	4.7	16.0	9.6	0.4	175	14.0	27	5.0	1,660	0.1
Iceland	0.2	20.9	6.9	1.8	39	14.1	34	0.3	1,690	0.02
Ireland	3.0	20.9	11.3	0.7	100	24.4	31	3.5	910	0.1
Norway	3.9	17.6	9.7	0.9	78	12.8	25	4.5	1,860	0.2
Sweden	8.0	14.3	10.4	0.8	88	12.9	21	8.8	2,500	0.3
United Kingdom	56.0	17.1	11.9	0.5	140	18.8	23	61.8	1,700	1.4
WESTERN EUROPE	149	17	11	0.8	88		24	163		5.5
Austria	7.4	17.2	13.1	0.4	175	25.5	24	8.0	1,210	0.2
Belgium	9.7	14.8	12.8	0.4	175	22.9	24	10.4	1,740	0.2
France	51.1	16.8	11.0	0.8	88	20.4	25	57.6	1,950	2.4
West Germany	58.6	19.7	11.9	0.6	117	22.8	23	62.3	1,750	1.7
Luxembourg	0.4	14.2	12.3	1.2	58	16.7	22	0.4	2,000	0.02
Netherlands	13.0	18.6	8.2	1.1	63	13.6	28	15.3	1,520	0.7
Switzerland	6.3	17.1	9.3	1.1	63	16.1	23	7.4	2,310	0.3
EASTERN EUROPE	104	17	10	0.8	88		25	116		4.0
Bulgaria	8.5	16.9	8.6	0.8	88	28.3	24	9.4	690	0.3

1970 WORLD POPULATION STATISTICS

Region or Country	Population Estimates Mid-1970 (Millions)†	Births per 1,000 population‡	Deaths per 1,000 population‡	Current Rate of Population Growth	Number of Years to Double Population □	Infant Mortality Rate (Deaths under one year per 1,000 live births)‡	Population under 15 Years (Per cent)♦	Population Projections to 1985 (Millions)†	Per Capita Gross National Product (U.S. $)§	Population Increase 1965-1970 (Millions)†
Czechoslovakia	14.7	14.9	10.7	0.7	100	22.1	25	16.2	1,110	0.5
East Germany	16.2	14.3	14.3	0.3	233	20.4	22	16.9	1,300	0.2
Hungary	10.3	15.1	11.2	0.4	175	35.8	23	11.0	900	0.1
Poland	33.0	16.2	7.6	0.9	78	33.4	30	38.2	780	1.5
Romania	20.3	26.3	9.6	1.3	54	59.5	26	23.3	720	1.3
SOUTHERN EUROPE	128	19	9	0.9	78		27	146		5.7
Albania	2.2	35.6	8.0	2.7	26	86.8		3.3	320	0.3
Greece	8.9	18.2	8.3	0.8	88	34.4	25	9.7	700	0.3
Italy	53.7	17.6	10.1	0.8	88	32.8	24	60.0	1,120	2.1
Malta	0.3	16.1	9.0	−0.8		27.4	32	0.3	570	−0.01
Portugal	9.6	20.5	10.0	0.7	100	59.2	29	10.7	420	0.3
Spain	33.2	20.5	8.7	1.0	70	32.0	27	38.1	680	1.6
Yugoslavia	20.6	18.9	8.6	1.1	63	61.4	30	23.8	530	1.1
U.S.S.R.	242.6	17.9	7.7	1.0	70	26.5	28	286.9	970	12.1
OCEANIA	19²	25	10	2.0	35		32	27		2.0
Australia	12.5	20.0	9.1	1.9	37	18.3	29	17.0	1,970	1.1
New Zealand	2.9	22.6	8.9	1.7	41	18.7	33	3.8	1,890	0.2

WORLD AND REGIONAL POPULATION (Millions)

	World	Africa	Asia	North America	Latin America	Europe	Oceania	USSR
Mid-1970	3,632	344	2,056	228	283	462	19	243
2000 Projections, U N Constant Fertility	7,522	860	4,513	388	756	571	33	402
2000 Projections, U N Medium Estimate	6,130	768	3,458	354	638	527	32	353

FOOTNOTES

† Estimates from United Nations. *World Population Prospects, 1965-85, As Assessed in 1968*, United Nations Population Division Working Paper No. 30, December 1969.

‡ Latest available year. Except for North American rates computed by PRB, world and regional estimates are derived from *World Population Prospects* (see footnote †). The country estimates are essentially those available as of October, 1969 in United Nations *Population and Vital Statistics Report*, Series A, Vol. XXI, No. 4, with some adjustments which were necessary in view of the deficiency of registration in some countries.

♦ Latest available year. Derived from *World Population Prospects* (see footnote †) and United Nations *Demographic Yearbook, 1967*.

§ 1967 data supplied by the International Bank for Reconstruction and Development.

□ Assuming continued growth at current annual rate.

* Non-sovereign country.

[1] Total reflects United Nations adjustments of discrepancies in international migration data.

[2] Regional population totals take into account small areas not listed on the Data Sheet.

[3] U.S. figures are based on data from the U.S. Bureau of the Census and the National Center for Health Statistics. The total mid-year population has not been adjusted to accommodate the estimated 5.7 million 'undercount' of the U.S. population in the 1960 census.

NOTE: In general, for many of the developing countries, the demographic data including total population, age reporting, and vital rates are subject to deficiencies of varying degrees. In some cases, the data are estimates of the United Nations Secretariat.

Selected Bibliography

1. INTRODUCTION TO DEMOGRAPHY AND POPULATION PROBLEMS

American Academy of Political and Social Science, 'World Population', *The Annals*, Vol. 369, January 1967.

APPLEMAN, PHILIP, *The Silent Explosion*, Beacon Press, Boston, 1965.

BATES, MARSTON, *The Prevalence of People*, Charles Scribner's Sons, New York, 1962.

BENJAMIN, BERNARD, *Demographic Analysis*, George Allen & Unwin Ltd., London, 1968.

BOGUE, DONALD J., *Principles of Demography*, John Wiley & Sons, Inc., New York, 1969.

BORGSTROM, GEORG, *The Hungry Planet*, The Macmillan Company, New York, 1965.

BROWN, HARRISON, *The Challenge of Man's Future*, The Viking Press, Inc., New York, 1954.

——, et al., *The Next Hundred Years*, The Viking Press, Inc., New York, 1957.

CHAMBERLAIN, N.W., *Beyond Malthus: Population and Power*, Basic Books Inc., New York, 1970.

CLARK, COLIN, *Population Growth and Land Use*, St Martin's Press, Inc., New York, 1967.

COOK, ROBERT C., and LECHT, J., *People!: An Introduction to the Study of Population*, Columbia Books, Washington, D.C., 1968.

COX, PETER R., *Demography*, Cambridge University Press, New York, 3rd ed., 1966.

DAVIS, KINGSLEY, 'Population', *Scientific American*, 1963.

DEEVEY, EDWARD S., JR, 'The Human Population', *Scientific American*, 1960.

EHRLICH, PAUL R., *The Population Bomb*, Ballantine Books, Inc., New York, 1968.

FARMER, RICHARD N., LONG, JOHN D., and STOLNITZ, GEORGE J., eds., *World Population—The View Ahead*, Bureau of Business Research, Indiana University, Indiana, 1968.

FISHER, TADD, *Our Overcrowded World*, Parent's Magazine Press, New York, 1969.

FREEDMAN, RONALD, ed., *Population: The Vital Revolution*, Doubleday & Company, Inc., New York, 1964.

HAUSER, PHILIP M., *Population Perspectives*, Rutgers University Press, New Brunswick, New Jersey, 1961.

——, ed., *The Population Dilemma*, Prentice-Hall, Inc., Englewood Cliffs, New Jersey, 2nd ed., 1970.

——, and DUNCAN, OTIS DUDLEY, eds., *The Study of Population: An Inventory and Appraisal*, University of Chicago Press, Chicago, 1959.

HEER, DAVID M., ed., *Readings on Population*, Prentice-Hall, Inc., Englewood Cliffs, New Jersey, 1968.

HUXLEY, JULIAN, *The Human Crisis*, University of Washington Press, Seattle, 1963.

KEYFITZ, NATHAN, and FLIEGER, WILHELM, *World Population: An Analysis of Vital Data*, University of Chicago Press, Chicago, 1968.

MALTHUS, THOMAS, HUXLEY, JULIAN, and OSBORN, FREDERICK, *Three Essays on Population*, Mentor Books, New York, 1960.

MCCORMACK, ARTHUR, *The Population Problem*, Thomas Y. Crowell Co., New York, 1970.

MORAN, WILLIAM E., JR, ed., *Population Growth—Threat to Peace?*, P. J. Kenedy & Sons, New York, 1965.

MUDD, STUART, ed., *The Population Crisis and the Uses of World Resources*, Indiana University Press, Bloomington, Indiana, 1964.

NAM, CHARLES B., ed., *Population and Society: A Textbook of Selected Readings*, Houghton Mifflin Company, Boston, 1968.

NICOL, HUGH, *The Limits of Man: An Enquiry into the Scientific Basis of Human Population*, Humanities Press, Inc., New York, 1967.

OSBORN, FAIRFIELD, *Our Plundered Planet*, Pyramid Publications, New York, 1968.

——, ed., *Our Crowded Planet: Essays on the Pressures of Population*, Doubleday & Co., Inc., New York, 1962.

PETERSEN, WILLIAM, *Population*, The Macmillan Company, New York, 2nd ed., 1969.

Population Reference Bureau, 'Spaceship Earth in Peril', *Population Bulletin*, Vol. XXI, No. 1, March 1969.

———, *World Population Data Sheet*, Washington, D.C.

PRESSAT, ROLAND, *Demographic Analysis*, Aldine Publishing Company, Chicago, 1969.

REGIER, HENRY, and FALLS, BRUCE J., eds., *Exploding Humanity: The Crisis of Numbers*, House of Anansi Press Press Limited, Toronto, 1970.

SAUVY, ALFRED, *Fertility and Survival: Population Problems from Malthus to Mao Tse-Tung*, Criterion Books, New York, 1961.

SAX, KARL, *Standing Room Only: The World's Exploding Population*, Beacon Press, Boston, 1960.

SILLS, DAVID L., ed., *International Encyclopedia of the Social Sciences*, Vol. 12, Crowell Collier and Macmillan, Inc., New York, 1968.

SPIEGELMAN, M., *Introduction to Demography*, Harvard University Press, Cambridge, 1968.

THOMLINSON, RALPH, *Demographic Problems; Controversy over Population Control*, Dickenson Publishing Co., Belmont California, 1967.

———, *Population Dynamics: Causes and Consequences of World Demographic Change*, Random House, Inc., New York, 1965.

THOMPSON, WARREN S., and LEWIS, DAVID T., *Population Problems*, McGraw-Hill Book Company, New York, 5th ed., 1965.

United Nations, *Demographic Yearbook*, United Nations, New York, published annually.

———, *The Determinants and Consequences of Population Trends*, United Nations, New York, 1953.

———, *Statistical Yearbook*, United Nations, New York, published annually.

U.S. Senate, Ninetieth Congress, Committee on Government Operations, Sub-Committee on Foreign Aid Expenditures, *Population Crisis* (The Gruening Hearings), 14 vols, Government Printing Office, Washington, D.C., 1965-8.

VOGT, WILLIAM, *People! Challenge to Survival*, William Sloane Associates, New York, 1960.

World Population Conference 1965, *Proceedings* (4 vols), United Nations, New York, 1966.

WRONG, DENNIS H., *Population and Society*, Random House, Inc., New York, 3rd ed., 1967.

YOUNG, LOUISE B., ed., *Population in Perspective*, Oxford University Press, New York, 1968.

2. WORKS BY GEOGRAPHERS

BEAUJEU-GARNIER, J., *Geography of Population*, St Martin's Press, New York, 1966.

CLARKE. JOHN I., *Population Geography*, Pergamon Press Ltd., London, 1965.

DEMKO, GEORGE J., et al., eds., *Population Geography: A Reader*, McGraw-Hill Book Company, New York, 1970.

GRIFFIN, PAUL F., ed., *Geography of Population*, Fearon Publishers, Palo Alto, California, 1969.

STAMP, DUDLEY L., *The Geography of Life and Death*, William Collins Sons & Co., Ltd., Fontana Library, London, 1964.

TREWARTHA, GLENN T., *A Geography of Population and World Patterns*, John Wiley & Sons, Inc., New York, 1969.

WILSON, MURRAY G. A., *Population Geography*, Thomas Nelson & Sons, Ltd., Melbourne, 1968.

WRIGLEY, E. A., 'Demographic Models and Geography', in Richard J. Chorley and Peter Haggett, eds., *Models in Geography*, Methuen Publications, London, 1967.

——, 'Geography and Population', in Richard J. Chorley and Peter Haggett, eds., *Frontiers in Geography Teaching*, Methuen Publications, London, 1967.

ZELINSKY, WILBUR, *A Prologue to Population Geography*, Prentice-Hall, Inc., Englewood Cliffs, New Jersey, 1966.

——, KOSINSKI, LESZEK, and PROTHERO, MANSELL R., eds., *Geography and a Crowding World: Essays on Population Pressures upon Resources*, Oxford University Press, New York, 1970.

3. HISTORICAL DEMOGRAPHY

CARR-SAUNDERS, ALEXANDER M., *World Population: Past Growth and Present Trends*, Barnes and Noble, Inc., New York, 1965. (First published in 1936.)

CIPOLLA, CARLO, *The Economic History of World Population*, Penguin Books, Inc., Baltimore, 1962.

Daedalus: Journal of the American Academy of Arts and Sciences, 'Historical Population Studies', Vol. 97, No. 2, Spring 1968.

GLASS, DAVID V., and EVERSLEY, D.C.C., eds., *Population in History/Essays in Historical Demography*, Aldine Publishing Co., Chicago, 1965.

HUTCHINSON, C. P., *The Population Debate,* Houghton Mifflin Company, Boston, 1967.

LORIMER, FRANK, 'The Development of Demography', in *The Study of Population,* edited by Philip M. Hauser and Otis Dudley Duncan, University of Chicago Press, Chicago, 1959.

MALTHUS, THOMAS R., *On Population,* edited and introduced by Gertrude Himmelfarb, Modern Library, New York, 1960.

MORRIS, JUDY K., 'Malthus in Retrospect', *Population Bulletin,* Vol. XXII, No. 1, 1966.

Population Reference Bureau, 'How Many People Have Ever Lived on Earth?' *Population Bulletin,* Vol. XVIII, No. 1, February, 1962.

———, 'Soviet Population Theory from Marx to Kosygin', *Population Bulletin,* Vol. XXIII, No. 4, 1967.

WRIGLEY, E. A., *Industrial Growth and Population Change,* Cambridge University Press, Cambridge, England, 1961.

4. FERTILITY AND MORTALITY

BENJAMIN, BERNARD, *Health and Vital Statistics,* George Allen & Unwin Ltd., London, 1968.

———, *Social and Economic Factors Affecting Mortality,* Humanities Press, Inc., New York, 1965.

GOODE, WILLIAM J., *World Population and Family Patterns,* The Free Press, New York, 1963.

GREEP, ROY O., *Human Fertility and Population Problems,* Schenkman Publishing Co., Inc., Cambridge, Mass., 1963.

Milbank Memorial Fund, *Thirty Years of Research in Human Fertility: Restrospect and Prospect,* Milbank Memorial Fund, New York, 1959.

NAG, MONI, *Factors Affecting Human Fertility in Non-Industrialized Societies: A Cross-Cultural Study,* Human Relations Area Files Press, New Haven, 1968.

SZABADY, EGON, ed., *Studies on Fertility and Social Mobility,* Akademie Kiado, Budapest, 1964.

United Nations, *Selected Papers and Summaries: Fertility, Family Planning and Mortality,* Proceedings of the Belgrade Population Conference, August 30-September 10, 1965, Vol. II, United Nations, New York, 1967.

———, 'The Situation and Recent Trends of Mortality in the World', *Population Bulletin,* No. 6 (1963), United Nations, New York, 1963.

WOOD, CLIVE, *Sex and Fertility*, Thames and Hudson Ltd., London, 1969.

World Health Organization, *Trends in the Study of Morbidity and Mortality*, Public Health Papers 27, World Health Organization, Geneva, 1965.

5. POPULATION, RESOURCES, AND ECONOMIC DEVELOPMENT

The American Assembly, *Overcoming World Hunger*, Prentice-Hall, Inc., Englewood Cliffs, New Jersey, 1969.

BARNETT, HAROLD J., and MORSE, CHANDLER, *Scarcity and Growth*, Johns Hopkins Press, Baltimore, 1963.

BORGSTROM, GEORG, *Too Many*, The Macmillan Company, New York, 1969.

BRIGGS, PETER, *Water, The Vital Essence*, Harper & Row, New York, 1967.

BROWN, LESTER R., *Man, Land and Food: Looking Ahead at World Food Needs*, Government Printing Office, Washington, D.C., 1963.

———, *Seeds of Change: The Green Revolution and Developments in the 1970s*, Praeger Publishers, Inc., New York.

CAREFOOT, G. L., and SPROTT, E. R., *Famine on the Wind*, Angus & Robertson Ltd., 1969.

COALE, ANSLEY J., and HOOVER, EDGAR M., *Population Growth and Economic Development in Low-Income Countries*, Princeton University Press, Princeton, 1958.

COCHRANE, WILLARD W., *The World Food Problem: A Guardedly Optimistic View*, Thomas Y. Crowell, New York, 1969.

DANSEREAU, PIERRE, *Challenge For Survival, Land, Air and Water for Man in Megalopolis*, Columbia University Press, New York, 1970.

DARLING, F. FRASER, and MILTON, JOHN P., eds., *Future Environments of North America*, Natural History Press, Garden City, New York, 1966.

DASMANN, RAYMOND F., *Environmental Conservation*, John Wiley & Sons, New York, 2nd ed., 1968.

DE CASTRO, JOSUE, *The Black Book of Hunger*, Beacon Press, Boston, 1969.

———, *The Geography of Hunger*, Little, Brown and Company, Boston, 1952.

DUMONT, RENE, and ROSIER, BERNARD, *The Hungry Future*, Praeger Publishers, Inc., New York, 1969.

EHRLICH, PAUL R., and ANNE H., *Population, Resources, Environment: Issues in Human Ecology*, W. H. Freeman and Co., San Francisco, 1970.

ENKE, STEPHEN, *Economics for Development*, Prentice-Hall Inc., Englewood Cliffs, New Jersey, 1963.

Food and Agriculture Organization (United Nations), *A Strategy for Plenty: The Indicative World Plan for Agricultural Development*, Rome, 1970.

FREEMAN, ORVILLE L., *World Without Hunger*, Praeger Publishers Inc., New York, 1968.

HOPCRAFT, ARTHUR, *Born to Hunger*, Pan Books Ltd., London, 1968.

KUZNETS, SIMON, *Economic Growth and Structure: Selected Essays*, W. W. Norton & Co., New York, 1965.

MEIER, GERALD M., *Leading Issues in Economic Development: Studies in International Poverty*, Oxford University Press, New York, 1970.

MOUNTJOY, A. B., *Industrialization and Underdeveloped Countries*, Hutchinson University Library, London, 1966.

MUDD, STUART, ed., *The Population Crisis and the Use of World Resources*, Indiana University Press, Bloomington, Indiana, 1964.

MYINT, H., *The Economics of the Developing Countries*, Hutchinson & Co., Ltd., London, 1964.

MYRDAL, GUNNAR, *Asian Drama*, 3 Vols, Pantheon Books, Inc., New York, 1968.

National Academy of Sciences, *Prospects of the World Food Supply: A Symposium*, Washington, D.C., 1966.

National Academy of Sciences—National Research Council, *Resources and Man*, W. H. Freeman and Co., San Francisco, 1969.

PADDOCK, WILLIAM and PAUL, *Famine—1975!*, Little, Brown & Co., Boston, 1967.

PINCUS, JOHN A., ed., *Reshaping the World Economy: Rich and Poor Countries*, Prentice-Hall, Inc., Englewood Cliffs, New Jersey, 1968.

PIRIE, N. W., *Food Resources Conventional and Novel*, Penguin Books, Inc., Baltimore, 1969.

POPKIN, ROY, *Desalination: Water for the World's Future*, Praeger Publishers, Inc., New York, 1968.

Population Reference Bureau, 'The Food-Population Dilemma', by Tadd Fisher, *Population Bulletin*, Vol. XXIV, No. 4, December 1968.

——, 'The Thin Slice of Life', *Population Bulletin*, Vol. XXIV, No. 5, December 1968.

Report of the Commission on International Development, Chairman, Lester B. Pearson, *Partners in Development*, Praeger Publishers, Inc., New York, 1969.

ROSTOW, W. W., *The Stages of Economic Growth*, Cambridge University Press, Cambridge, England, 1960.

SHEPARD, PAUL, and MCKINLEY, DANIEL, eds., *The Subversive Science*, Houghton Mifflin Co., Boston, 1969.

SIMPSON, DAVID, 'The Dimensions of World Poverty', *Scientific American*, Vol. 219, No. 5, 1968.

TAYLOR, GORDON R., *The Doomsday Book*, Thames and Hudson Ltd., London, 1970.

United Nations, *Man and Hunger*, FAO, Rome, revised ed., 1961.

———, *Six Billions to Feed*, FAO, Rome, 1962.

VIDAL, GORE, *Reflections upon a Sinking Ship*, Heinemann Ltd., London, 1969.

WARD, BARBARA, *The Rich Nations and the Poor Nations*, Canadian Broadcasting Corporation, Toronto, 1961.

6. POPULATION POLICY AND FERTILITY CONTROL

Agency for International Development, *Population Programs Assistance*, AID, Bureau for Technical Assistance, Office of Population, Washington, D.C., 1969.

BEHRMAN, S. J., ed., *Fertility and Family Planning: A World View*, University of Michigan Press, Ann Arbor, Michigan, 1969.

BERELSON, BERNARD, et al., eds., *Family Planning and Population Programs*, University of Chicago Press, Chicago, 1966.

BOGUE, DONALD J., ed., *Mass Communication and Motivation for Family Planning*, Community and Family Study Centre, Chicago, 1967.

BRAYER, FRANKLIN T., ed., *World Population and United States Government Policy and Programs*, Georgetown University Press, Washington, D.C., 1968.

DAVIS, KINGSLEY, 'Population Policy: Will Current Programs Succeed?', *Science*, November 10, 1967.

DRAPER, ELIZABETH, *Birth Control in the Modern World: The Role of of the Individual in Population Control*, Penguin Books, Inc., New York, 1965.

DUBOS, RENE, *Man, Medicine, and Environment*, Praeger Publishers, Inc., New York, 1968.

EWALD, WILLIAM R., JR, *Environment and Policy: The Next 50 Years*, Indiana University Press, Bloomington, Indiana, 1968.

FAGLEY, RICHARD, *Population Explosion and Christian Responsibility*, Oxford University Press, New York, 1960.

HARDIN, GARRETT, ed., *Population, Evolution, Birth Control: A Collage of Controversial Readings*, W. H. Freeman & Co., San Francisco and London, 1969.

HAUSER, PHILIP M., ed., *Population and World Politics*, The Free Press, New York, 1958.

HOYT, ROBERT G., ed., *The Birth Control Debate*, National Catholic Reporter, Kansas City, 1969.

MAURY, MARION, *Birth Rate and Birth Right*, MacFadden-Bartwell Corp., New York, 1963.

ORGANSKI, KATHERINE and A. F. K., *Population and World Power*, Alfred A. Knopf, Inc., New York, 1961.

POHLMAN, EDWARD, *The Psychology of Birth Planning*, Schenkman Publishing Co., Inc., Cambridge, Mass., 1969.

Population Association of America, 'Progress and Problems of Fertility Control Around the World', *Demography* (Special issue), Vol. 5, No. 2 (1968), Population Association of America, New York.

QUINN, FRANCIS X., ed., *Population Ethics*, Corpus Books, Washington, D.C., 1968.

ROCK, JOHN, *The Time Has Come: A Catholic Doctor's Proposals to End the Battle over Birth Control*, Alfred A. Knopf, Inc., New York, 1963.

SANGER, CLYDE, *Half a Loaf: Canada's Semi-Role Among Developing Countries*, The Ryerson Press, Toronto, 1969.

SPITZER, W. O., ed., *Birth Control and the Christian: A Protestant Symposium on the Control of Human Reproduction*, Tyndale House Publishers, Wheaton, Illinois, 1969.

TIETZE, C., and LEWIT S., 'Abortion', *Scientific American*, Vol. 220, No. 1, 1969.

7. BIBLIOGRAPHIES

Foreign Policy Association, 'The World Population Crisis', *Intercom*, Vol. 10, No. 4, July-August 1968.

Office of Population Research, Princeton University, and Population Association of America, Inc., *Population Index*, Princeton, New Jersey, (quarterly).

Population Council and International Institute for the Study of Human Reproduction, Columbia University, *Current Publications in Population/Family Planning*, Columbia University Press, New York, (monthly).

Population Reference Bureau, Inc., 'A Sourcebook on Population', *Population Bulletin*. Vol. XXV, No. 5, 1969.

ZELINSKY, WILBUR, *A Bibliographic Guide to Population Geography*, University of Chicago, Department of Geography Research Paper No. 80, 1962.

8. PERIODICALS

Demography, Population Association of America, Washington, D.C., (quarterly).

Family Planning Perspectives, Centre for Family Planning Development, Technical Assistance Division of Planned Parenthood-World Population, New York, (quarterly).

Population Bulletin, Population Reference Bureau, Washington, D.C., (bi-monthly).

Population Chronicle, Population Council and International Institute for the Study of Human Reproduction, Columbia University. Population Council, New York, (monthly).

Population Index, Office of Population Research, Princeton University and Population Association of America, Inc., Office of Population Research, Princeton University, Princeton New Jersey, (quarterly).

Population Review, Indian Institute for Population Studies, Gandhinagar, Madras, India, (bi-annual).

Population Studies, Population Investigation Committee, London School of Economics, London, England, (quarterly).

Studies in Family Planning, Population Council, New York, (published irregularly).

List of Contributors

Index